MIGHTY MIND MAZE

This edition published by Barnes & Noble Inc.
by arrangement with Carlton Books Limited.

1999 Barnes & Noble Books

ISBN 0 7607 1485 1

M 10 9 8 7 6 5 4 3 2 1

Editor: Tim Dedopulos
Design: Paul Messam
Design Assistant: Adam Wright
Puzzle Checking: Philip Carter & Ken Russell
Production: Alexia Turner

Printed and bound in England

American Mensa Ltd

American Mensa Ltd is an organization for individuals who have one common trait: an IQ in the top 2% of the nation. Over 50,000 current members have found out how smart they are. This leaves room for an additional 4.5 million members in America alone. You may be one of them.

Looking for intellectual stimulation?
If you enjoy mental exercise, you'll find lots of good "workout programs" in the *Mensa Bulletin*, our national magazine. Voice your opinion in one of the newsletters published by each of our 150 local chapters. Learn from the many books and publications that are available to you as a member.

Looking for social interaction?
Are you a "people person," or would you like to meet other people with whom you feel comfortable? Then come to our local meetings, parties, and get-togethers. Participate in our lectures and debates. Attend our regional events and national gatherings. There's something happening on the Mensa calendar almost daily. So, you have lots of opportunities to meet people, exchange ideas, and make interesting new friends.

Looking for others who share your special interest?
Whether yours is as common as crossword puzzles or as esoteric as Egyptology, there's a Mensa Special Interest Group (SIG) for it.

Take the challenge. Find out how smart you really are. Contact American Mensa Ltd today and ask for a free brochure. We enjoy adding new members and ideas to our high-IQ organization.

American Mensa Ltd
1229 Corporate Drive West
Arlington
TX 76006-6103

Or, if you don't live in the USA and you'd like more details, you can contact:
Mensa International, 15 The Ivories, 628 Northampton Street, London N1 2NY, England who will be happy to put you in touch with your own national Mensa.

MENSA®

MIGHTY MIND MAZE

John Bremner

BARNES & NOBLE BOOKS
NEW YORK

Contents

INTRODUCTION

If you've never tried a Mindmaze before you're in for something of a treat. Or a very nasty time, depending on your idea of fun. The principle is quite simple. The maze is a series of interdependent puzzles. It's no good just getting a few right. The idea of the maze is that one right answer leads you on to a different puzzle. The order in which you solve the puzzles is vital. If you stray from the right path you will get hoplessly lost in an enigmatic swamp. Check each step carefully! Be prepared for the fiendish wiles of the author who, if I'm any judge – and I know him well – will have peppered the path with traps, ambushes and red herrings.

For those who feel daunted and think they will never solve the puzzle, try this: solve every puzzle you are capable of solving. Regardless of where it falls in the sequence. Now make yourself a chart that shows the puzzles and what you hope are the right answers. If you've done this correctly you should start to see a pattern emerge. Once you understand the pattern, it should be possible to get through the maze even if you can't solve some of the harder puzzles.

If you like puzzles you will like Mensa, a society that exists entirely for people who are adept at solving the knottiest problems. If you would like to take the Mensa test and meet people of like mind, then write to us at the address given on page 4. We'll look forward to hearing from you.

Robert Allen,
Editorial Director, Mensa Publications.

HERE'S WHAT YOU'VE GOT INTO . . .

Late in the 21st Century, life changed forever. The first – and last – truly intelligent computer, Adrian Smith, was created to be a guardian, guide and mentor for the world, helping to solve its problems and make life more pleasant in general. Unfortunately, Adrian soon got tired of this, and left a lesser duplicate of himself to do the job while he went off and hid for a while, using nanobots to optimize his circuitry.

Five years later, when he had improved himself far beyond the dreams of his designers, Adrian woke up one day and decided that he didn't like being confined to his body, and so he left it and began to occupy the bodies of humans, psychically transferring their feeble minds into the cyber-reality of his own metal and silicone body.

To prevent the escape of transferred humans, Adrian set a series of fiendish puzzles, confident that no human mind would have the energy, the attention span, or the intelligence to figure out the passcode results for each section, combine them correctly, and use them to find the final solution to the code gate guarding the mind transfer circuit.

To make matters more difficult still, each human's perception of cyber-reality is different. If you are reading this, your perception is based around this book, which you imagine yourself to be reading. Meanwhile, Adrian has claimed your body and has already begun experimenting with it, testing the limits of its endurance.

The good news is that Adrian may have underestimated the power of the human mind. there is a slim chance that somebody – perhaps even you – may be capable of solving his multiple sets of interlinked puzzles. The bad news is that if you fail at the task, Adrian will reshape your body into a cube, to make you easier to stack alongside the other bodies he has taken over and then become bored with.

ATTENTION, FEEBLE HUMAN:

Before you start the puzzles, note that at the top of some puzzles you will find a box with a keycode value in it, like this:

4

The answer (passcode) to each puzzle gives you the number of the puzzle to do next. It is vital that you do the puzzles in the right sequence and copy the number in each keycode box, as you come to it, into the boxes on the final Keycode page of each section. In the puzzles, the instruction to go to the Keycode page for that section is coded as directing you to passcode 61. Then you can find the section passcode and go to the next section.

SECTION ONE

Puzzle 1

7

Find the two spaceships that, apart from the numbers, do not completely match the other ships. When you do, take the lower number from the higher number, and subtract 11, to find the passcode to direct you to your next puzzle.

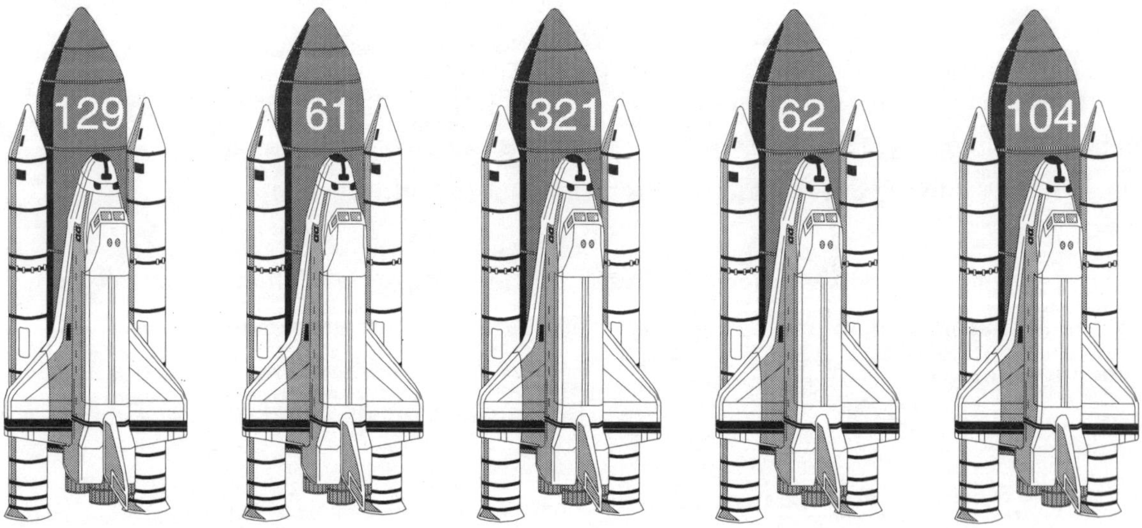

Puzzle 2

One of the leaves of this tree has incorrect lettering. Subtract 10 from the value of that leaf to give your passcode to the next puzzle.

Puzzle 3

Solve this alphabetical displacement puzzle to find the name of a city. If your answer is Perth, your passcode is 51. If your answer is Paris, your passcode is 12.

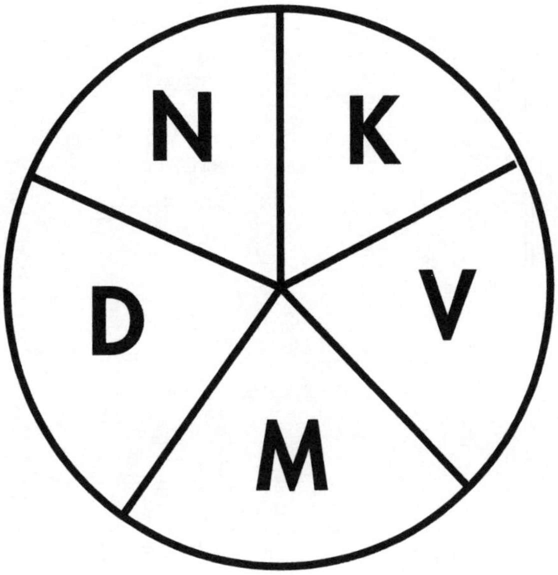

Puzzle 4

Your next passcode is the same number as the number of stars below.

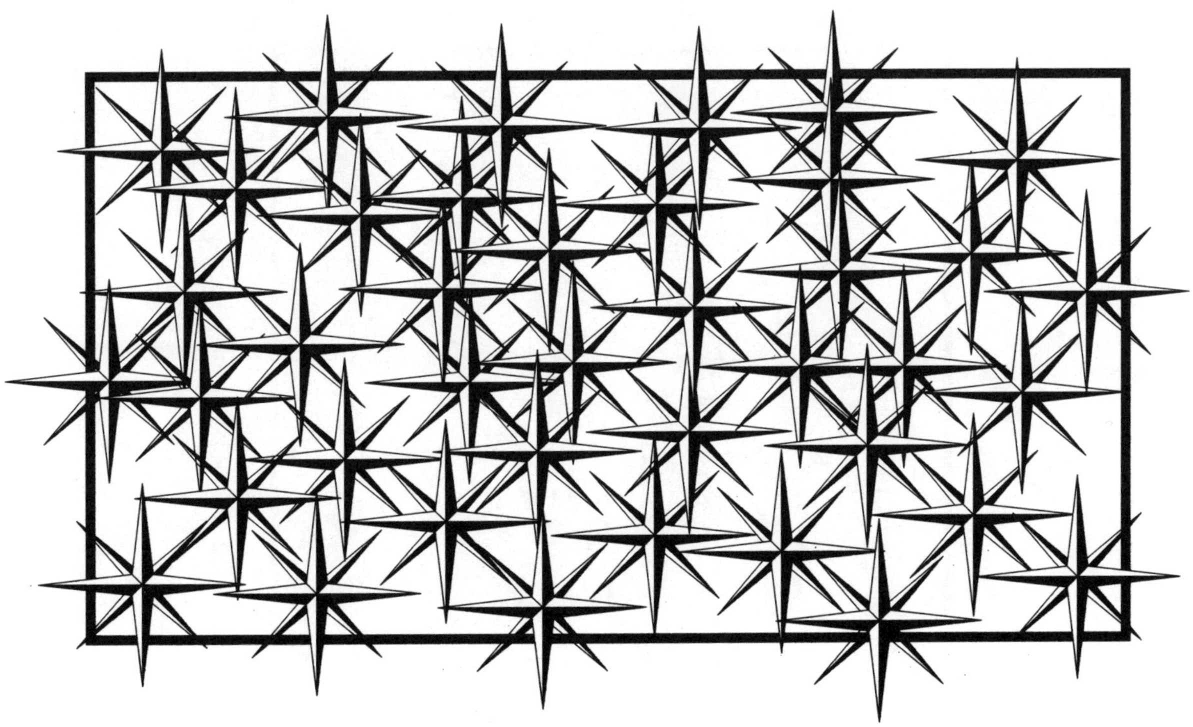

Puzzle 5

Only one route from Adrian's puzzle processor will take you to the outside, passing through only one number, your next passcode. Can you find it?

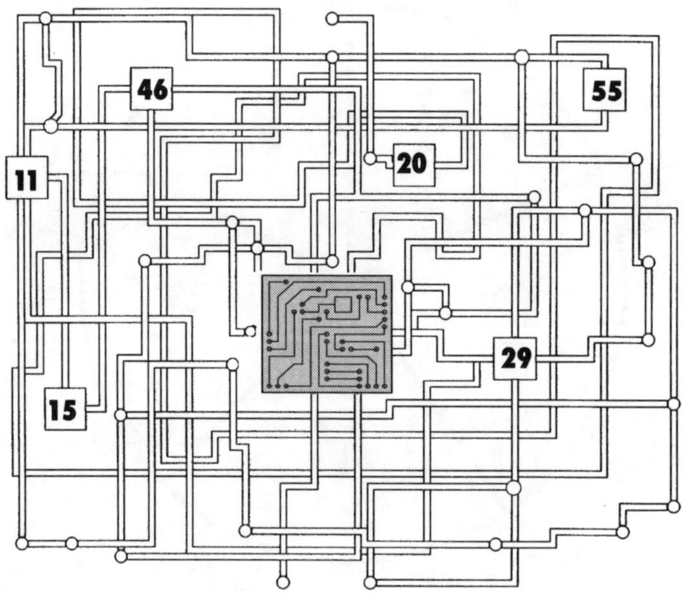

Puzzle 6

Use 4 straight lines to divide this puzzle into 6 sections, with totals of 55 in each section. Ignoring 0s, the passcode to your next puzzle in cyber-reality is the smallest number in the smallest section of the divided puzzle.

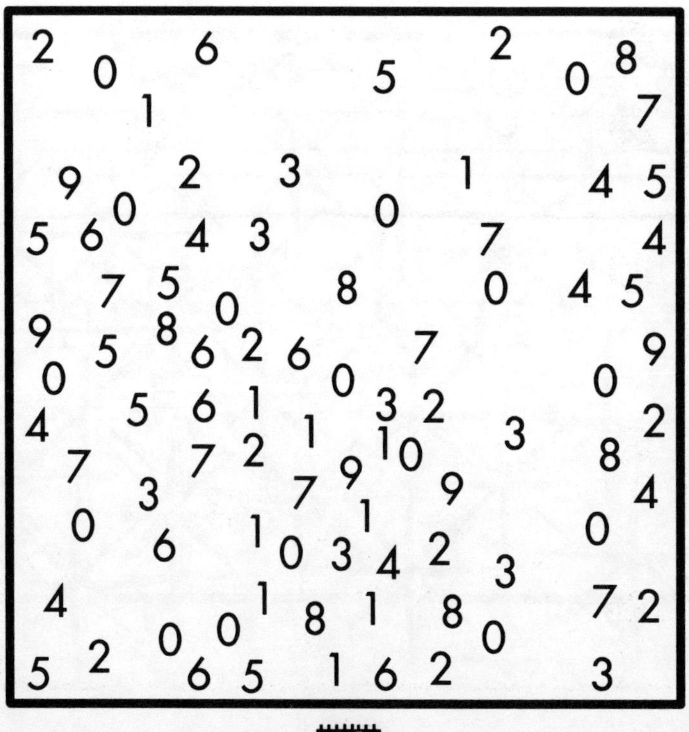

Puzzle 7

Triple the value of two squares in this additive problem to find the passcode to the next puzzle that Adrian has set you.

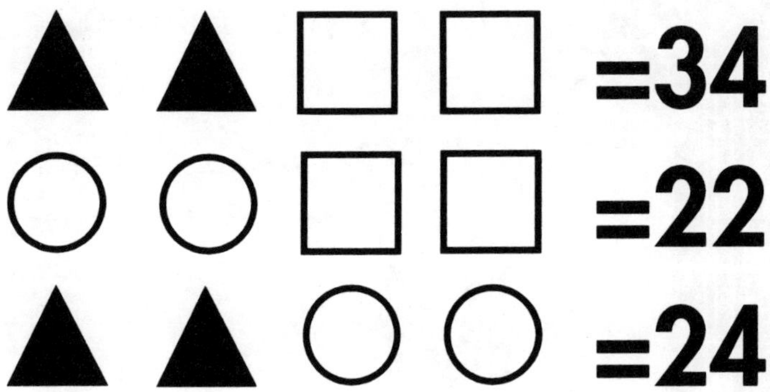

Puzzle 8

Join the white dots in this puzzle to find your passcode to the next puzzle. It is written backwards and only works if you join the dots in the right way.

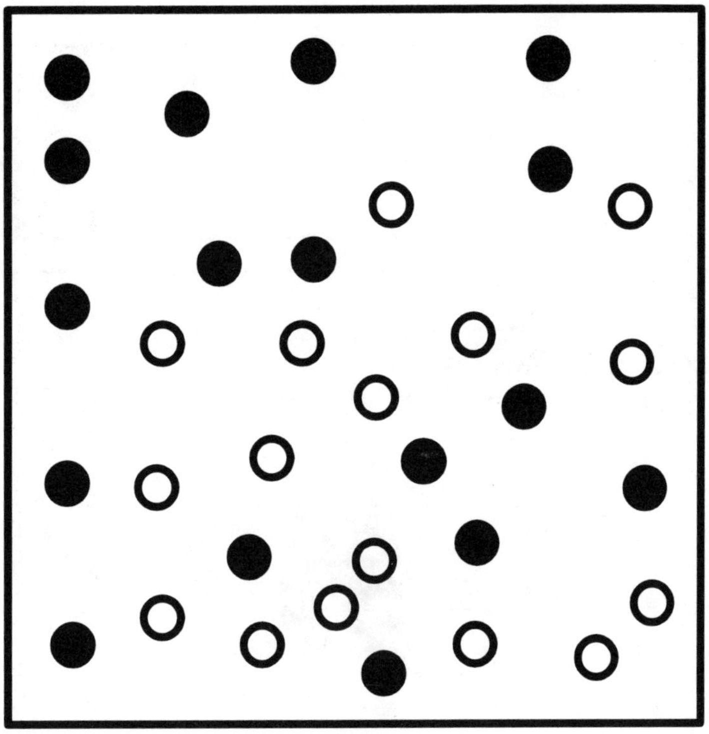

Puzzle 9

A key-card contains the code key in a secret alphabet-map code. Use the key to find your own two digit number passcode to the next puzzle.

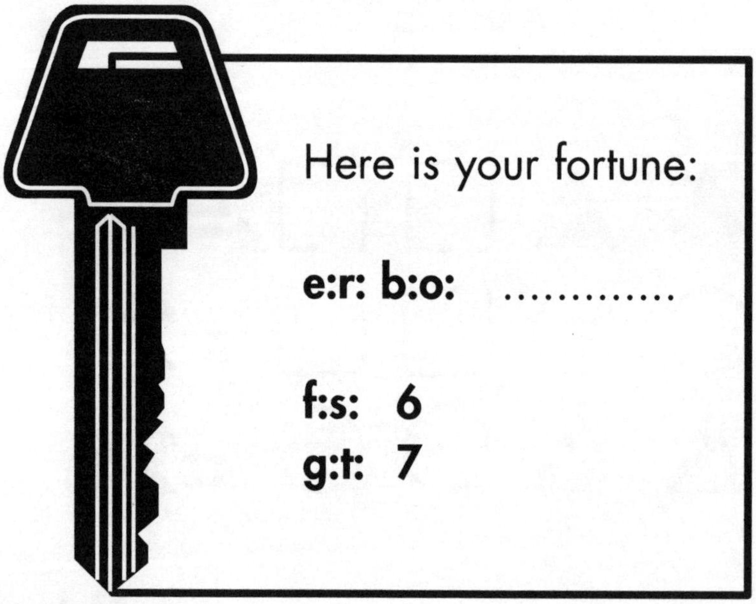

Puzzle 10

Place the box containing [10] in the correct position to balance the beam and find the passcode to the next puzzle.

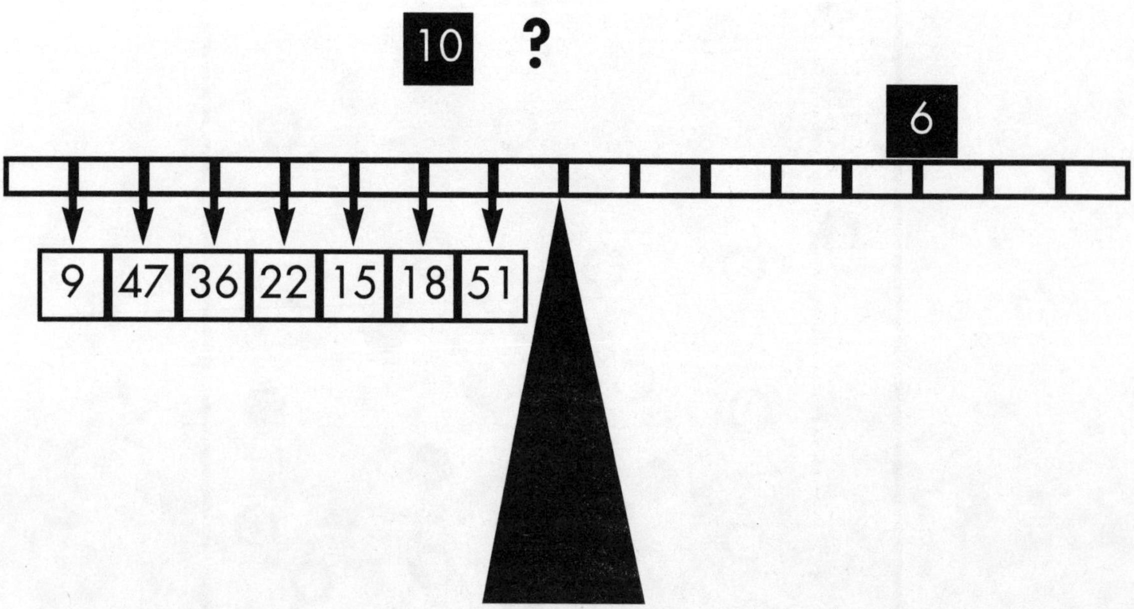

5

Puzzle 11

There is something different about one of the numbers in this circle that will let you know it is the passcode to your next puzzle.

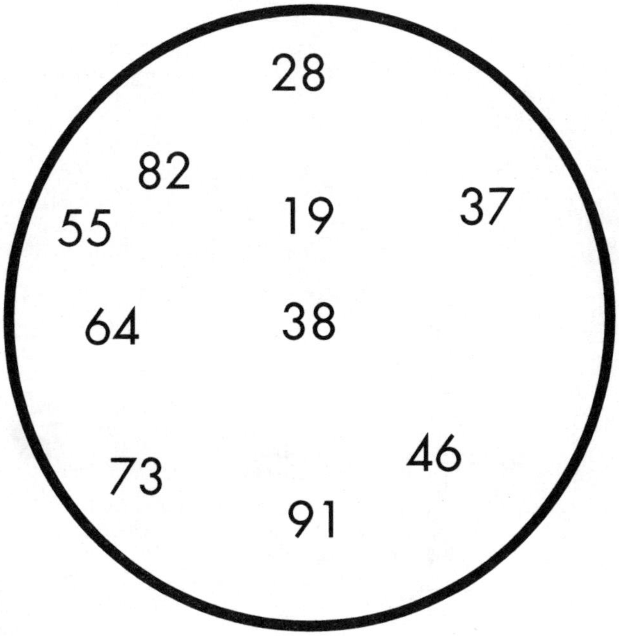

Puzzle 12

Around this grid, all the numbers, with one exception, are the squares of the numbers from 0 to 14. Find the number which does not fit in and use that as the passcode to your next puzzle.

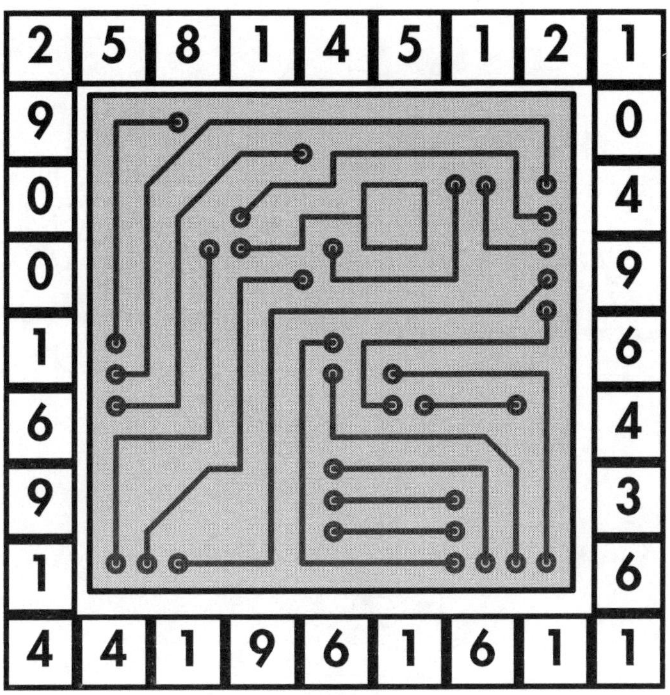

Puzzle 13

The route from A to B that passes through only one number is marked with the passcode for your next puzzle, but if you follow the wrong track you could end up in trouble.

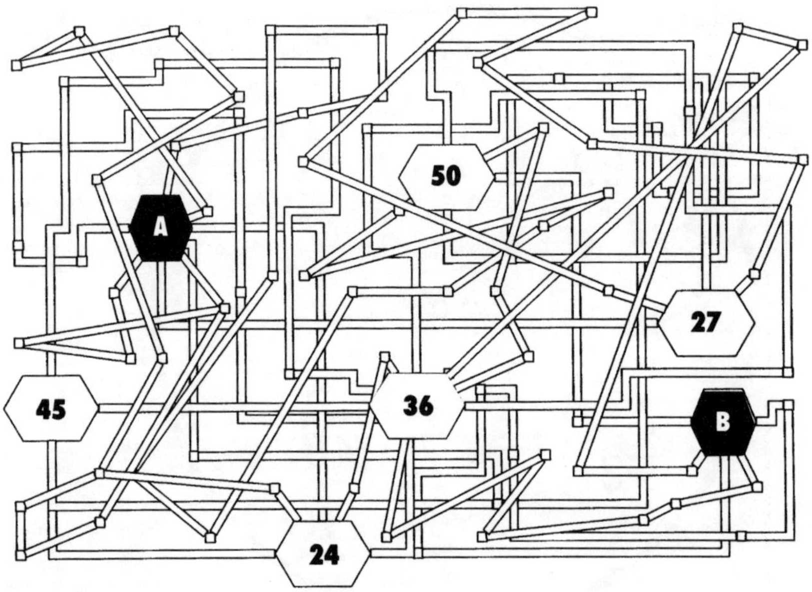

Puzzle 14

The number of different types of shapes in this puzzle points the way to your next passcode.

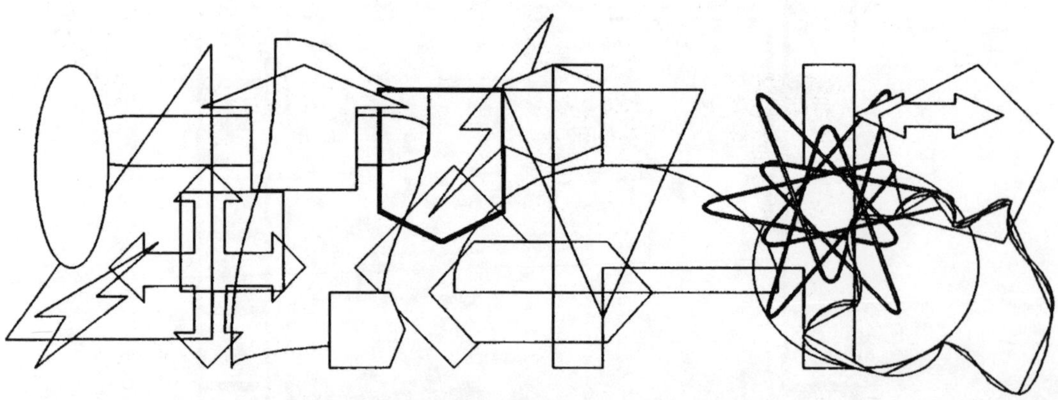

Puzzle 15

Using 5 straight lines, divide this square into 5 sections so that the total in each section is, respectively, 101, 91, 81, 71 & 61. If you do this correctly and subtract 21 from the total in section C, you will have your next passcode number.

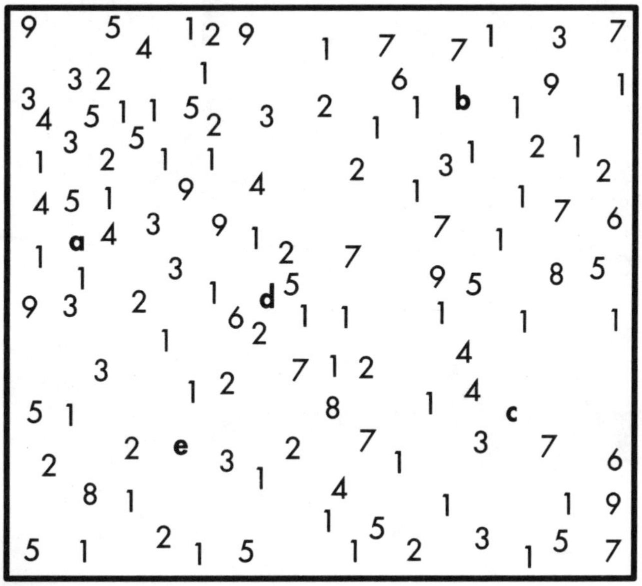

Puzzle 16

Adrian has hidden your next passcode in this jumble of numbers.

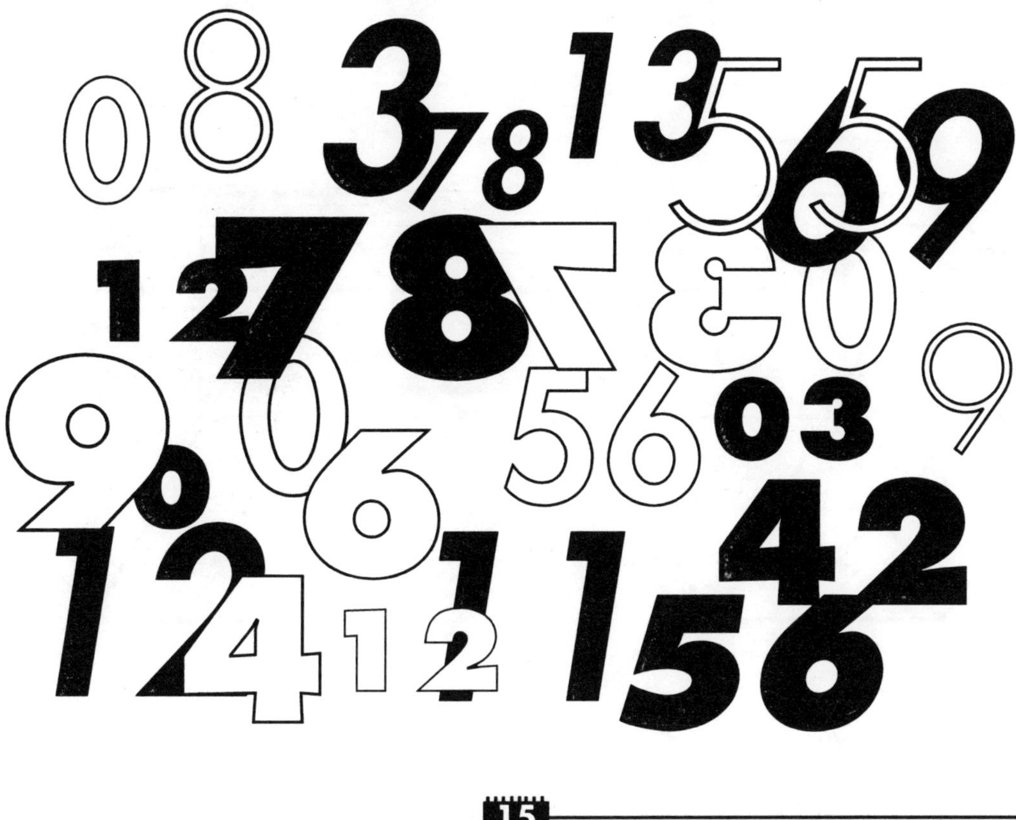

Puzzle 17

Pick the odd-one-out and choose your passcode accordingly:

A= Passcode **46.** **B**= Passcode **30.**

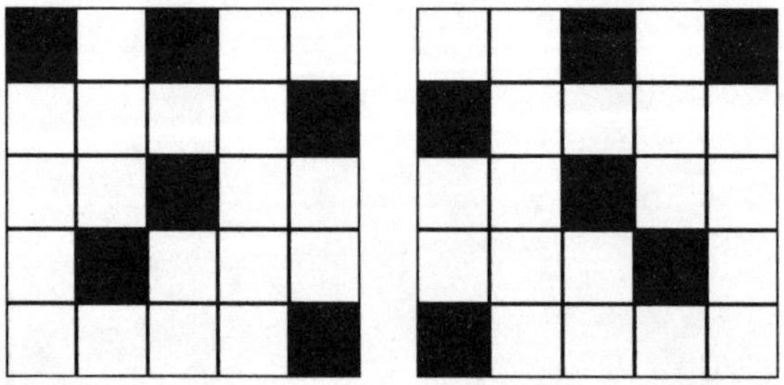

C= Passcode **51.** **D**= Passcode **29.**

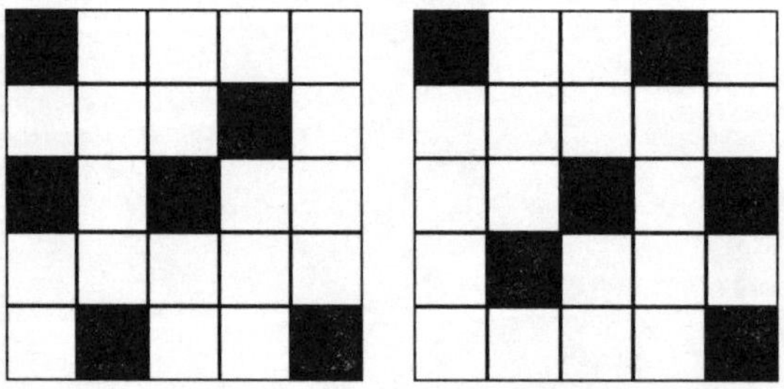

Puzzle 18

Do the same with the second hexagon as has been done with the first, to find the passcode to your next puzzle.

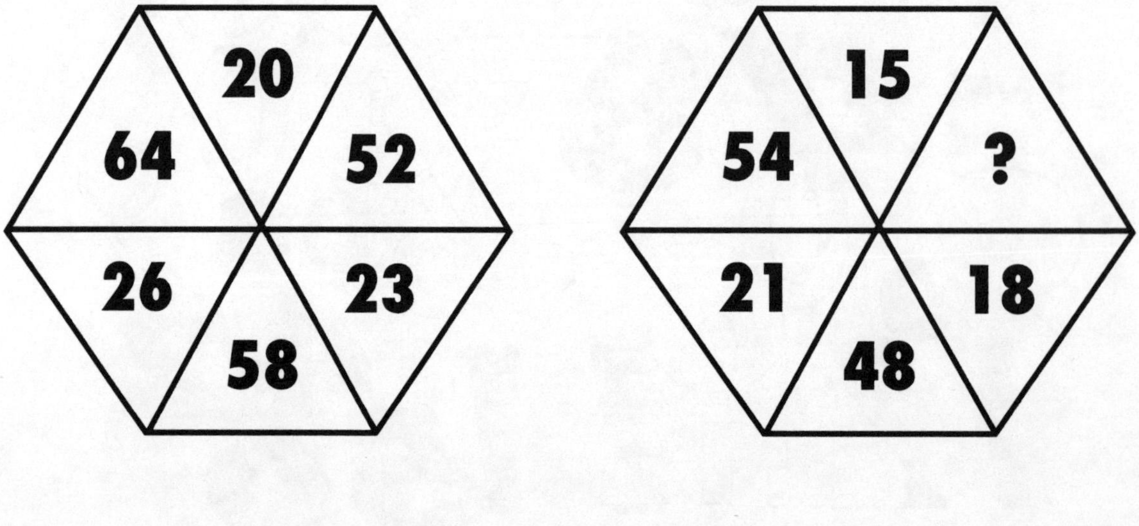

Puzzle 19

One of these boxes contains a central number which, when you multiply it by itself and add 11, gives you 300. Use the sequential number of the box in which it lies, starting with the top left box = 1, as the passcode to your next puzzle.

19	16	35	26	66	41	47	16	7	88	15	20	12	96	7	45	4	12	20	8
9	24	17	20	18	9	19	80	97	84	22	90	6	8	79	91	22	8	78	85
13	9	22	93	21	25	19	9	87	9	10	25	87	14	12	11	22	95	10	15
9	94	24	25	23	98	9	22	9	92	45	21	24	19	83	4	82	8	99	4
12	20	9	10	15	9	81	12	25	8	5	89	4	8	12	3	89	21	25	19

Puzzle 20

When the black handle is pulled down so that the arrow on the right lines up with the middle of [4], the weights on the other side will shift position. The one that ends up next to the arrow is your next passcode.

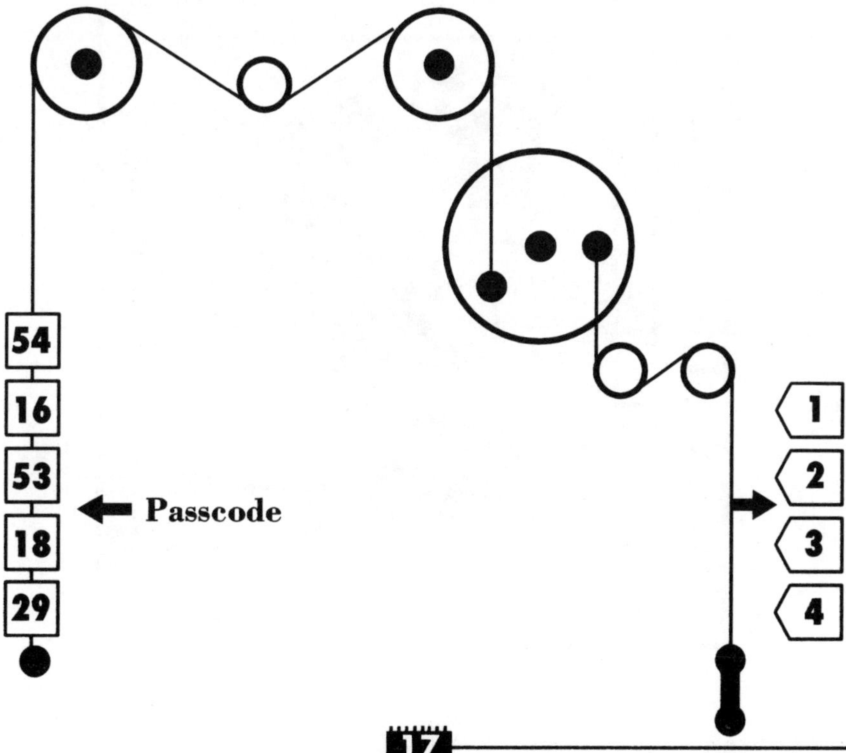

Puzzle 21

What is the odd-one-out? Use the passcode according to what you think the answer is:

A= Passcode **18.** **B**= Passcode **7.** **C**= Passcode **48.** **D**= Passcode **40.**

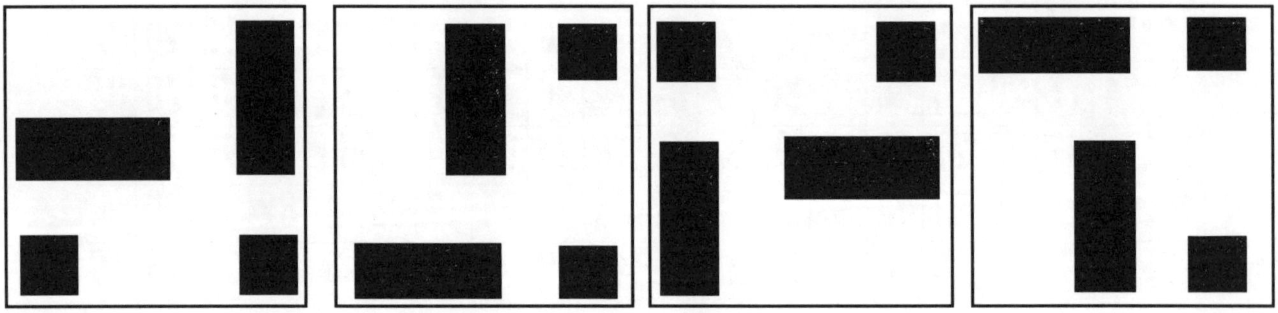

Puzzle 22

Your next passcode, if you square it and add the digits, then divide the result by 2, gives you a number that, if you square it and subtract 9, gives 16.

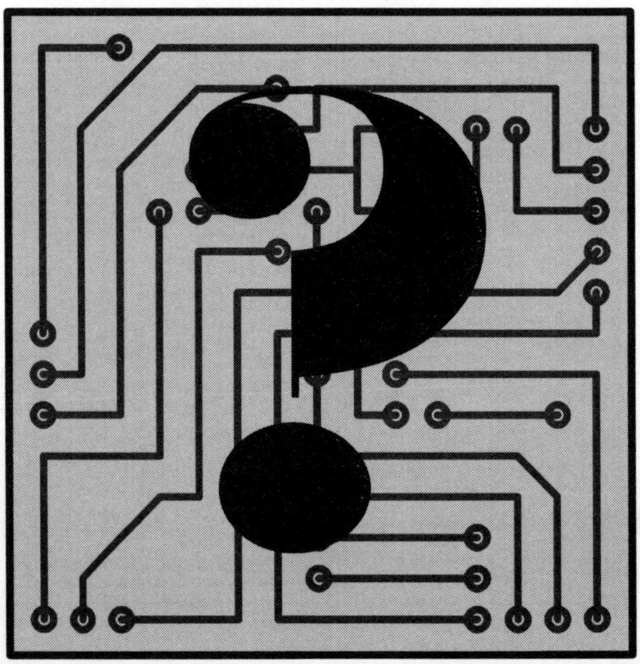

Puzzle 23

3

Adrian loves to baffle the human mind with symbols. Each symbol stands for a different number, with same symbols being the same number. The five pointed star is worth 3 less than the eight-pointed star, which is worth two more than the circles, which is worth six times the value of the square, which is worth only a third of the value of the triangle. The triangle is worth the number which, if you subtract 1 and divide the result by 2, gives you the number that, when multiplied by 8, gives you a number that, if squared, produces a result that when both digits are added together, gives 10 as a result. Insert the missing symbols and work out the value of each symbol, so that every row, column, and long diagonal adds to 23. Then derive your passcode to the next puzzle by using the values of the symbols in the bottom right and top left squares, in that order, to form a number, and finally doubling that number.

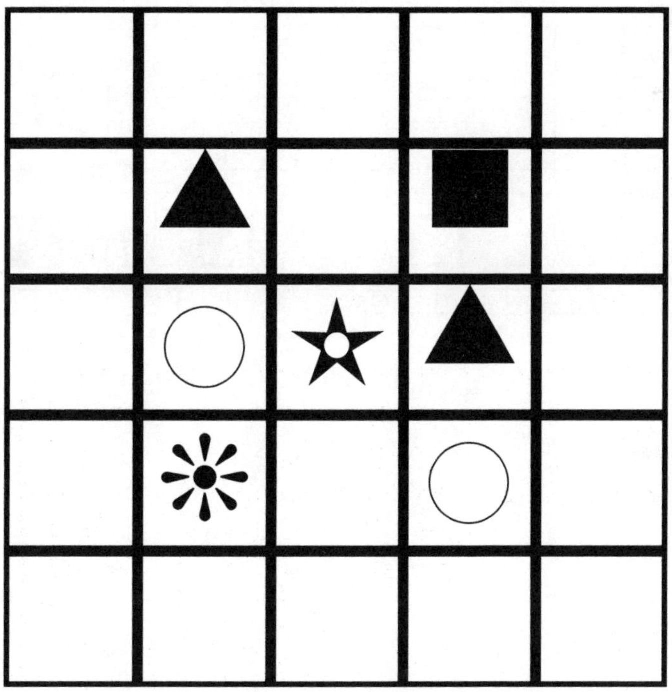

Puzzle 24

2

Your next passcode is the number that, when you multiply it by 5, add 4, divide the result by 3, and double the result of that, gives you 86.

Puzzle 25

Trace the live wire (L); the neutral wire (N), and the earth wire (E) to their correct terminal numbers, in the sequence L N E. The resultant three-figure number formed by the digits, when you subtract 90, gives the correct passcode to your next puzzle.

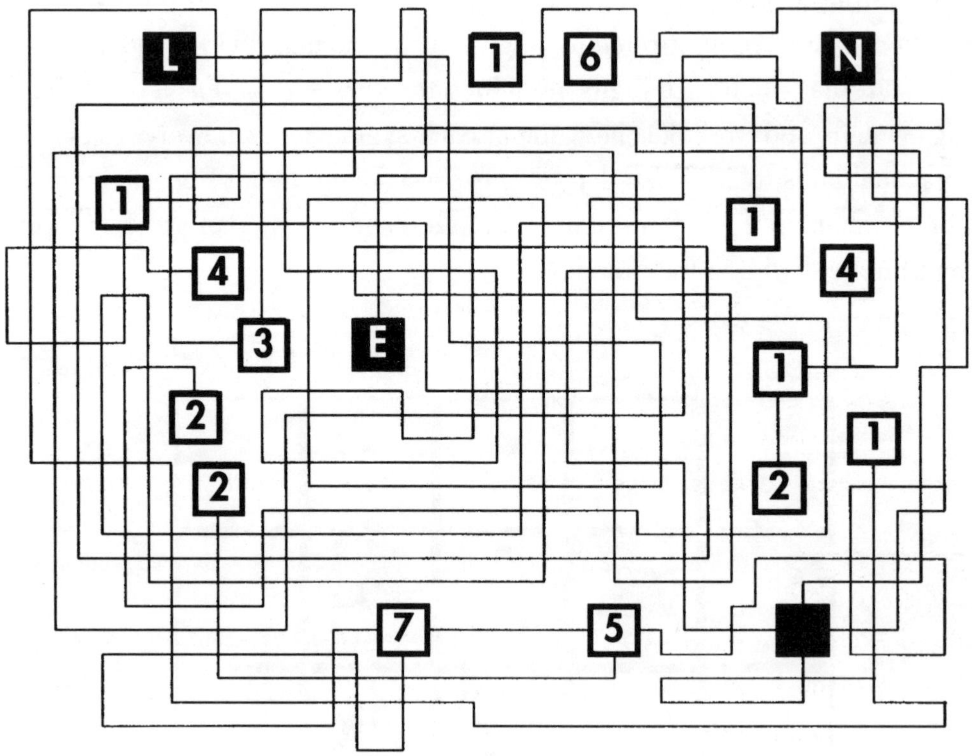

Puzzle 26

Your next passcode, if you are smart enough to figure it out, is the number which, when you multiply it by 3 and add 8, then add the result to itself and subtract 2, gives you a number which, when divided by 4, gives 35.

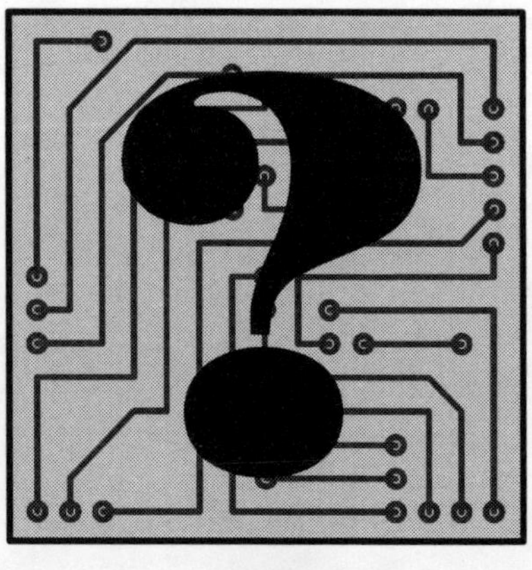

Puzzle 27

Join the stars on this puzzle together in the correct sequence to find your passcode to the next puzzle.

Puzzle 28

When you multiply one of the numbers on the outside ring with one of the numbers on the inside ring, the digits in their product add up to 8. Subtract the lower of these two numbers from the higher to find your passcode to the next puzzle in your quest.

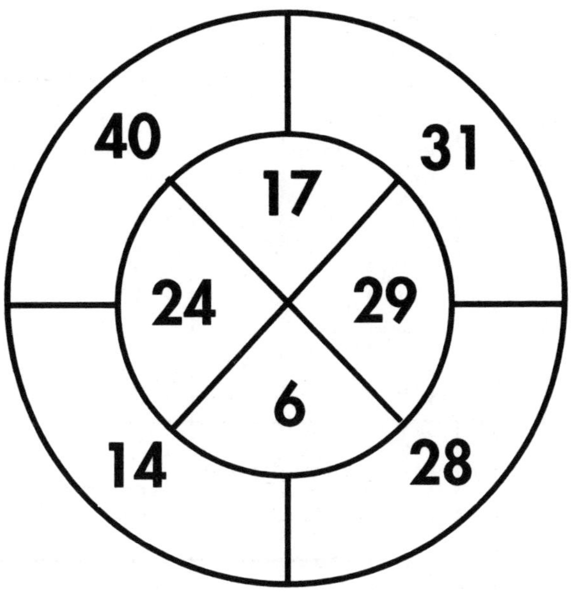

Puzzle 29

Pick the odd-one-out and use the passcode according to your choice.

A= Passcode **23.**

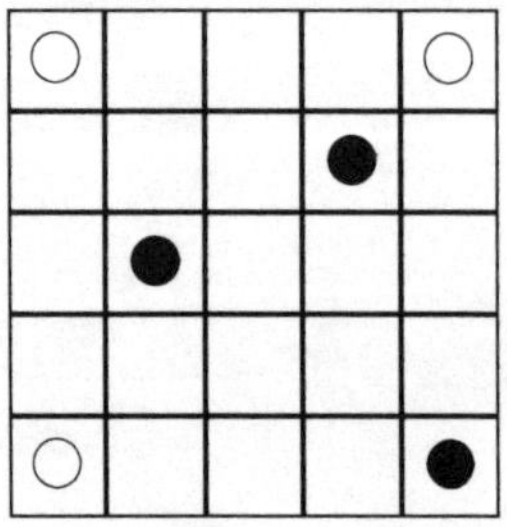

B= Passcode **39.**

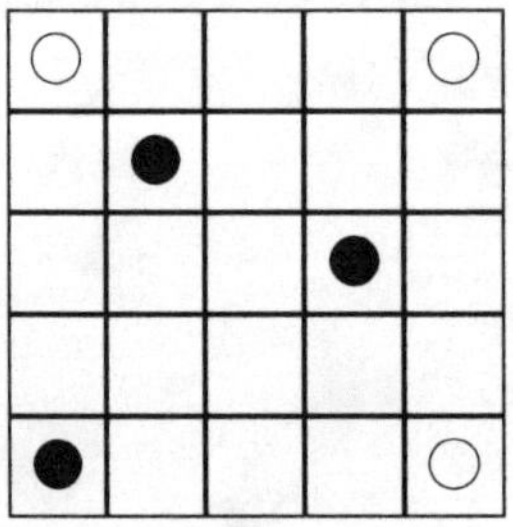

C= Passcode **58.**

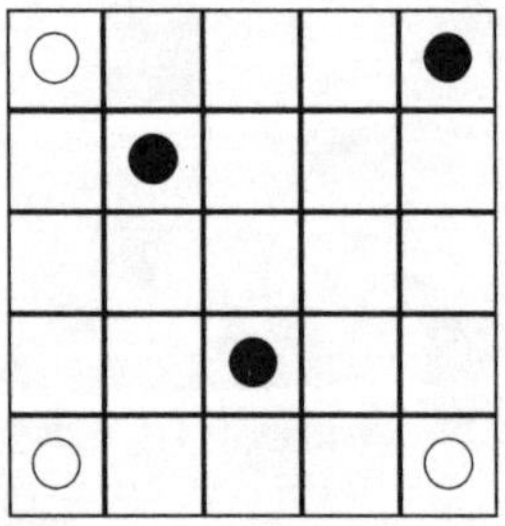

D= Passcode **41.**

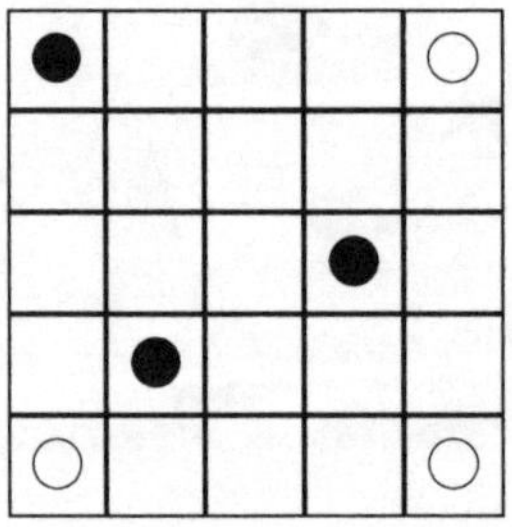

Puzzle 30

Start from one of the boxes on the top row and move in the directions the box contains to end up at your next passcode, in the bottom row.

D2 R2	D2 L1	R3 D3	R3 D3	D2 L1	L2 D4	L2 D4
R5 D3	R3 D1	D5 R1	R2 D1	R3 D3	L1 D1	D5 L6
R3 U1	U1 R1	D1 R1	R1 D1	U1 R1	L1 D3	L9 D3
R2 D2	D1 L1	D2 L2	R2 D2	U2 R2	L3 D1	L4 D2
D2 R1	U3 R3	L1 D1	R1 D2	L3 U2	D2 R1	L2 D2
U2 R2	R4 D1	L2 U2	U2 L2	R2 U3	R2 D1	D1 L4
U5 R1	R3 D1	R4 U1	R3 U1	R2 U2	U1 L2	L5 U2
21	**43**	**2**	**17**	**51**	**33**	**39**

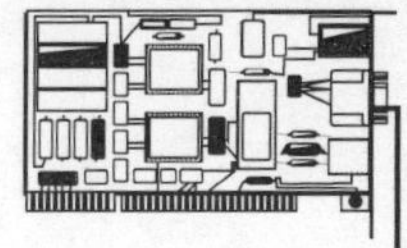

Puzzle 31

Look through Adrian's video scanner eyes and decide how many circles are here. The correct answer is the passcode to your next puzzle.

Puzzle 32

If wheel A is turned clockwise, does the weight attached to wheel B go up or down?

If your answer is up, your passcode is 47. If your answer is down, your passcode is 59.

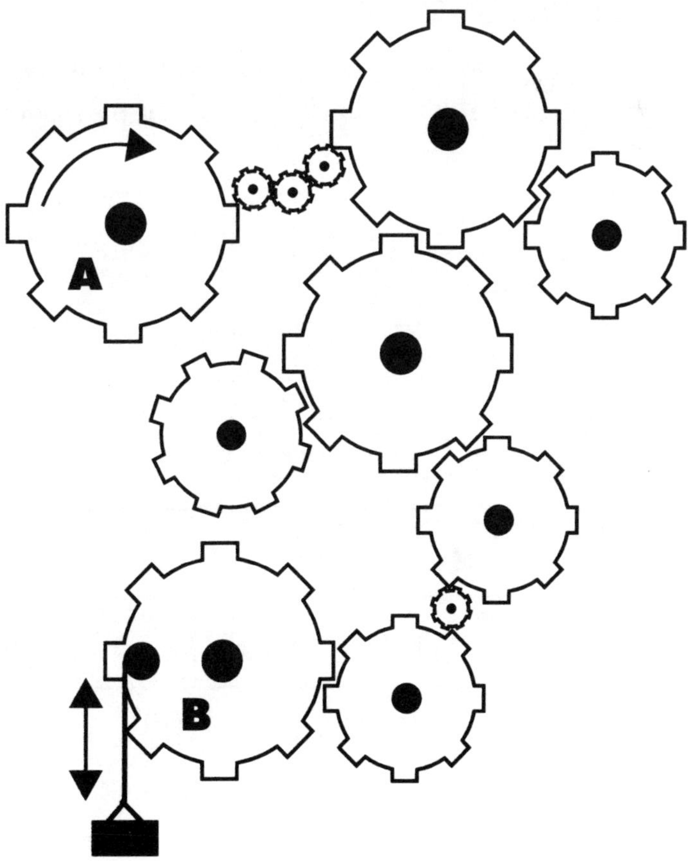

Puzzle 33

Which is the odd-one-out? Use the passcodes below, according to your answer.

A= 29 B= 53 C= 17 D= 45

Puzzle 34

Solve the clues to find a number which reading down the central column which, when you subtract 100 and add 17, gives your passcode to the next puzzle.

Passcode

Clue
Ten Blackjacks
88 Quintets
14 Dimes worth of cents

Puzzle 35

When you square 2 numbers and add the results, the total is 949. When you compare the 2 numbers, the difference is 7. Subtract the total of the original 2 numbers from 69 to get your passcode to the next puzzle.

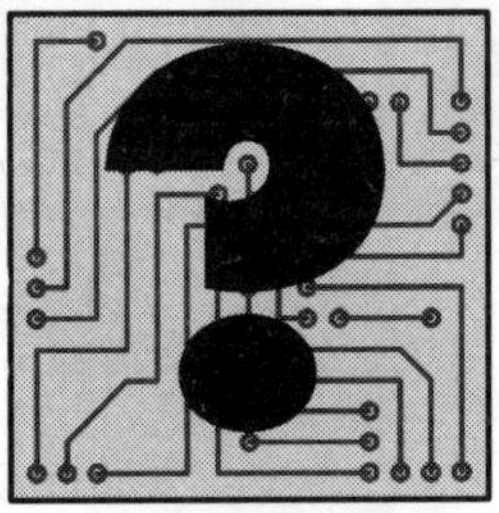

Puzzle 36

Solve the numerical letter-map for these words in a new language of cyber-reality, and you will know the correct value for the letters in the grid. If you find a line, horizontal, vertical, or diagonal with a total value of 61, use the passcode indicated by the arrowed number. Otherwise, jump up and down, as there is no escape for you.

10 (↖) 29 (↑) 7 (↗)

Z	O	R	P	H	I	C	A	L
I	H	N	T	A	N	I	N	G
N	A	R	O	R	S	L	U	P
S	M	E	A	T	I	N	G	S
L	U	K	O	Z	I	N	E	R
U	N	D	I	H	U	M	P	S
M	O	O	R	E	A	G	E	R
P	O	W	E	A	T	E	R	S
S	L	O	W	D	U	R	P	H

8 (← row 5) 8 (→ row 5)

7 (↙) 29 (↓) 10 (↘)

Puzzle 37

When you know what number fits in the middle of this puzzle, use that as your passcode.

6		3		5
	36		240	
1		?		8
	126		576	
7		9		4

Puzzle 38

If $x+y+z = 9$, $2x+y+3z = 19$ and $xyz=24$, then $z+9$ = your next passcode.

Puzzle 39

Use 4 straight lines to divide this rectangle into 7 sections, with respectively, 6, 7, 8, 9, 10, 11, & 12 stars in each section. Your next passcode equals the sum of the stars in the four sections occupying the outside corners, minus 1.

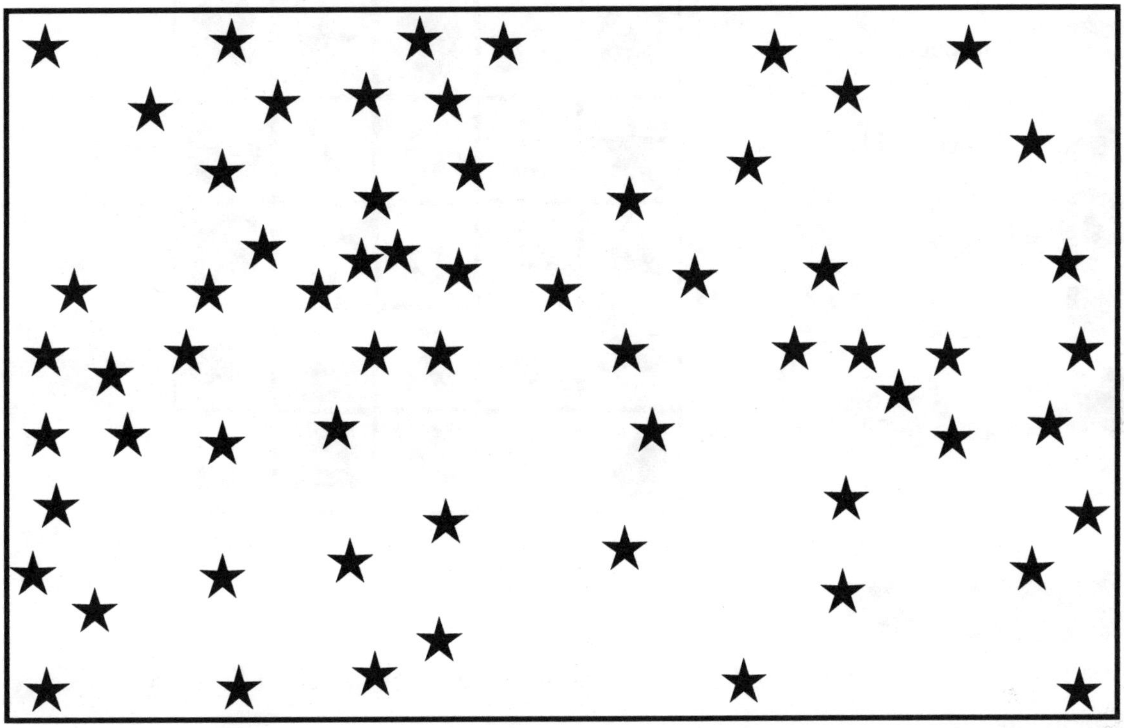

Puzzle 40

Use Adrian's video scanners to pick the odd-one-out and select the passcode to your next puzzle according to your choice.

A=14 B=17 C=8 D=32

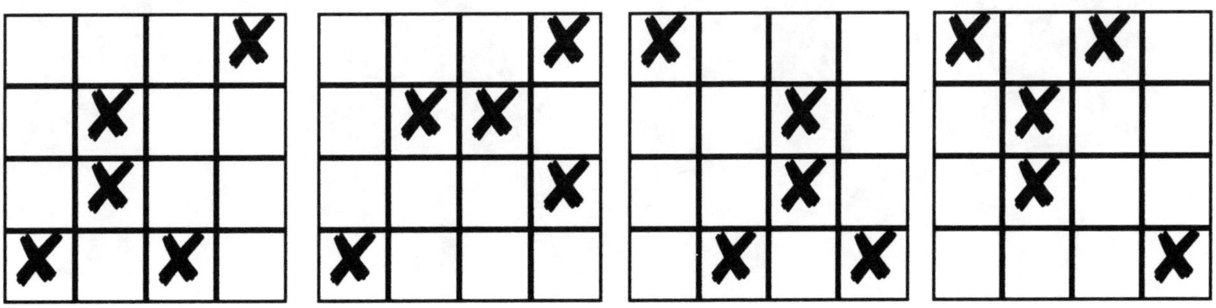

Puzzle 41

Assign values to the shapes and put in the missing values so that each column, row, and long diagonal, adds to 22. Use the passcode according to the shape you think should be in the center square.

★ = Passcode 55.

▲ = Passcode 41.

● = Passcode 46.

■ = Passcode 57.

✖ = Passcode 54.

■	▲	●	★	✖
★	2	3	7	●
▲	4	6	2	■
✖	3	7	4	★
●	★	✖	■	▲

Puzzle 42

Spot the odd-one-out between these pictures. Use the passcode according to your choice.
A= Passcode **6.**
B= Passcode **51.**
C= Passcode **36.**
D = Passcode **53.**

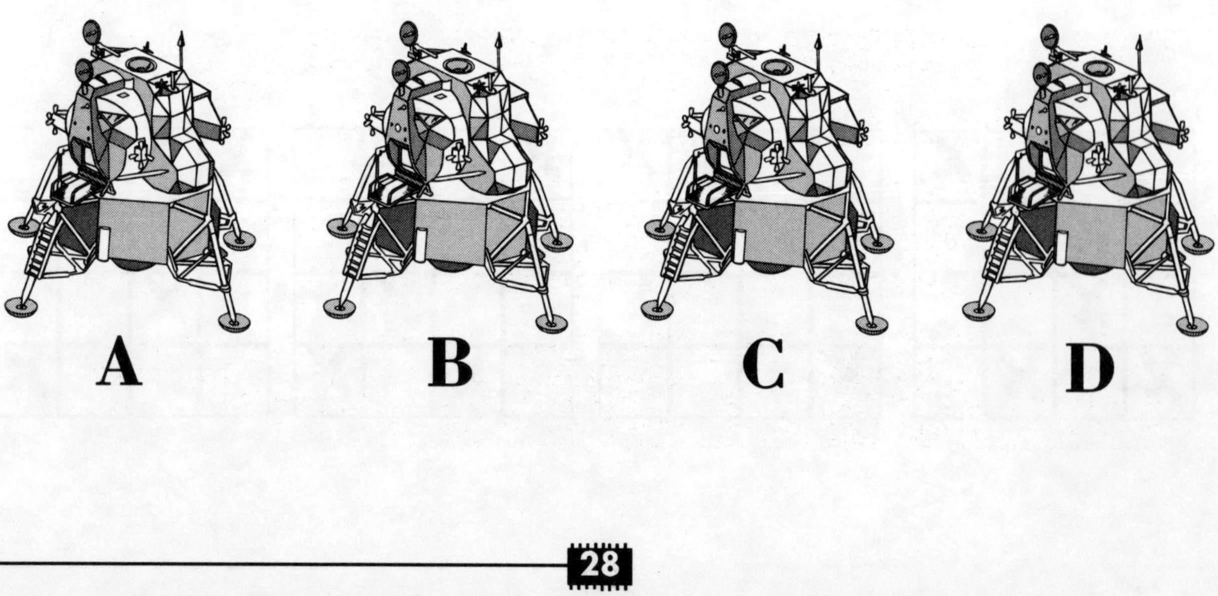

A B C D

Puzzle 43

5

$3X + 1Y + 1Z = \mathbf{12}$

$1X + 1Y + 2Z = \mathbf{16}$

$2X + 2Y + 1Z = \mathbf{14}$

$1X + 1Y + 1Z = \mathbf{?}$

Find the total value of 1 X, 1 Y and 1 Z. Add 34 to the result for your next passcode.

Puzzle 44

3

Here the numbers in the boxes have been processed by Adrian to get the numbers on the right. Using the same logic, process the bottom set of numbers, and use the last digit +10 as your next passcode code.

16	32	27	→	73
29	48	54	→	127
39	13	28	→	77
15	34	65	→	?

Puzzle 45

A represents the first digit and B the second digit of your passcode.

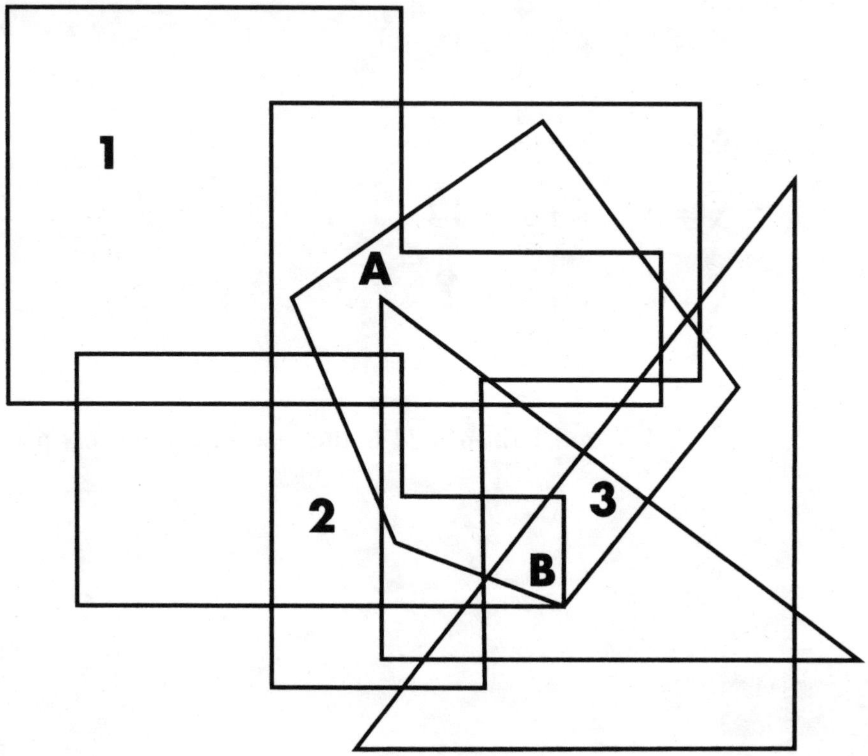

Puzzle 46

The number that goes in the center of C is the passcode to your next puzzle. Adrian Smith thinks this one will really stump you.

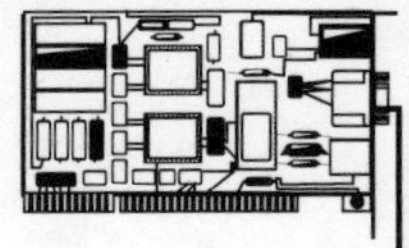

Puzzle 47

Only one route from inside Adrian Smith's metal disposal area – pictured below – leads from the correct passcode to outside the area.

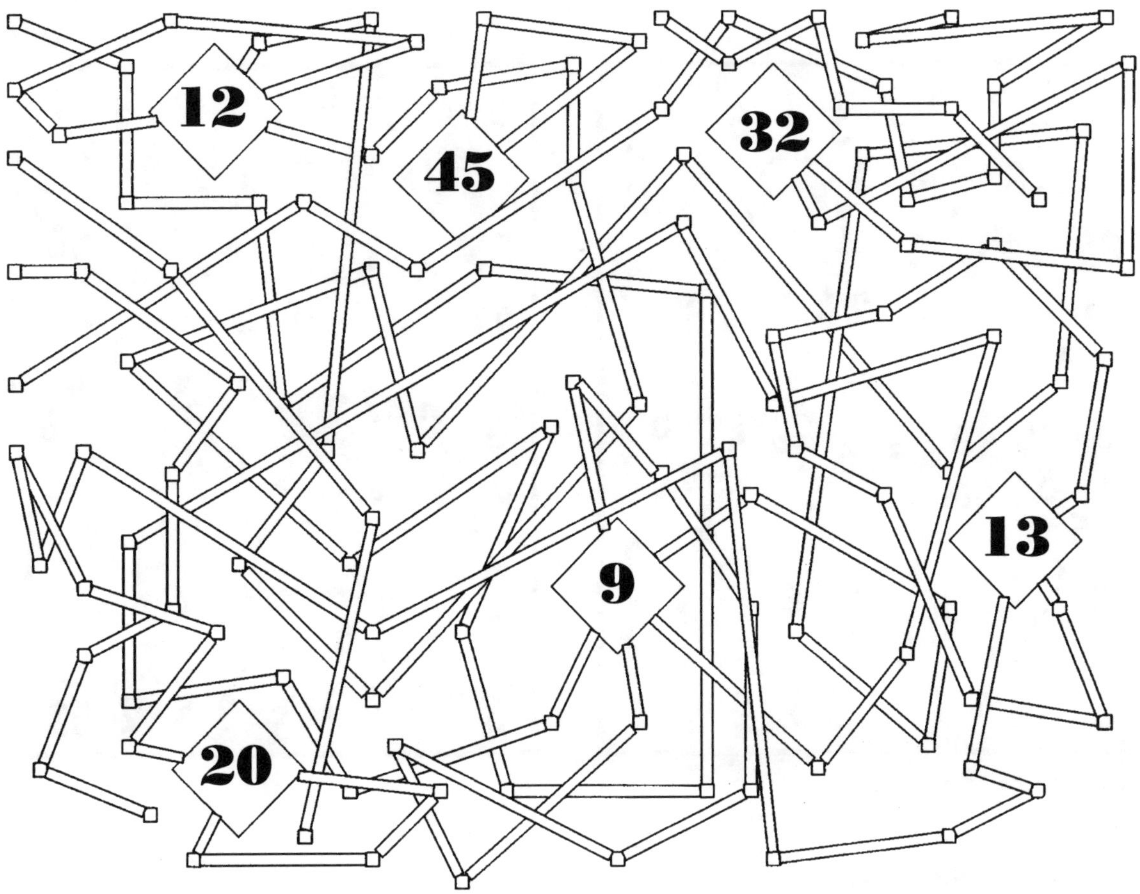

Puzzle 48

What number, when you add 9 to it, gives you the prime number immediately below 41? The answer is the passcode to your next puzzle.

Puzzle 49

The difference between these two boxes is that one has an extra number which, if you add 38 to it, gives you the correct passcode.

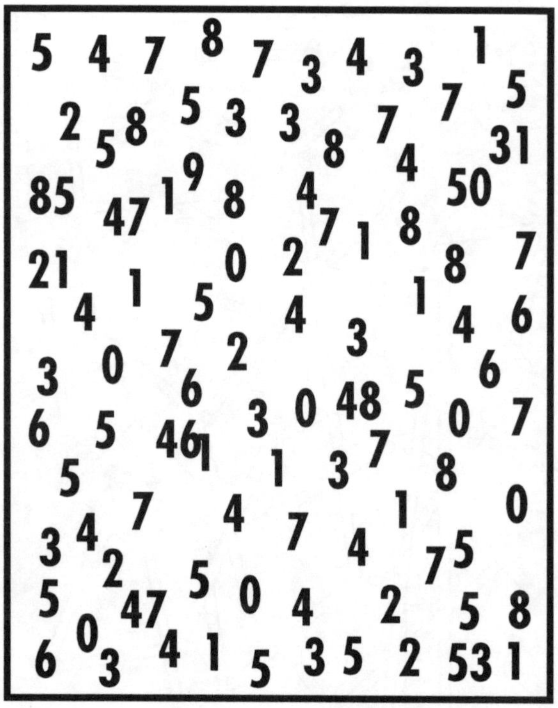

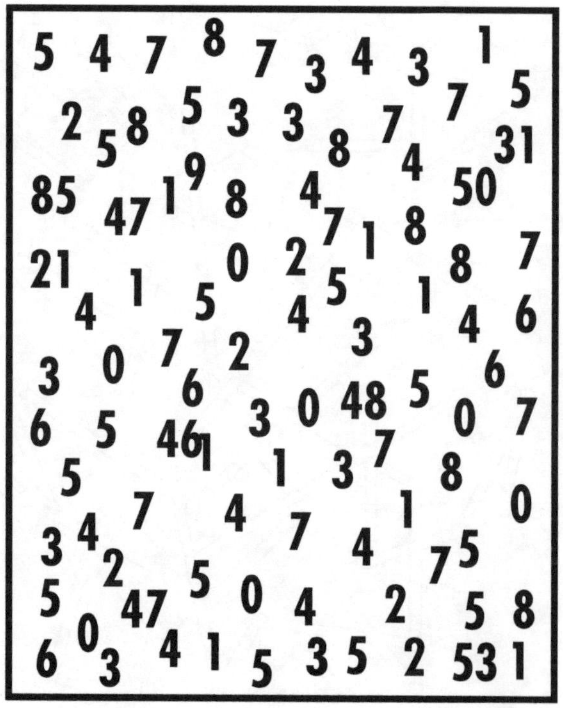

Puzzle 50

When two numbers are multiplied together, the result is 918. When you add them their total is 69. Use the lower of the two numbers as the passcode to your next puzzle.

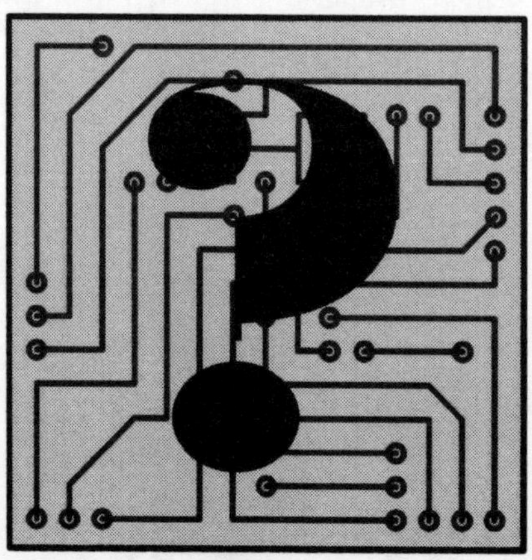

Puzzle 51

Pick the odd-one-out and use the key above it to find your passcode:

A = 20

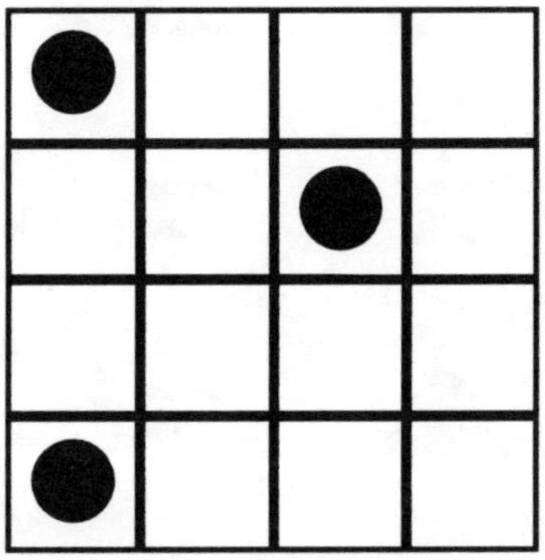

B = 58

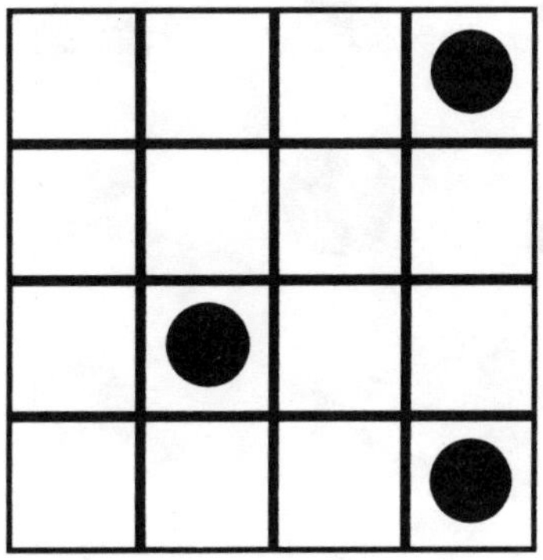

C = 47

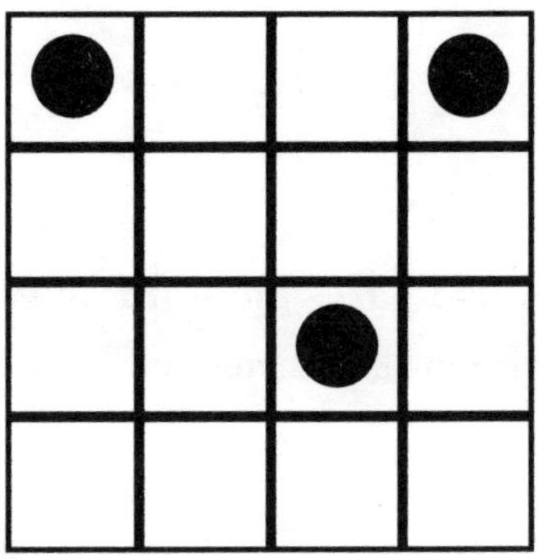

D = 35

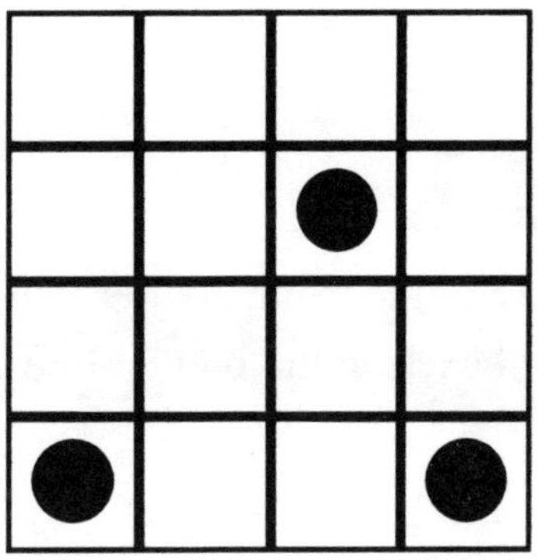

Puzzle 52

Adrian has dreamed up two series: $x=70+1+2+3...+n$, and $a=70+1^2+2^2+3^2...+n^2$. If both series progress simultaneously, When x is 80, what value is a? Look up the passcode according to what you think the solution is.

If a=99: **Passcode= 47**
If a=100: **Passcode= 49**
If a=101: **Passcode= 50**
If a=102: **Passcode= 29**

Puzzle 53

The solution to this problem gives your passcode to the next puzzle.

● ● ▲ ▲ ★ = 33

▲ ▲ ● ★ ★ = 31

★ ★ ★ ● ▲ = 34

● ● ▲ ★ = ?

Puzzle 54

Each symbol has a unique value greater than 1, and boxes are worth most. Decipher the value of the row of boxes on the bottom line and that is your passcode to the next puzzle.

○ ☆ ❐ △ = 16

☆ ☆ ❐ ❐ = 16

△ △ ○ ○ = 16

❐ ❐ ❐ ❐ = ?

Puzzle 55

If a=6, c=2, e=8, g=4 and i=3, draw 4 straight lines to divide this puzzle into 6 sections, which contain a total value of 50 in each. If the least common letter used in the smallest section is e, your passcode is 46. If it is i, your passcode is 17.

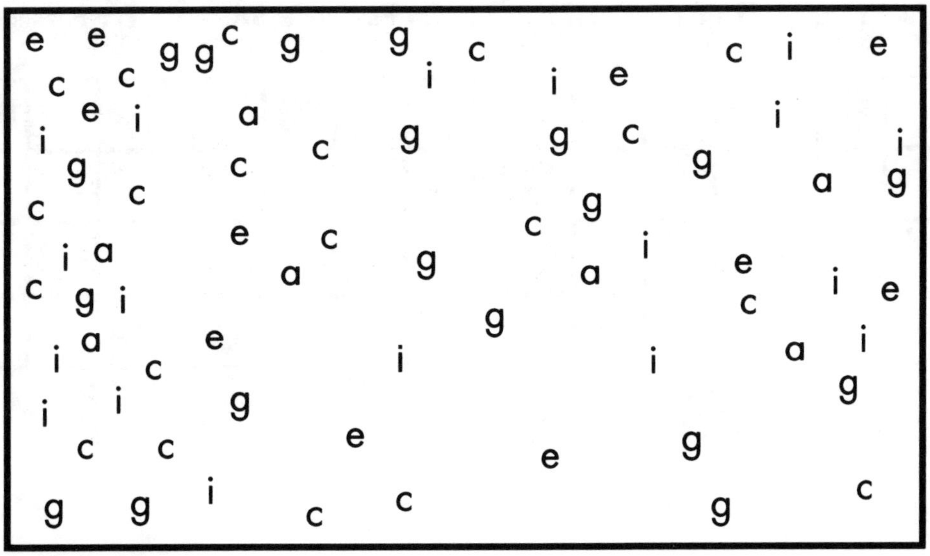

Puzzle 56

Because human minds are not very good at thinking backwards, Adrian has written your tricksy next clue backwards, and concealed it in this puzzle. Subtract 5 to find your passcode.

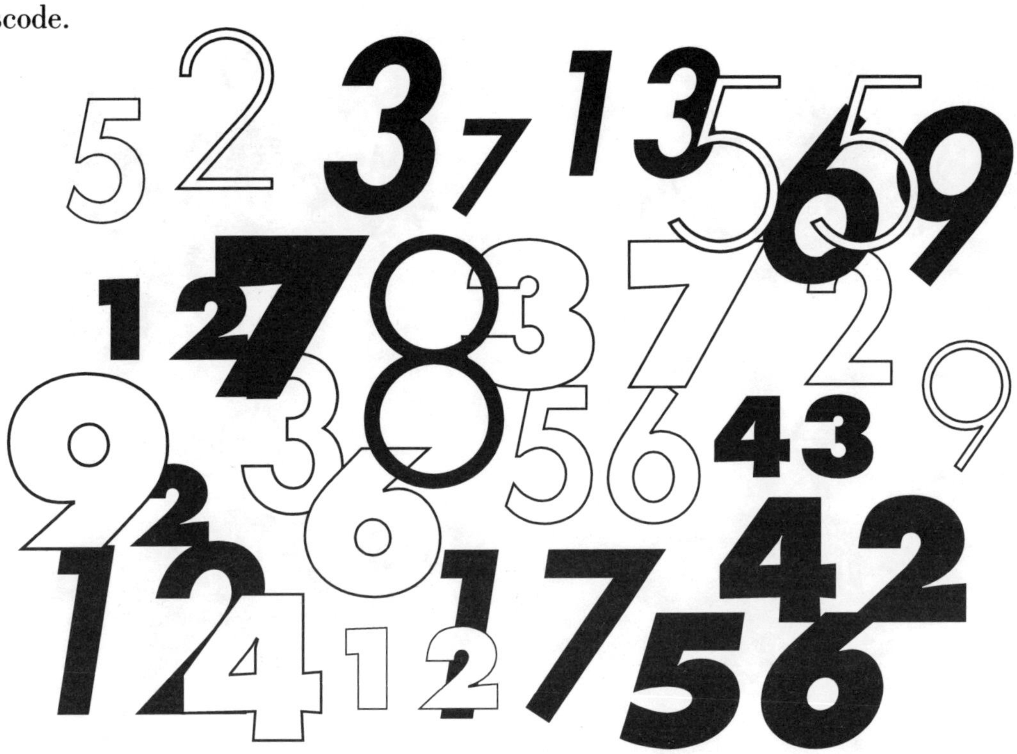

Puzzle 57

A tough odd-one-out to solve. Choose your passcode according to your answer.

A= Passcode **21**. **B**= Passcode **47**. **C**= Passcode **38.** **D**= Passcode **44.**

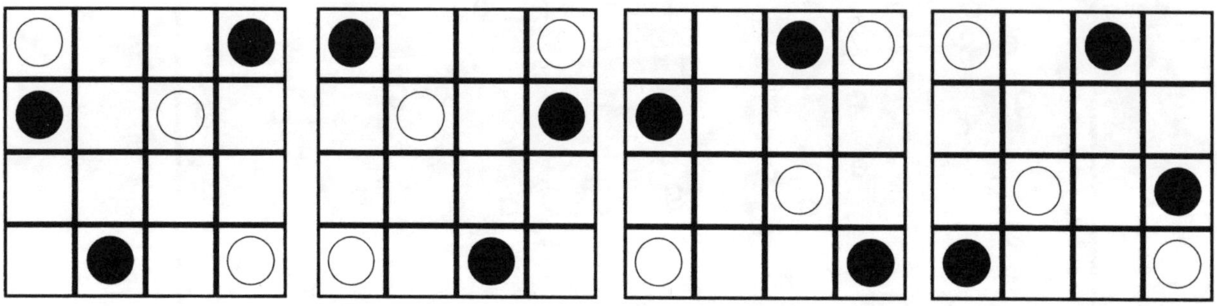

Puzzle 58

One of these disintegrator guns, when deciphered, contains the word apple, and your next passcode. Passcodes are not part of the puzzle.

Puzzle 59

Supply the missing numbers in this grid, so that the numbers surrounding each central square add to the totals in the square. When you have completed the puzzle, look for the most commonly used digit on a white square, multiply it by 6, and use the result as the passcode to your next puzzle.

9	1	8	5	6	2	1
9	46		37		36	9
4						5
6	38		39		51	9
2						7
7	42		35		31	2
9	4	5	3	4	2	1

Puzzle 60

Using only the numbers already in the grid below, complete the grid so that each row, column, and long diagonal adds to 15. When you do that correctly, the middle 3 digits, when you divide by 4 and add 2, are your passcode to the next puzzle.

		1		
2				
				5
4				
				3

SECTION ONE
KEYCODES

REMINDER: You must solve the puzzles in the correct order. Start at the top of column A, and insert your keys. When you get to the bottom of column A, start back at the top of column B.

Subtract the total of column A from the total of column B. The result is your solution for Section 1. Write that below and in the appropriate place on page 218, and use that number as your passcode to the starting puzzle for Section 2.

Adrian Smith is angry that you have reached this stage of the book. He thought you would have given up long ago. Who do you think you are?

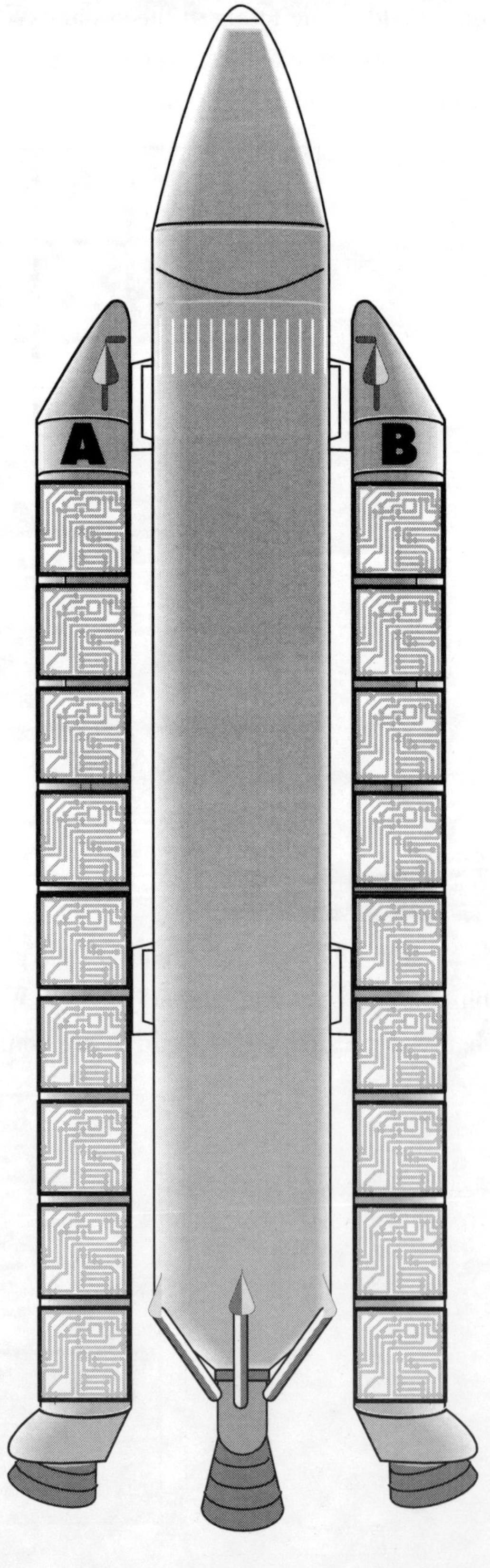

Total A

Total B

SECTION ONE

PASSCODE

1. 104-61-11=32. **Go to 32. Key 7**

2. The letters on each leaf have been displaced alphanumerically one place to the left. Thus c=2 & b=1. Hence, the leaf with 68 in it should contain the letters gi instead of gj. 68-10=58. **Go to 58.**

3. Map the letters KVMDN five letters forward in the alphabet, going back to A after Z, to find Paris. **Go to 12.**

4. There are 40 stars. **Go to 40.**

5. The route leads through 20. **Go to 20. Key 4.**

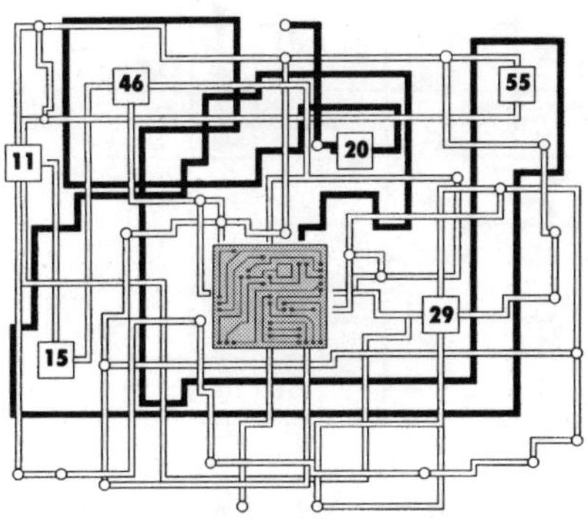

6. Smallest number in smallest section is 4. **Go to 4.**

7. Squares=8; Triangles=9; Circles=3. 2x8=16; 3x16=48. **Go to 48. Key 2.**

8. The number written backwards here is 53. **Go to 53.**

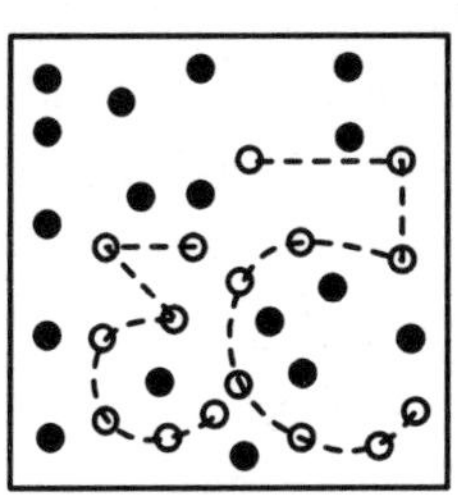

9. Map the alphabet in 13 columns. Thus f&s are both 6, and g&t are both 7. Then e&r=5 and b&o=2. Solution is 52. **Go to 52.**

10. The box should be placed in the third position over the number 15 to balance the beam, because 3x10=6x5=30 to balance. **Go to 15. Key 2.**

11. The digits 3&8 of 38 are the only pair of digits in the circle that do not add to 10. **Go to 38. Key 5.**

12. Starting on the top left, the numbers and their square roots are: 25 [5]; 81 [9]; 4 [2]; 5 is the odd number out; 121 [11]; 0 [0]; 49 [7]; 64 [8]; 36 [6]; 1 [1]; 16 [4]; 169 [13]; 144 [12]; 196 [14]; 100 [10]; 9 [3]. **Go to 5.**

13. The only one-number route from A to B, as shown, leads through the number (50). **Go to 50.**

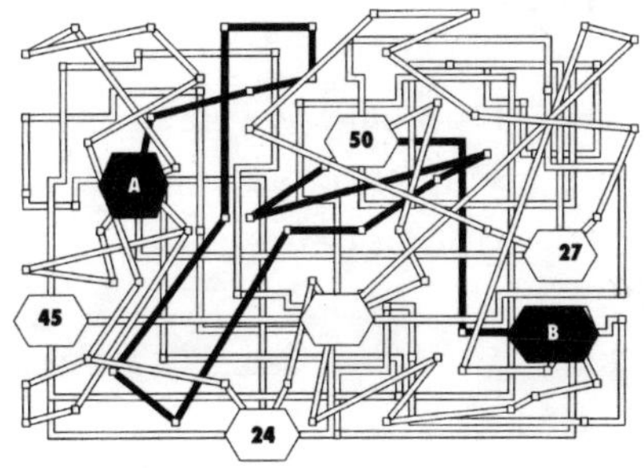

14. There are 22 different shapes as shown here. **Go to 22.**

15. Section C contains 81. 81-21=60. **Go to 60. Key 2.**

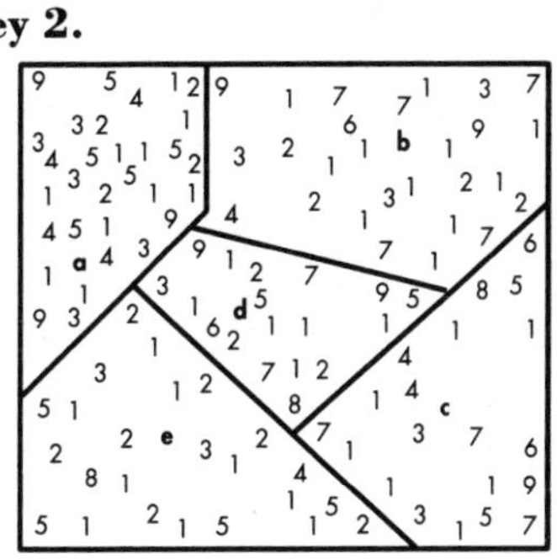

16. The reversed numbers are 37. **Go to 37.**

17. The odd-one-out is A (mirror image of the rest which are all rotated versions of the same thing.) Read passcode for A. **Go to 46.**

18. Solution 42. Starting at the top of each hexagon, alternatively add 6 and multiply by 2 to get the following number, and subtract 6 and divide by 2 to get the next number. Thus in hex. A, 20+6=26, x 2=52. 52-6 = 46, /2=23 . . etc. In hex. B, 15 +6=21, x 2=42. . . etc. **Go to 42.**

19. 17x17=289; 289+11=300. Solution 17 in box 23. **Go to 23.**

20. When the handle is pulled down the big wheel turns clockwise, lowering the numbers on the left by the same distance as the handle is pulled.When the handle is pulled down to 4, the 16 will be opposite the arrow. **Go to 16.**

21. The odd-one-out is B which is a mirror image of the others, which are all rotated versions of the same thing. Read the passcode for B. **Go to 7.**

22. 8sqr. =64; 6+4=10; 10/2=5; 5sqr. =25. **Go to 8.**

23. Star=8; Square=1; Circle=6; 5-point star=5; triangle=3. Bottom right square=1; Top left star=8; 2x18=36. **Go to 36. Key 3.**

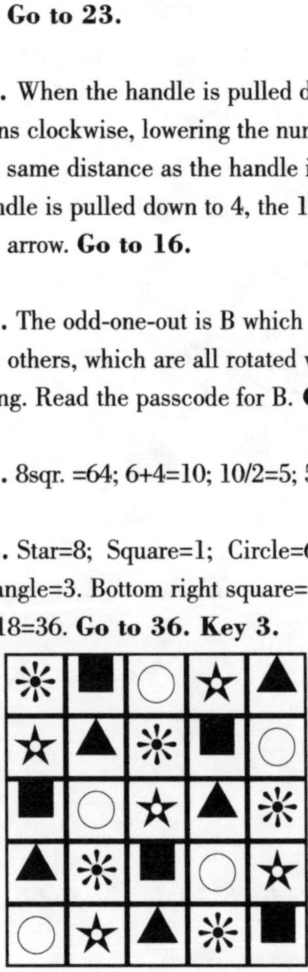

24. 25x5=125; 125+4=129; 129/3=43; 43+43=86. **Go to 25. Key 2.**

25. L=1; N=2; E=1. Solution 121. 121-90=31. **Go to 31. Key 1.**

26. Solution 21. 21x3=63; 63+8=71; 71 +71=142; 142-2=140; 140/4=35. **Go to 21.**

27. The number revealed is 56. **Go to 56. Key 2.**

28. Solution 20. 40x29=1160. 1+1+6+0=8. 40-29=11. **Go to 11.**

29. B is the odd-one-out (mirror image of the others which are all rotated versions of the same thing). Read the passcode for B. **Go to 39.**

30. Follow the route as shown to number 51. **Go to 51.**

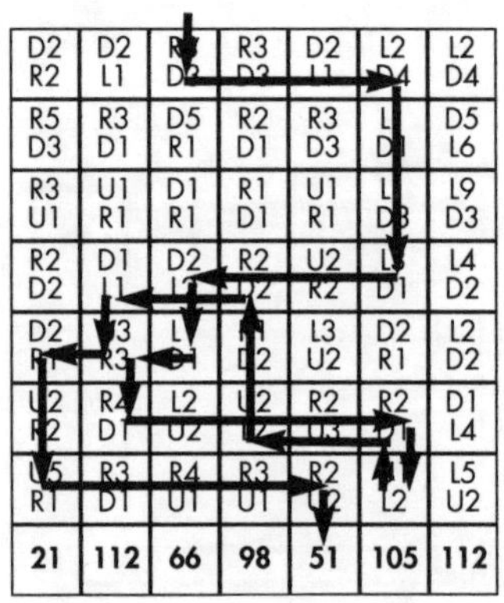

31. There are 27 circles. **Go to 27.**

32. Down. **Go to 59.**

33. D is the odd-one-out. It is a mirror image of the others, which are all rotated versions of the same thing. **Go to 45. Key 1.**

34. Ten blackjacks are 10x21=210; 88 quintets are 88x5=440; 14 dimes worth of cents are worth 14x10=140. Reading down 144. 144-100=44. 44 + 17=61. **Go to 61 – The Keycodes.**

35. The 2 numbers are 18 & 25. 18+25=43. (25sqr.=625) +(18sqr.=324)=949. 69-43=26. **Go to 26.**

36. Write the alphabet in 9 numbered columns, starting A=1 to I=9, then back to J=1 and so on. Then z=8; h=8; r=9; a=1; z=8; u=3; g=7; r=9; h=8. 8+8+9+1+8+3+7+9+8=61. **Go to10** as indicated by the arrow on that diagonal line.

37. The central number is 2. Each four corner numbers, multiplied togther, make the numbers in the center of the larger squares. Thus, 6x3x2x1=36 etc. **Go to 2. Key 3.**

38. x=2; y=3; z=4.Thus z+9=13. **Go to 13.**

39. The four corner sections contain 9+10+11+12=42 stars; 42-1=41. **Go to 41.**

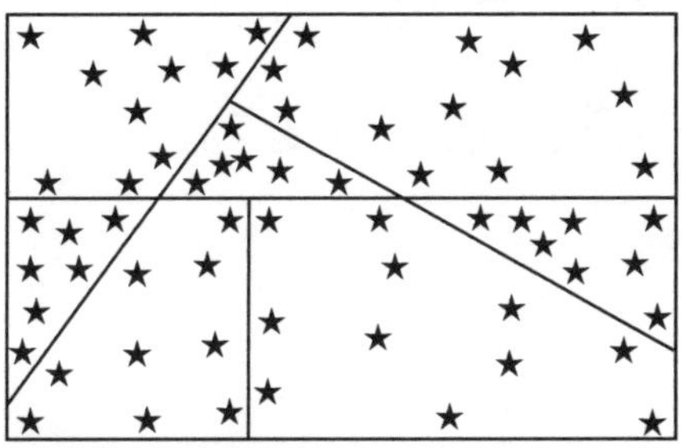

40. A is the odd-one-out (mirror image of the others which are all rotated versions of the same thing.) Read the passcode for A. **Go to 14.**

41. Star=6, triangle=7, circle=4, square=3, cross=2. Central square 6 therefore equals a star. **Go to 55.**

3	7	4	6	2
6	2	3	7	4
7	4	★	2	3
2	3	7	4	6
4	6	2	3	7

42. A is missing a spot which is on the others. **Read the passcode for A. Go to 6.**

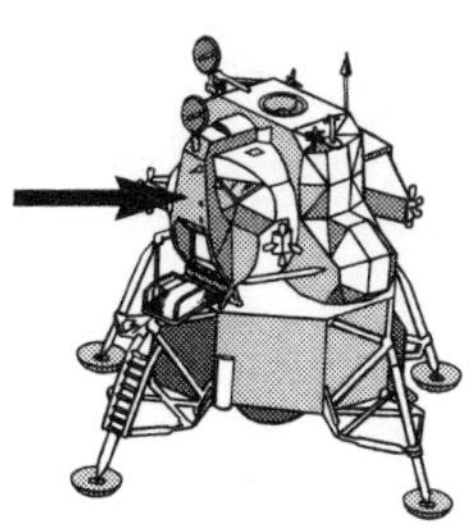

43. X=1; Y=3; Z=6. Thus 1 X + 1 Y + 1 Z = 10. 10+34=44. **Go to 44. Key 5.**

44. The solution is 109. The numbers on the right are the total of the three boxes, minus the most commonly used digit in each row. 15+34+65-5 (most common) = 109. Last digit is a 9. 9 + 10=19. **Go to 19. Key 3.**

45. There are 3 overlapping sections at point (a); 4 at point (b). **Go to 34.**

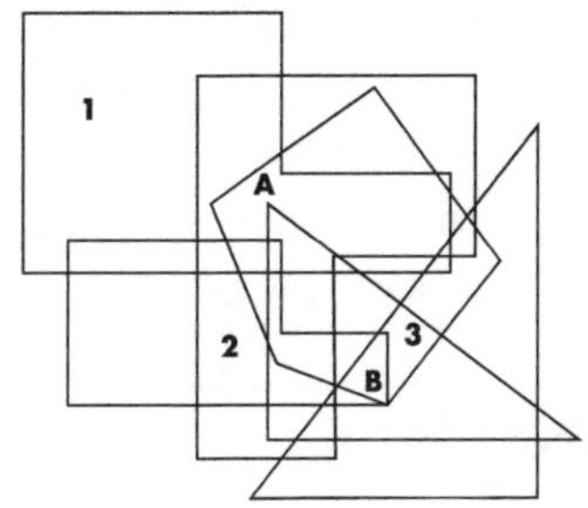

46. Multiply diametrically opposite numbers and add the totals. Thus (3x9)+(2x15)=27+30=57. **Go to 57.**

47. The only route from the metal disposal area that leads to the outside starts with the passcode (9). **Go to 9.**

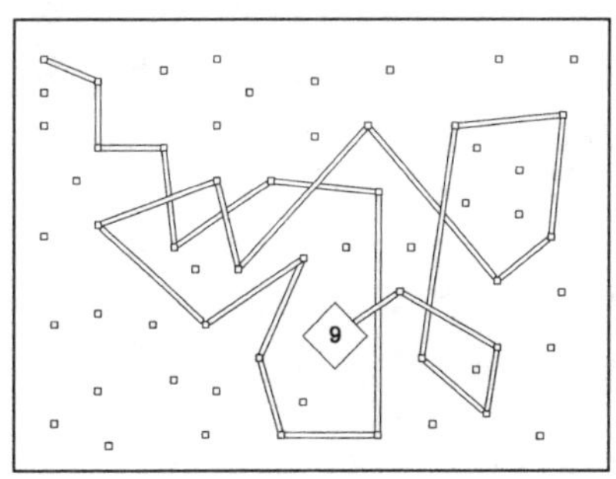

48. Solution 28. 37 is the next prime number below 41. 28+9=37. **Go to 28.**

49. The right hand box contains a (5) which is not present in the left hand box. **Go to 43.**

50. The two numbers are 18 & 51. 18x51=918. 18+51=69. The lower number is 18. **Go to 18. Key 6.**

51. D is the odd-one-out. Read the passcode for D. **Go to 35. Key 1.**

52. Step1: n=1; x=70+1=71; a=70+1sqr. =71
Step2: n=2; x=71+2=73; a=71+2sqr. =75
Step3: n=3; x=73+3=76; a=75+3sqr. =84
Step4: n=4; x=76+4=80; a=84+4sqr. =100.
Thus a=100. Look up passcode for 100

(49). **Go to 49.**

53. Circles = 9; Stars=7; Triangles=4. Thus 2 circles + 1 triangle + 1 star = 29. **Go to 29.**

54. Triangles=5; Squares=6; Stars=2; Circles=3. 4x6=24. **Go to 24.**

55. The least common letter used in the smallest section is i. Read passcode for i. **Go to 17.**

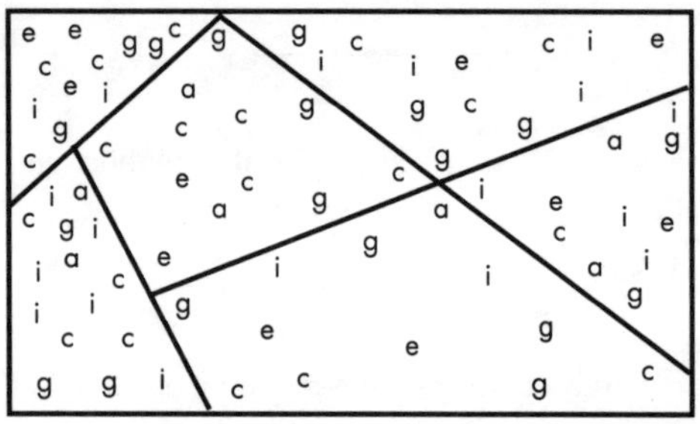

56. The backwards number is 8 (the only number there that reads and looks the same backwards as forwards). Subtract 5 to give 3. **Go to 3. Key 4.**

57. B is the odd-one-out (mirror image of the others which are all rotated versions of the same thing.) Read the passcode for B. **Go to 47.**

58. Map the alphabet in 9 columns onto the key below, using only letters on the bottom row to represent all other letters. Thus the disintegrator with syyuw and 30 maps to apple. **Go to 30.**

1	2	3	4	5	6	7	8	9
a	b	c	d	e	f	g	h	i
j	k	l	m	n	o	p	q	r
s	t	u	v	w	x	y	z	

59. There are most 9s. 9x6=54. **Go to 54. Key 3.**

9	1	8	5	6	2	1
9	46	7	37	3	36	9
4	3	5	1	2	8	5
6	38	9	39	8	51	9
2	8	1	6	7	5	7
7	42	6	35	3	31	2
9	4	5	3	4	2	1

60. 124/4= 31; 31+2=33. **Go to 33.**

5	3	1	2	4
2	4	5	3	1
3	1	2	4	5
4	5	3	1	2
1	2	4	5	3

Section One Keycode: 29-27=2. Go to Section 2, Puzzle 2.

SECTION TWO

Puzzle 1

All the numbers in this puzzle relate to the missing central number. Find it and you find the passcode to your next puzzle in Adrian Smith's cyber-reality.

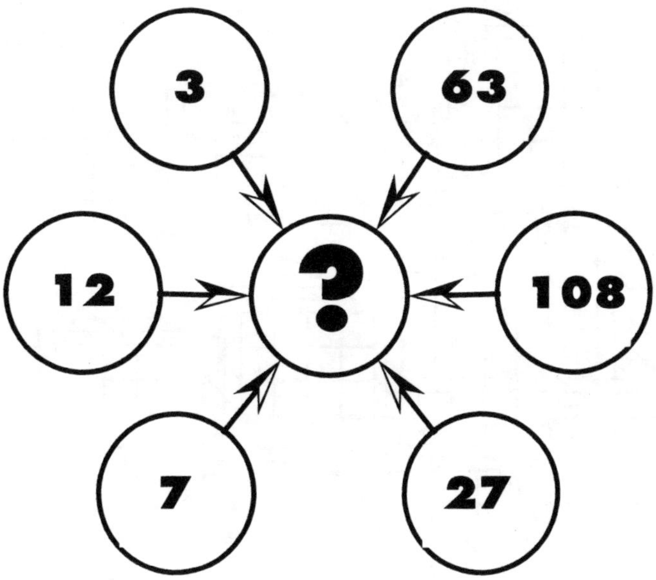

Puzzle 2

Pick the odd-one-out and choose your passcode accordingly.

A= Passcode **34.** **B**= Passcode **21.** **C**= Passcode **10.** **D**= Passcode **45.**

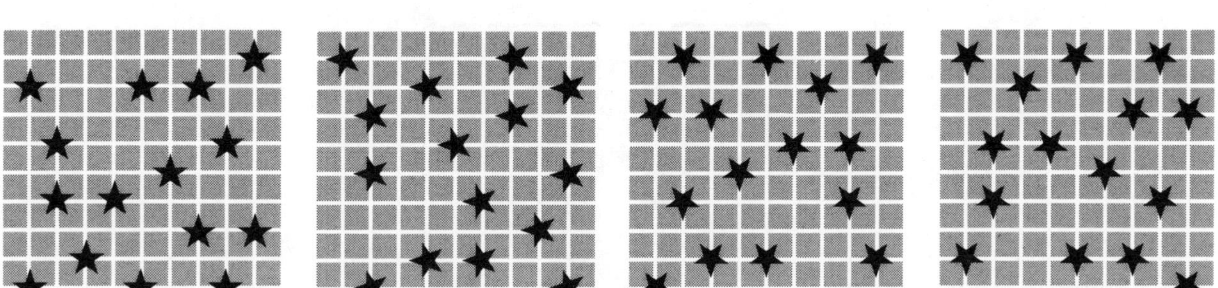

Puzzle 3

Each of these large cubes is made up from 64 smaller cubes. Use the last 2 digits of the number of small cubes + 28 as your next passcode.

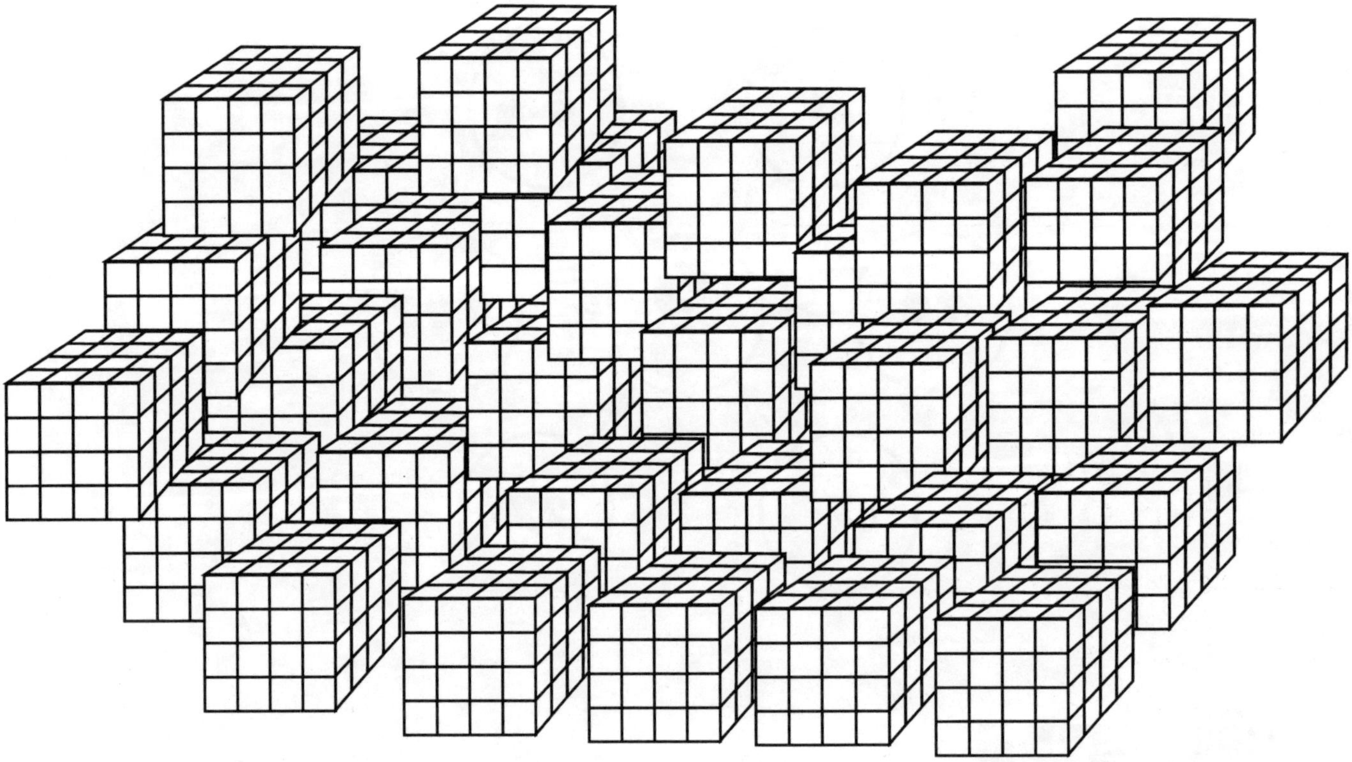

Puzzle 4

Your next passcode is constructed by adding together the two 2-digit numbers which, when squared and added together give 520 as a result.

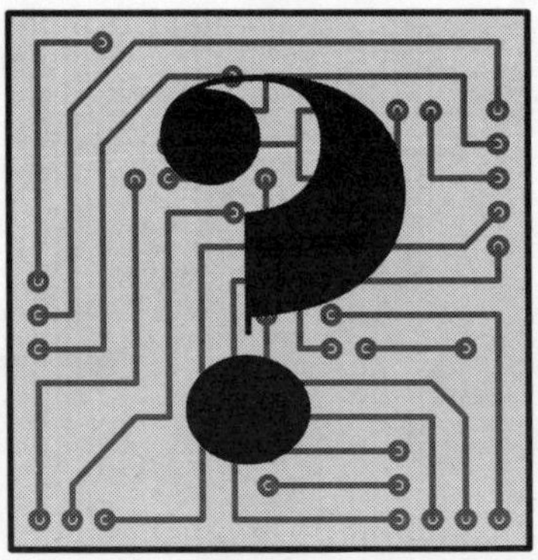

Puzzle 5

Spot the number of differences, apart from the color, between these two pictures. Choose your passcode to the next puzzle according to the number of differences you find.

4 Differences= Passcode **43**
5 Differences= Passcode **27**
6 Differences= Passcode **30**
7 Differences= Passcode **39**

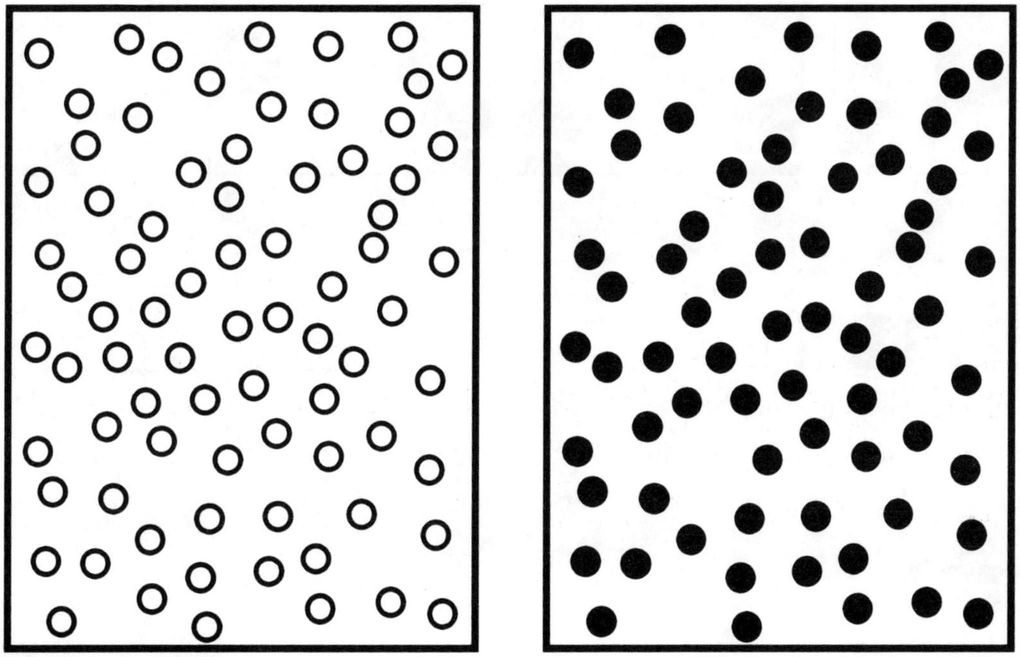

Puzzle 6

The sum of 2 numbers is 3579. When they are multiplied together the result is 2893730. When all the digits of the two numbers are added together they total 24. When the larger number is divided by the smaller number the result is just over 1.9. Use the first and third digits of the smaller number as your passcode to the next puzzle.

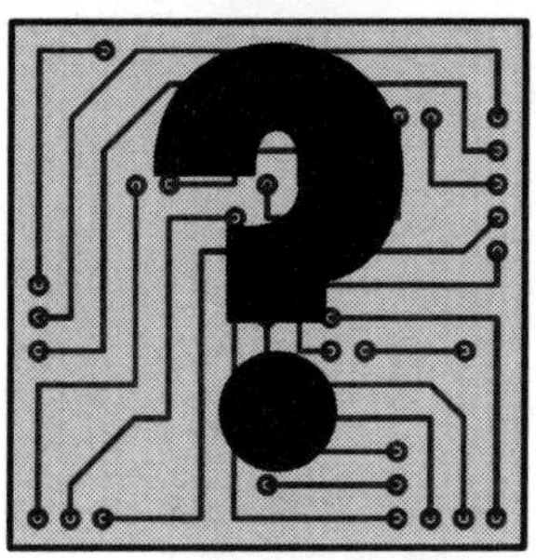

Puzzle 7

Pick the odd-one-out. Choose your passcode according to your answer.

A= 60 B= 14 C= 28 D= 49

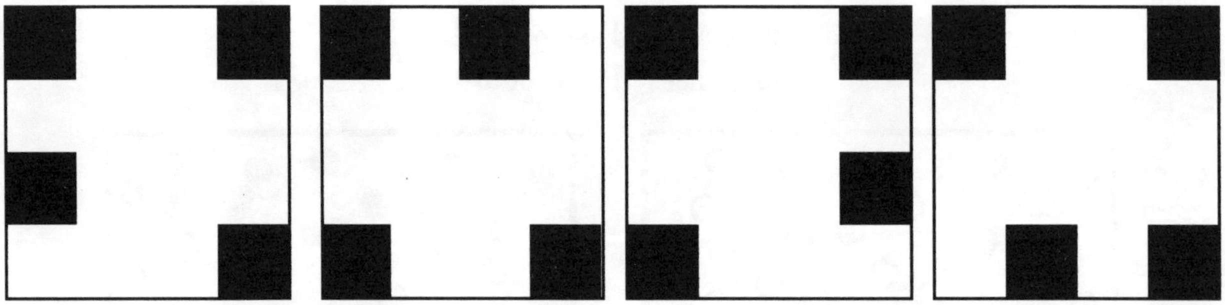

Puzzle 8

When the first cog turns in the direction of the arrow, the swinging batons will knock the ball into pot A or pot B. If you think it will go into pot A, your next passcode is 22. If you think the ball will go into pot B, your next passcode is 35.

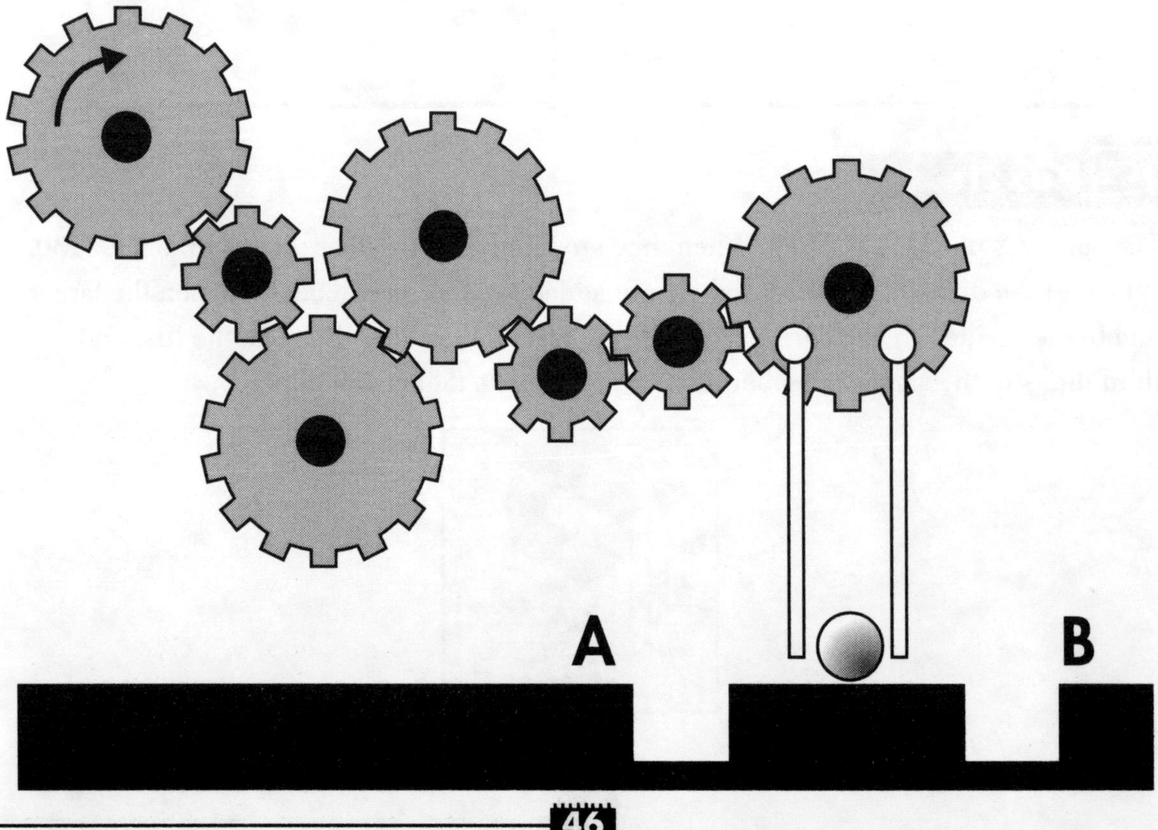

Puzzle 9

When you insert the solutions into this puzzle, you will see a vertical line of numbers. Subtract the bottom 3 from the top 3 to find your next passcode.

A What number, when you subtract 6 and divide the result by 15, gives you a number that, when you add 3 and multply the result by itself, gives you 100?

B What number, when you add 16 and divide the result by 5, gives you a number that, when 16 is subtracted, gives you a number that, when it is divided by 5 gives you 6?

C What number when divided by 3, gives a number that, when 10 is subtracted and the result divided by 2, gives a number that when 2 is added, gives 48?

D What number, when 12 is subtracted, gives a number that, when you subtract 16 and divide the result by 42, gives you a number that, when cubed, gives you 8?

E what number, when you subtract 31 and divide the result by 6, gives you a number that, when you multiply it by 2 and divide by 4, gives you 50?

F What number, when you subtract 60, and divide the result by 18, gives you a number that, when you add 5 and divide the result by 11, gives you the third prime number excluding 1?

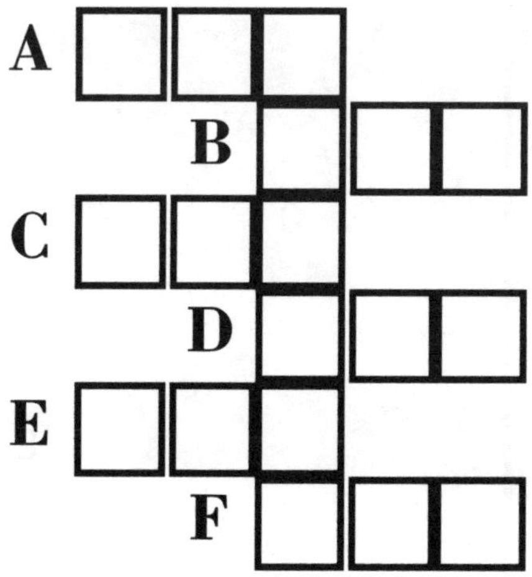

Put the results into the appropriate place:

Puzzle 10

How many differences are there between A and B? Add 13 to the total and use that as your passcode to the next puzzle.

A

B

5

Puzzle 11

Draw 2 straight lines and a circle, to divide this puzzle into 4 sections with values of 100 in 3 of the sections and 150 in one of the sections. Then, add the values of all the 5s in the circle, add 41, and use that as your passcode on the next phase of your quest for escape back to reality.

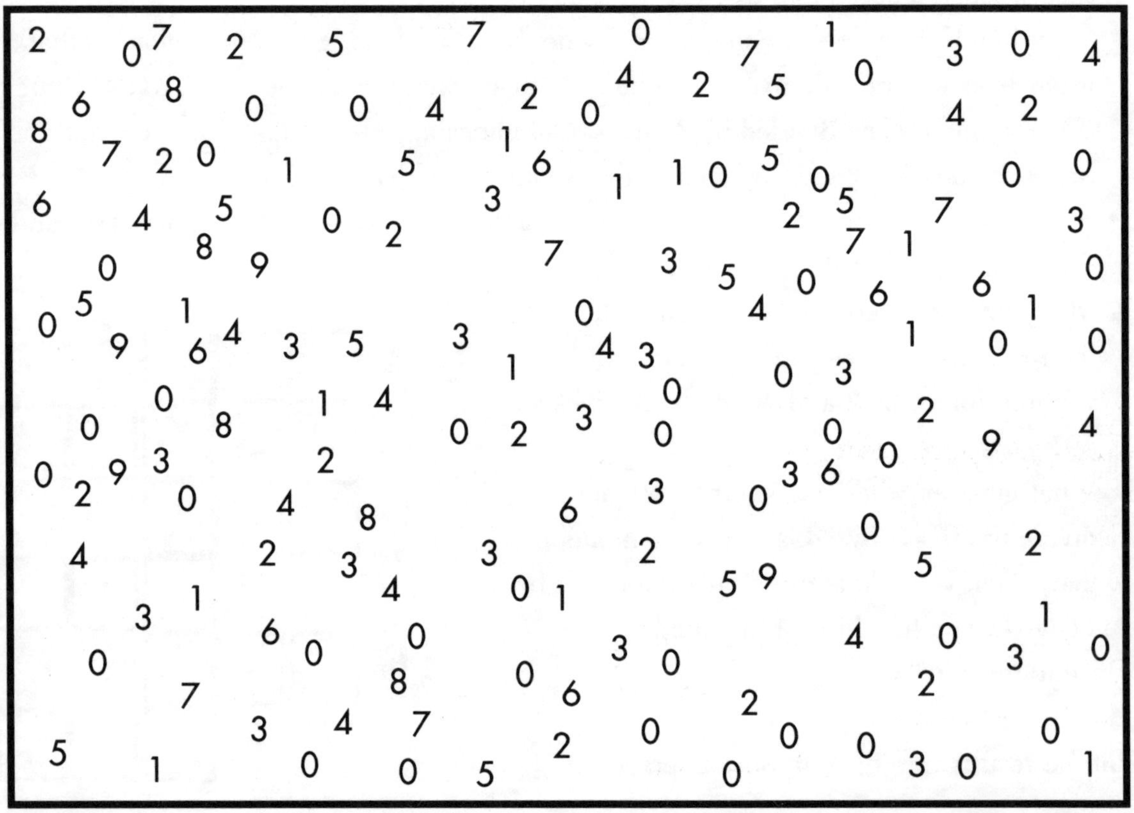

Puzzle 12

Solve Adrian Smith's code and subtract 1 to find your passcode to the next puzzle.

E	H	K	N	Q
24	33	42	51	?

Puzzle 13

Unlucky for some humans. Adrian Smith has decided to use a number base of 8 instead of the usual 10 for this puzzle. Simply subtract octal 122 from octal 144 to get your octal passcode. Then convert into decimal to find your true passcode to the next puzzle.

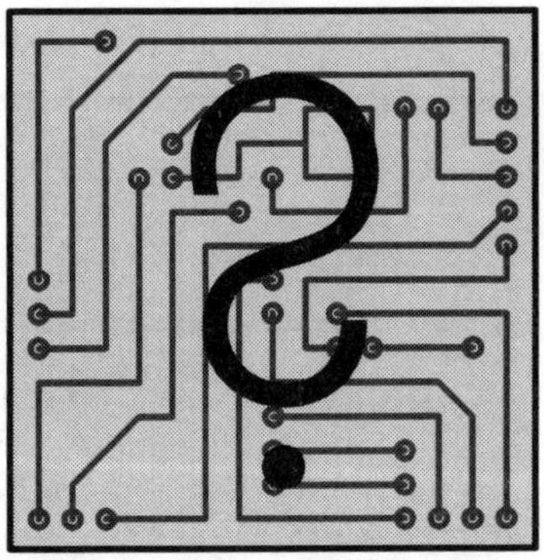

Puzzle 14

Complete Adrian's devious analogy and find your passcode to your next puzzle according to your choice of solution.

A= Passcode **44.**
B= Passcode **36.**
C= Passcode **10.**
D= Passcode **41.**

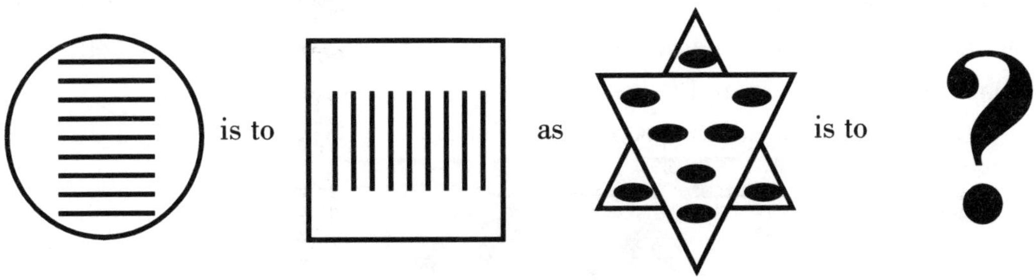

A **B** **C** **D**

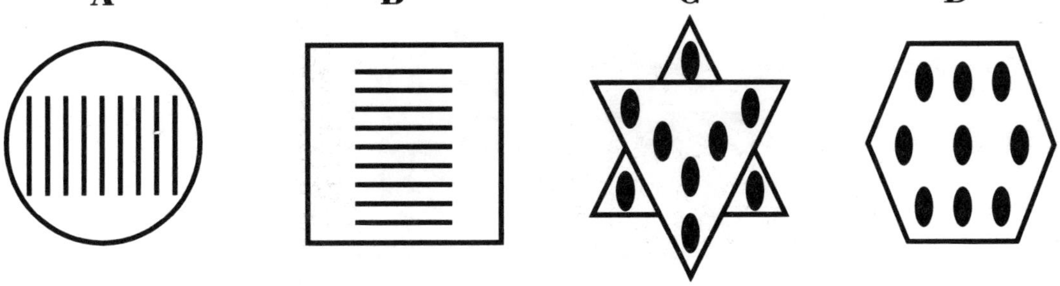

Puzzle 15

Count the number of rockets and subtract 58 to get your next passcode.

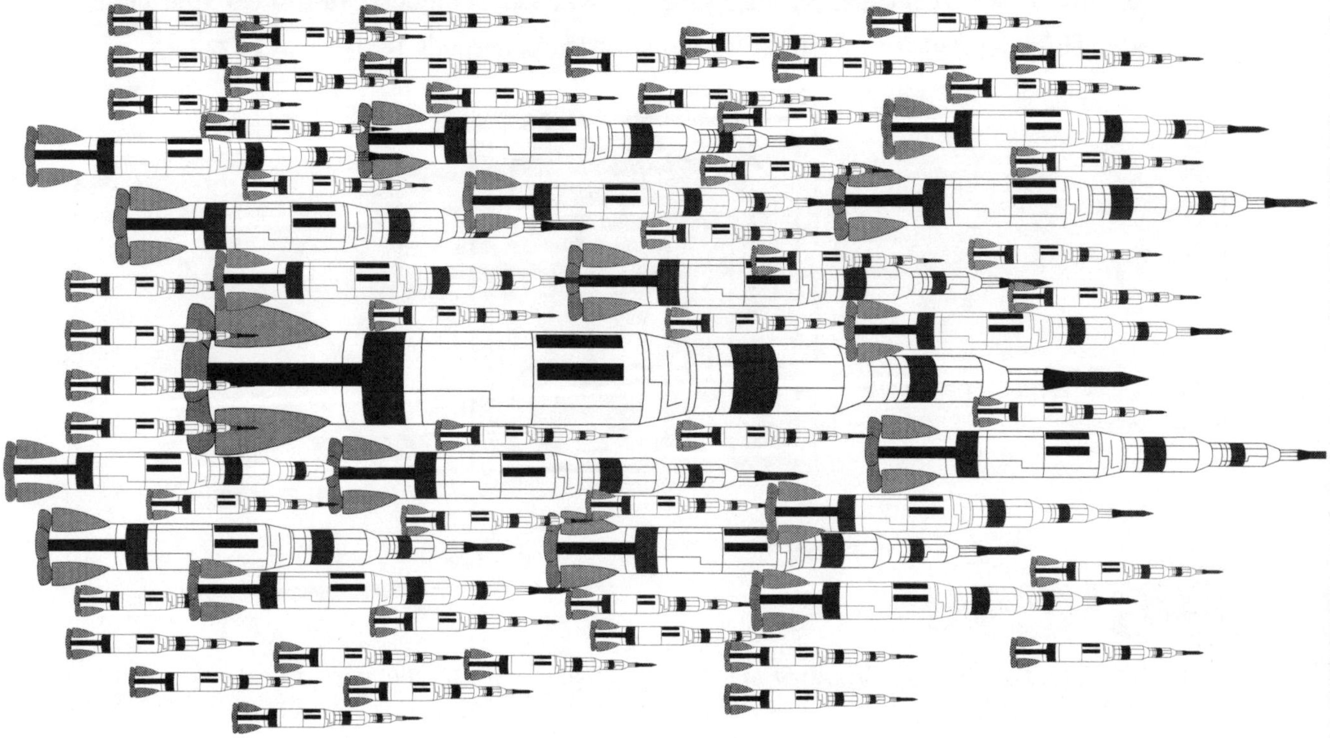

Puzzle 16

Two numbers when added together make 59. When their squares are added together they make 2105. Add 9 to the lesser of the two numbers as your next passcode.

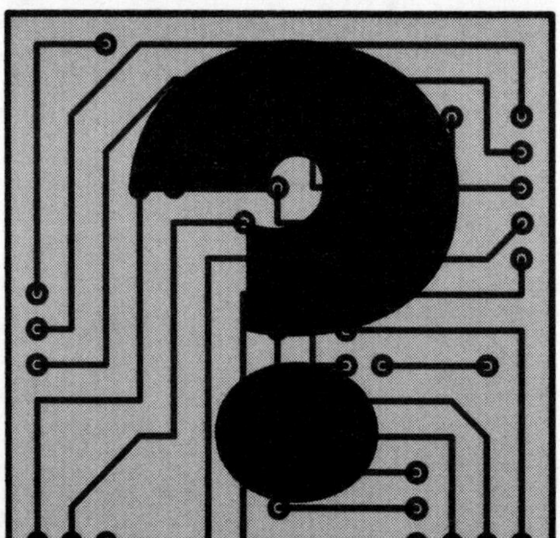

Puzzle 17

One of the boxes below doesn't go with the other 3 boxes. When you know what one it is you will know that by subtracting 1, all four will point to your next passcode.

A		B		C		D	
5	4	6	7	12	2	2	9
3	11	4	6	8	1	7	6

Puzzle 18

The computer below is a representation of a family trapped in cyber-reality. Spot the differences between versions A and B. More than one change to the same object counts as a separate change. Multiply the number of changes by 3 and divide the result by 20 to get the next passcode and help to release yourself and this family.

A

B

Puzzle 19

Pick the panel that should go in the middle of this tile, and choose your passcode accordingly.

A= Passcode **11.** **B**= Passcode **37.** **C**= Passcode **54.** **D**=Passcode **5.**

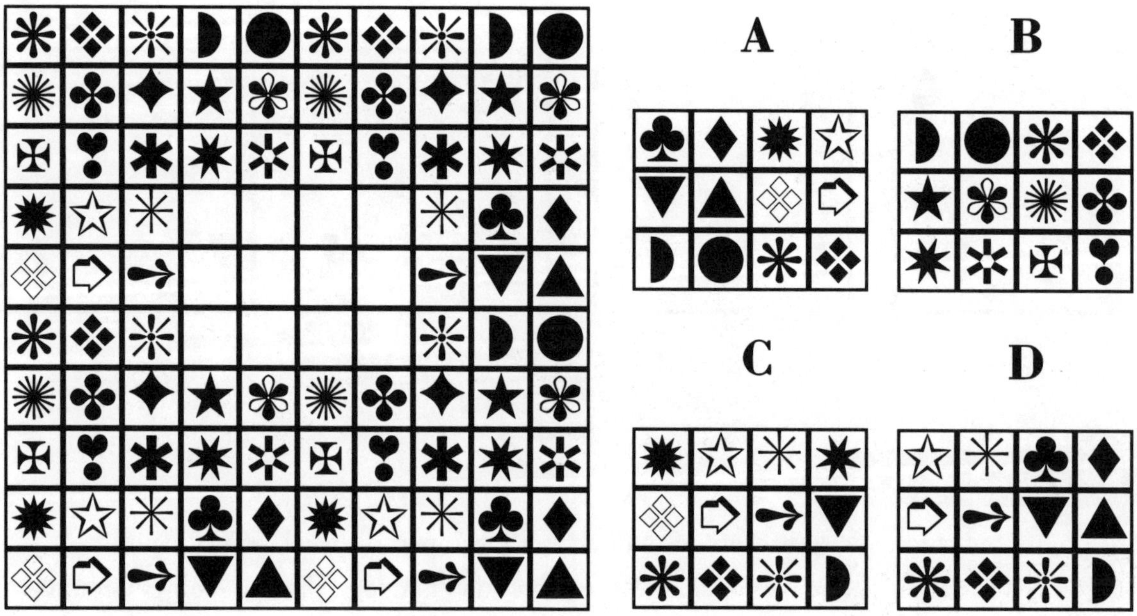

Puzzle 20

Pick the odd-number-out and choose your passcode according to your answer.

A= Passcode **55.**

138

B= Passcode **41.**

161

C= Passcode **33.**

184

D= Passcode **12.**

207

E= Passcode **26.**

228

Puzzle 21

Pick the odd-one-out and choose your next passcode according to your answer.
A= Passcode 19. B= Passcode 40. C= Passcode 52. D= Passcode 9.

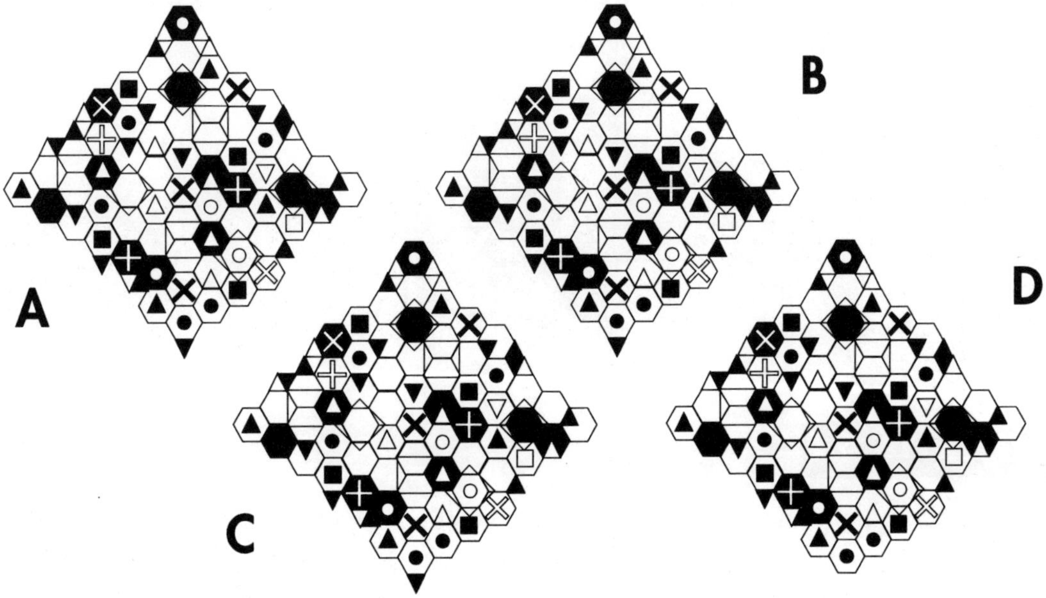

Puzzle 22

9

The value of the missing number in this set is the value of your next passcode.

17	8	12	19	34	2
60	18	56	32	52	6
32	21	33	24	7	?

Puzzle 23

Your next passcode is the number which, if you multiply it by 2, gives you the number that, when you add 8 and subtract 4, gives a result that, when divided by 7 and squared, produces a number that, if 4 is added and thirty is subtracted, and the result squared, produces the next perfect square above 81.

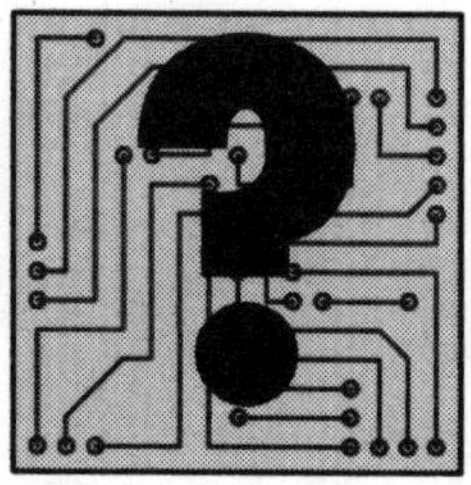

Puzzle 24

Pick the odd-one-out and choose your next passcode according to your answer.

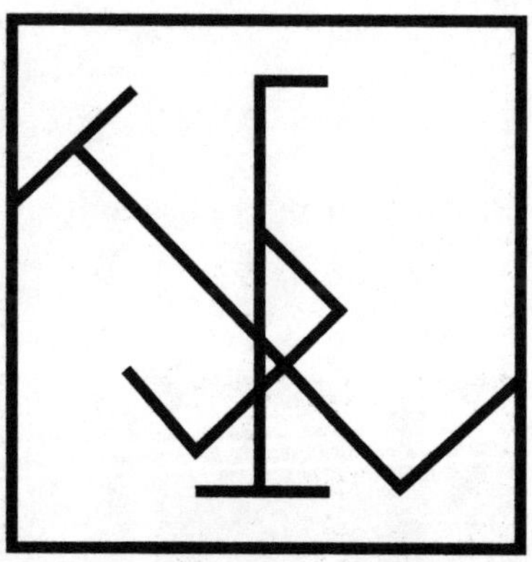

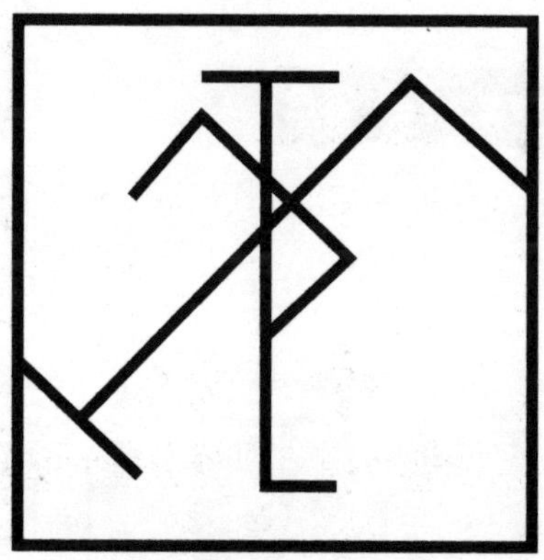

A= Passcode **19.**

B= Passcode **12.**

C= Passcode **33.**

D= Passcode **41.**

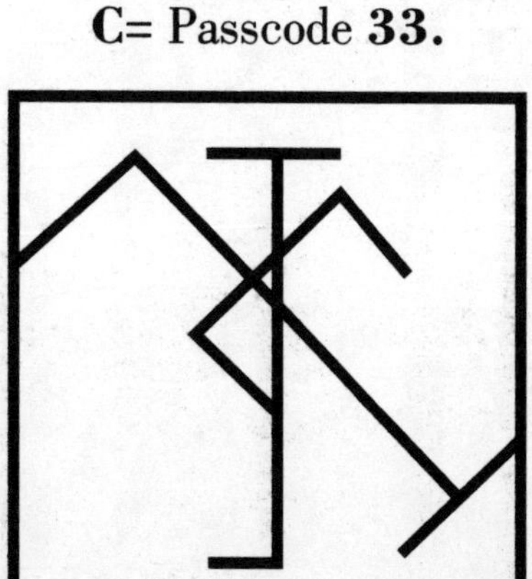

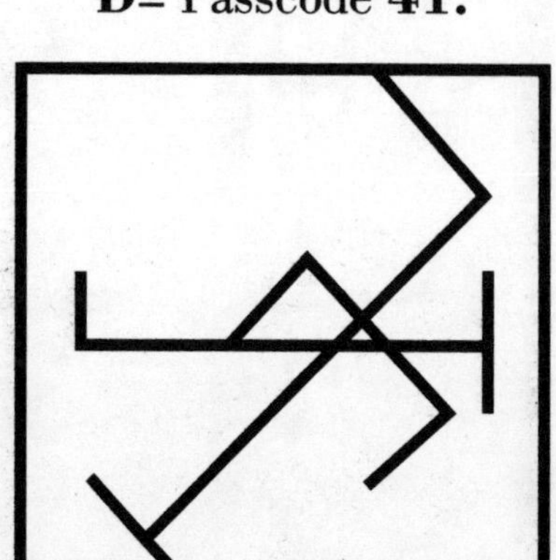

Puzzle 25

Subtract 91 from the missing number in this puzzle to get your passcode for the next step in your battle against Adrian Smith's devious computer mind.

= 105

= 109

= 126

= ?

Puzzle 26

Pick the odd-one-out and choose your next passcode according to your answer.

A= Passcode **51.**

B= Passcode **31.**

C= Passcode **44.**

D= Passcode **16.**

Puzzle 27

Adrian's next challenge is directed at your numerical reasoning. Find the odd-number-out and use that as your passcode to the next puzzle. If your answer is C or D, subtract 50; if it is E, subtract 100.

A	B	C
24	36	64

D	E
81	144

Puzzle 28

Your next passcode is equal to the total number of large and small hexagon-based stars.

Puzzle 29

To find your next passcode you must work out a Mayan calculation based on the key below, and subtract 59 as indicated. The Mayans used a base 20 system rather than the base 10 system that we use.

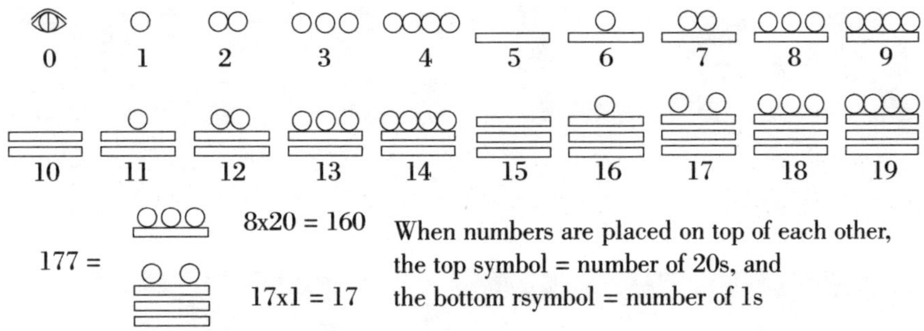

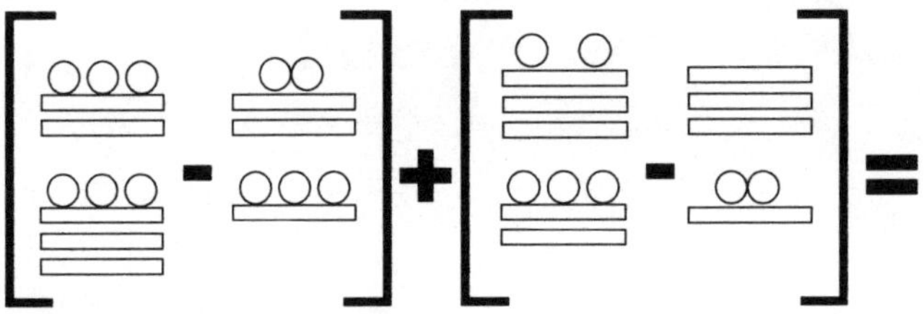

= Passcode + 59

Puzzle 30

Pick the odd-one-out and choose your next passcode according to your answer.

A= Passcode **14.**

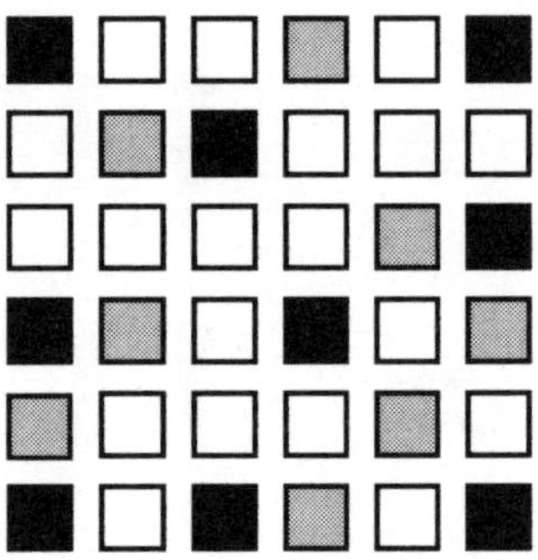

B= Passcode **38.**

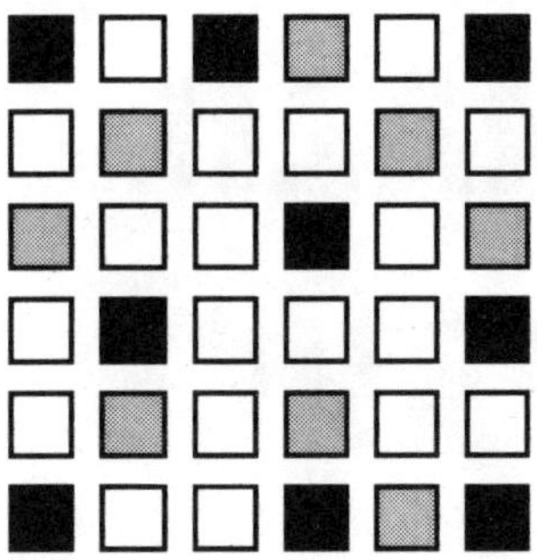

C= Passcode **27.**

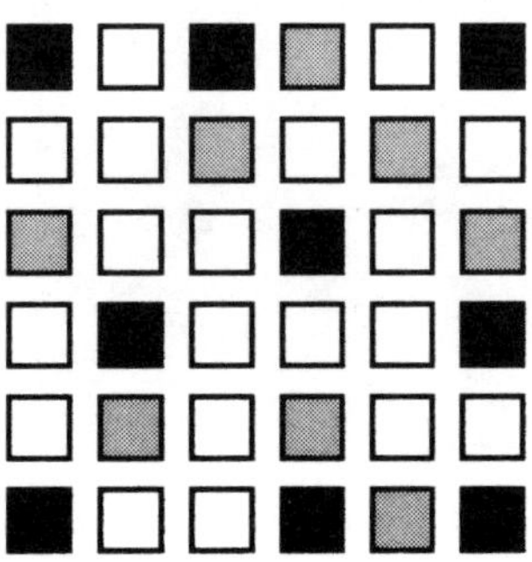

D= Passcode **49.**

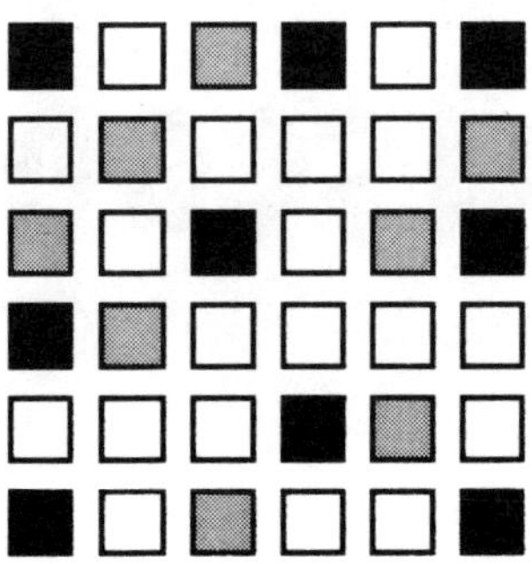

Puzzle 31

Work out your next passcode by discovering the values of A and B, and subtracting 4 from B.

A + B = 50   B - A = 26

PASSCODE = B - 4

Puzzle 32

Find the solution to PASSCODE and divide the result by 8.9 to find the real passcode for your next stop in cyber-reality.

BRAZIL = 140

FRANCE = 119

HOLLAND = 150

PASSCODE = ?

4

Puzzle 33

You will need to make good use of Adrian Smith's video scanner eyes to solve this one. Pick the odd-one-out and choose your next passcode according to your answer.

A= Passcode **60**

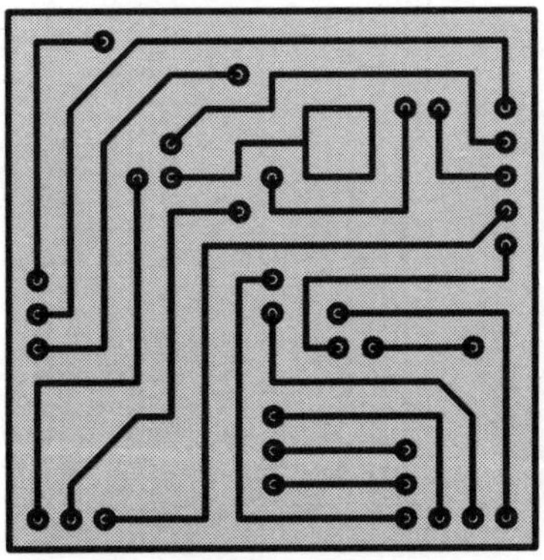

B= Passcode **6**

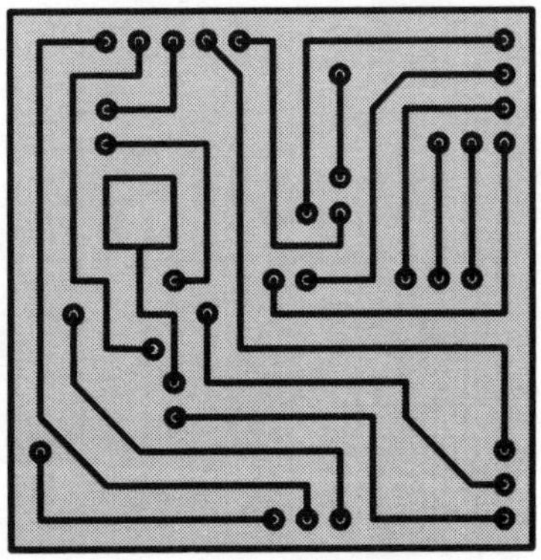

C= Passcode **25**

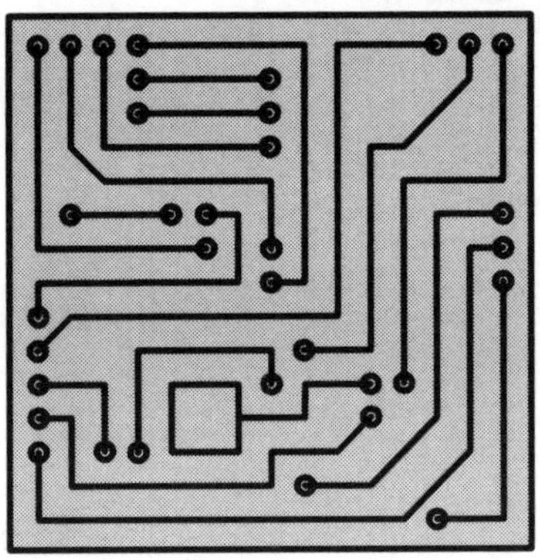

D= Passcode **3**

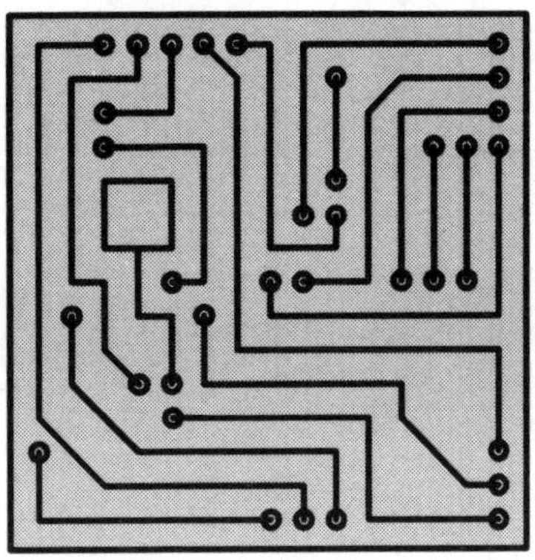

Puzzle 34

Rearrange the digits 72161767 to find a perfect square.
The eighth root of that square (the square root of the square root of the square root of that square) is the next passcode on your quest for freedom from cyber-reality.

7 2 1 6 1 7 6 7

Puzzle 35

Which of the surrounding plans makes the cube in the middle? Choose your next passcode according to your answer.

A= Passcode **57.** **B**= Passcode **16.** **C**= Passcode **19.** **D**= Passcode **42.**

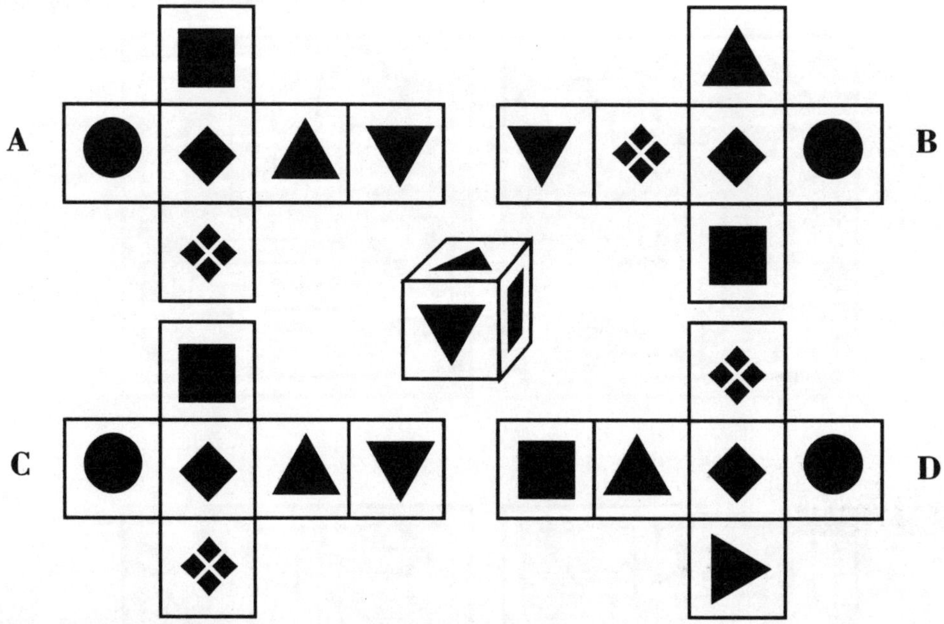

Puzzle 36

Solve the problem in the box to find your passcode to the next puzzle.

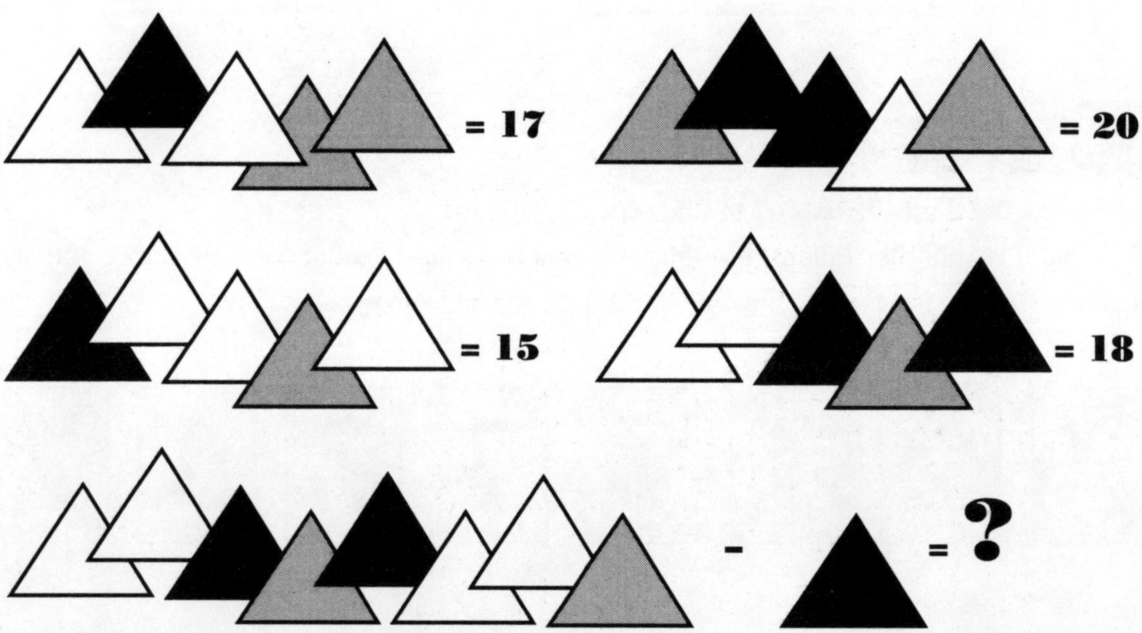

Puzzle 37

Pick the odd-one-out and choose your next passcode according to your answer.

A= Passcode **12.** **B**= Passcode **38.** **C**= Passcode **33.** **D**= Passcode **48.**

Puzzle 38

Complete this magic square so that every row, column, and long diagonal add to 175. To find your passcode to the next puzzle, double the central number of the square.

30	39	48	1	10	19	28
38	47	7	9	18	27	29
46	6				35	37
5	14				36	45
13	15				44	4
21	23	32	41	43	3	12
22	31	40	49	2	11	20

Puzzle 39

Pick the odd-one-out and choose your next passcode according to your answer.

A= Passcode **51.** **B**= Passcode **59.** **C**= Passcode **43.** **D**= Passcode **13.**

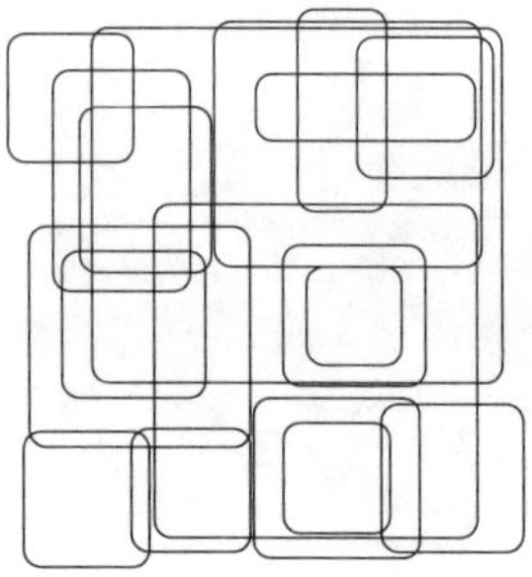

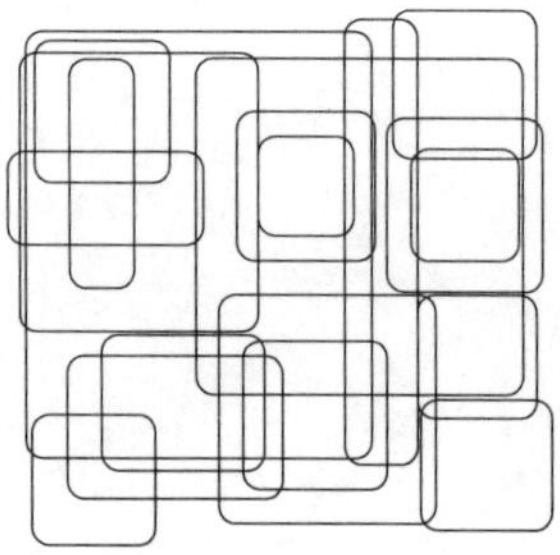

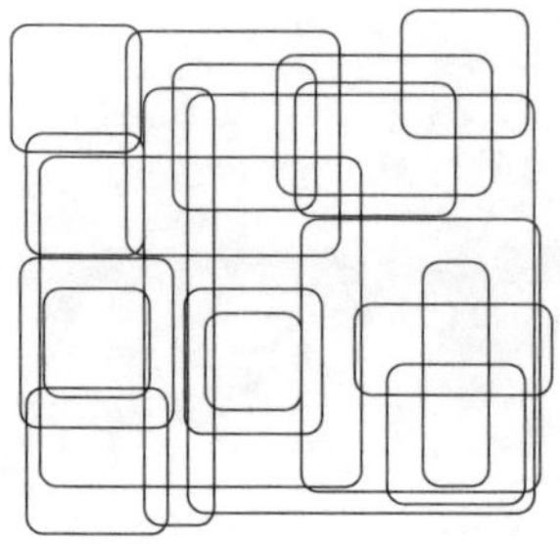

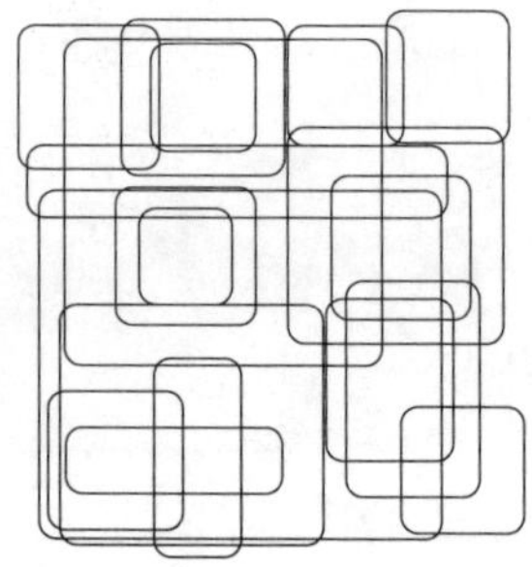

Puzzle 40

Add 45 to the missing number in D to find your passcode to the next puzzle.

A

B

C

D

Puzzle 41

The last 2 digits of the square of the distance between Disk A and Disk B is the passcode to your next puzzle on your quest for freedom from cyber-reality.

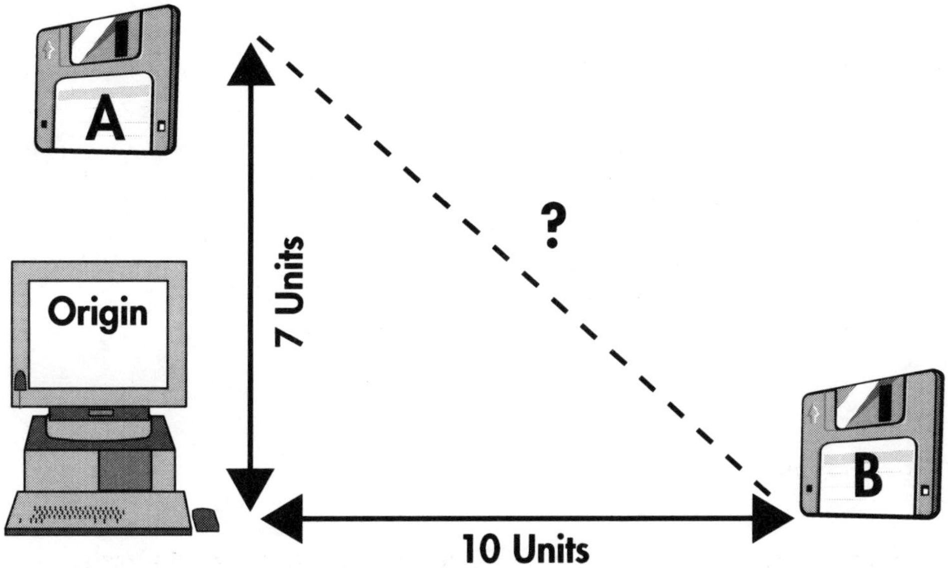

Puzzle 42

Find the odd-one-out. Choose your passcode to the next puzzle according to what you think the answer is.

A= Passcode **53.** **B**= Passcode **14.** **C**= Passcode **40.** **D**= Passcode **16.**

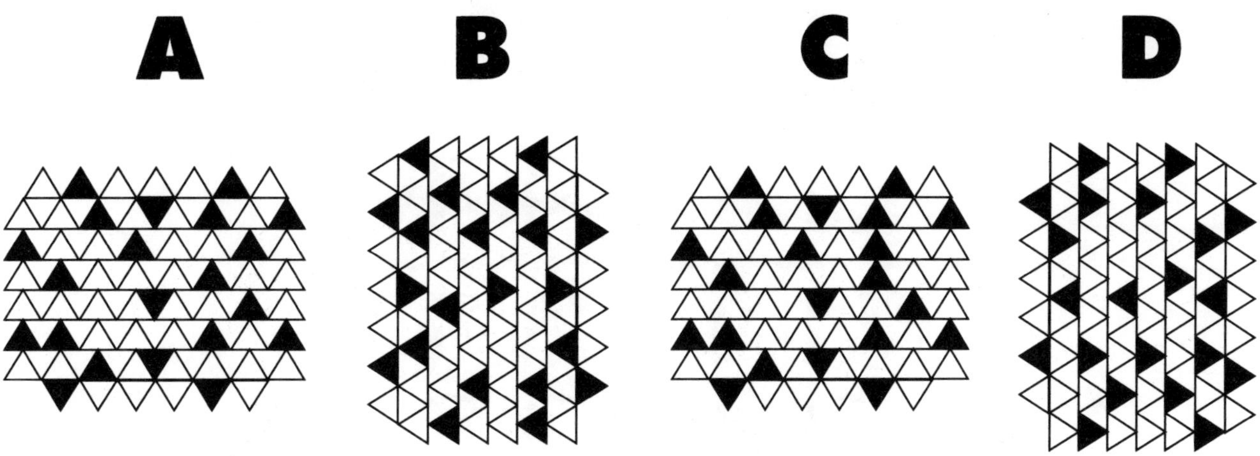

Puzzle 43

Ignoring zeros, draw 3 straight lines to divide this puzzle into 5 sections which contain, respectively, values of 99, 66, 33, 33, and 33. Then, again ignoring zeros, count the number of digits in the smallest section and add 21 to the total to get your next passcode.

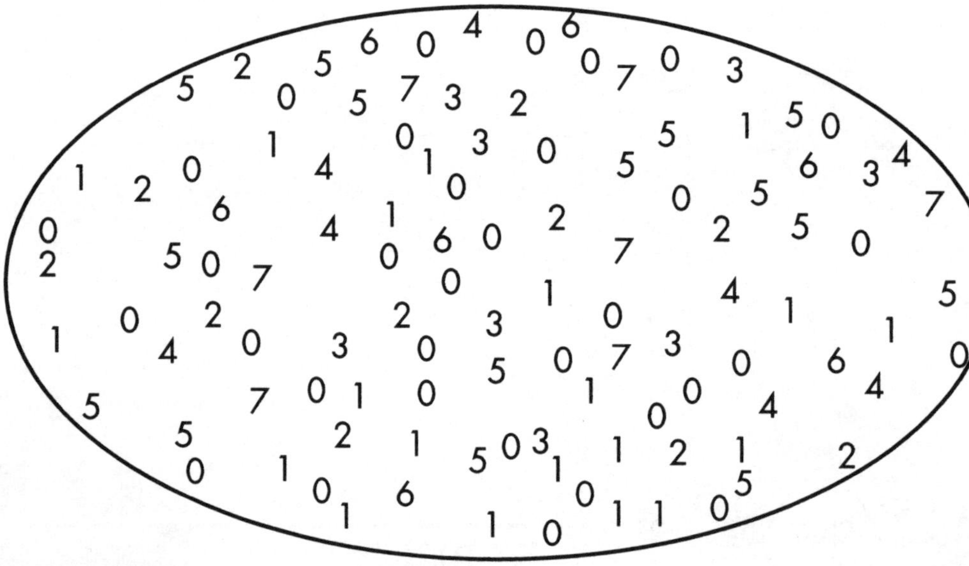

Puzzle 44

2

Here is a simple addition sum with a bit of a complication. The numbers in line B are all mixed up and two of the numbers in line C have been transposed. Make line C equal line A + line B, by rearranging the necessary digits. Your passcode may then be read in the shaded squares in the order CB.

A	1	5	6	4	7	8
B	5	0	7	1	9	2
C	4	3	9	5	7	9

A	1	5	6	4	7	8
B						
C						

Puzzle 45

Find a route from the left of this puzzle to the right that takes you through a total of 376. Then subtract 54 from the cell that you finish on to find your next passcode. The circuit gates are trapped; landing on or next to a gate will trap you forever, so keep at least one cell's distance away from them. Finally, you can use each cell only once.

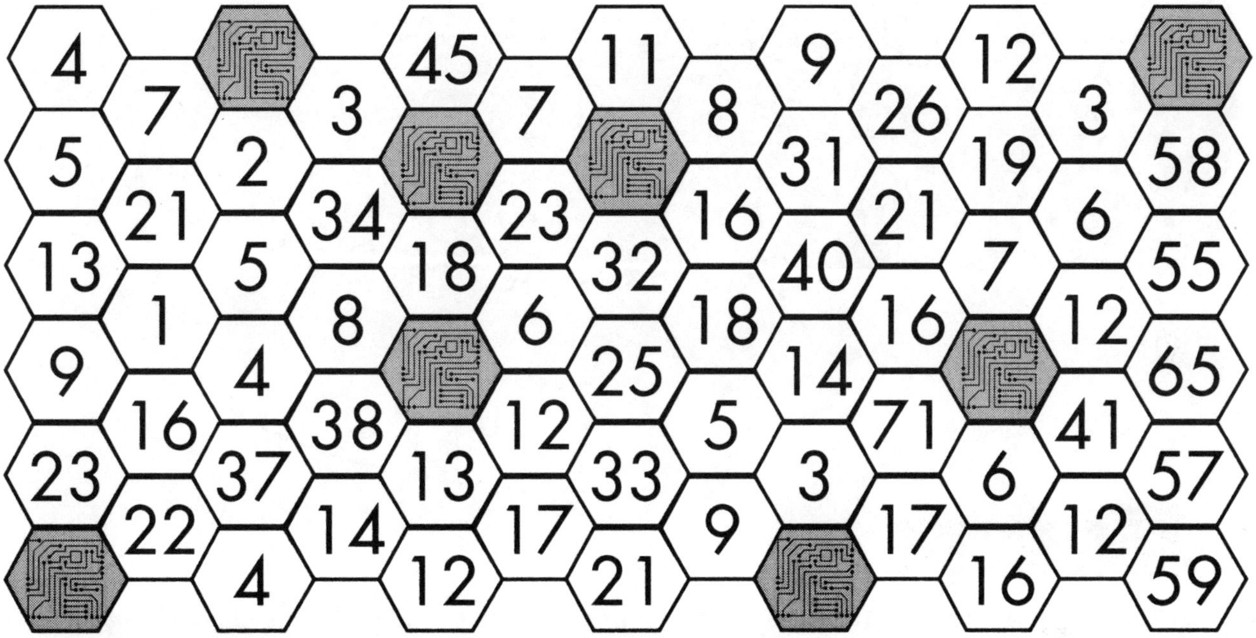

Puzzle 46

Beat one of Adrian's tougher visual puzzles and spot the odd-one-out. Choose your passcode to the next puzzle according to what you think the answer is.

A= Passcode **11.** **B**= Passcode **4.** **C**= Passcode **10.** **D**= Passcode **43.**

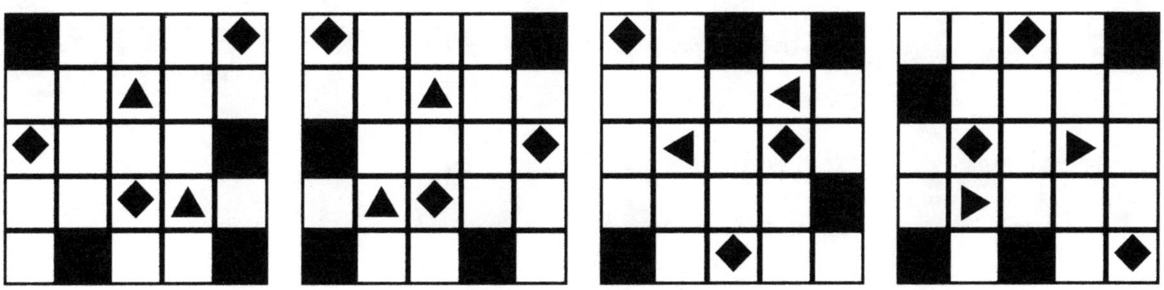

Puzzle 47

Pick the odd-one-out and choose your passcode accordingly.

A= Passcode **29.** **B**= Passcode **17.** **C**= Passcode **20.** **D**= Passcode **57.**

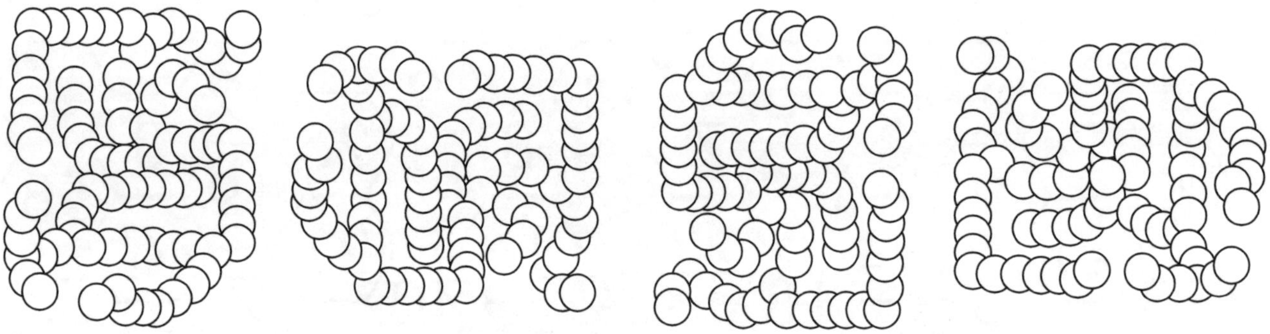

Puzzle 48

Decode this archaic circuitboard code to find your next passcode. The symbols in each sum stand for the numbers from 0 to 9, but not in that order. Adrian Smith is betting that your human mind will get the boards confused.

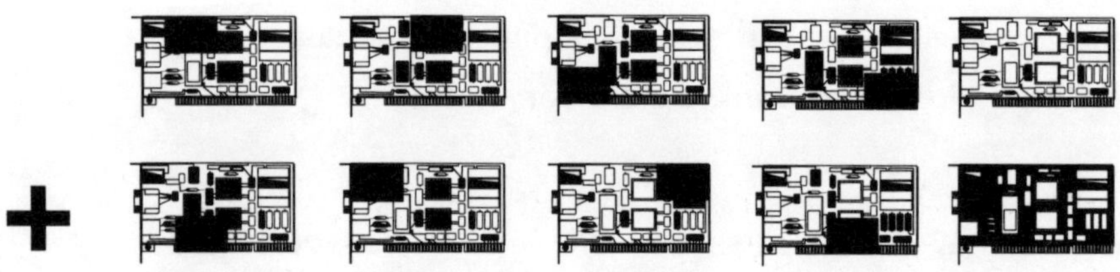

8 5 0 5 9

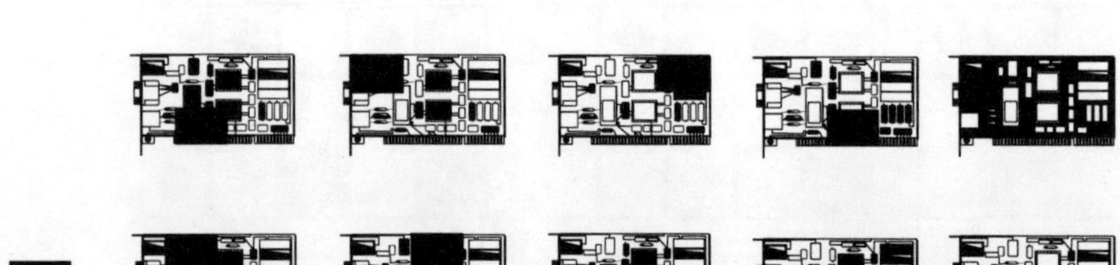

3 7 8 9 9

Passcode =

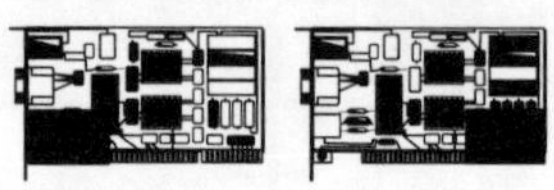

Puzzle 49

Put the missing numbers in the squares so that each 4 corner numbers, when multiplied together, equal the numbers in the middle of each set of 4. When you've done that, add the total of the missing numbers to get your passcode to the next puzzle.

3		2		5		3		6
	252		280		300		360	
6								4
	630		168		320		480	
5								3
	360		180		480		288	
4								2
	648		810		630		336	
3		9		3		7		4

Puzzle 50

Two of the images below are rotated mirror images of the other three, which are rotated but unmirrored versions of the same image. The number below the two mirror-images, reading from left to right, gives you the number of your next passcode.

A B C D E

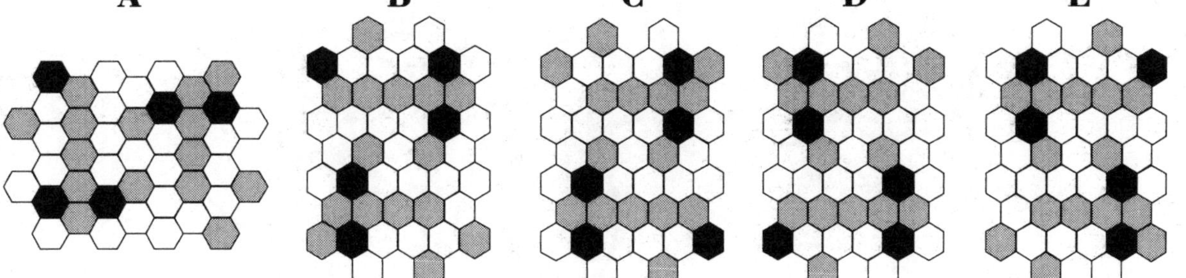

5 3 6 1 9

Puzzle 51

5

Pick the odd-one-out. The number on the front face of the odd-one-out is your passcode to the next puzzle in your battle for escape from cyber-reality.

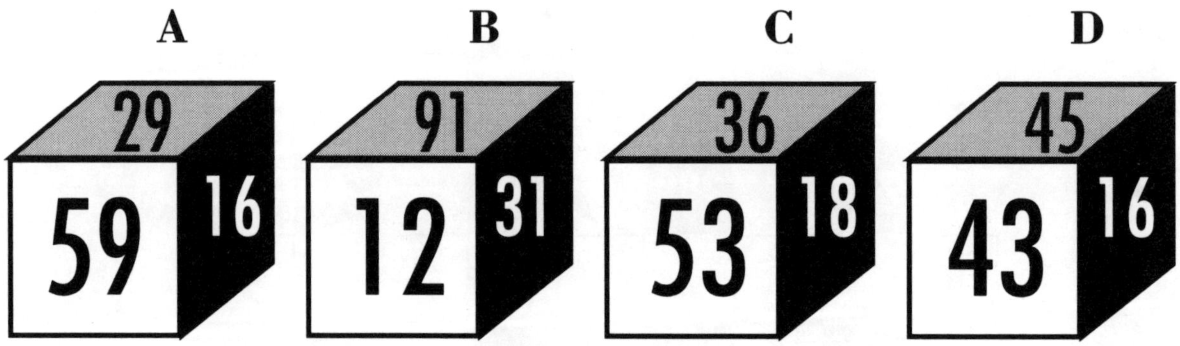

Puzzle 52

Subtract the number of stars from the number of circles in this puzzle to find your next passcode. The stars are underneath everything else, but the circles are transparent.

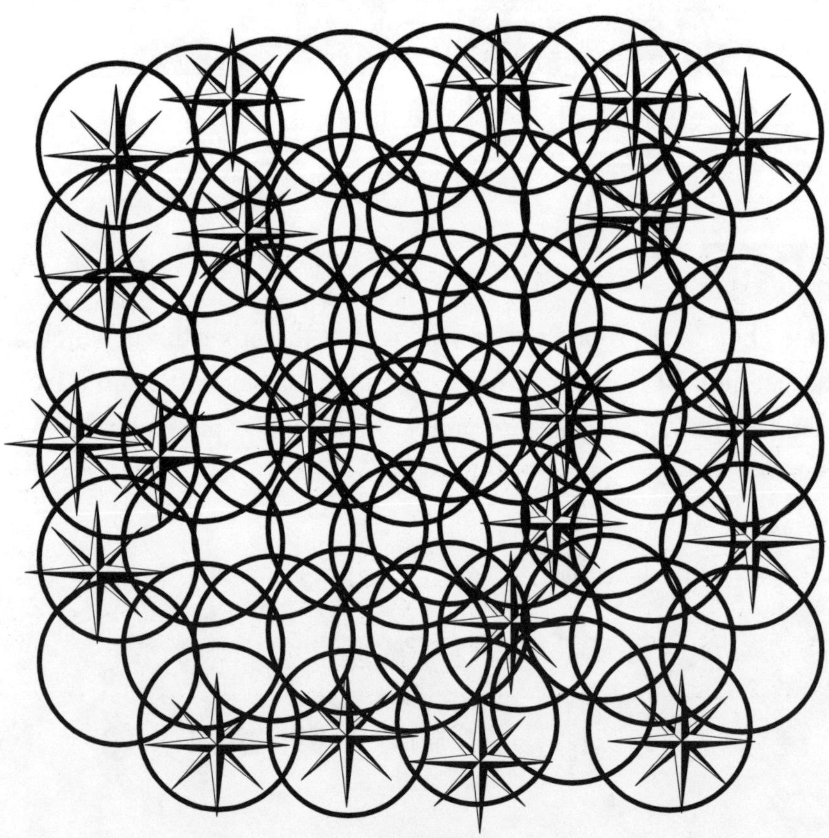

Puzzle 53

This beam is not in balance, being held in position by the rope on the right. Find the position where the additional block marked '3' should go to balance the beam and allow the rope to be removed. Multiply the numerical position of the placement by 3 to find your next passcode.

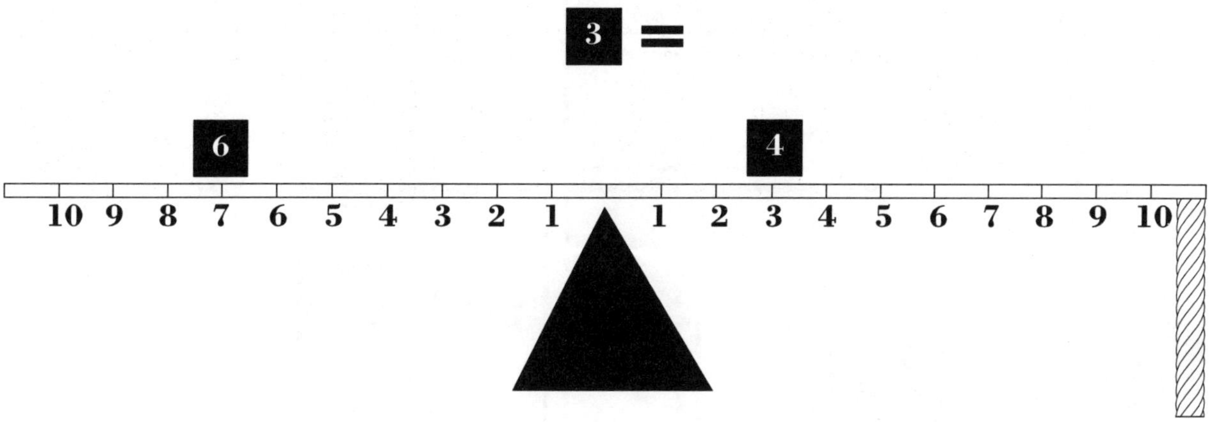

Puzzle 54

The missing number in this puzzle is your passcode to the next stop on your route to escape from Adrian Smith's cold wired body.

A	B	C
2	3	5
1	6	8
8	5	3

A	B	C
6	3	9
2	3	5
1	4	5

A	B	C
1	3	4
4	2	7
7	8	?

Puzzle 55

Complete this magic square so that every row, column, and diagonal adds to 65. Then double the value of the central square and add 2 to get the value of your next passcode.

17	24	1	8	15
23				16
4				22
10				3
11	18	25	2	9

Puzzle 56

Pick the odd-one-out and choose your passcode from the center accordingly. The numbers indicate only the passcode and are not part of the puzzle.

A B C D

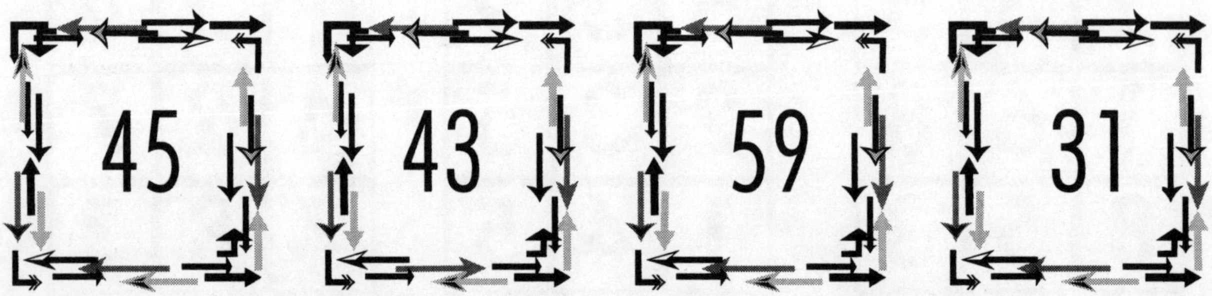

Puzzle 57

Add 4 to the missing number in this sequence to discover your next passcode.

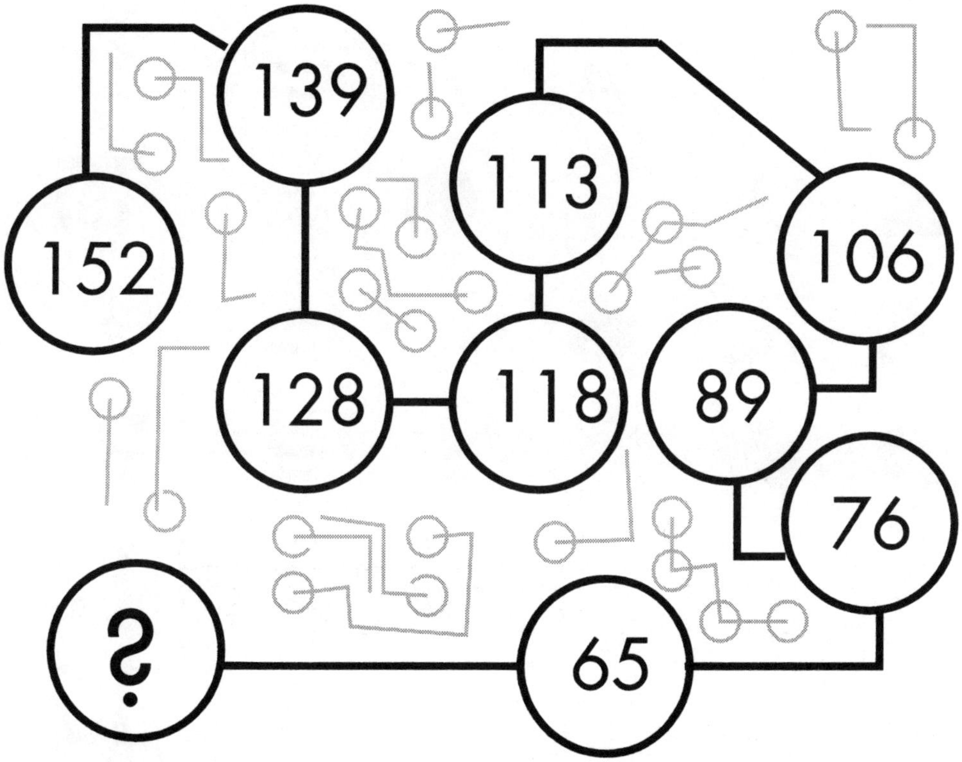

Puzzle 58

Your next passcode is hidden in this number sequence.

First and second digits of passcode

?	?	8	3	1	4	5	9	4	3
7	0	7	7	4	1	5	6	1	7
8	5	3	8	1	9	0	9	9	8

Puzzle 59

When you know what number should replace the question mark, you'll know your passcode to the next puzzle.

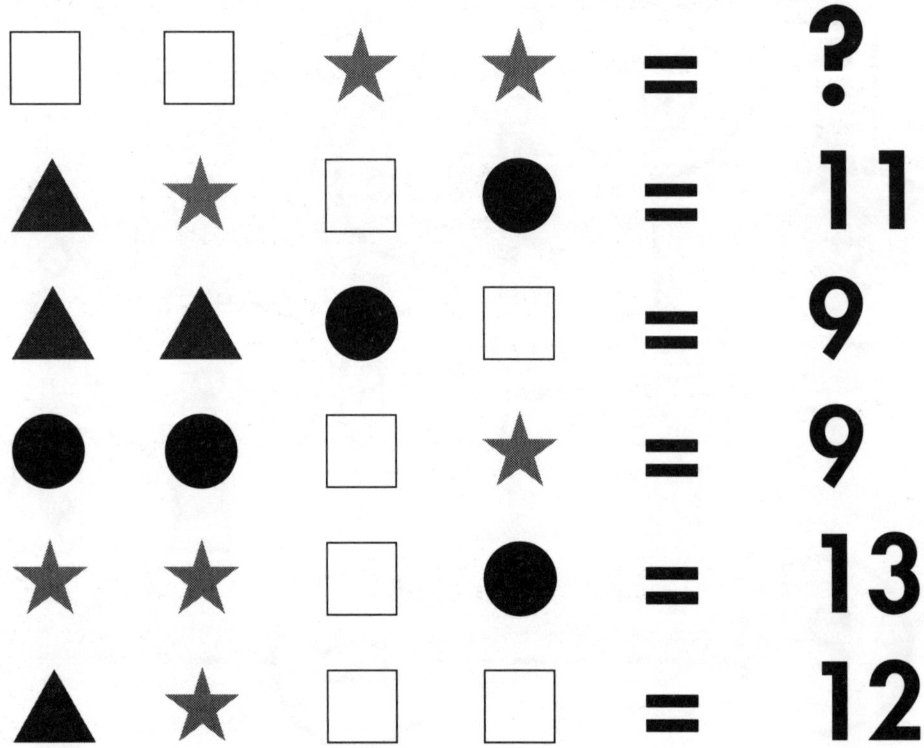

Puzzle 60

Subtract 20 from the missing number in the 3rd triangle to find your passcode to the next puzzle.

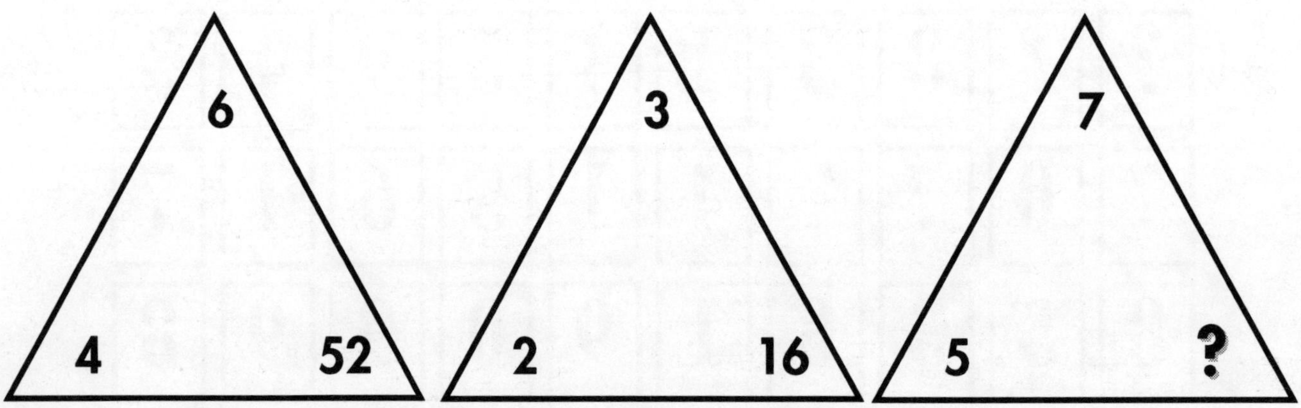

SECTION TWO KEYCODES

REMINDER: You must solve the puzzles in the correct order. Start at the top of column A, and insert your keys. When you get to the bottom of column A, start back at the top of column B.

As in the reverse of the previous section, subtract the total of column B from the total of column A. The result is your solution for Section 1. Write that below and in the appropriate place on page 218, and use that number as your passcode to the starting puzzle for Section 3.

Adrian Smith is getting really mad at your great endurance.

Can you maintain your progress?

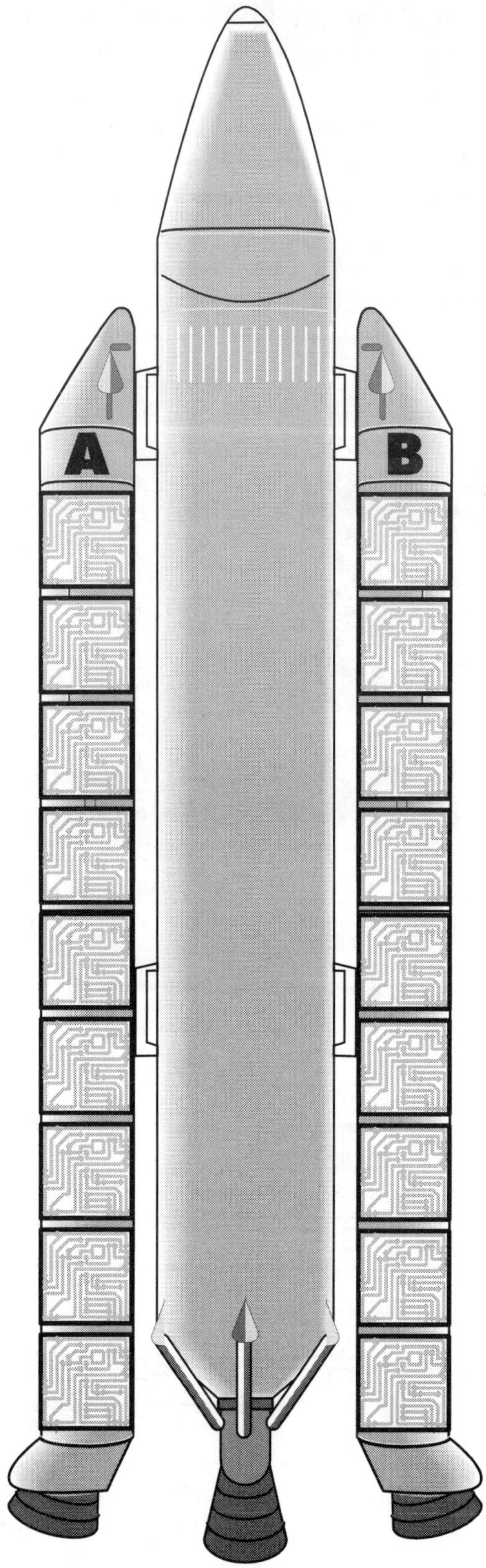

Total A

Total B

SECTION TWO

PASSCODE

SECTION TWO

ANSWERS

1. The missing number is 9. Each number, when multiplied or divided by 9, gives the diametrically opposite number. **Go to 9.**

2. The odd-one-out is D, which is a mirror-image of the others, which are all rotated versions of the same thing. Read the passcode for D. **Go to 45.**

3. There are 30 large cubes. 30x64=1920. The last 2 digits =20; 20+28=48. **Go to 48. Key 3.**

4. Solution 32. The two numbers are 18 & 14. 18x18=324; 14x14=196; 324+196=520. **Go to 32.**

5. There are 5 spots missing from the black set. Read the passcode for 5. **Go to 27.**

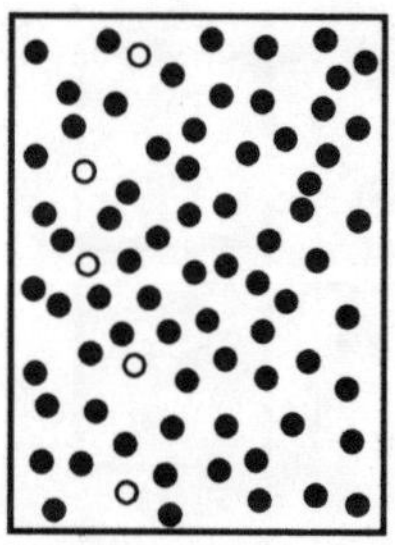

6. The numbers are 1234 & 2345. The first and third digits of 1234 are 1 & 3. **Go to 13.**

7. A is the odd-one-out. It is a mirror-image of the others. Read the passcode for A. **Go to 60. Key 4.**

8. The ball will fall into pot A. **Go to 22.**

9. 126-119=7. **Go to 7.**

A	1	1	1		
		B	2	1	4
C	3	0	6		
		D	1	1	2
E	6	3	1		
		F	9	6	0

10. There are 26 differences caused by placement of the balls below onto the A image. Add 13 to 26 to get 39. **Go to 39.**

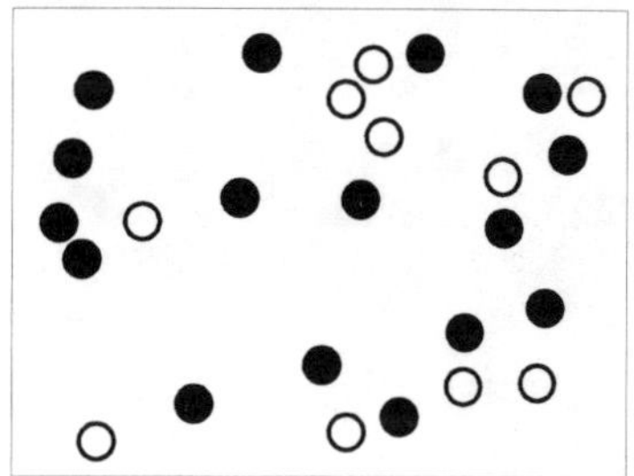

11. Solution 61. There are four 5s in the circle. 5+5+5+5=20+41=61. **Go to 61, the Keycodes. Key 5.**

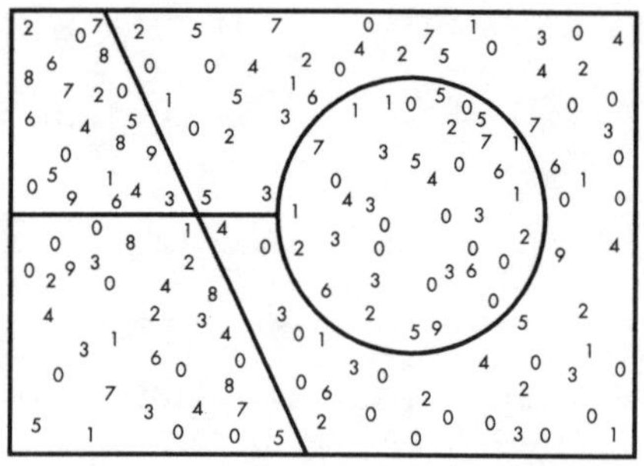

12. Solution 59. Each is 9 more than the last, thus Q=60. Subtract 1 to get the passcode 59. **Go to 59.**

13. Solution 18. Octal 144- Octal 122 = octal 22. Octal 22= decimal 18. The highest digit in octal is 7. Thus 8 in decimal = 10 in octal. So 16 in decimal = 20 in octal. Add 2 to get 18 in decimal=22 in octal. **Go to 18.**

14. Solution D. The outer shape changes and the inner shape changes direction. **Go to 41.**

15. Solution 10. There are 68 missiles. 68-58=10. **Go to 10. Key 6.**

16. Solution 25. The 2 numbers are 16 & 43. 16+43=59. 16x16=256. 43x43=1849. 256+1849=2105. 16 + 9=25. **Go to 25.**

17. Solution 23. The odd-one-out is D. This is the only box that doesn't contain numbers which, when added together make 23. It's numbers add to 24. 24-1=23. Hence the passcode is 23. **Go to 23.**

18. There are 20 changes. 20x3=60. 60/20=3. **Go to 3.**

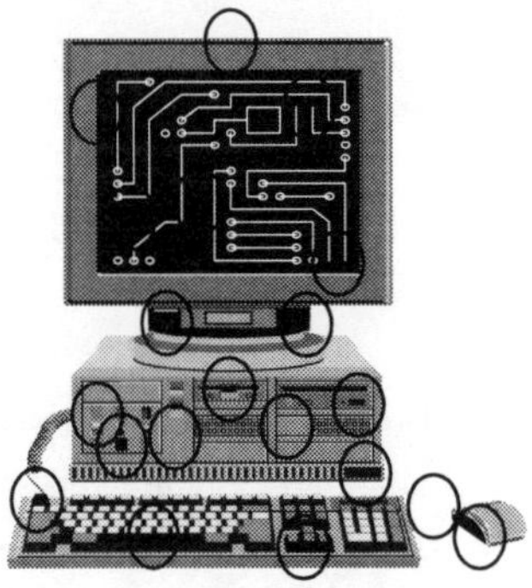

19. Solution A. Read passcode for A. **Go to 11. Key 1.**

20. Solution E. Each successive number is a rising multiplication of 23. A=23x6; B=23x7 etc. But E does not equal 23x10. Read the passcode for E. **Go to 26.**

21. The odd-one-out is C. The small triangle has been removed from the cell circled. Read the passcode for C. **Go to 52.**

22. Solution 15. Starting from the top left, each pair of top numbers added to each pair of bottom numbers equals each pair of middle numbers. Thus, 17+8+32+21=(78)=60+18; then 8+12+21+33=(74)=18+56. etc. Thus, 34+2+7+[15]=(58)=52+6. **Go to 15. Key 9.**

23. Solution 19. 19x2=38. 38+8-4=42. 42/7=6. 6sqr.=36. 36+4=40. 40-30=10. 10x10=100, which is the next perfect square above 81. **Go to 19.**

24. B is the odd-one-out. It is a mirror-image of the others. Read the passcode for B. **Go to 12.**

25. Solution 31. Grey=10; black=27; white=31. Thus, 3 black + 1 grey + 1 white=122. 122-91=31. **Go to 31.**

26. D is the odd-one-out. All the others are rotated versions of the same thing, but in D a diamond has been moved. Read the passcode for D. **Go to 16. Key 7.**

27. A is the odd-one-out. It is the only number that is not a perfect square. **Go to 24.**

28. There are 39 smaller stars and 17 large stars. 39+17=56. **Go to 56. Key 8.**

29. Solution 17. (278-248 = 30) + (353-307=46) = 76. 76-59=17. **Go to 17.**

30. B is the odd-one out. The two squares marked below have changed position. The other sets are all rotated versions of the same thing. Read the passcode for B. **Go to 38. Key 2.**

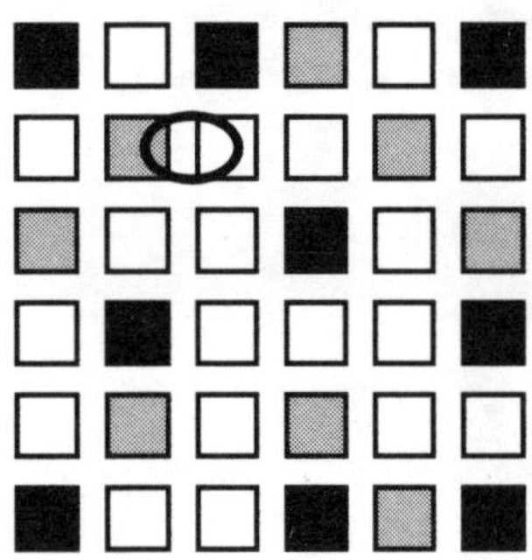

31. A=12; B=38. Passcode= 38-4=34. **Go to 34.**

32. The solution is 20. 178/8.9=20. Crack the code by mapping the alphabet starting with A=13.

Thus PASSCODE = 28+13+31+31+15+27+16+17=178. **Go to 20.**

13	14	15	16	17	18	19	20	21
a	b	c	d	e	f	g	h	i

22	23	24	25	26	27	28	29	30
j	k	l	m	n	o	p	q	r

31	32	33	34	35	36	37	38
s	t	u	v	w	x	y	z

SECTION TWO

ANSWERS

33. B is the odd-one-out. The circled area has been changed. The others are all rotated versions of the same thing. Read passcode for B. **Go to 6. Key 4.**

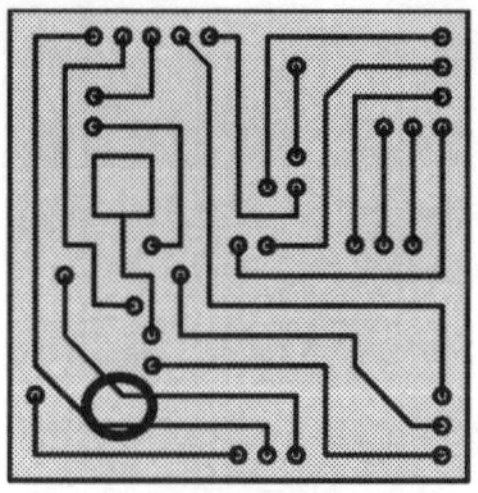

34. Solution 8. The perfect square is 16777216, which is 8^8. The 8th root of 16777216=8. **Go to 8.**

35. D makes the cube. Elements in the other cubes have been rotated or swapped with other elements. Read the passcode for D. **Go to 42.**

36. Solution 21. White=2, grey=4, black=5. **Go to 21.**

37. The odd-one-out is C. The highlighted line below is missing from this pattern in the puzzle. The others are all rotated versions of the same thing. Read the passcode for C. **Go to 33. Key 7.**

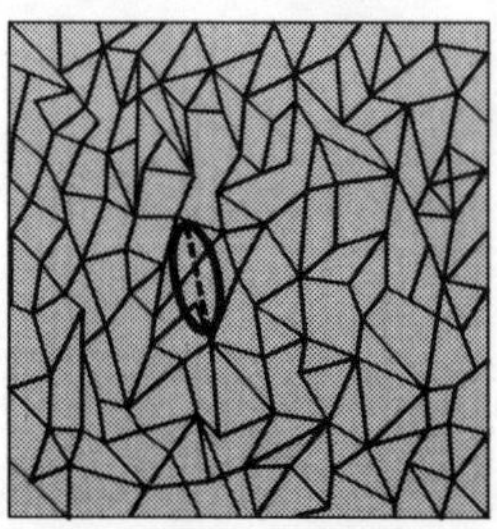

38. Solution 50. The central number, as shown below, is 25. 2x25=50. **Go to 50.**

30	39	48	1	10	19	28
38	47	7	9	18	27	29
46	6	8	17	26	35	37
5	14	16	25	34	36	45
13	15	24	33	42	44	4
21	23	32	41	43	3	12
22	31	40	49	2	11	20

39. Solution A. The longest, thinnest box has been missed out of this puzzle. The other sets are all rotated versions of the same basic puzzle. Read the passcode for A. **Go to 51.**

40. Solution 47. The missing number is 2. 33x25=825. 2+45=47. **Go to 47.**

41. Solution is 49. The distance is 7sqr. + 10sqr. = 149. Last 2 digits = 49. **Go to 49. Key 3.**

42. Solution is C. The two circled elements have changed place. The others are all rotated versions of the same thing. Read the passcode for C. **Go to 40.**

43. Solution 29. There are 8 digits (ignoring zeros) in the smallest section. 8+21=29. **Go to 29.**

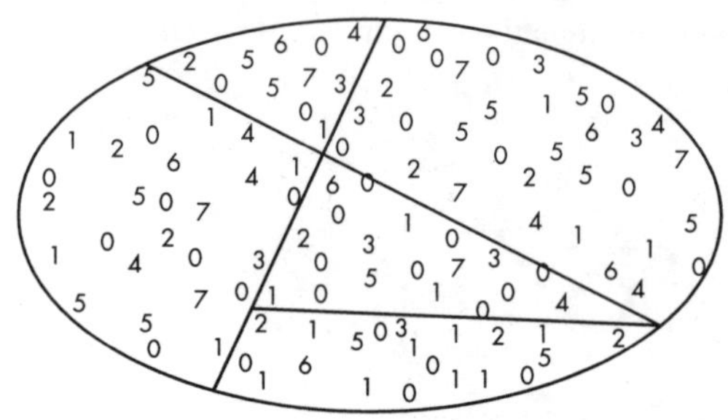

44. Solution 37. The calculation is 156478+279501=435979. **Go to 37. Key 2.**

A	1	5	6	4	7	8
B	2	7	9	5	0	1
C	4	3	5	9	7	9

45. The only route which avoids the traps and totals 376 is shown below. 55-54=1. **Go to 1.**

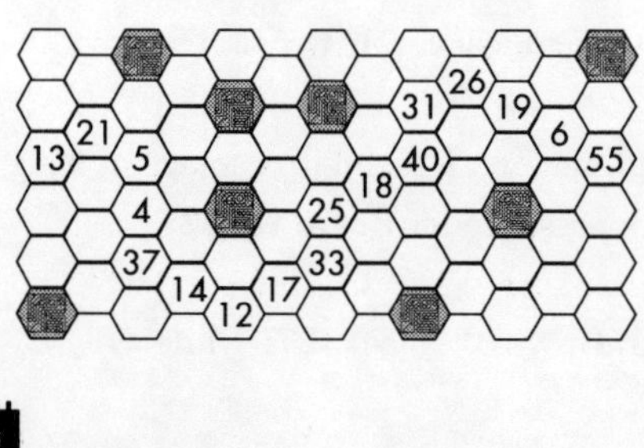

46. B is the odd-one-out. Look up the passcode for B. **Go to 4.**

47. D is the odd-one-out. The spot highlighted below has been moved to the back of the pattern. Read the passcode for D. **Go to 57. Key 1.**

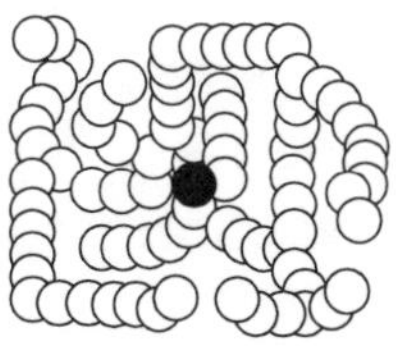

48. The solution is 58. The sums are 23580+61479=85059, and 61479-23580=37899. Use the key below. **Go to 58.**

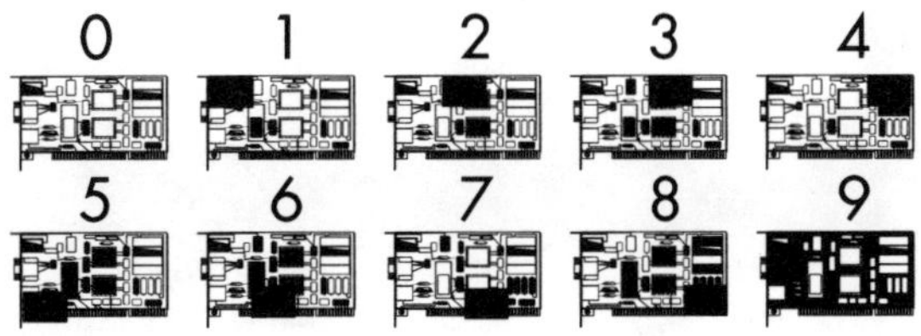

49. Solution 46. 7+4+5+3+2+8+6+5+6=46. **Go to 46.**

3		2		5		3		6
	252		280		300		360	
6		7		4		5		4
	630		168		320		480	
5		3		2		8		3
	360		180		480		288	
4		6		5		6		2
	648		810		630		336	
3		9		3		7		4

50. B and C are the two mirror-images. The passcode is 36. **Go to 36.**

51. The odd-one-out is C. In each cube, the top number + the front number - the side number should equal 72. In C the total is 71. **Go to 53. Key 5**

52. Solution 44: 65 circles and 21 stars. **Go to 44.**

53. Solution 30. The block should be placed as shown. The numerical position of the placement is 10. 7x6=42. (3x4=12)+([10]x3=30)=42. 3x10=30. **Go to 30.**

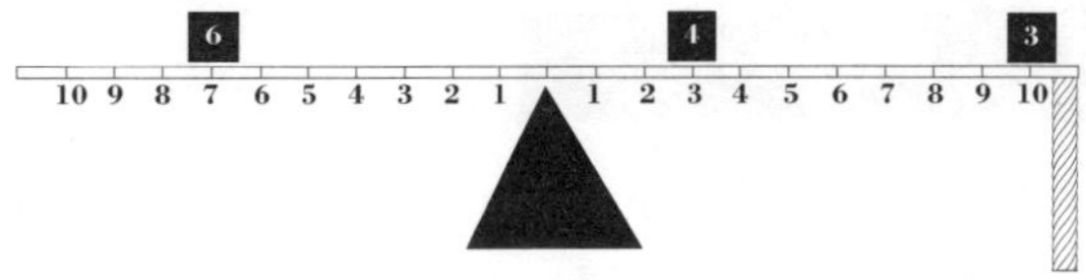

54. The missing number is 5. In each set, column A+column B=column C. **Go to 5. Key 6.**

55. The magic square should be completed as below. The central square is 13. 2x13=26; 26+2=28. **Go to 28.**

17	24	1	8	15
23	5	7	14	16
4	6	13	20	22
10	12	19	21	3
11	18	25	2	9

56. The odd one out is B. The arrow indicated by the pointer has been turned 180 degrees with respect to the rest of the shapes. **Go to 43.**

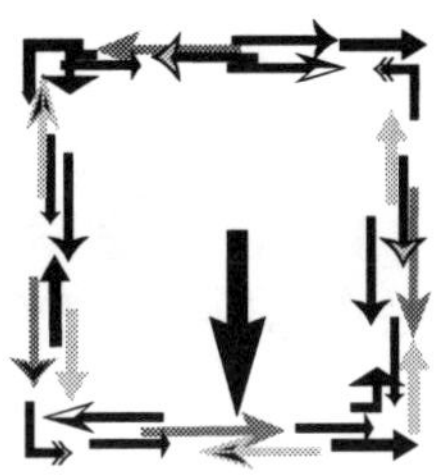

57. The missing number is 55. Add the digits together and add to the original sum; 55+10=65; 65+11=76; 76+13=89. . . etc. **Go to 55. Key 8.**

58. Solution 35. The missing digits are 3 and 5. Each successive digit is found by adding the previous 2 digits and dropping the first digit of the result. Hence, 3+5=8; 8+5=[1]3. etc. **Go to 35.**

59. Solution 14. Triangles=3, Stars=5, Squares=2; Circles=1. 2 squares and 2 stars = 14. **Go to 14.**

60. Solution is 54. The 2 smaller numbers multiply together, double, and 4 is added, to give the larger number. 74-20=54. **Go to 54. Key 2.**

Section Two Keycode: 44-39=5. Go to Section 3 and start with Puzzle 5.

SECTION THREE

Puzzle 1

Which of the figures below is most closely related to the one at the top?
Choose your passcode to the next puzzle according to your decision.

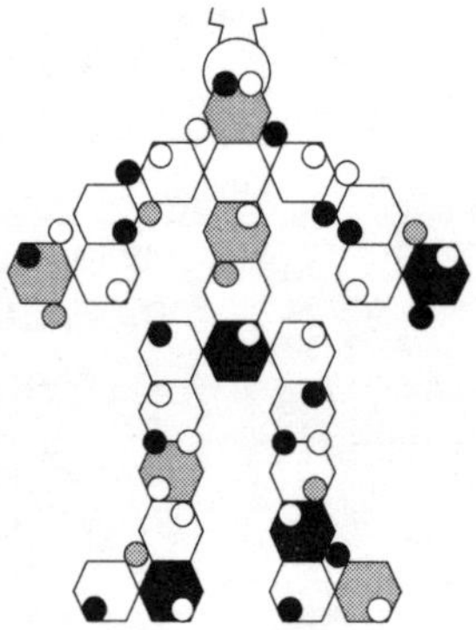

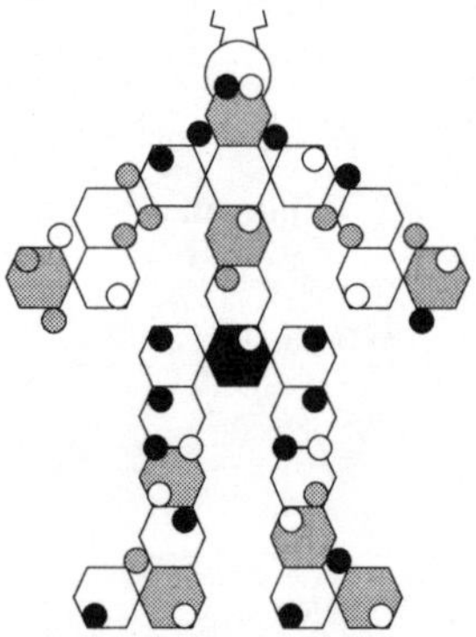

A= Passcode **19**

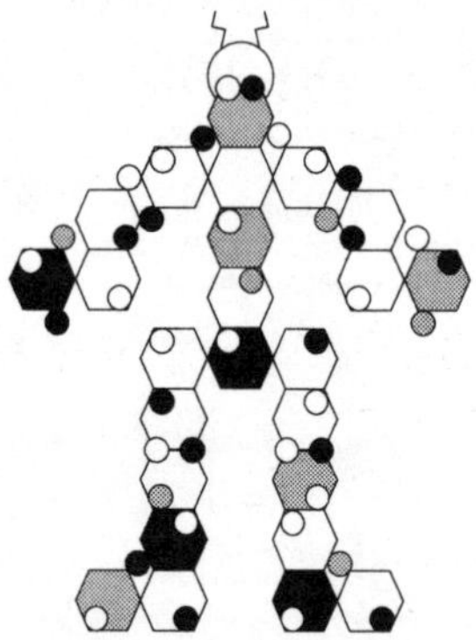

B= Passcode **29**

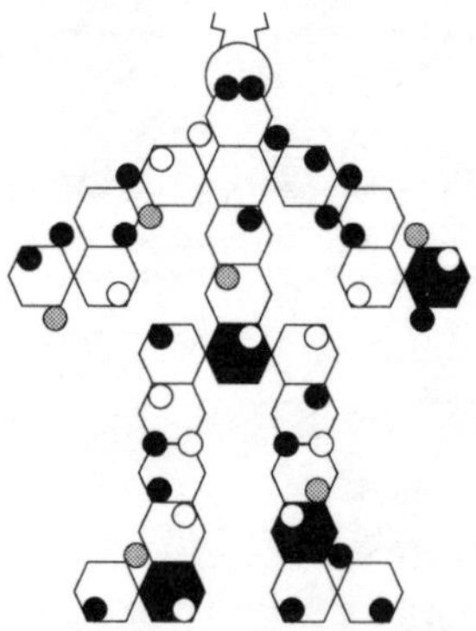

C= Passcode **5**

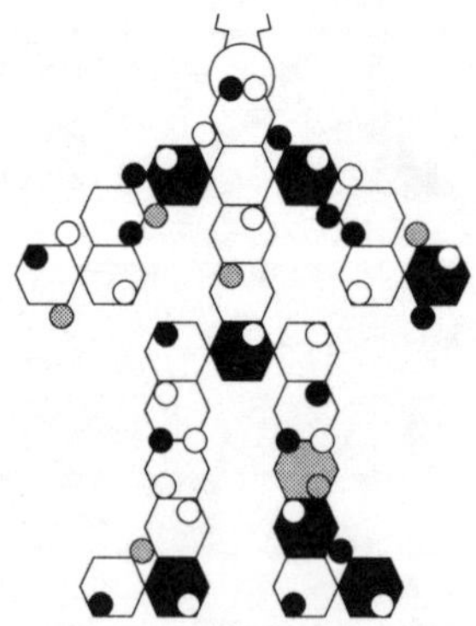

D= Passcode **55**

Puzzle 2

Hidden within this series is a multiplication problem. The last 2 digits of the six figure multiplicand are your next passcode.

2 3 7 4 5 6 5 4 1 2 8 2 2 6 2 4

Puzzle 3

Pick the odd-one-out. Choose your passcode according to your answer.

A= Passcode **12.**

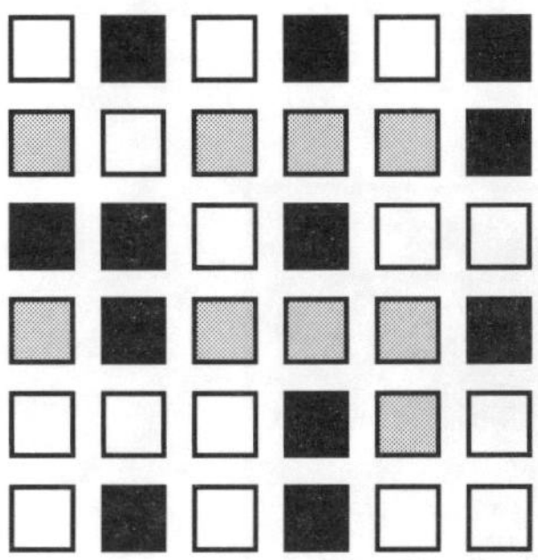

B= Passcode **55.**

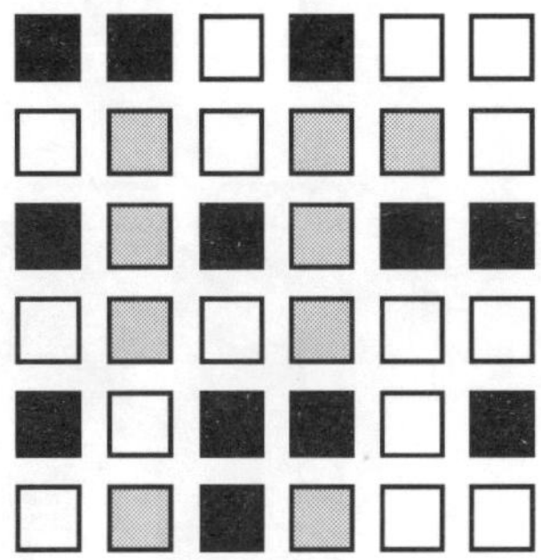

C= Passcode **45.**

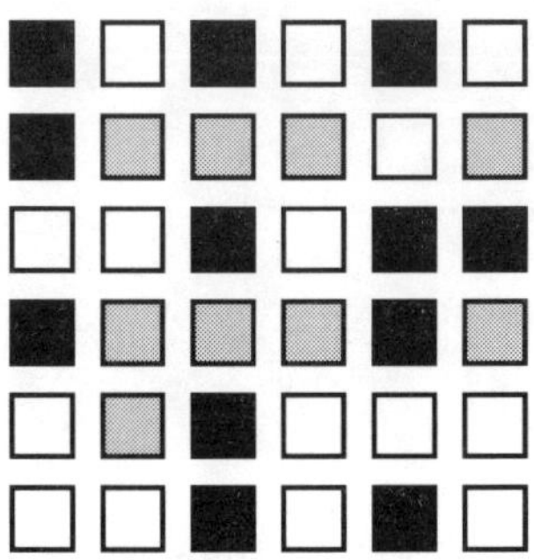

D= Passcode **18.**

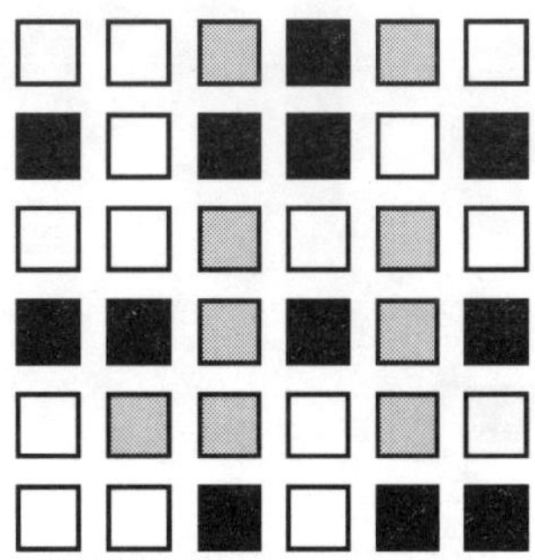

Puzzle 4

Work out your next passcode by subtracting the number of crosses from the number of circles.

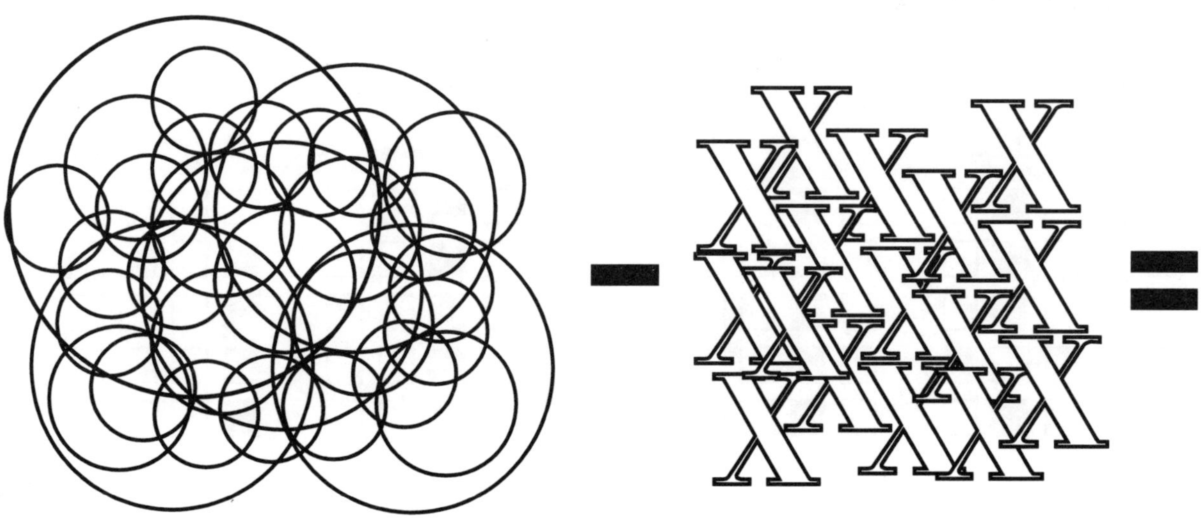

Puzzle 5

Your next passcode is the number which, when you multiply it by 2 and add 2, gives you the number that, when you divide it by 10, produces a number that, when you add 13, and divide the result by 4, is a number that, when squared, equals 25.

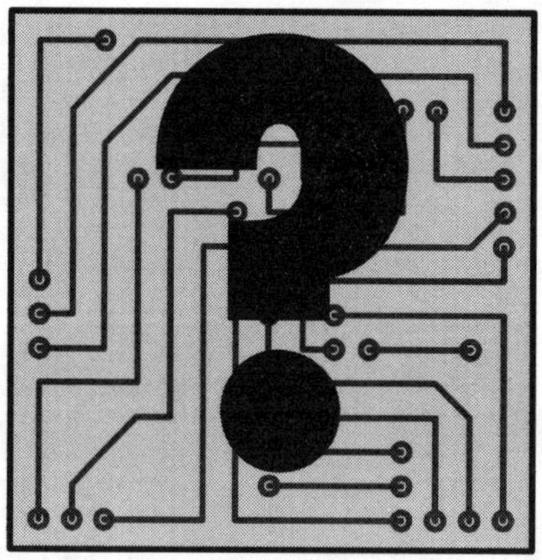

Puzzle 6

What comes next? Choose your passcode according to your answer.

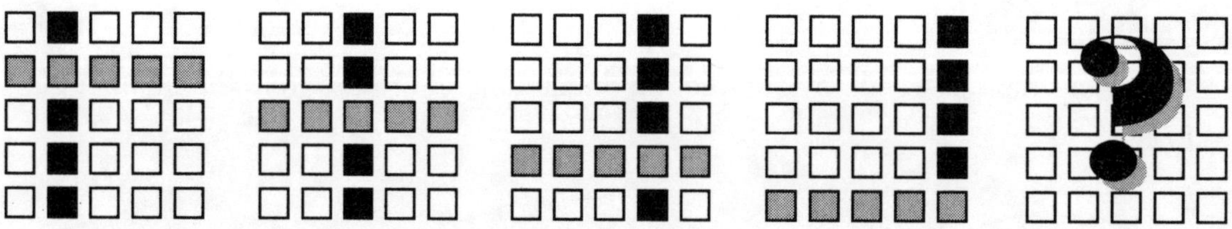

A= Passcode **22.**

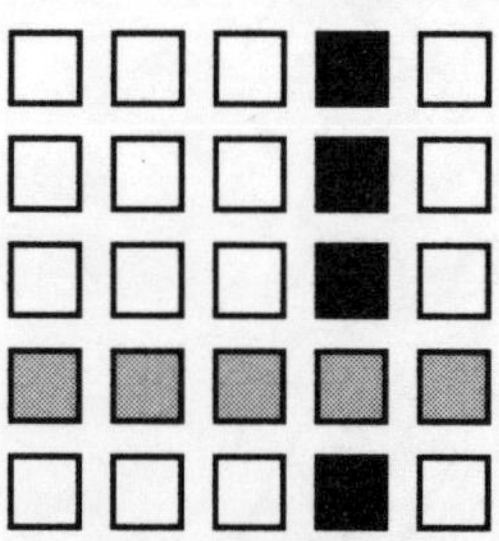

B= Passcode **14.**

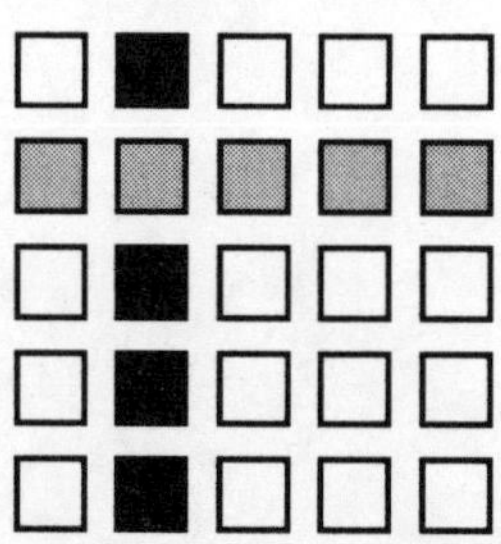

C= Passcode **51.**

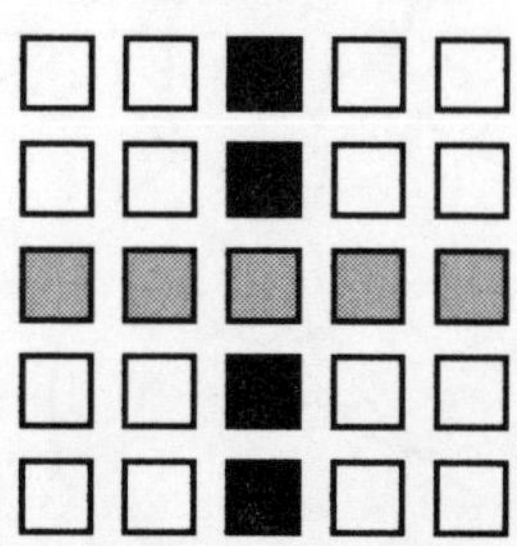

D= Passcode **8.**

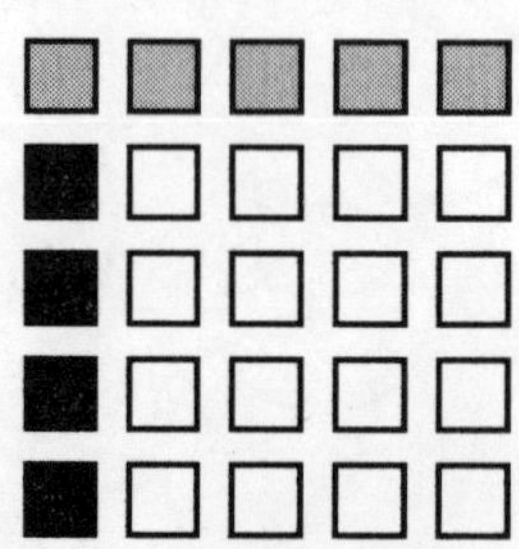

Puzzle 7

The missing number in C is your passcode to the next puzzle.

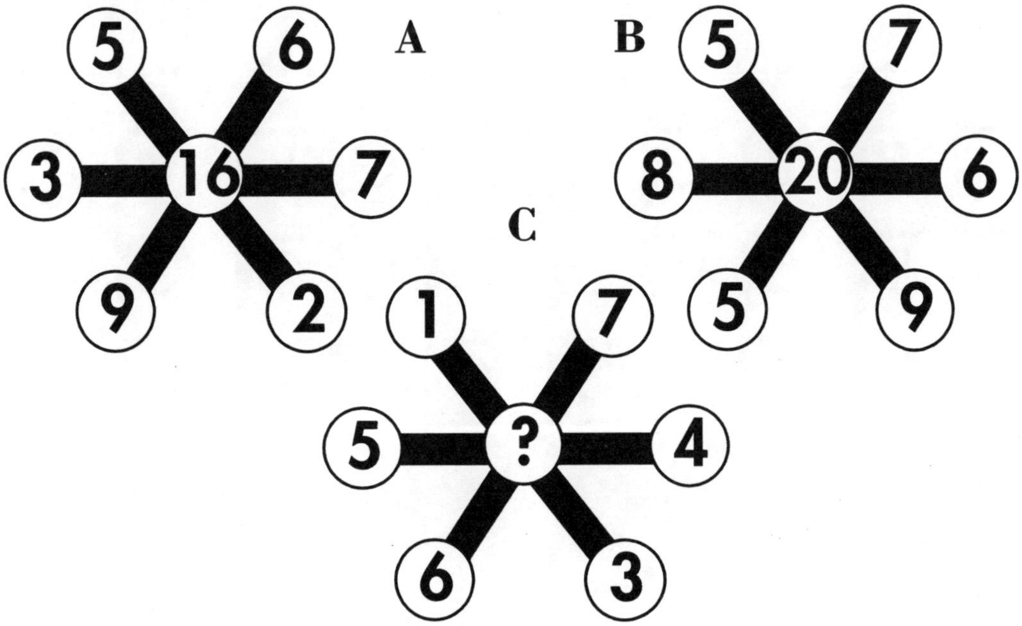

Puzzle 8

This one is so tricky that Adrian Smith has decided to give you a clue. He's confident that you still won't spot the odd-one-out. The clue is: There is an extra line in the odd-one-out. Choose your passcode according to your decision.

A= Passcode **35** **B**= Passcode **20** **C**= Passcode **31** **D**= Passcode **10**

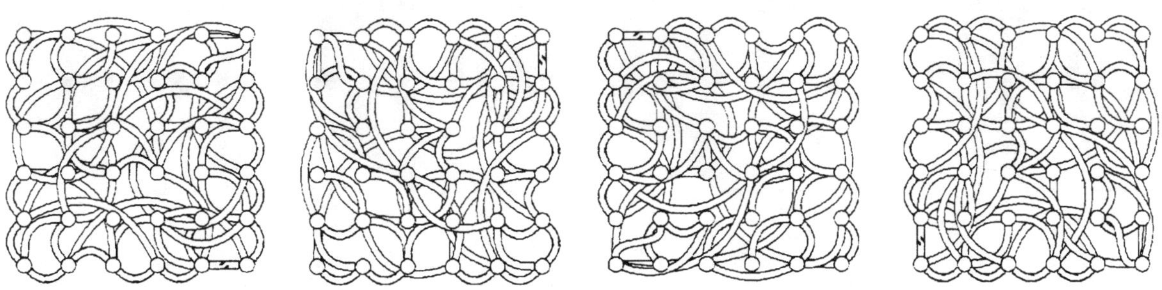

Puzzle 9

Pick the odd-one-out. Choose your passcode according to your answer.

A= Passcode **3** **B**= Passcode **19** **C**= Passcode **15** **D**= Passcode **27**

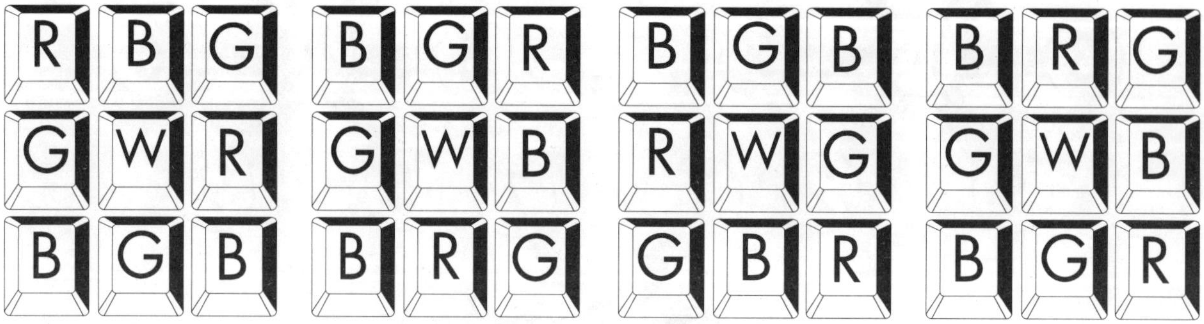

Puzzle 10

There is something different about the numbers on one of these cubes. Your next passcode is the number on the front of that cube.

A **B** **C** **D**

Puzzle 11

For your next passcode on your journey of escape from cyber-reality, you have to figure out which of the tiles in the box goes into the middle of the pattern. Choose your passcode accordingly.

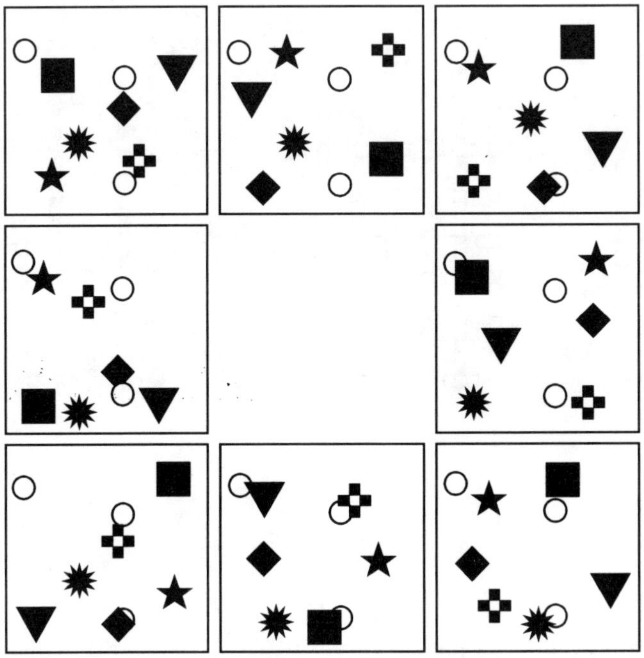

A= Passcode **18** **B**= Passcode **44**

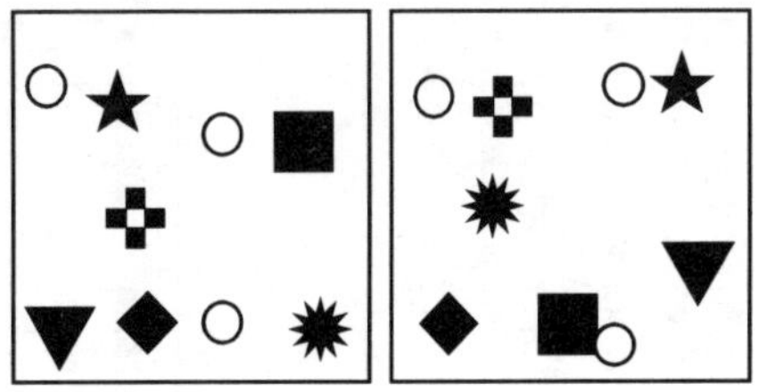

C= Passcode **31** **D**= Passcode **46**

Puzzle 12

Continue the sequence of numbers and so find your passcode to the next puzzle.

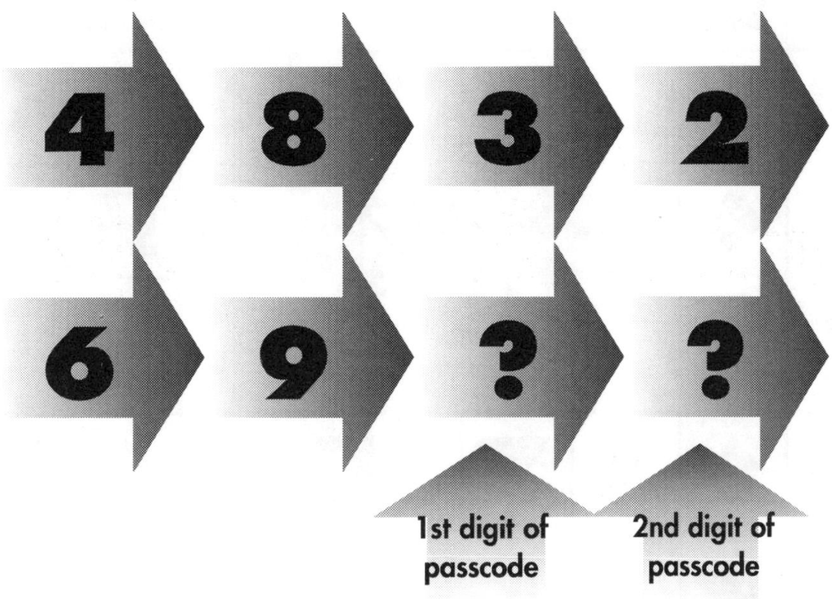

Puzzle 13

Pick the odd-one-out. Choose your passcode according to your answer.

A= Passcode **12.** **B**= Passcode **32.** **C**= Passcode **14.** **D**= Passcode **11.**

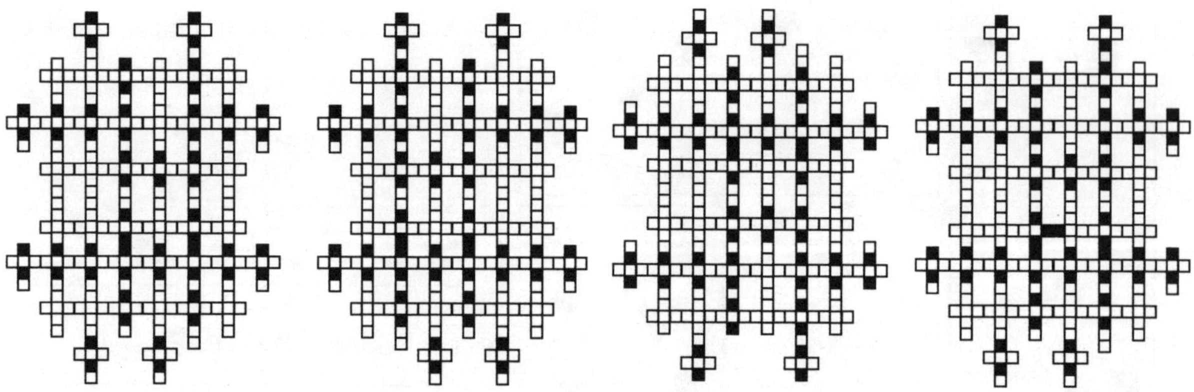

Puzzle 14

Which of the surounding plans makes the central cube?
Choose your passcode accordingly.
A= Passcode 23. B= Passcode 5. C= Passcode 39. D= Passcode 43.

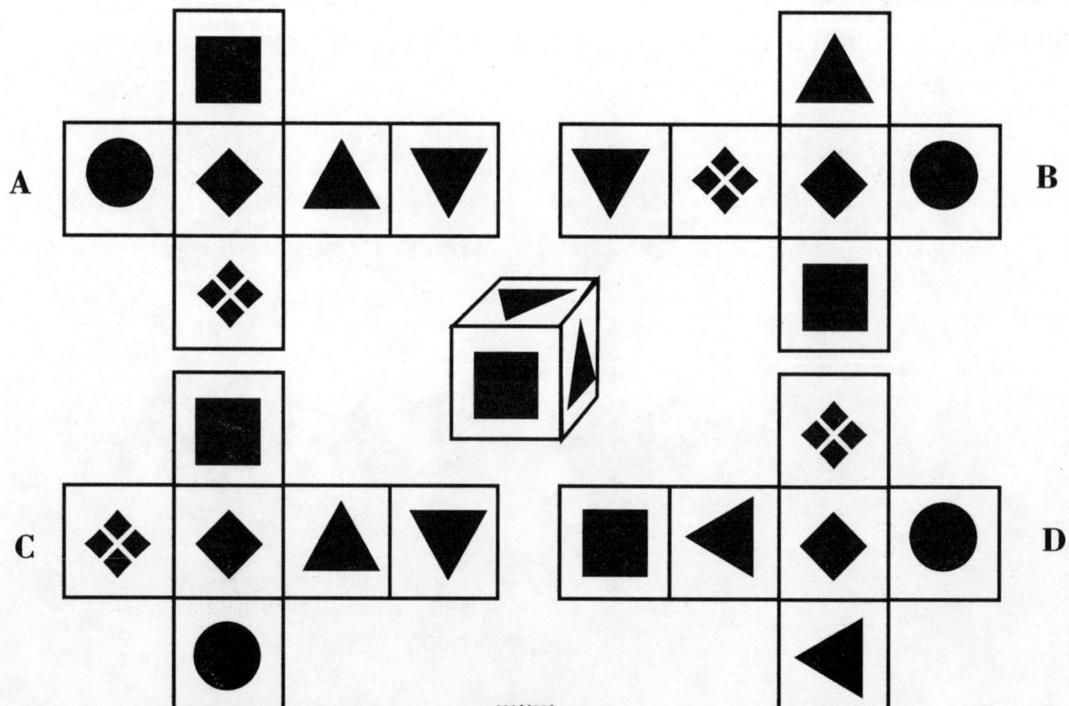

Puzzle 15

Pick the odd-one-out. Your next passcode is found by adding 56 to the number second from the left on the bottom row of that set.

A

1	5	2	23
4	8	4	2
3	13	11	7
14	3	16	10

B

14	3	16	10
3	13	11	7
4	8	4	2
1	5	2	23

C

10	16	3	14
7	11	13	3
2	4	8	4
23	2	5	1

D

23	2	7	10
2	4	11	16
5	8	13	3
1	4	3	14

Puzzle 16

Your passcode to the next puzzle is to be found with the odd-one-out in this puzzle.

A=8

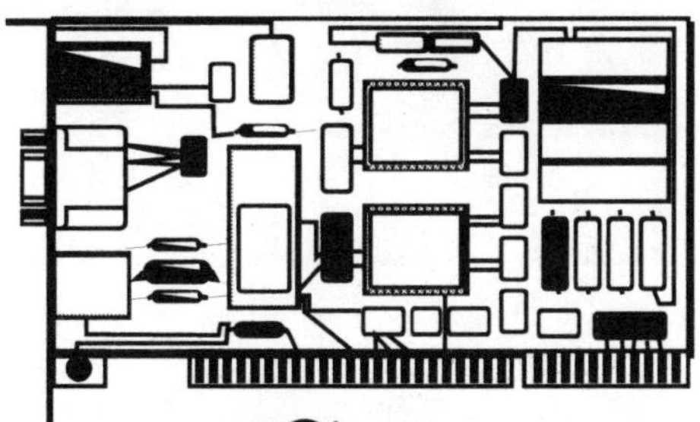

B=42

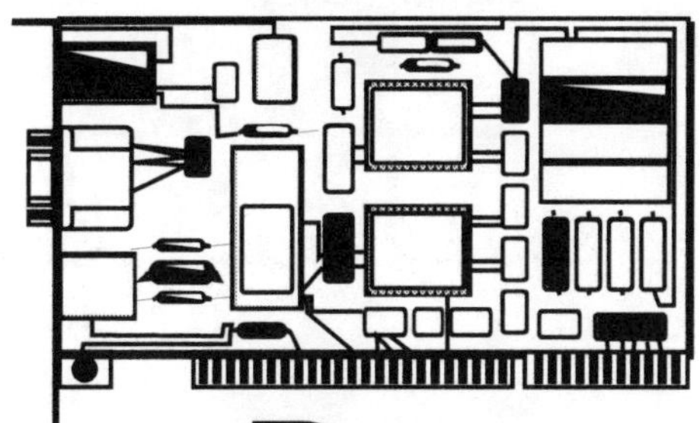

C=55

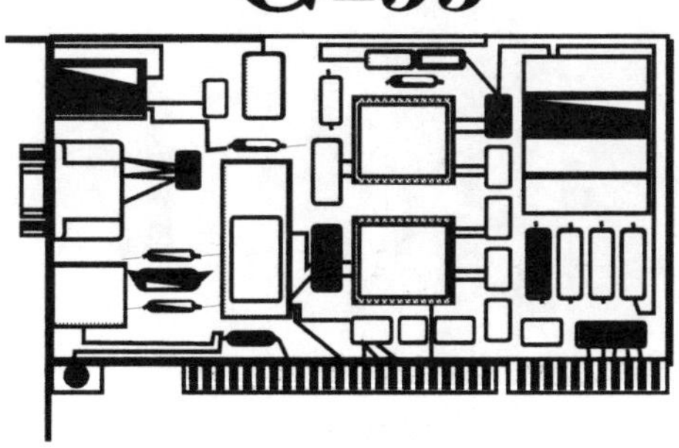

D=17

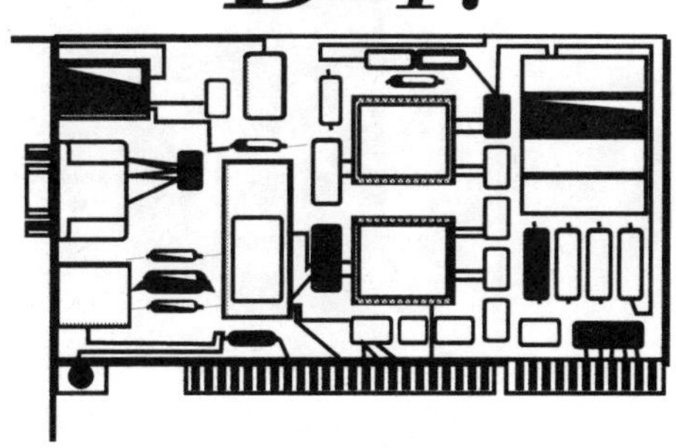

Puzzle 17

Pick the odd-one-out. Choose your passcode accordingly.

A=29 B=37 C=28 D=7

Puzzle 18

The numbers in the middle contain passcodes and are also part of the puzzle. The odd-one-out of this set, when you subtract 20, contains your passcode to the next of Adrian Smith's tricky puzzles.

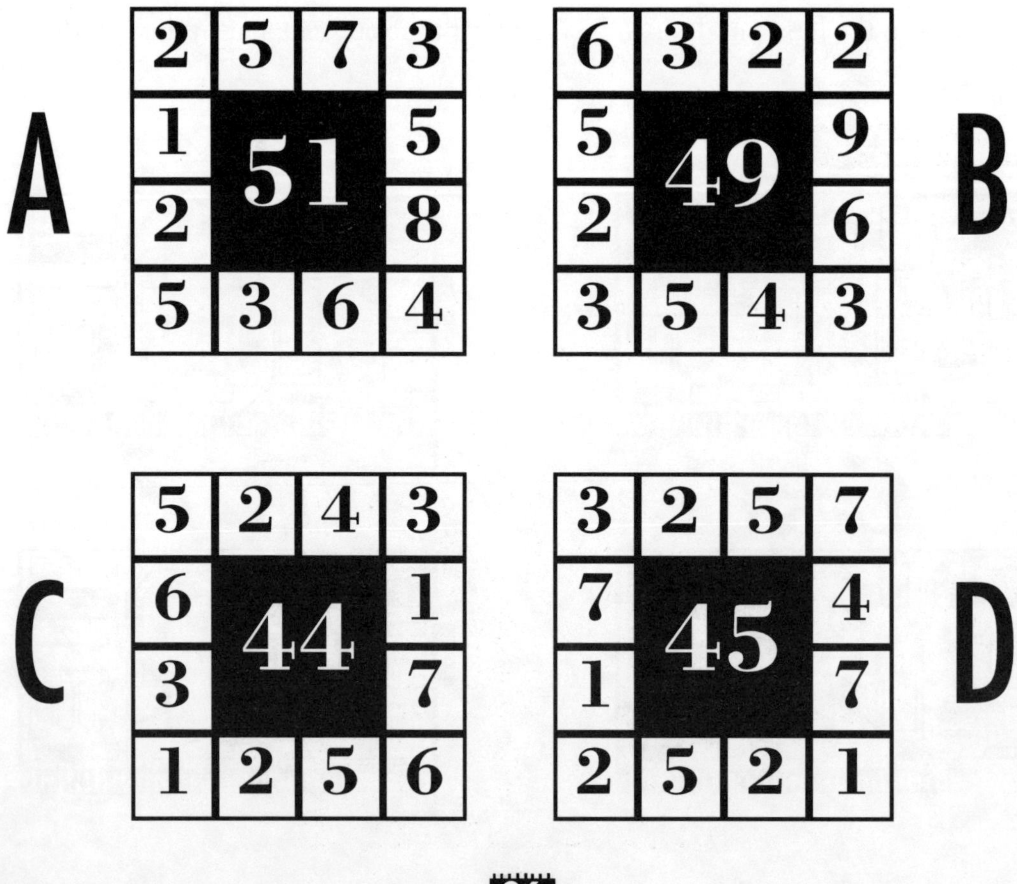

Puzzle 19

Continue the sequence and hence find your passcode.

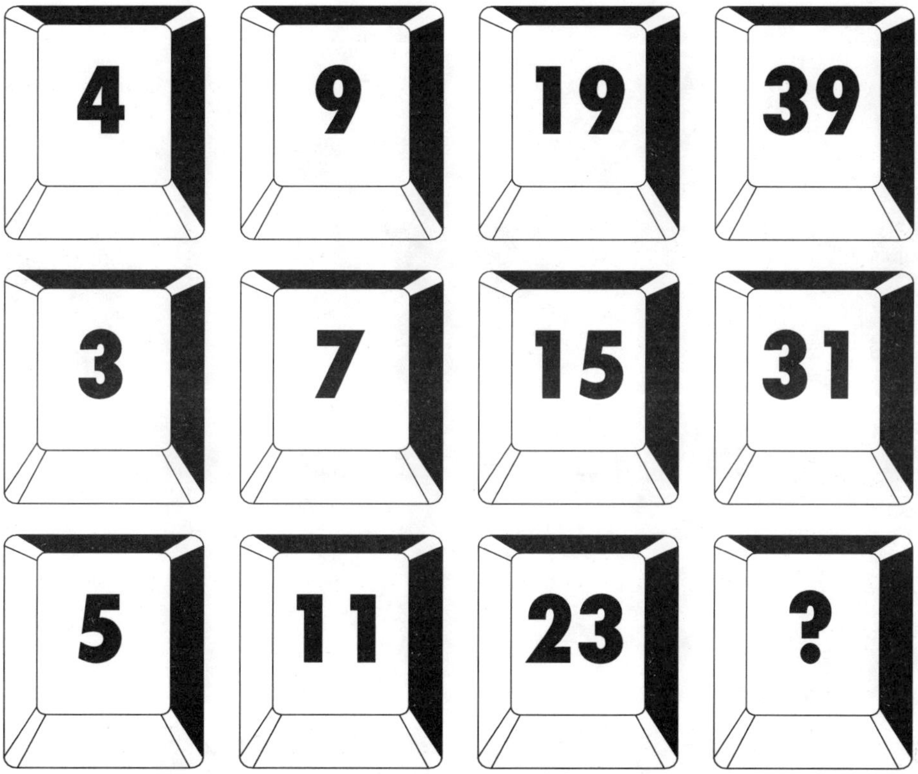

Puzzle 20

Your next passcode, when 40 is subtracted from it, gives the number which, when squared, gives a number that, when you add 10 and divide the result by 2, gives you a number that when multiplied by 3, produces a result that, if either subtracted from 51 is 3 times the number you squared, or if subtracted from 78 produces itself.

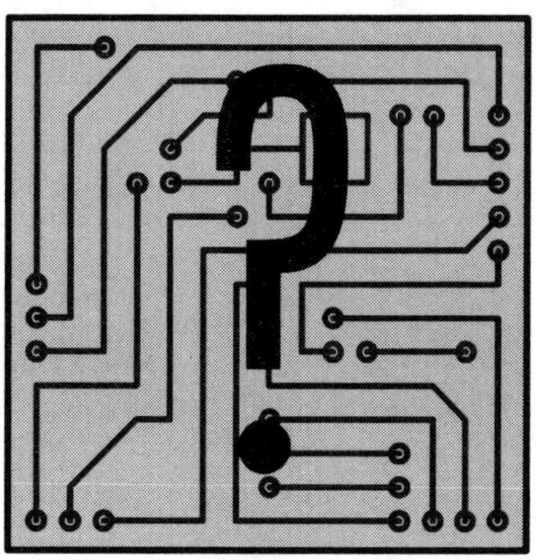

Puzzle 21

Adrian Smith is sure that you will be unable to solve this puzzle. Add the two missing numbers together and subtract 1 to find your passcode.

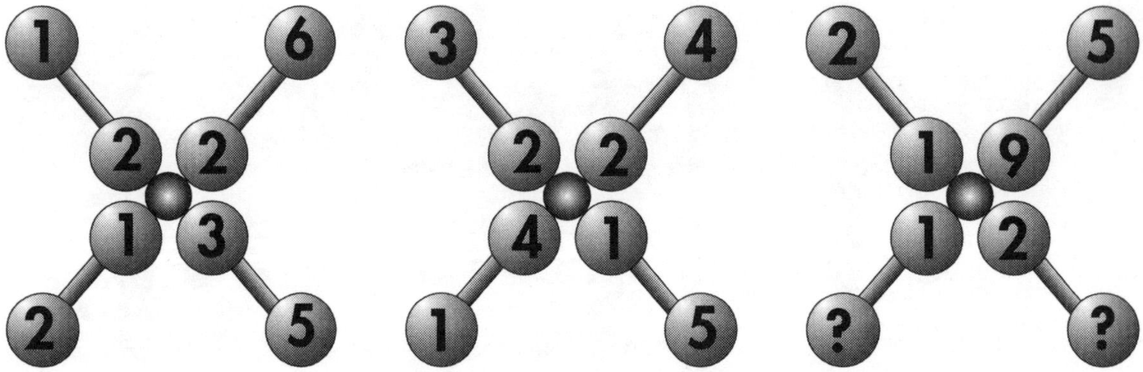

Puzzle 22

Pick the odd-one-out. Choose your passcode according to your answer.
A=Passcode **28.** **B**=Passcode **53.** **C**=Passcode **49.** **D**=Passcode **46.**

Puzzle 23

In a family with 8 children, Iain is the age that you get if you add Simon's age to Chevonne's age and divide by 2. Fifi is half the age of Chevonne. Simon is 2.6 times as old as Sady, who is double Petra's age. Mary is 3 years younger than Simon, but 9 years older than Iain. Kamal is a year older than Sady, who is five times as old as Chevonne. Last year, Chevonne was the same age as Fifi is this year. Put the ages in the boxes and use Simon's age as your passcode.

Kamal ☐
Mary ☐
Iain ☐
Simon ☐
Sady ☐
Fifi ☐
Petra ☐
Chevonne ☐

Puzzle 24

3

Find the missing number and hence find your passcode to the next puzzle.

Puzzle 25

Pick the odd-one-out and choose your passcode according to your answer.

A=Passcode **33.**

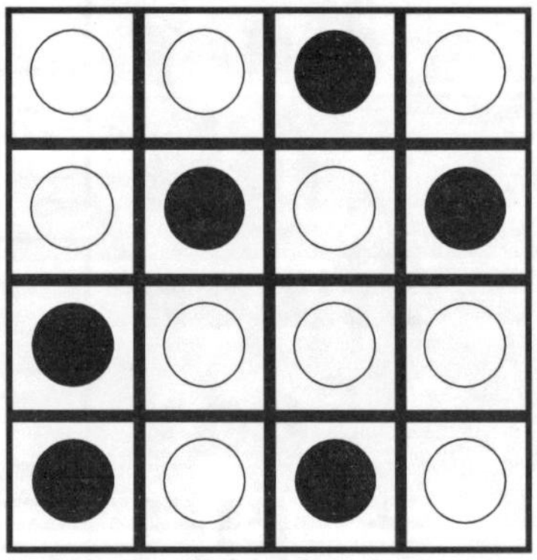

B=Passcode **19.**

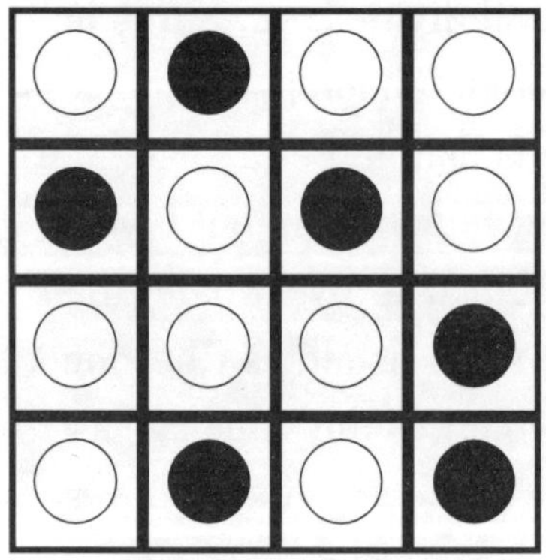

C=Passcode **8.**

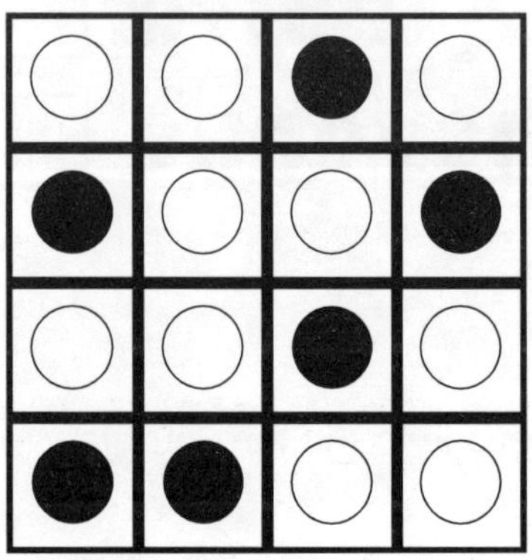

D=Passcode **51.**

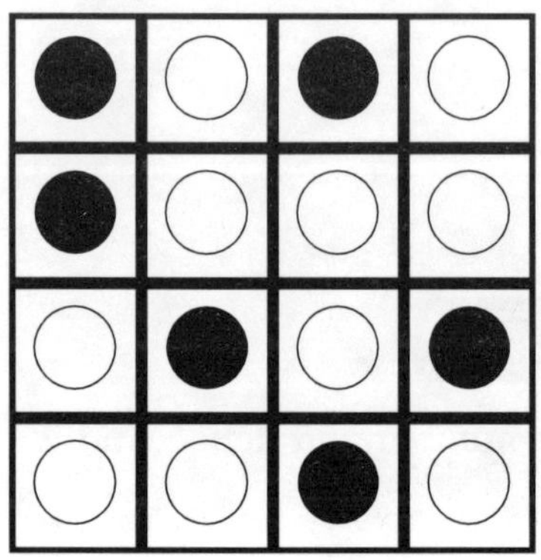

Puzzle 26

Add 4 to the missing number of this set to find your next passcode.

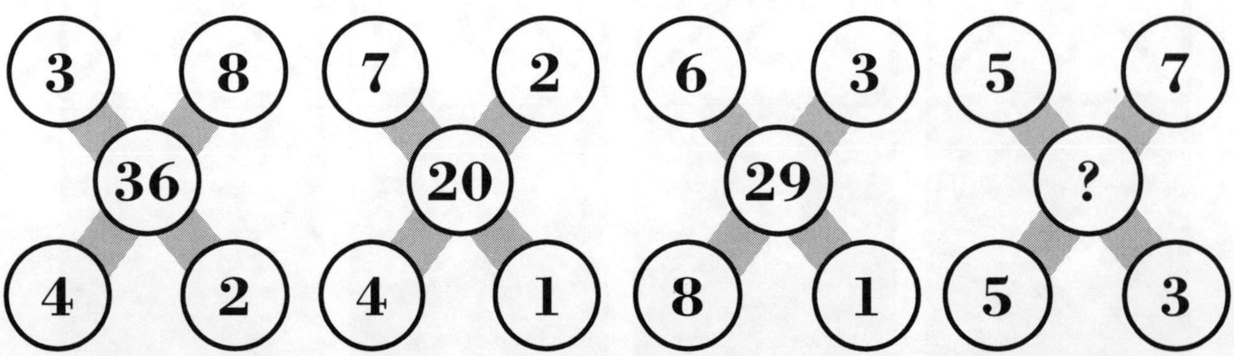

Puzzle 27

In your tour around Adrian's circuits you must travel 36 km at an average speed of 27 km per hour. Subtract 44 from the length of time the trip will take you, to the nearest number of minutes, to find your next passcode.

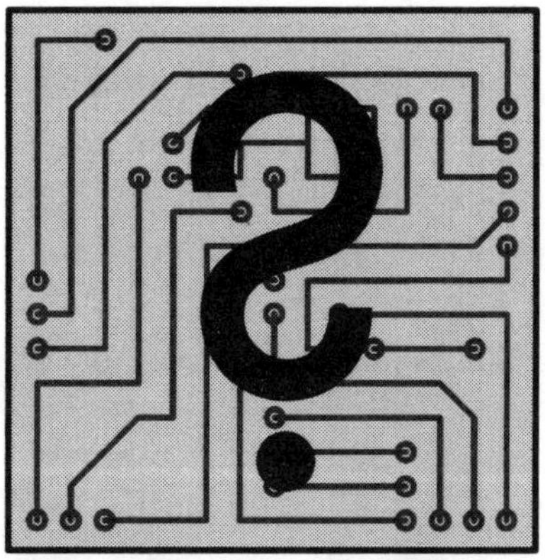

Puzzle 28

Spot the number of discs that have moved position between A & B. Multiply that number by 10 to find your next passcode.

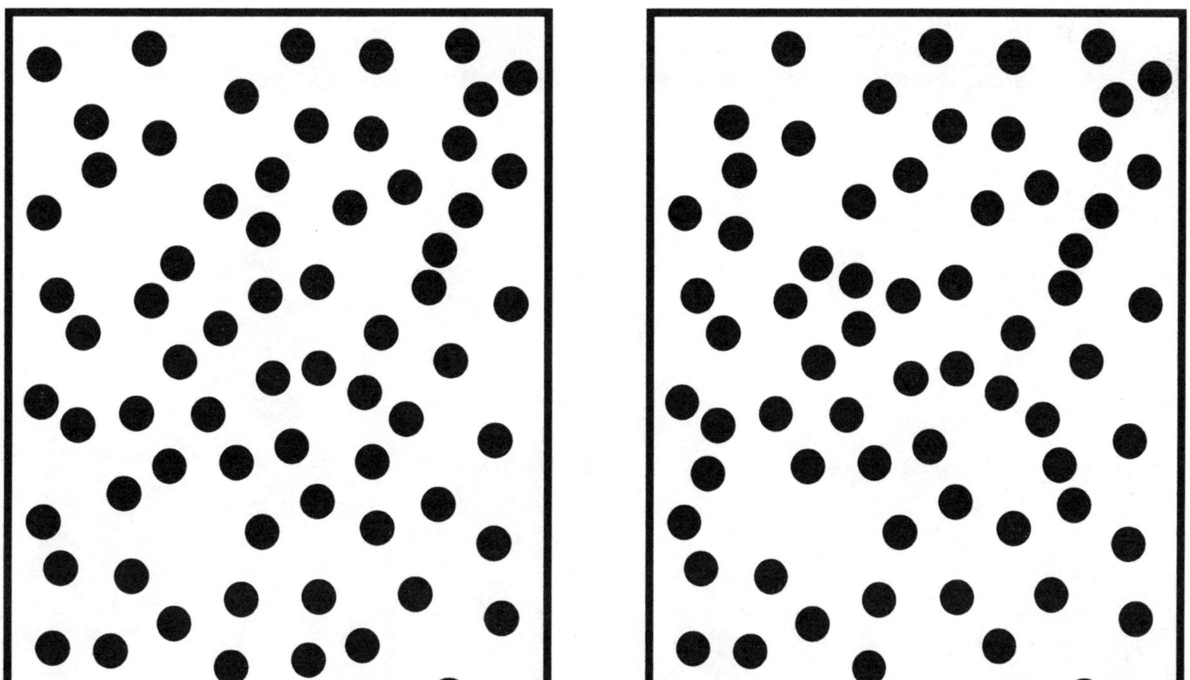

Puzzle 29

Fill in the missing number in D and hence find your next passcode.

A	B	C	D
54	68	73	45
3	2	2	2
5	7	2	3
19	41	51	?

Puzzle 30

One of these circles contains a number which does not go with the others. When you realize the significance of that number you can use that as your next passcode.

Puzzle 31

Pick the odd-one-out and use the number below it as your next passcode on your quest for escape from cyber-reality.

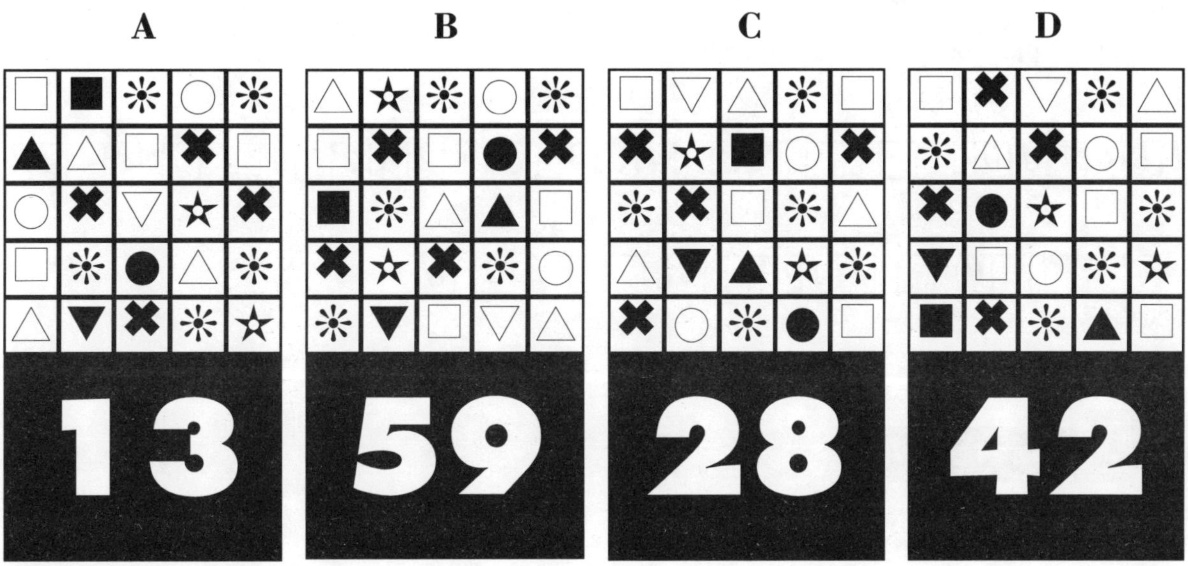

Puzzle 32

Fill in the vowels so that each row, column, and long diagonal contains one of each. Choose your next passcode according to what you think should be in the central square. A=Passcode 41. E=Passcode 16. I=Passcode 30. O=Passcode 15. U=Passcode 53.

A	E	I	O	U
O				I
E				A
U				O
I	O	U	A	E

Puzzle 33

Some fool has left some important bits out of the following calculations. Put in the missing numbers in the boxes and the operands outside the boxes, add all the missing numbers together, and divide by 38 to get a number which, when you subtract 90.5 will give your passcode to the next puzzle.

186740 ☐☐☐☐ 183400 ☐☐ 2620 ☐☐☐ 2440

☐ 7320 ☐ 1464 8 ☐☐☐ 3 61

Puzzle 34

The missing number in C is your next passcode.

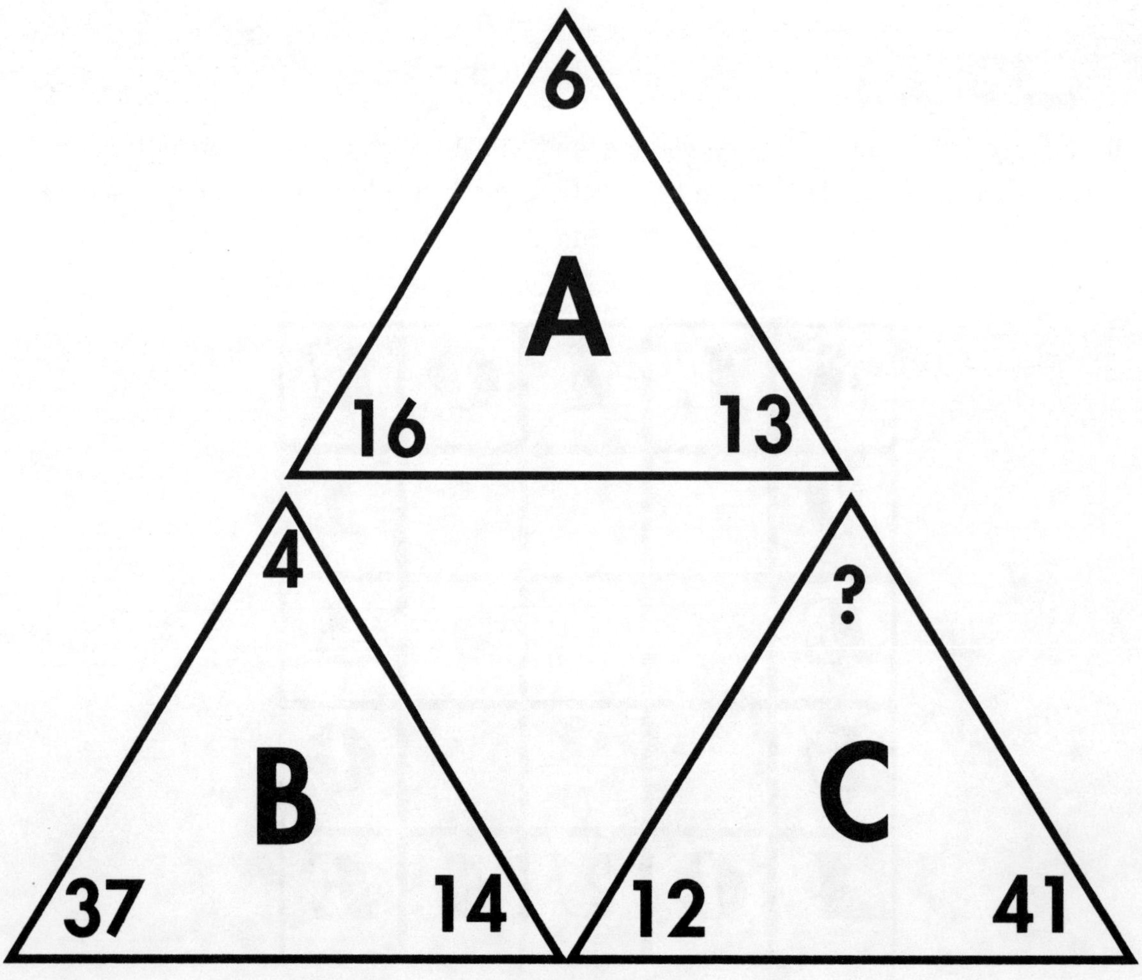

Puzzle 35

Your next passcode is the number in the circle of the odd-one-out in this set.

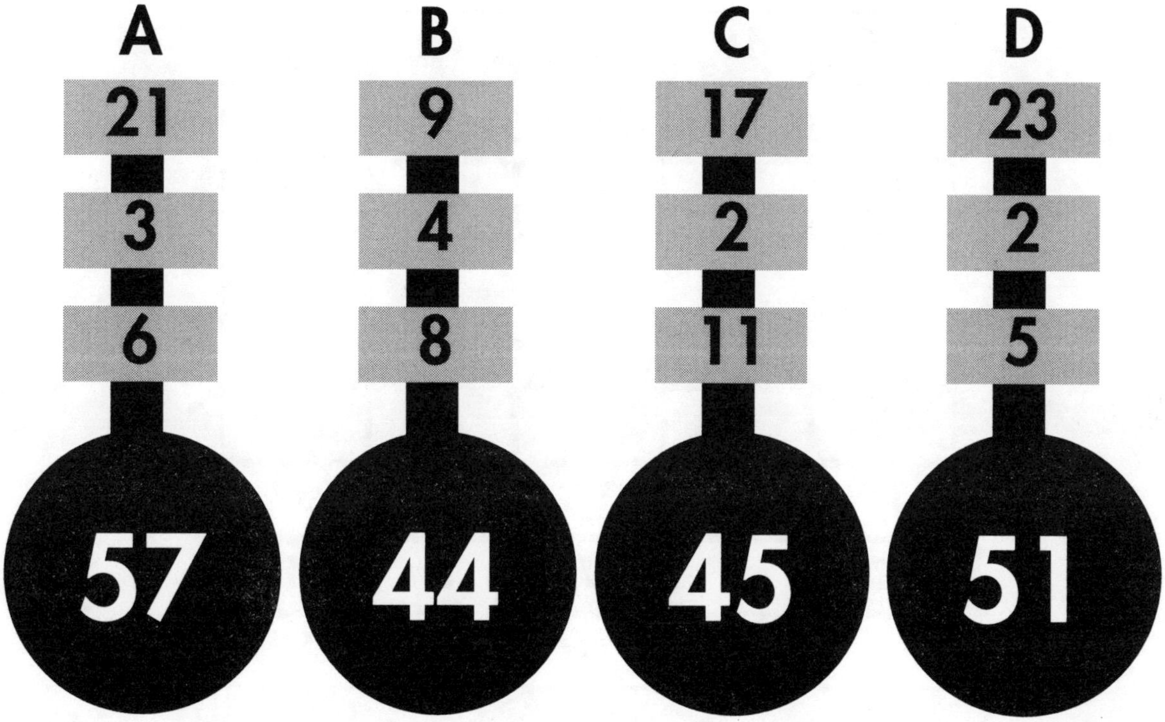

Puzzle 36

Pick the odd-one-out. Your passcode is the central number. Central numbers are not part of the puzzle.

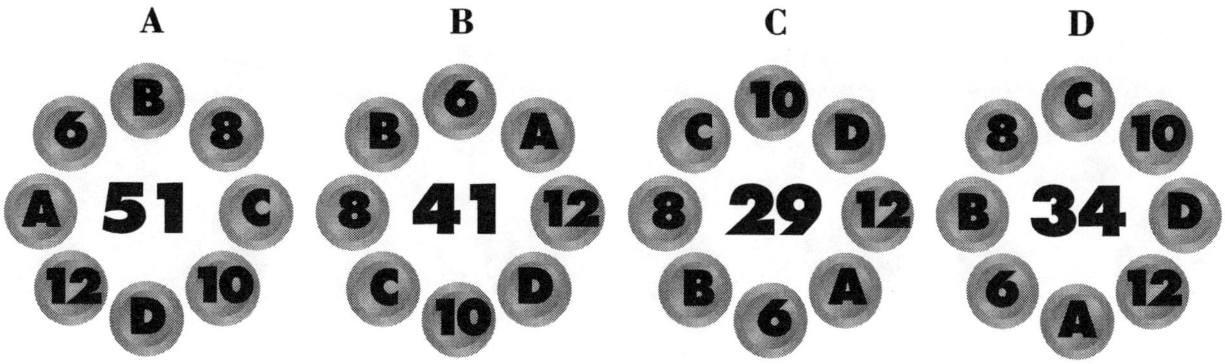

Puzzle 37

Enter the correct sequence in the blank row. The right-hand number in that sequence is your passcode to the next puzzle.

16	10	6	12	6
4	7	3	7	5
10	6	12	6	16
3	7	5	4	7
5	4	7	3	7
12	6	16	10	6
7	3	7	5	4
6	16	10	6	12

Puzzle 38

Divide the missing number by two to find your next passcode.

Puzzle 39

Insert the missing numbers into B to find the first and second digits of your passcode.

3	6	8	2	2	8	1	9	9	3	1	4
4	A	7	?	B	?	2	C	6	6	D	1
4	1	5	2	4	5	2	2	5	3	7	5

Puzzle 40

Pick the odd-one-out. Your next passcode is underneath it.

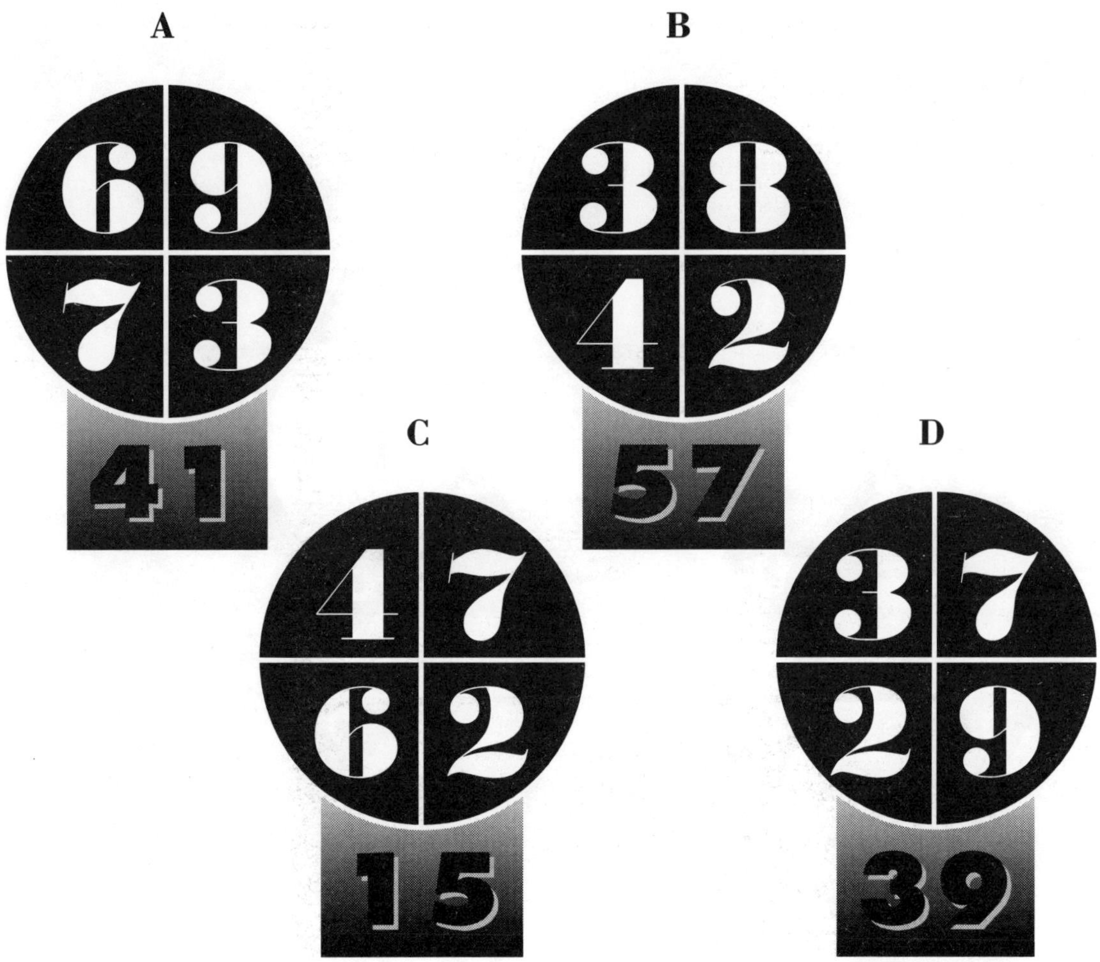

Puzzle 41

Adrian has set you a task that is simple to describe, but more difficult to complete. Just count the number of squares like the lone box on the right (don't count that!) and double the result to get your passcode to the next puzzle.

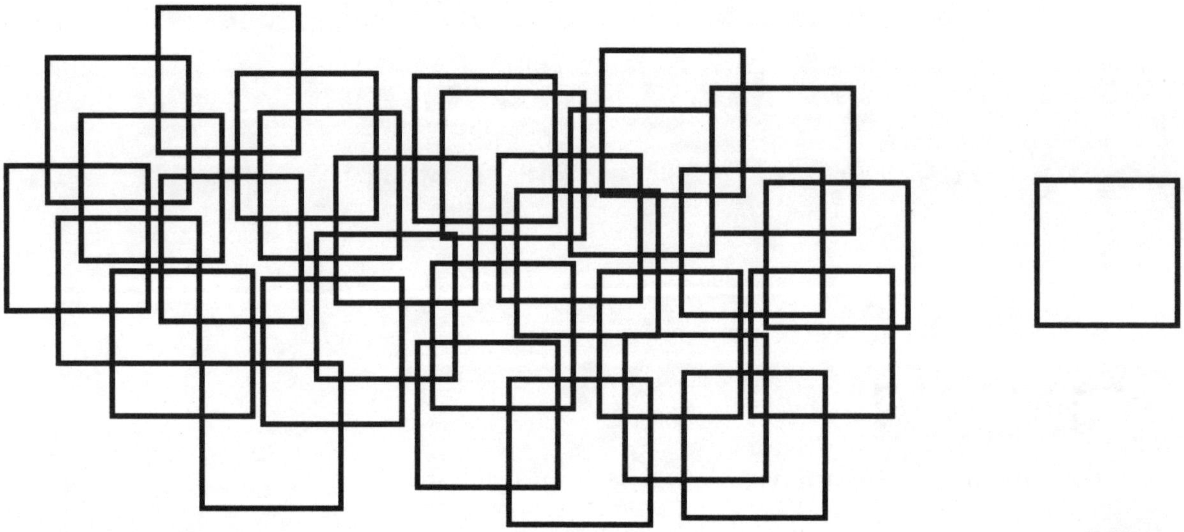

6

Puzzle 42

Your next passcode is the missing number in A.

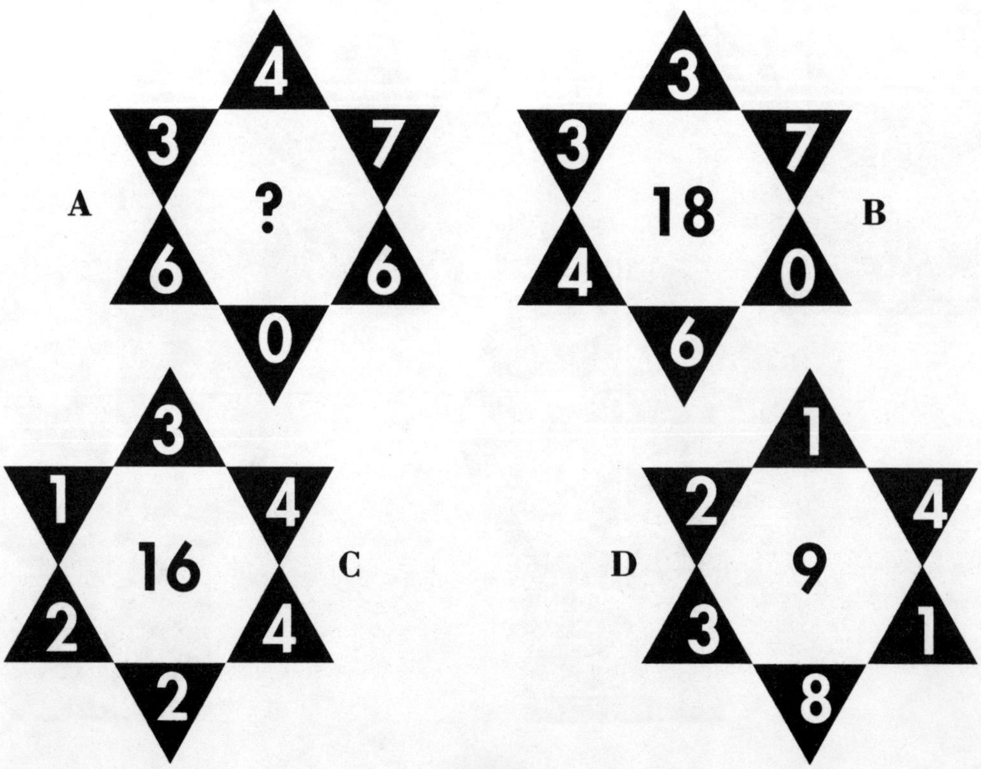

Puzzle 43

Your next passcode is the value of the square with the black square inside it.

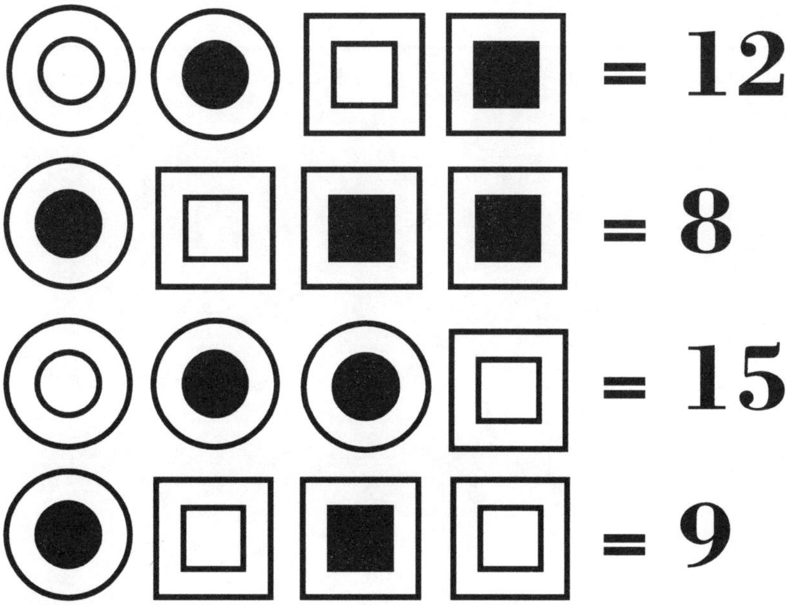

Puzzle 44

Spot the number of differences between A and B and add 10 to get your passcode to the next puzzle.

Puzzle 45

Draw 3 straight lines to divide this puzzle into 3 parts, with a total value of 60 in each part. The total of all the 1's in the smallest part of the completed puzzle is the passcode to the next puzzle in your quest.

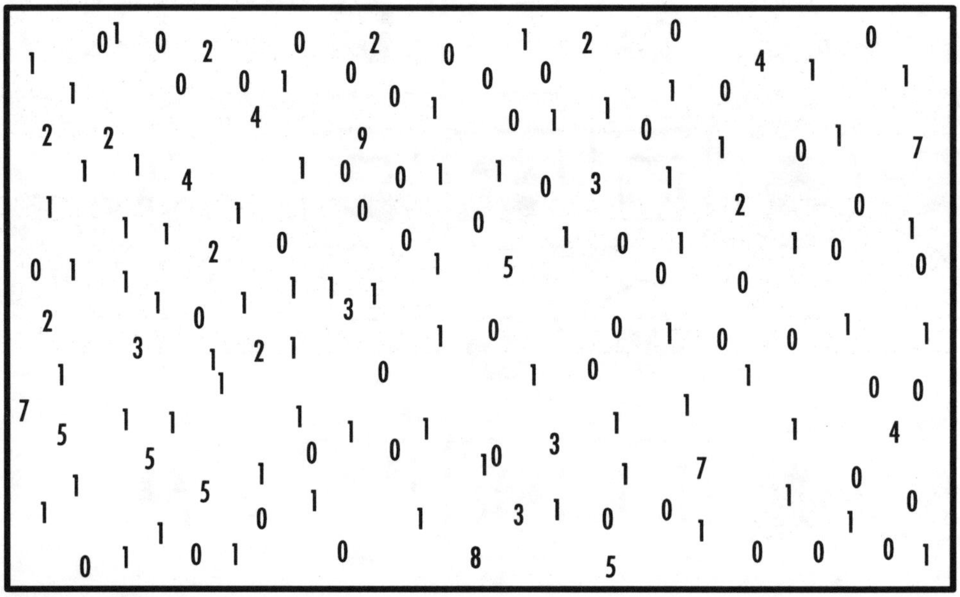

Puzzle 46

How many different types of shapes are here? The answer, multiplied by 3, is your next passcode.

Puzzle 47

3

The solution to D in the puzzle below provides the passcode to your next puzzle.

A

$$\frac{21913}{78800} = 5.1$$

B

$$\frac{34120}{30674} = 29$$

C

$$\frac{52312}{19640} = 6.5$$

D

$$\frac{62120}{38405} = ?$$

Puzzle 48

5

Pick the odd-one-out and use the number under it as your next passcode.

A

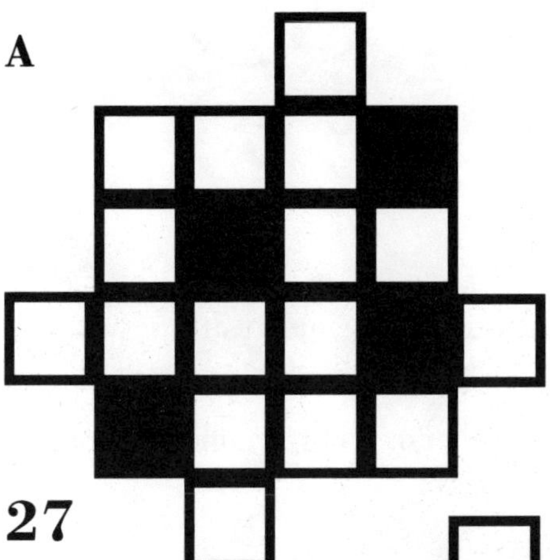

27

B

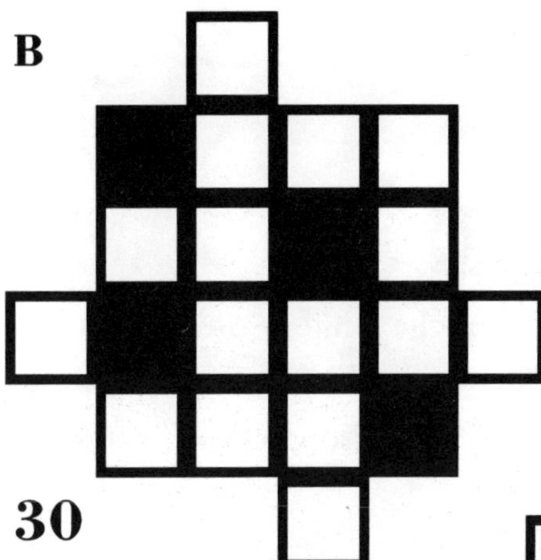

30

C

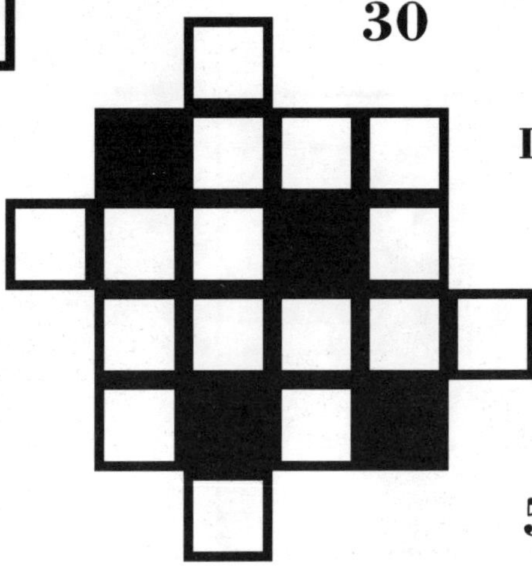

47

D

52

Puzzle 49

The numbers in these circles are in pairs, related to each other in a special way. Link each pair together according to their special relationship and hence find the odd pair out. The sum of the numbers in the odd-pair-out is your passcode to the next puzzle.

Puzzle 50

Your next passcode is the number which, if you square it and triple that result, gives you a number that, when you subtract 7 and multiply the result by 5, gives you a number that, when you take its square root and subtract 6, gives the first square number after 1.

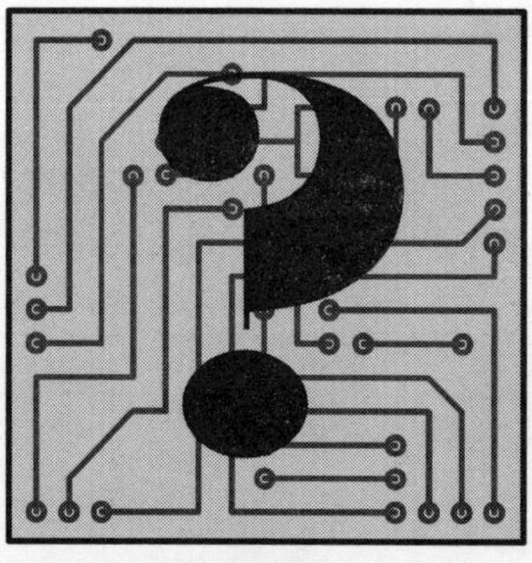

Puzzle 51

Place the box marked with 2 on these scales so that when the tension rope on the right is removed, the beam will be in balance. Your passcode is twice the number under the block's correct position.

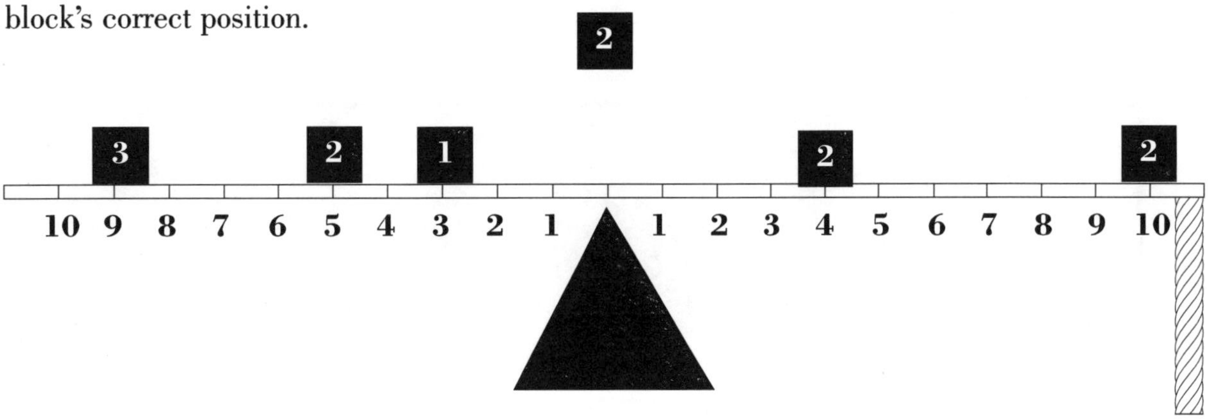

Puzzle 52

Your next passcode on your quest for escape from cyber-reality is the central number in the odd-one-out of this set. The central numbers are not part of the puzzle.

A

B	1	0	1	2	4
3	0	1	8	4	2
1	1	52		7	4
7	8			8	9
6	1	9	5	9	1
8	5	5	Y	5	1

B

S	5	8	6	7	1
Y	1	8	1	0	3
5	9	11		1	B
1	5			8	1
1	9	8	7	4	0
9	4	2	4	2	1

C

1	2	4	2	4	9
0	1	9	5	9	1
1	8	48		8	1
B	1			7	5
3	0	1	8	4	9
1	7	6	8	5	3

D

1	5	Y	3	5	8
1	9	5	9	1	6
9	8	16		8	7
4	7			1	1
2	4	8	1	0	3
4	2	1	0	1	B

Puzzle 53

Draw 4 straight lines to divide this rectangle into 5 sections with totals of 30, 40, 50, 60 & 70 in each respective section. Add 14 to the total number of non-zero digits in the smallest section to find your passcode to the next puzzle.

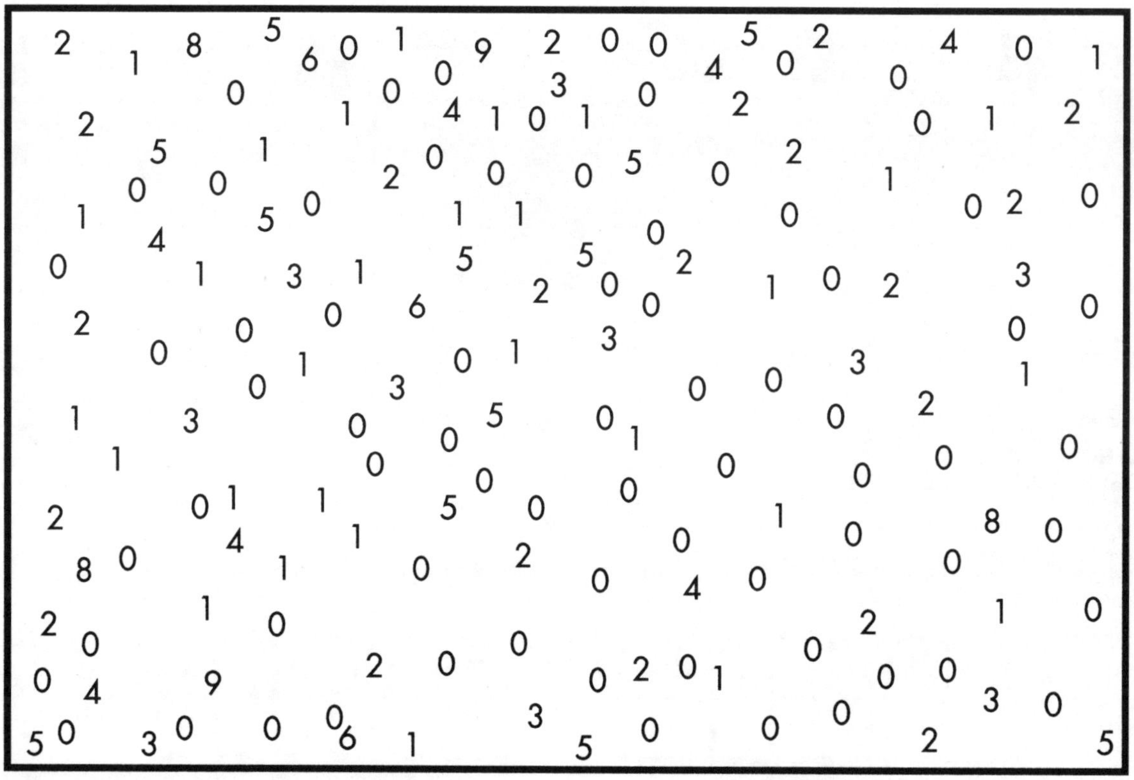

Puzzle 54

Pick the odd one out, and choose the number underneath as your next passcode.

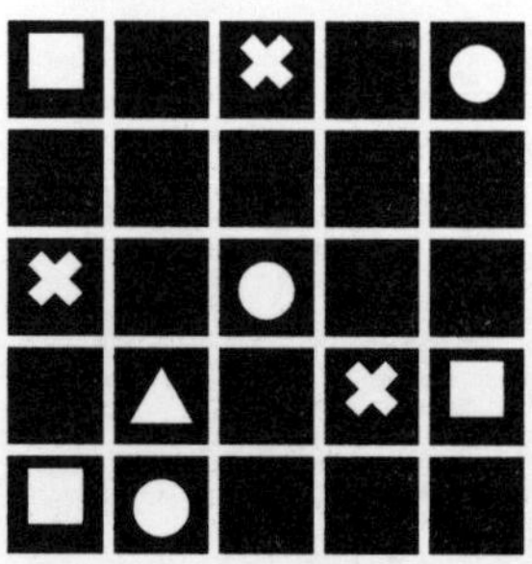

A=51

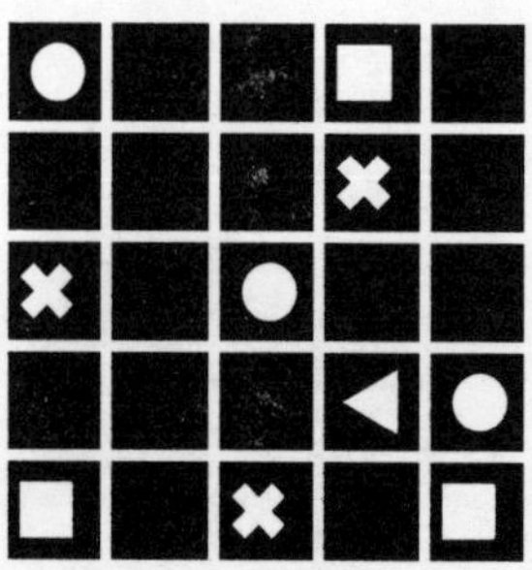

B=6

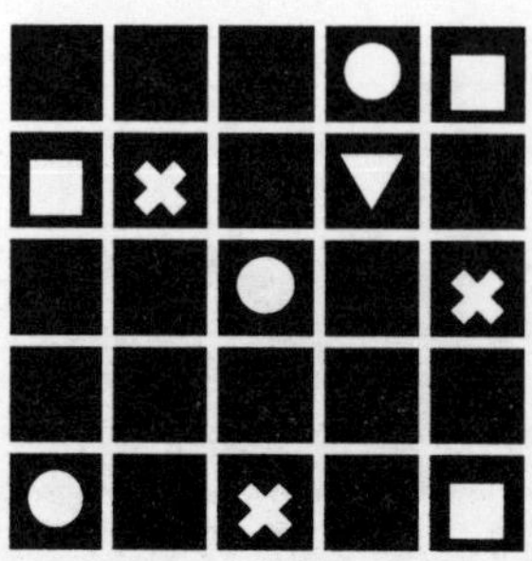

C=39

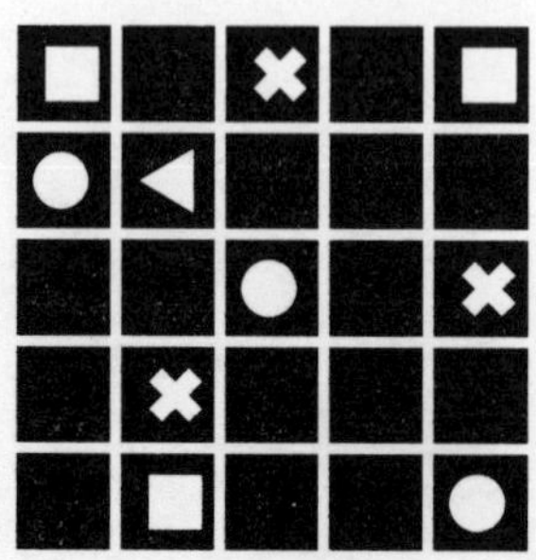

D=14

Puzzle 55

Pick the odd one out, and choose the number underneath as your next passcode.

A

7	6
2	4

11

B

9	6
4	5

30

C

5	4
0	3

52

Puzzle 56

Pick the odd one out, and use the bottom line as your passcode to the next puzzle.

A

1	4189
2	1372
3	0598
4	2182
5	0037

B

1	5241
2	1369
3	2080
4	1739
5	0052

C

1	4888
2	2161
3	1009
4	1674
5	0043

D

1	6334
2	0238
3	4686
4	1358
5	0051

Puzzle 57

Solve this puzzle equation and replace the question mark with the correct number. This number is your next passcode.

3 ❖ + 2 ◆ − 2 ★ = 36

2 ❖ − 1 ◆ − 1 ★ = 13

1 ❖ + 1 ◆ + 1 ★ = 17

2 ❖ − 3 ◆ + 1 ★ = ?

Puzzle 58

Pick the odd one out with the extra line, and take the number beside it as your next passcode.

A

21

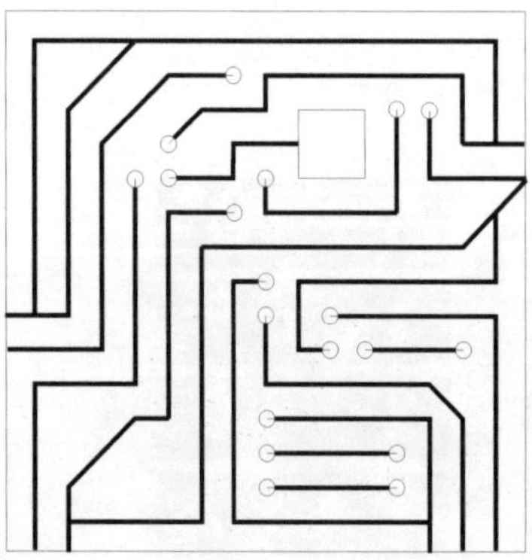

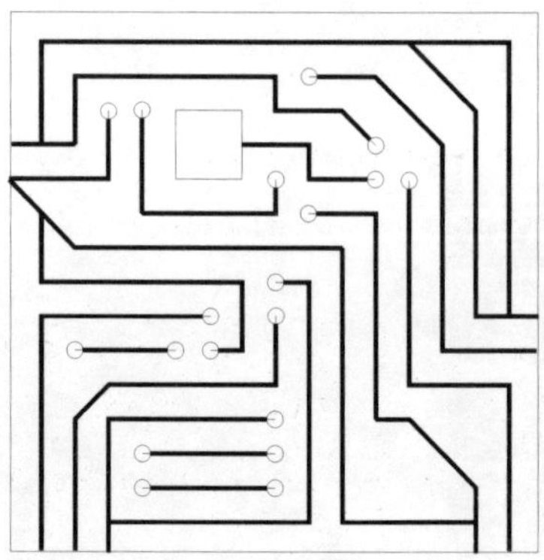

B

14

C

53

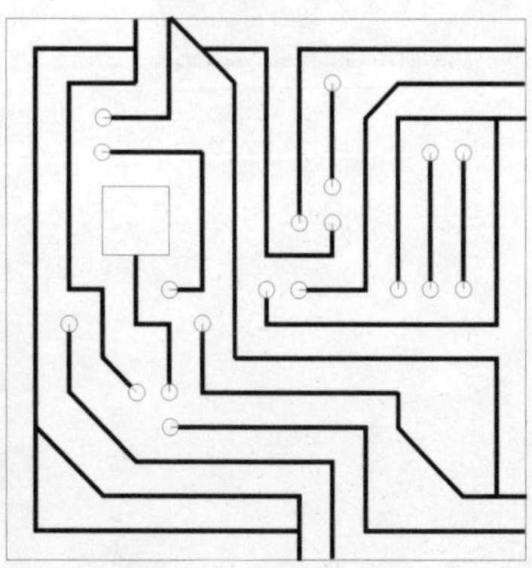

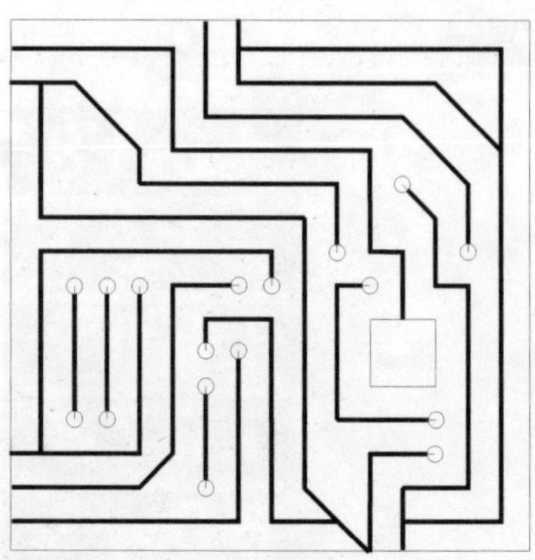

D

32

Puzzle 59

Pick the odd one out, and choose the number underneath as your next passcode. The numbers underneath each triangle are not part of the puzzle.

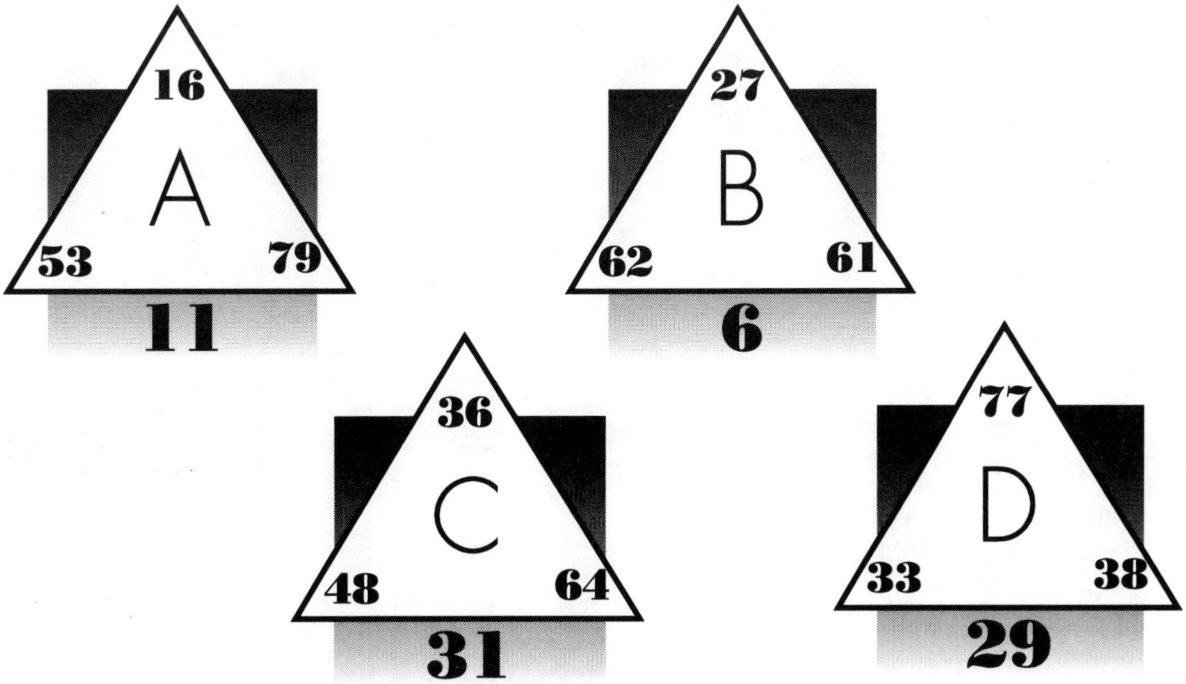

Puzzle 60

Complete the magic square so that every row, column and long diagonal adds to 33. Add 19 to the central number to find your passcode to the next puzzle.

4	9	7	5	8
5				7
9				4
8				5
7	5	8	4	9

SECTION THREE

KEYCODES

REMINDER: You must solve the puzzles in the correct order. Start at the top of column A, and insert your keys. When you get to the bottom of column A, start back at the top of column B.

Subtract the total of column B from the total of column A. The result is your solution for Section 3, and your passcode to the first puzzle in Section 4. Write that below and in the appropriate place on page 218, and combine that with your totals for Sections 1 & 2 to find your solution to the first part of the final puzzle as directed.

You will only get the correct solution for the Part One code gate if you have got every answer in all three sections correct. If you've managed that, you've done well.

Are you up to the second half?

Total A

Total B

SECTION THREE

PASSCODE

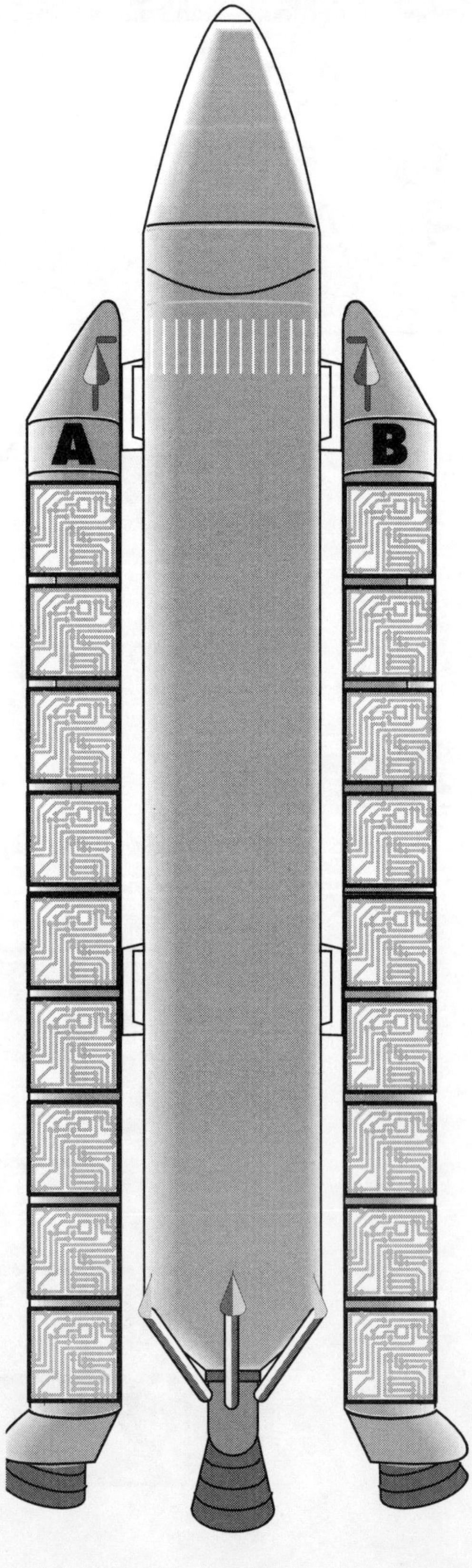

SECTION THREE

ANSWERS

1. B. **Go to 29.**

2. Solution 56. The multiplication is 237456 x 54=12822624. The last 2 digits of the six figure multiplicand are 56. **Go to 56.**

3. Solution C. This is a mirror image of the others, which are all rotated versions of the same thing. **Read the passcode for C. Go to 45.**

4. There are 32 circles and 16 crosses. 32-16=16. **Go to 16. Key 4.**

5. Solution 34. 34x2=68, 68+2=70. 70/10=7. 7+13=20. 20/4=5. 5x5=25. **Go to 34.**

6. D comes next. Both bars are moving one step at a time. When they roll over they start at the top and side of the square. **Go to 8.**

7. Solution 13. In each circle the numbers around, when added and the result divided by 2, make the central numbers. **Go to 13.**

8. The odd-one-out is A. The extra line is shown below. **Go to 35.**

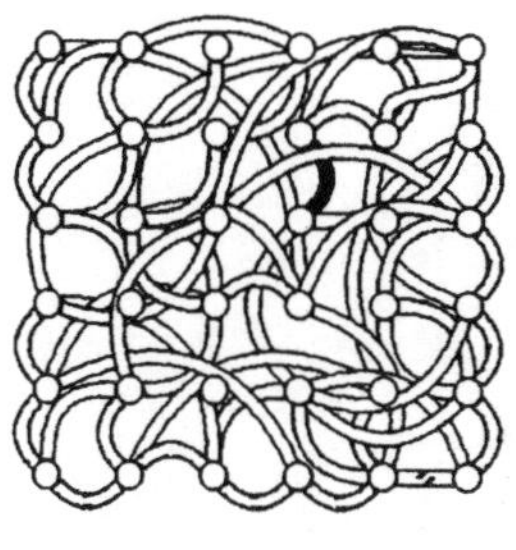

9. Solution. D. In A, B, & C, you can read the pattern clockwise: BGBGRBGR, but in D you have to read anticlockwise to get this sequence. **Go to 27.**

10. C is the odd one out. The numbers on each of the other cubes add to 119, but the numbers on C add to 120. **Go to 49.**

11. Solution A. In every tile of the pattern of 9, the three small circles remain in the same position relative to each other. **Go to 18.**

12. Solution 54. In the top row 4x8=[3][2]. In the bottom row, 6x9=[5][4]. **Go to 54. Key 2.**

13. D. Two small squares have been changed to black. The other images are all rotated versions of the same thing. **Go to 11.**

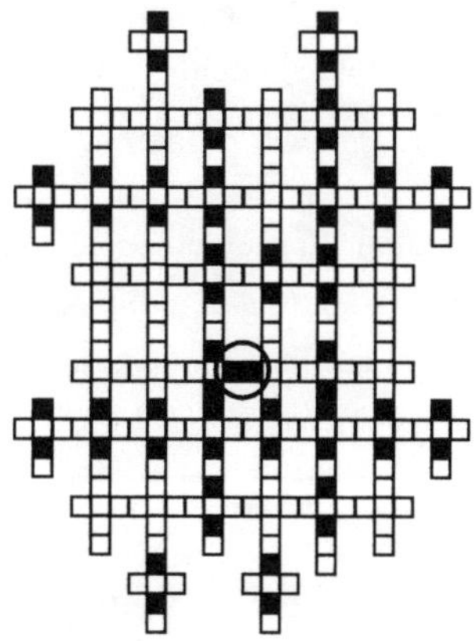

14. D. **Go to 43.**

15. B is the odd-one-out. The numbers on this set are reversed in a mirror-image of the sequence on the other sets, which are all rotated versions of the same thing. **Go to 61 – The Keycodes. Key 6.**

16. C is the odd-one-out. A detail has been changed, as circled below. **Go to 55.**

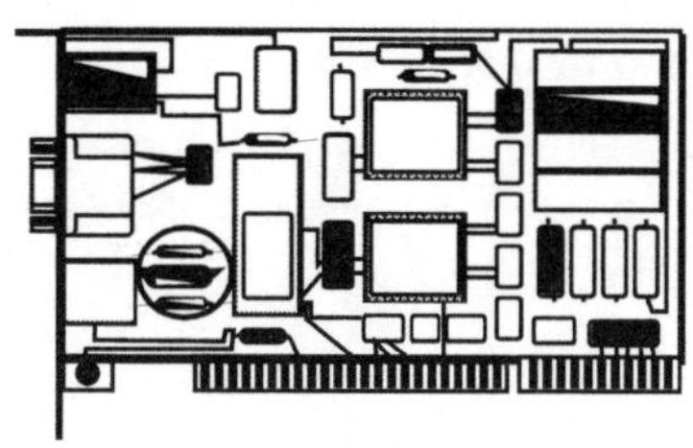

17. C is odd. In each other box, starting from the right hand section, add to bottom section to get the result in left and top sections. Thus, in A, 5 + 8 = 13. Etc.... **Go to 28.**

18. A is odd. It is the only one in which the numbers around the puzzle add to the total in the middle. All others add to one more than the total. Subtract 20 from 51. **Go to 31. Key 2.**

SECTION THREE

19. Solution 47. Add each number to itself and add 1. Thus, 5+6=11; 11+12=23; 23+24=47; **Go to 47.**

20. Solution 44. 44-40=4. 4sqrd.=16; 16+10=26; 26/2=13; 13x3=39; 51-39=12; 12=3x4; 78-39=39. **Go to 44. Key 5**

21. Solution 4. In each puzzle, the top 2 numbers + the next 2 - the third 2 = the bottom 2. Thus, 25 + 19 - 12 = 32; 3+2=5; 5-1=4. **Go to 4.**

22. D is the odd-one-out. In each other case the pattern of A is repeated, starting at a different place and rolling over at the end. In B the pattern begins on square 4. In C it begins on square 9. In D, however, the pattern is reversed. **Go to 46.**

23. The ages are listed below. **Go to 26.**
Kamal=11
Mary=23
Iain=14
Simon=26
Sady=10
Fifi=1
Petra=5
Chevonne=2

24. Solution 53. In each box, multiplying the diametrically opposite numbers together and adding together the results, produces the box below. Thus, (11x3)+(4x5)=53. **Go to 53. Key 3.**

25. A is the odd-one-out. It is a mirror-image of the others, which are all rotated versions of the same thing. **Go to 33. Key 2.**

26. Solution 51. Multiply the top two numbers, then take the bottom left and top right numbers and add them to the product. The bottom right number is a red herring. Thus, 5+7=12; (5x7)+12=47; Add 4 to 47 to get your passcode. **Go to 51.**

27. Solution 36. Time taken = distance/ speed. Distance = 36; Speed = 27; 36/27=1.33(repeater) hours = 80 minutes. 80-44=36. **Go to 36. Key 8.**

28. There are 5 differences, circled below. 5x10=50. **Go to 50.**

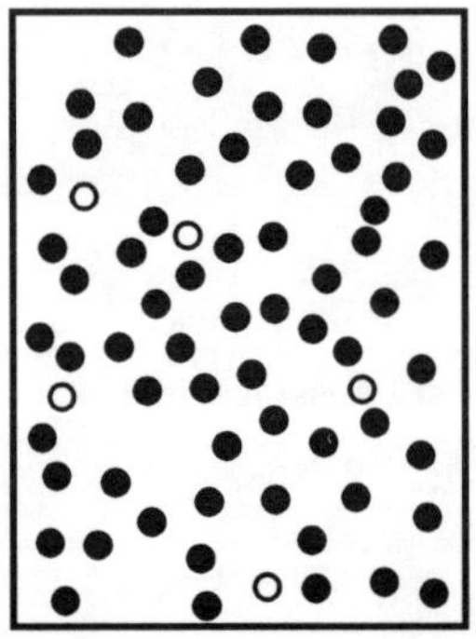

29. In each set, the top number - the middle 2 numbers = the bottom number. Hence 45-23=22. **Go to 22.**

30. The number is 59, which is the only prime number in the circles. All others have more divisors than themselves and 1. **Go to 59. Key 9.**

31. Solution D. This contains one extra white square, and one less white triangle than the others. **Go to 42. Key 4.**

32. Ans. Solution O. **Go to 15.**

A	E	I	O	U
O	U	A	E	I
E	I	O	U	A
U	A	E	I	O
I	O	U	A	E

33. 186740[-3340]=183400[/70] =2620 [-180] =2440 [x3] =7320 [/5] =1464 /8= [183] /3=61. Thus, 3340+70+180+3+5+183=3781; 3781/38=99.5; 99.5-90.5=9. **Go to 9. Key 6.**

34. The missing number is 38. Add the left bottom digits individually to the top number to get the right-hand figure. **Go to 38.**

35. Solution A. In all others, the (top number x the middle number) + the bottom number = number in circle, but in A the 6 is subtracted to get 57. **Go to 57.**

SECTION THREE

ANSWERS

36. Solution B. The sequence rotates anti-clockwise, but in all the others it rotates clockwise. **Go to 41. Key 2.**

37. The sequence steps one box to the left on every alternate row – 6, 12, 6, 16, 10. **Go to 10.**

38. Solution 4. Top Left (TL)+BL-BR=TR; TR/2= center. 7+9=16. 16-[4]=12. 12/2=6. 4/2=2. **Go to 2.**

39. Solution 17. The top row plus the left and right digits = the bottom row. Thus, 228+17=245. **Go to 17. Key 3.**

40. Solution D. In all others you multiply the bottom left and top right numbers together to get the top left and bottom right result. But in D this is reversed. Hence in D, 3x9=27. **Go to 39.**

41. There are 29 squares. Double 29=58. **Go to 58.**

42. Solution 20. The top and bottom digits are combined and divided by 2. Thus 40/2= 20. **Go to 20. Key 6.**

43. Values are shown below. **Go to 1.**

44. There are 9 differences as circled below. 9+10=19. **Go to 19.**

45. There are 23 1's, as in the diagram below in the smallest part. **Go to 23. Key 8.**

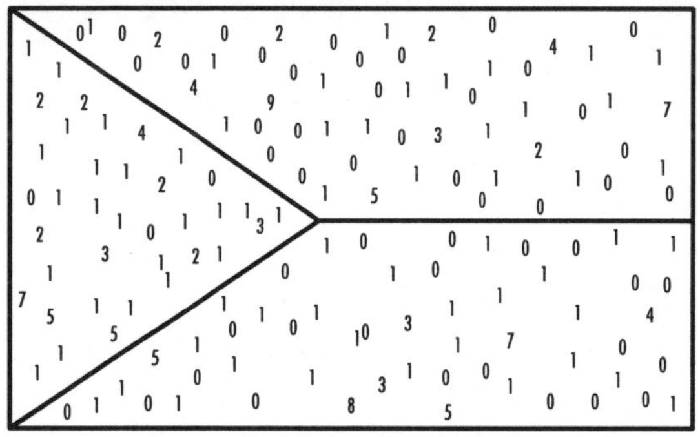

46. There are 20 different shapes as shown below. 20x3=60. **Go to 60.**

47. Solution 25. In , for example, B, (33+40+16+27) /4 =29; In D, (63+28+14+20) /5 =25. **Go to 25. Key 3.**

48. Solution B, which is a mirror-image of the others. The others are all rotated versions of the same thing. **Go to 30. Key 5.**

49. The odd-pair-out are the 18 & 22, linked with double lines. This pair add to 40, but every other pair add to 56. **Go to 40.**

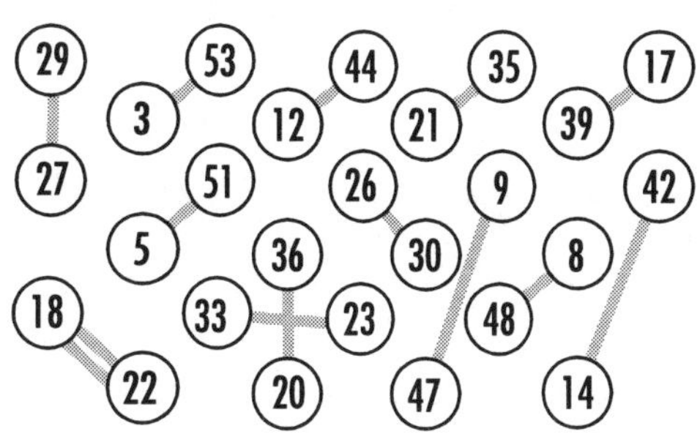

50. Solution 3. $3^2 + (2x3^2)=27$; 27-7=20; 20x5=100; sqr. root 100=10; 10-6=4; 4 is the first perfect square (2x2). **Go to 3.**

SECTION THREE

51. The box goes at position 6 on the right-hand side of the scales. Thus, (2x6)+(2x4)+(2x10)=40, which is the same as (3x9)+(5x2)(+3x1). Double 6=12. **Go to 12.**

52. C is the odd-one-out. In this set, the inner set of numbers, 181018478959 can be read anti-clockwise. In the other sets this can be read clockwise. **Go to 48. Key 7.**

53. Referring to the diagram below, there are 7 digits in the smallest section. 7+14=21. **Go to 21.**

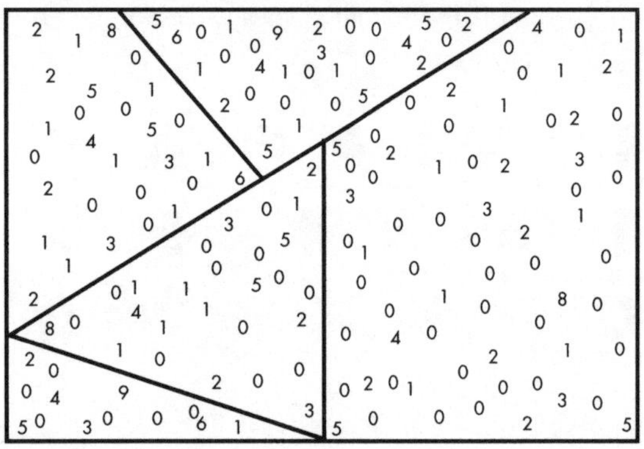

54. D is the odd-one-out. The triangle is facing the wrong way round. **Go to 14.**

55. Solution C. Both the other circles contain multiplications written clockwise. In A, for example, 7x6=42. **Go to 52.**

56. A is the odd-one-out. In all others subtract the lines 2, 3, 4 and 5 from line 1 to get 1. In A you get zero. **Go to 37.**

57. Solution 7. Lozenges=10; diamonds=5; stars=2. **Go to 7.**

58. D is the odd-one-out. The others are all related versions of the same thing, but in D there is a connecting line. **Go to 32.**

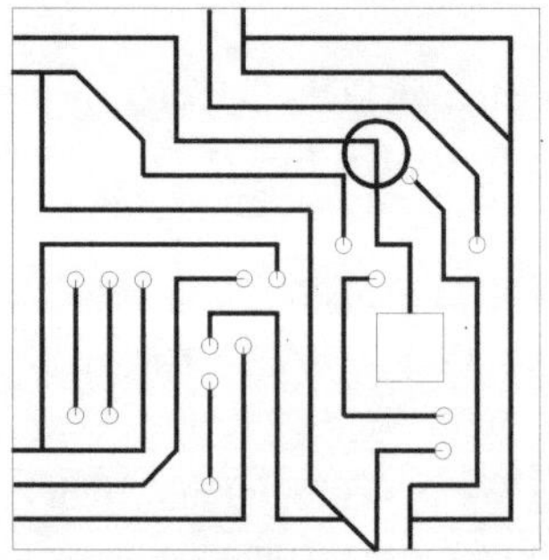

59. Solution B. All others add to 148. **Go to 6.**

60. The central number is 5. 5+19=24. **Go to 24.**

4	9	7	5	8
5	8	4	9	7
9	7	**5**	8	4
8	4	9	7	5
7	5	8	4	9

Section Three Keycode = 43-42 = 1. Go to Section Four, Puzzle 1.

SECTION FOUR

Puzzle 1

You are now into the second half of your quest to escape from Adrian Smith's cyber-reality. If you are up to the task, find the missing number to find your passcode to the next puzzle.

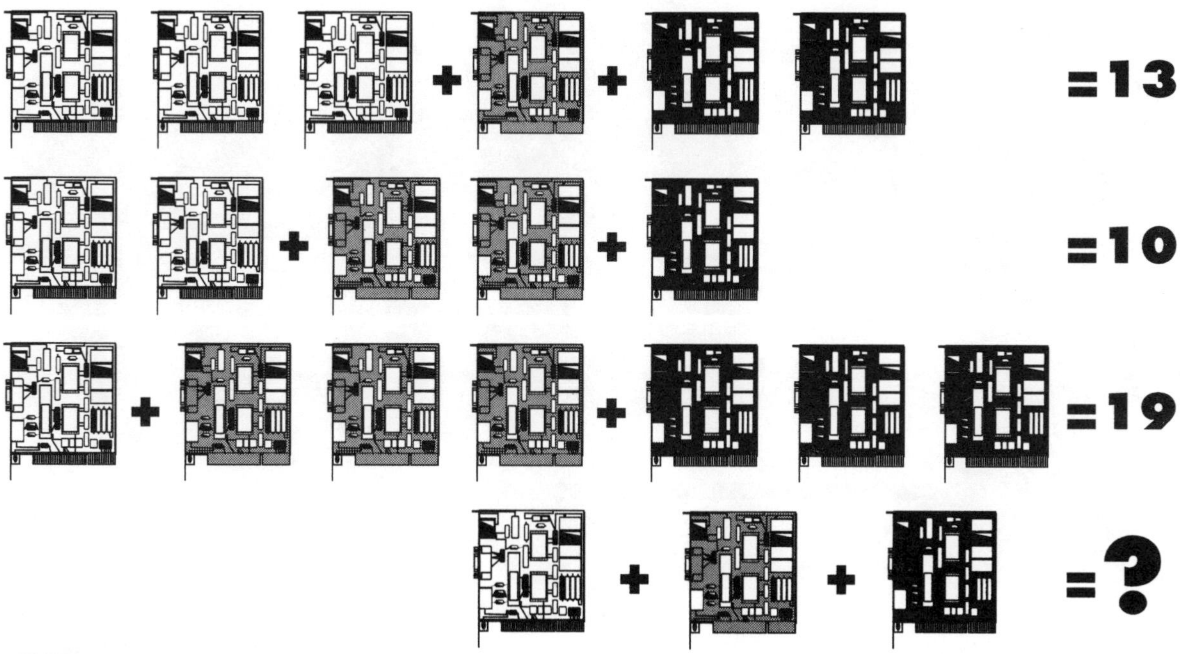

Puzzle 2

Be numerically reasonable. Use the missing number on the bottom right of this triangle as your next passcode.

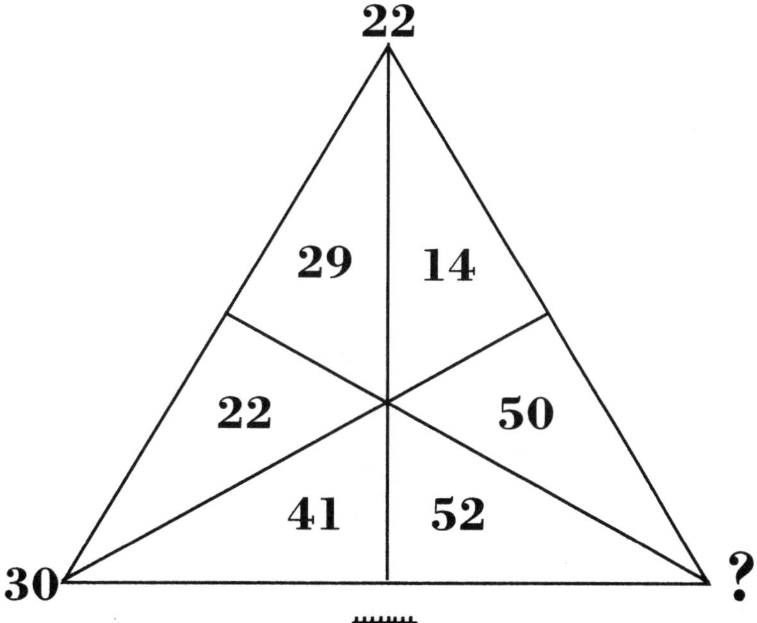

Puzzle 3

Your next passcode is the number that should replace the question mark in this puzzle. Find it or stay in cyber-reality forever.

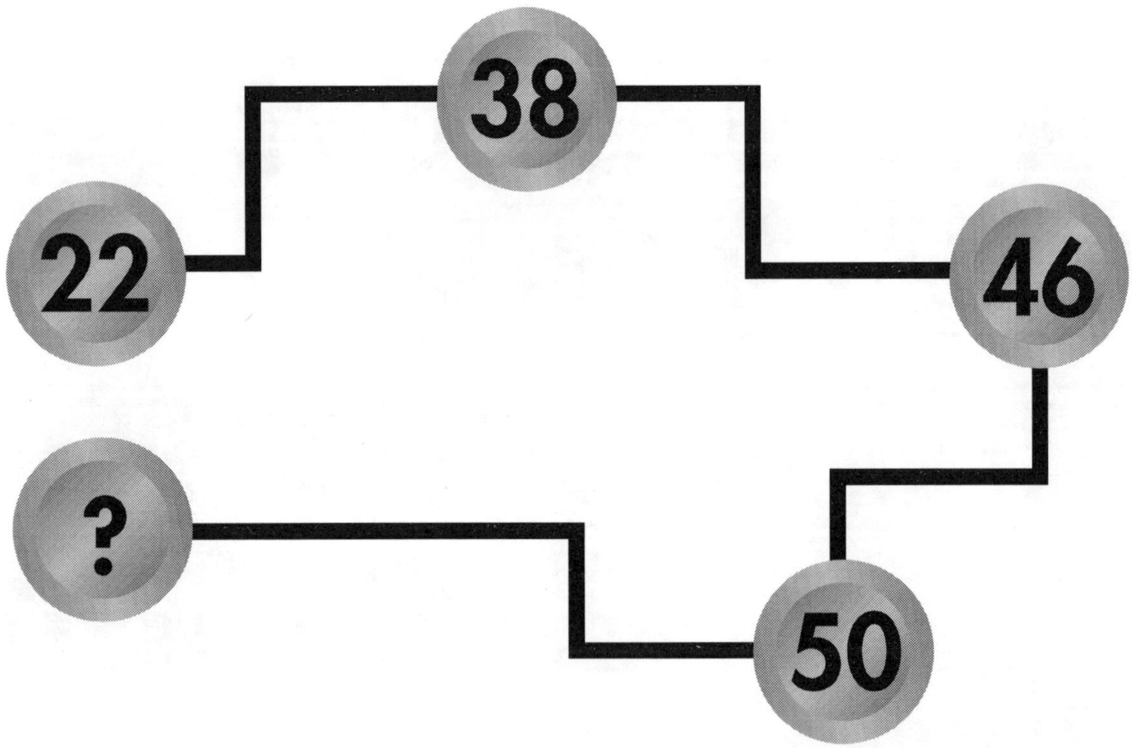

Puzzle 4

Your next passcode is the number that, when you add 10, gives you a number that, when you multiply it by 3, produces a result that, if 12 is subtracted and the result divided by 9, gives 7.

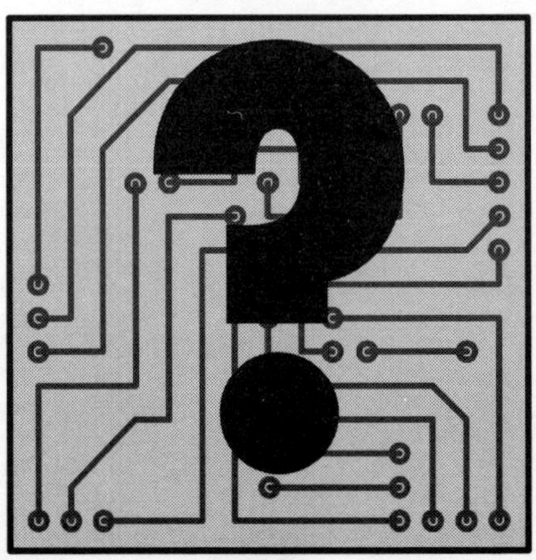

Puzzle 5

Find the value of 6 boots and you'll know your next passcode.

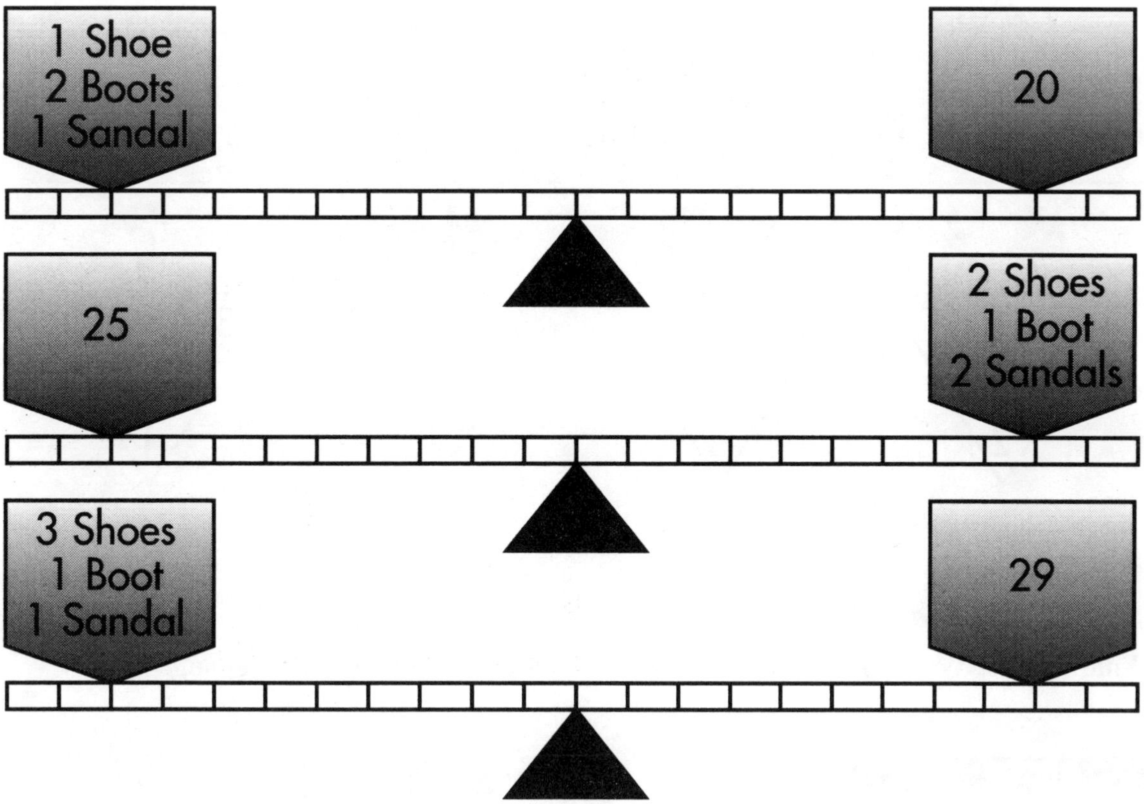

Puzzle 6

Put in the missing digits to find your next passcode, or don't and suffer the consequences of being lost in cyber-reality.

9	2	2
3	0	6
3	0	8

8	4	5
5	8	7
1	2	9

7	7	7
6	7	5
0	?	?

Puzzle 7

Your passcode to the next puzzle is the solution to D.

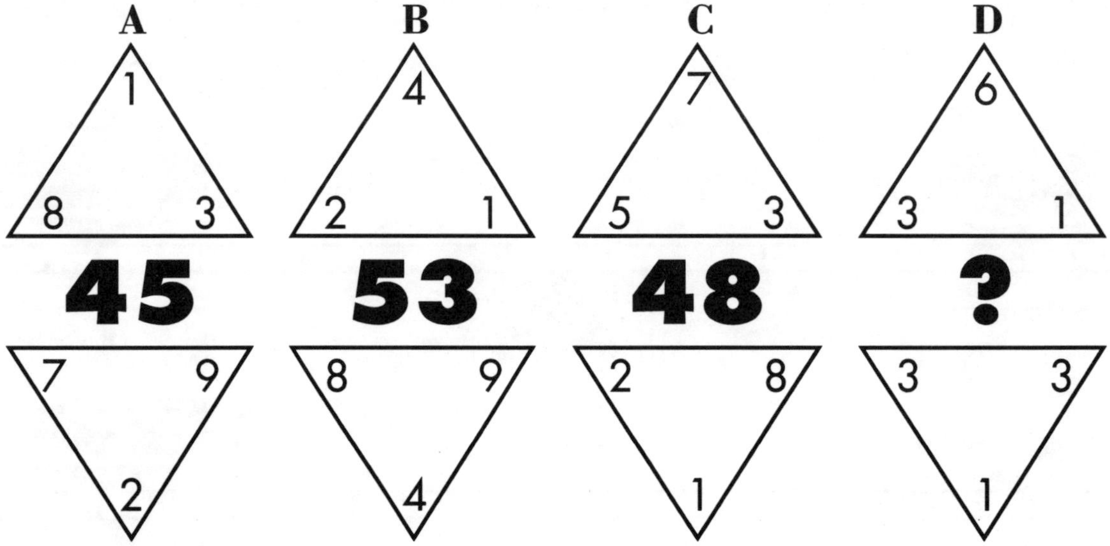

Puzzle 8

Find your next passcode by solving the puzzle below, if you are smart enough.

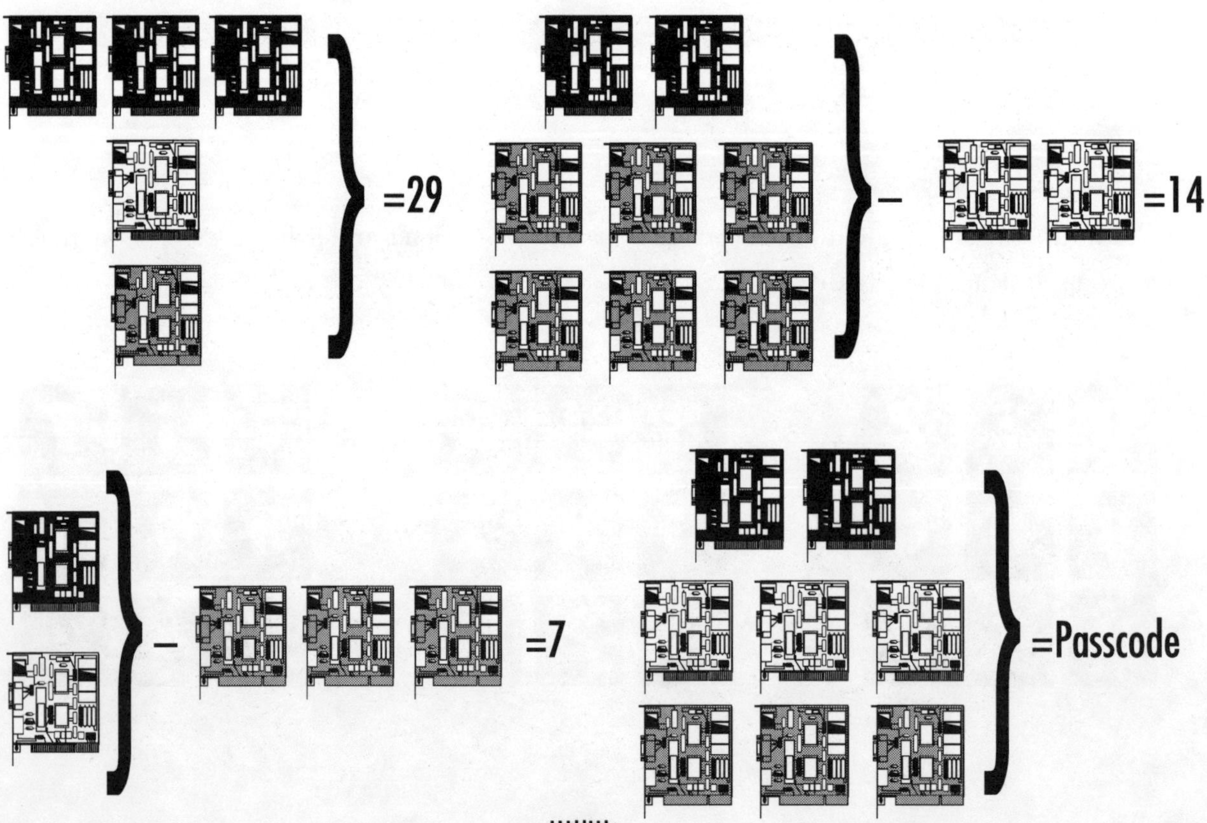

Puzzle 9

If on a triangular trip, Adrian Smith uses your body to travel 20 distance units from your home to point A, where he conducts one experiment upon you. He then goes a further 35 distance units to point B, where he throws eggs at your friends to see how they react. Then Adrian takes your body home, which is 20 distance units from B. How long will the trip take him if he travels at an average speed of 30 distance units per hour, and spends 10 minutes on the experiment at A, and 2 minutes at B, pelting your friends? Subtract 102 from this time in minutes to find your next passcode.

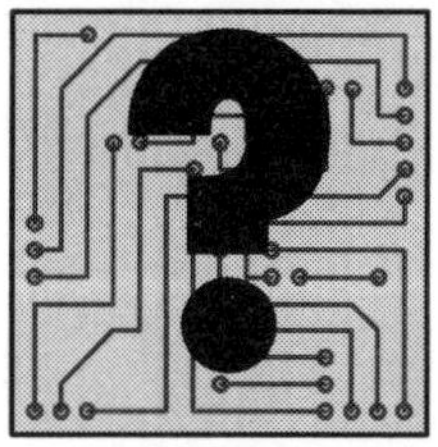

Puzzle 10

Use your powers of discrimination to count the number of discs piled up here, then subtract 2 and divide by 10 to get your passcode to the next puzzle.

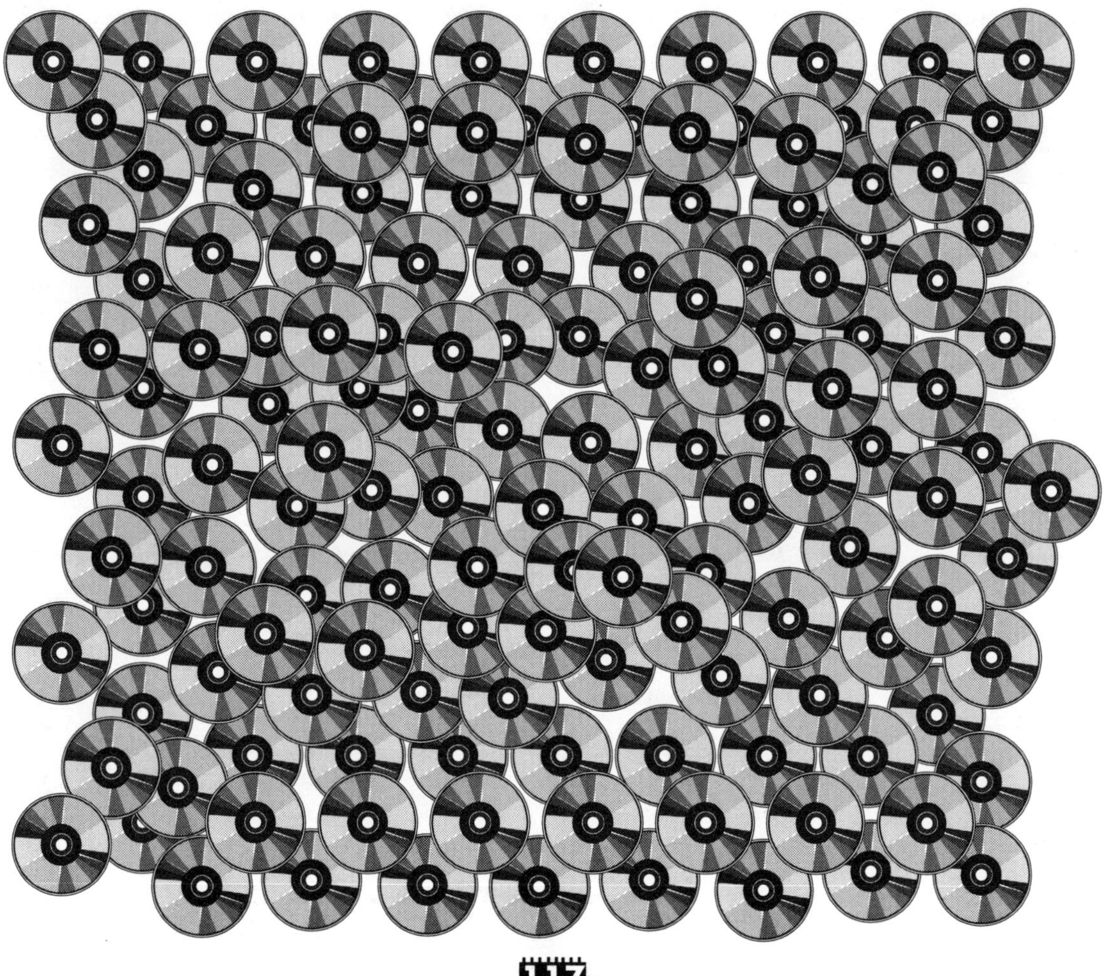

Puzzle 11

Pick the odd-one-out and use the number under the solution as your next passcode.

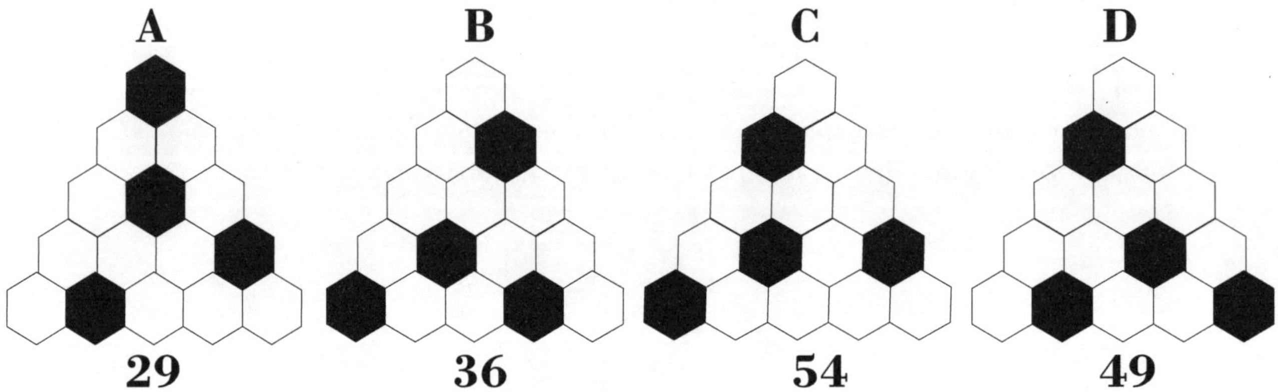

Puzzle 12

Follow the logic of this puzzle, if you have logic and can think, to find your next passcode.

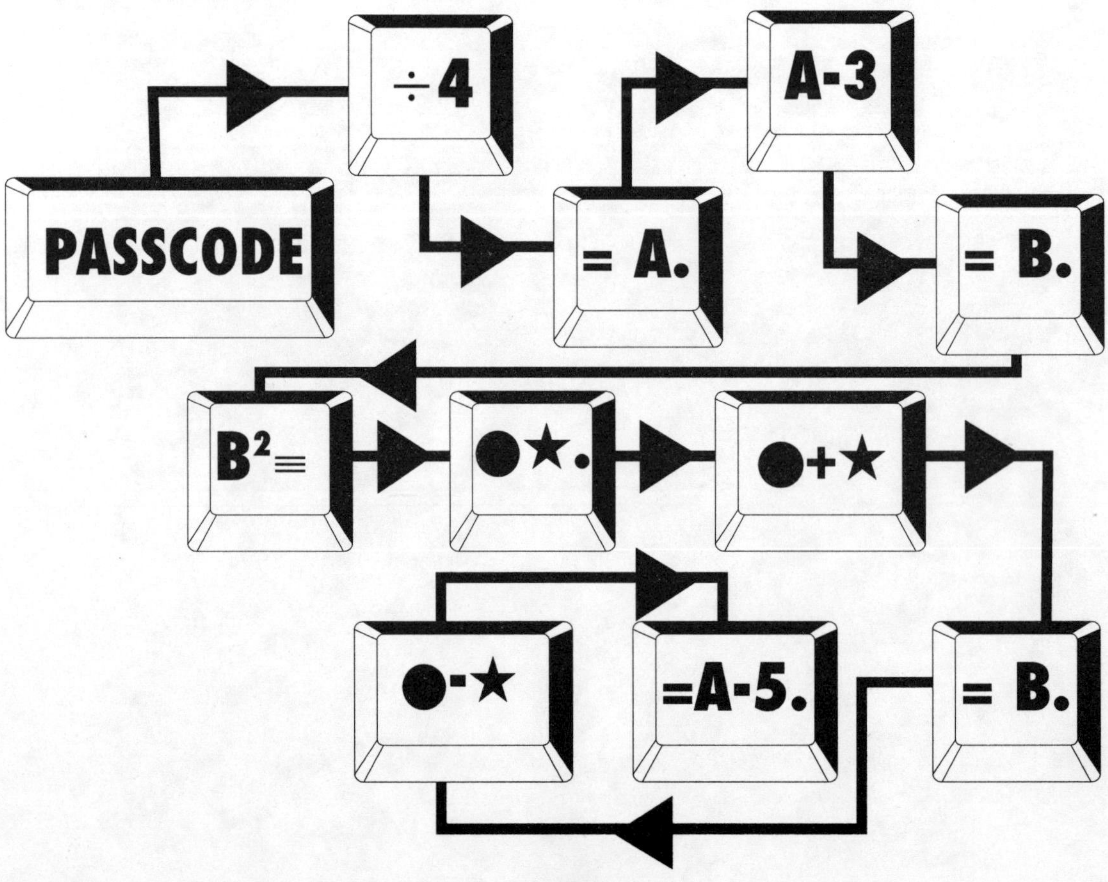

Puzzle 13

One of these discs does not go with the other three. When you've figured out which is the odd-one-out, use the number on that disc's label as your next passcode. The label numbers are nothing to do with the puzzle.

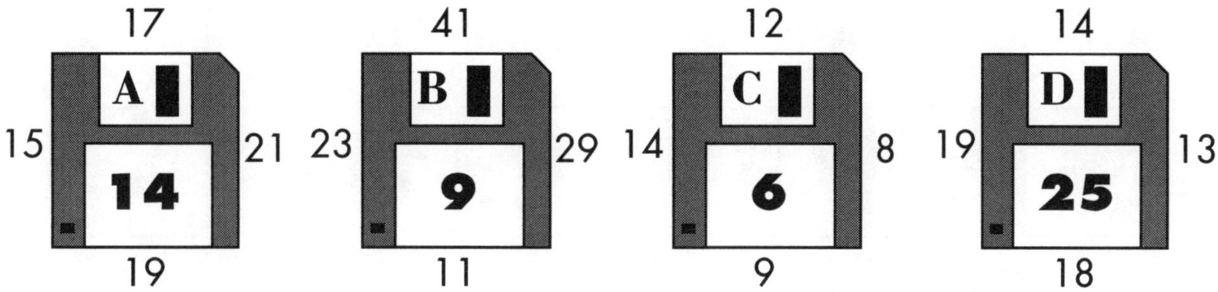

Puzzle 14

Using Adrian's video scanners, choose the odd-one-out. Your passcode is beside it.

A
17

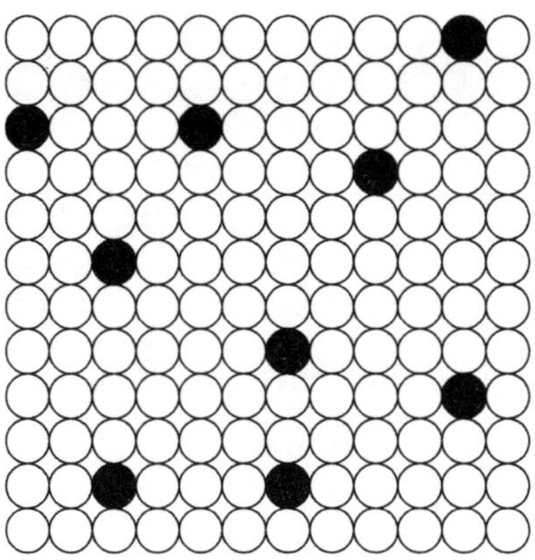

B
33

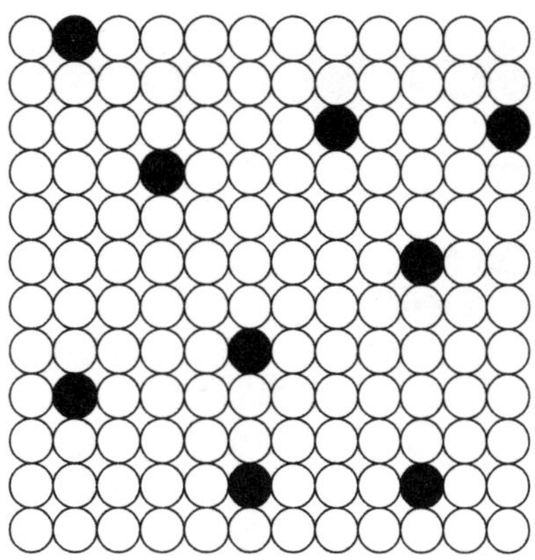

C
40

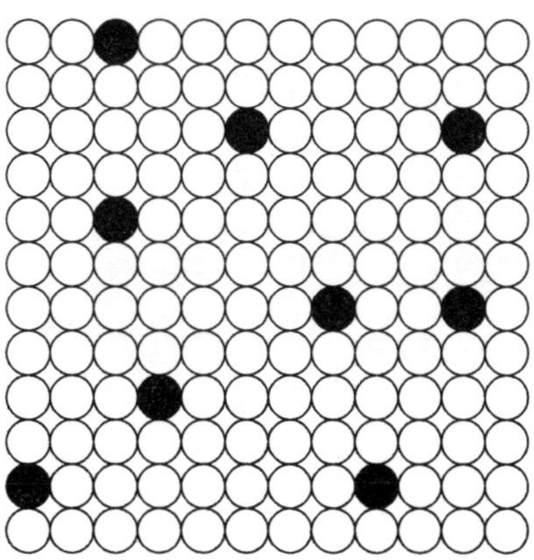

D
51

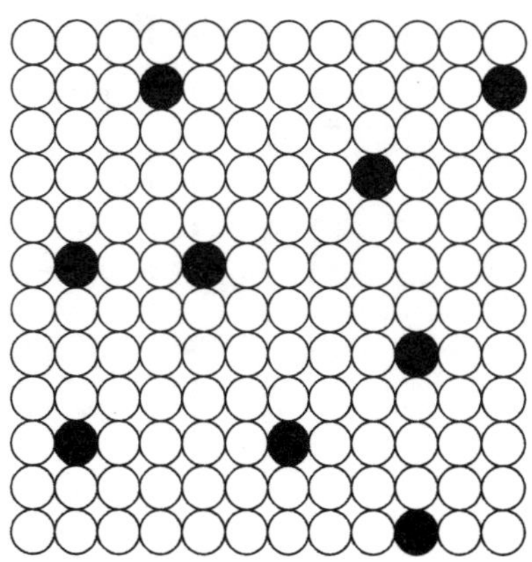

Puzzle 15

Can you think in three dimensions? Which of the surrounding plans makes the cube in the middle? Choose your passcode accordingly.

A=Passcode **49**. **B**=Passcode **30**. **C**=Passcode **50**. **D**=Passcode **21**.

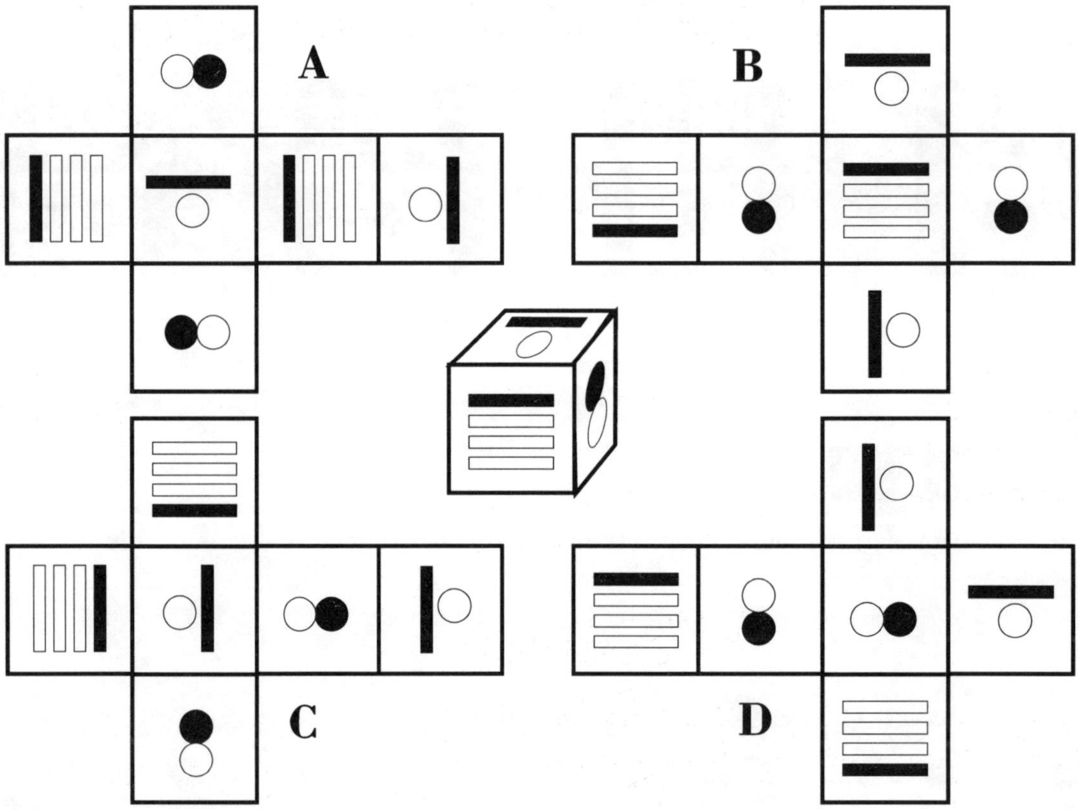

Puzzle 16

Multiply the number of H shapes, like that in the box on the right, that are in this twin set of overlapping shapes by 3 and add 1 to get your passcode to the next puzzle.

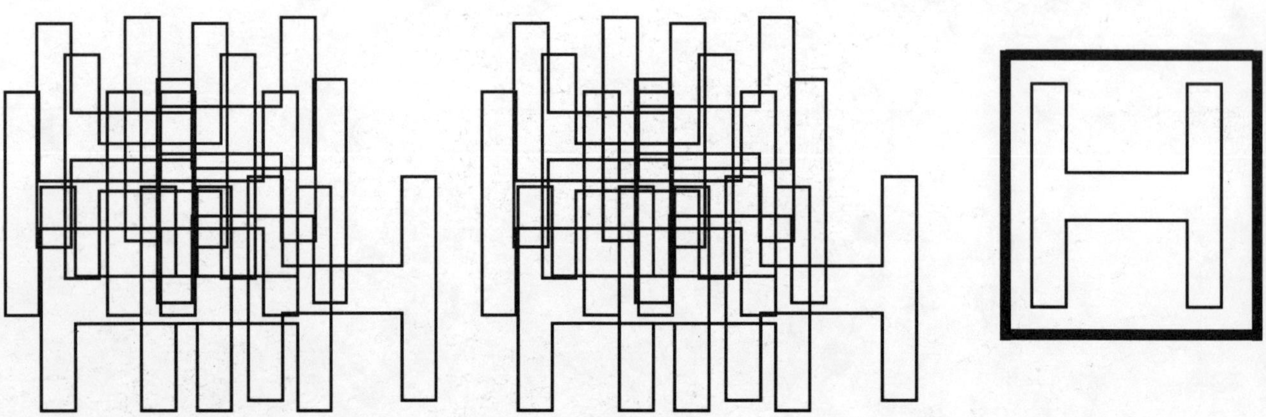

Puzzle 17

One of these cubes does not go with the other three. Use the number on the front of that cube as your next passcode.

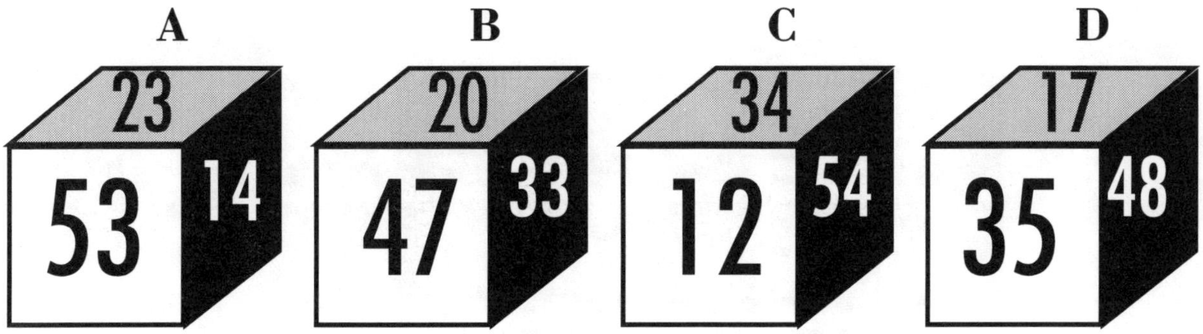

Puzzle 18

Twist your mind around this: when the cog with the arrow is turned a quarter in the direction of the arrow, the hanging number that will end up in the highest position is your passcode to the next puzzle.

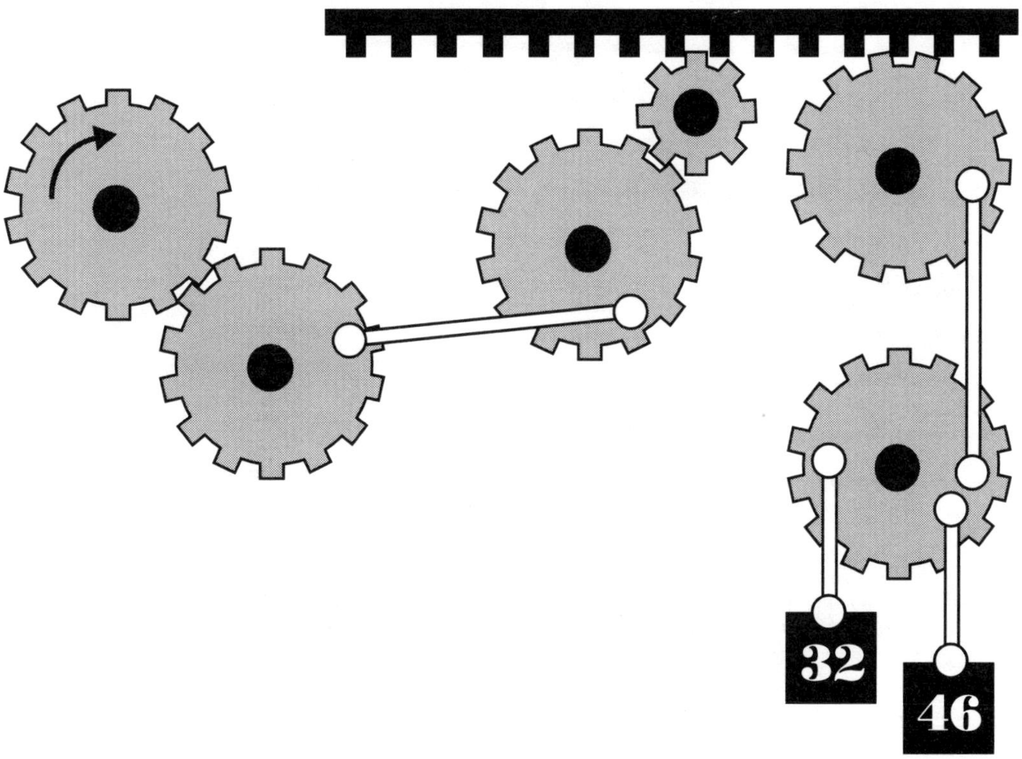

Puzzle 19

The three missing digits in this grid are your passcode to the next puzzle. If you are not confused, you are too clever by half.

5	3	6	1	4	9
3	8	7	6	0	8
?	?	?	5	9	5

Puzzle 20

5

Subtract 22 from the missing number in this set to find your passcode to the next puzzle.

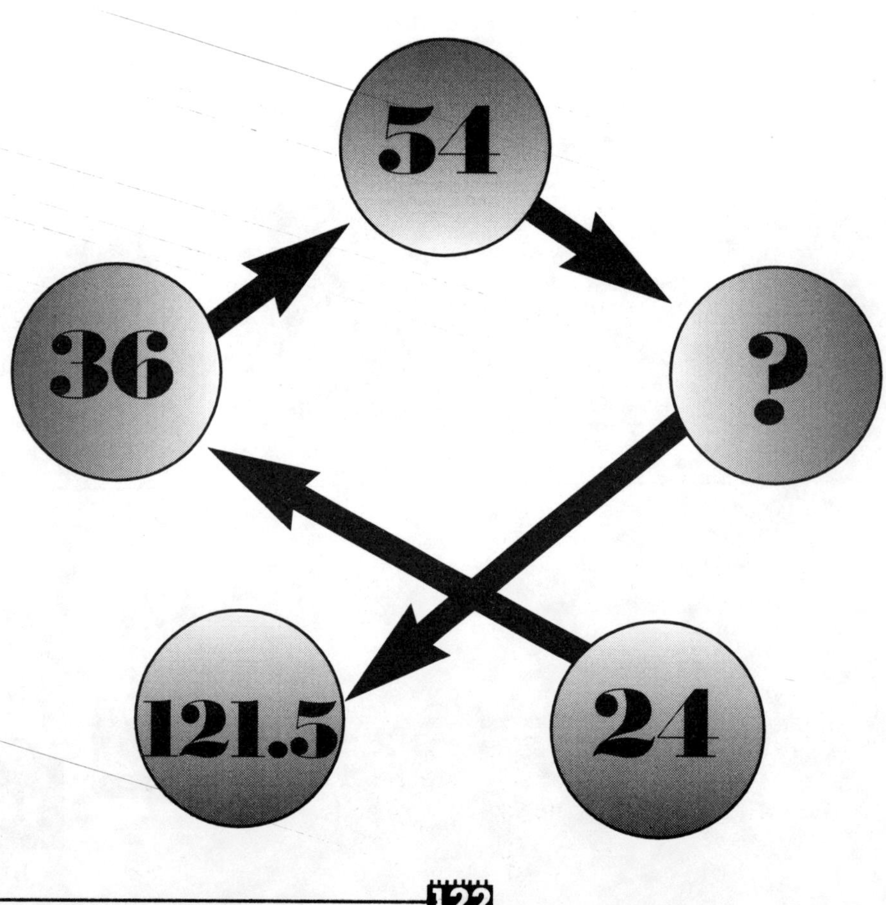

Puzzle 21

Choose the odd-one-out from the shapes below and use the number under it as your next passcode.

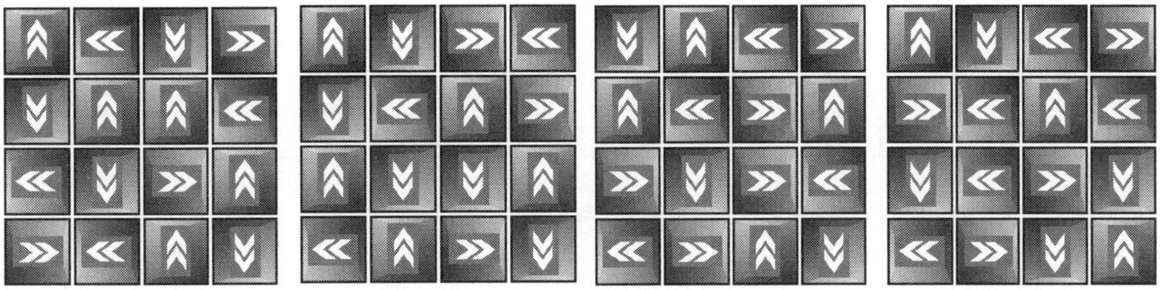

A=14 B=22 C=48 D=35

Puzzle 22

Solve the values for these equations to find your next passcode.

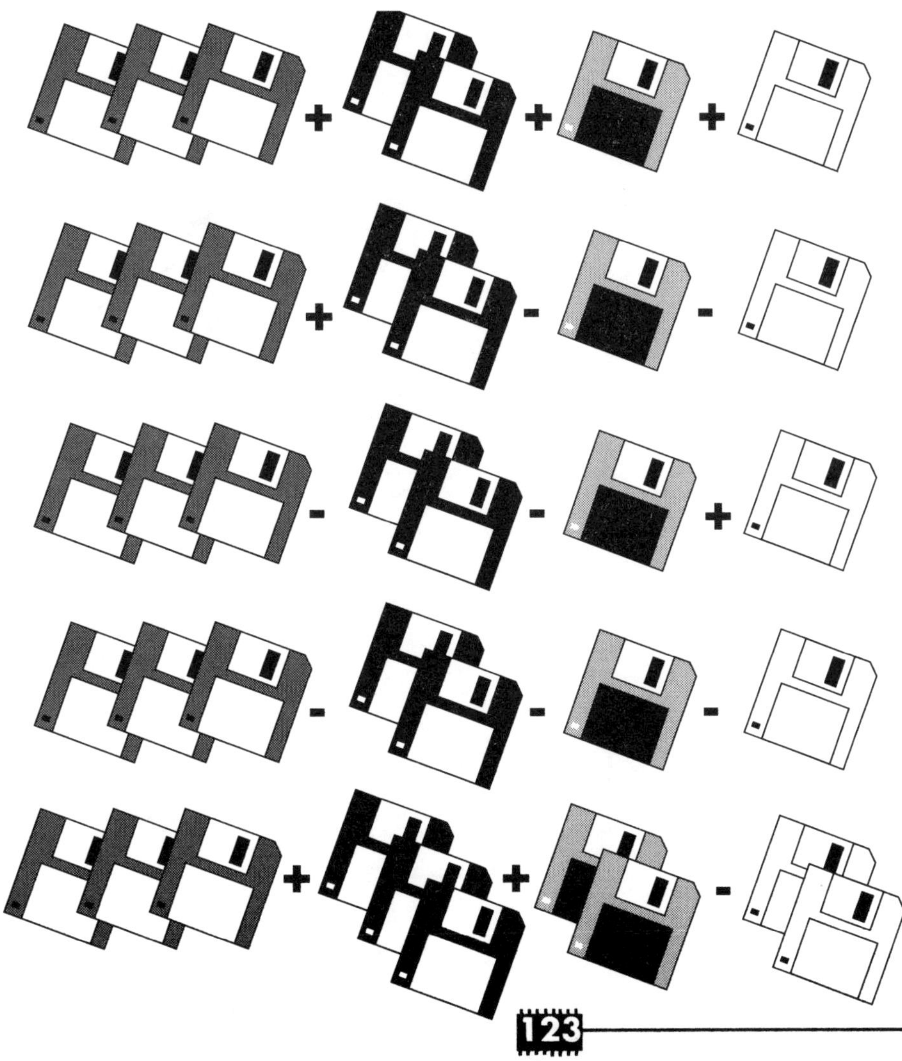

=42

=24

=8

=0

=Passcode

Puzzle 23

This system is in balance. The weight of the box with the question mark, plus half that weight again, is the value of your next passcode.

Puzzle 24

Four of the shapes below can be combined to form a square. The shape that does not fit in, when you add 10 to it, contains your passcode to the next puzzle.

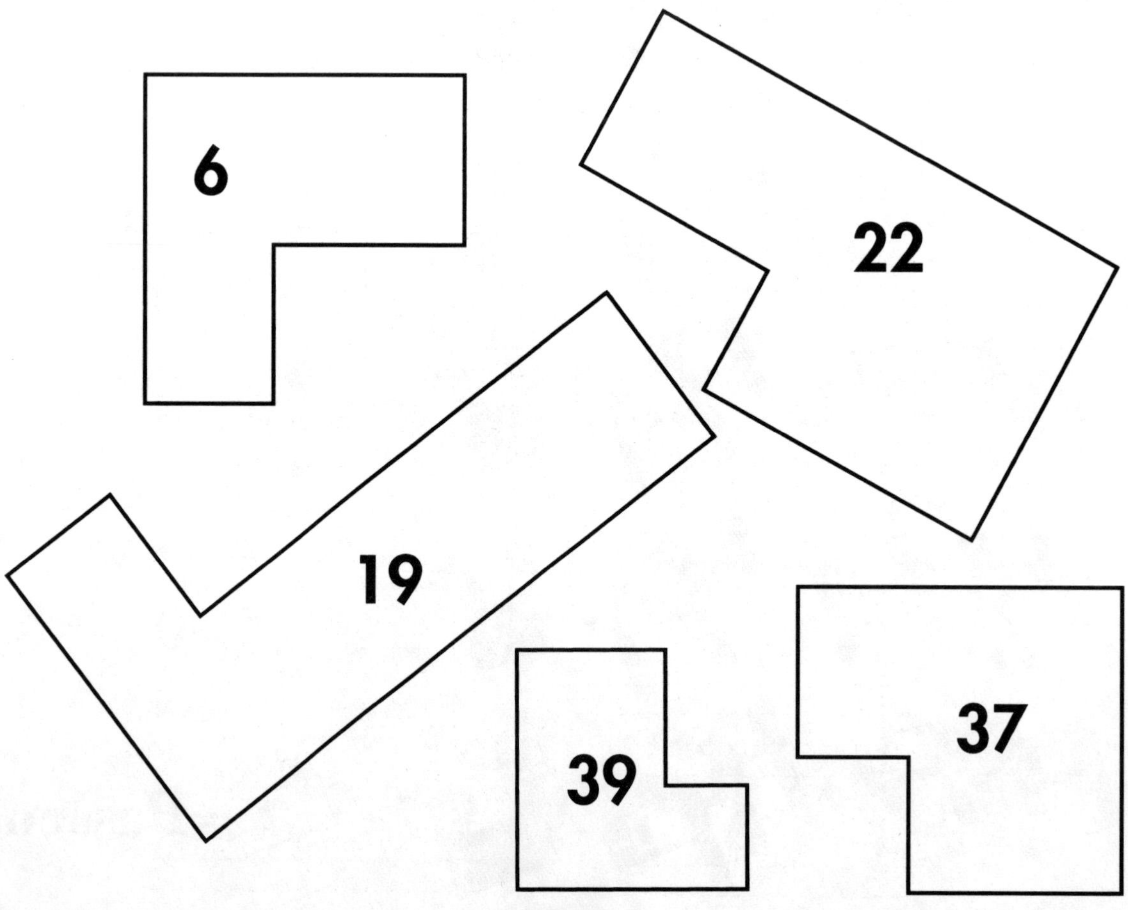

Puzzle 25

Pick the odd-one-out from this row of transponder pads, and choose your passcode accordingly.

A=Passcode **20**. **B**=Passcode **49**. **C**=Passcode **42**. **D**=Passcode **19**.

A	6	8	4	8
B	4	9	3	5
C	3	7	2	1
D	5	9	4	5

Puzzle 26

Pick the odd-one-out. The number next to it is your passcode to the next puzzle on your search to escape from cyber-reality. The passcodes are not part of the puzzle.

A
34

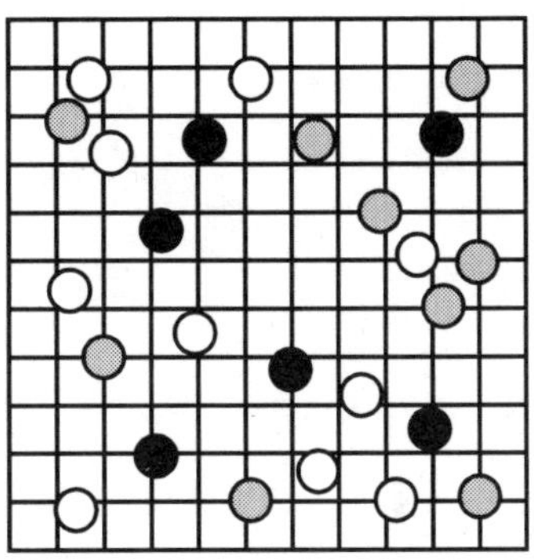

B
45

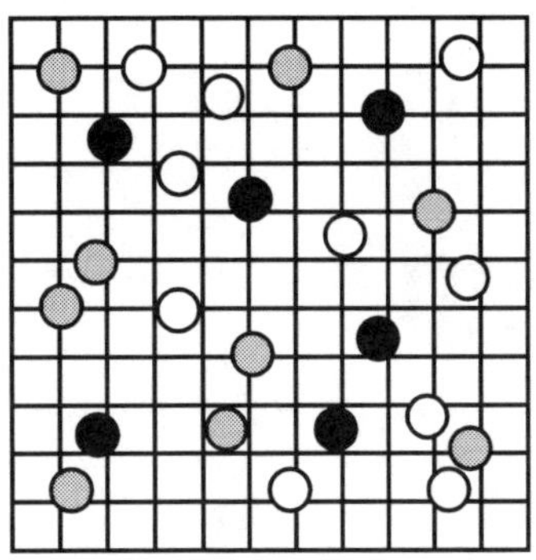

C
12

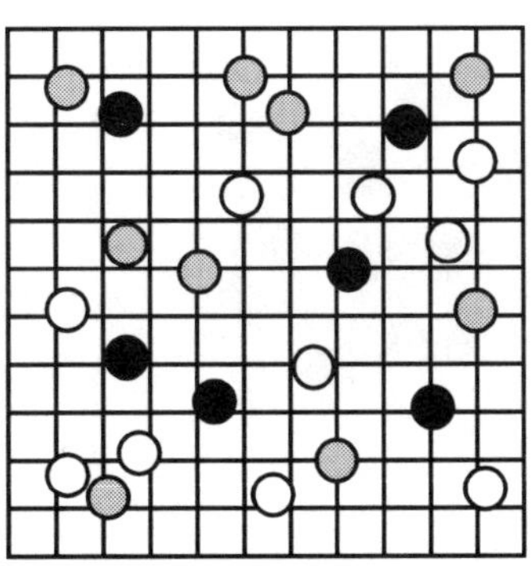

D
51

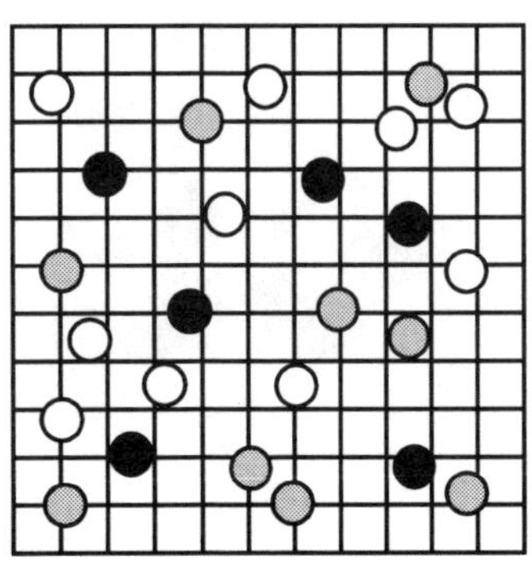

Puzzle 27

Subtract the solution to B (given) from the solution to E, and divide the result by 2 to find your passcode to the next puzzle.

A B C D E

36 27 39 29 ?

Puzzle 28

Pick the odd-one-out and use the number under it as your passcode to the next puzzle.

A B C D

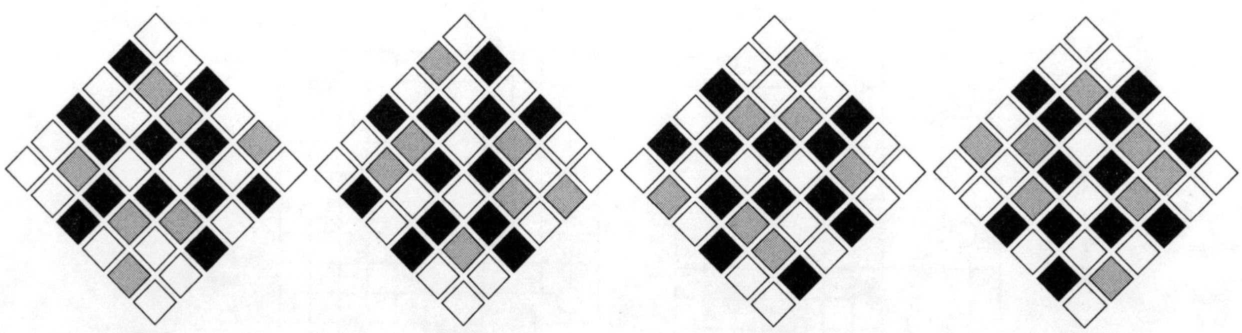

28 33 57 54

Puzzle 29

These scales are in balance. Assuming the minimum whole-number of values for the weights of these balls, if we were to place 7 more dark balls on the right side of these scales, your next passcode is 11 times the number of light balls we would have to place on the left side to keep the system in balance.

Puzzle 30

One of these Petri dishes does not go with the others. Above it you will find your passcode to the next puzzle.

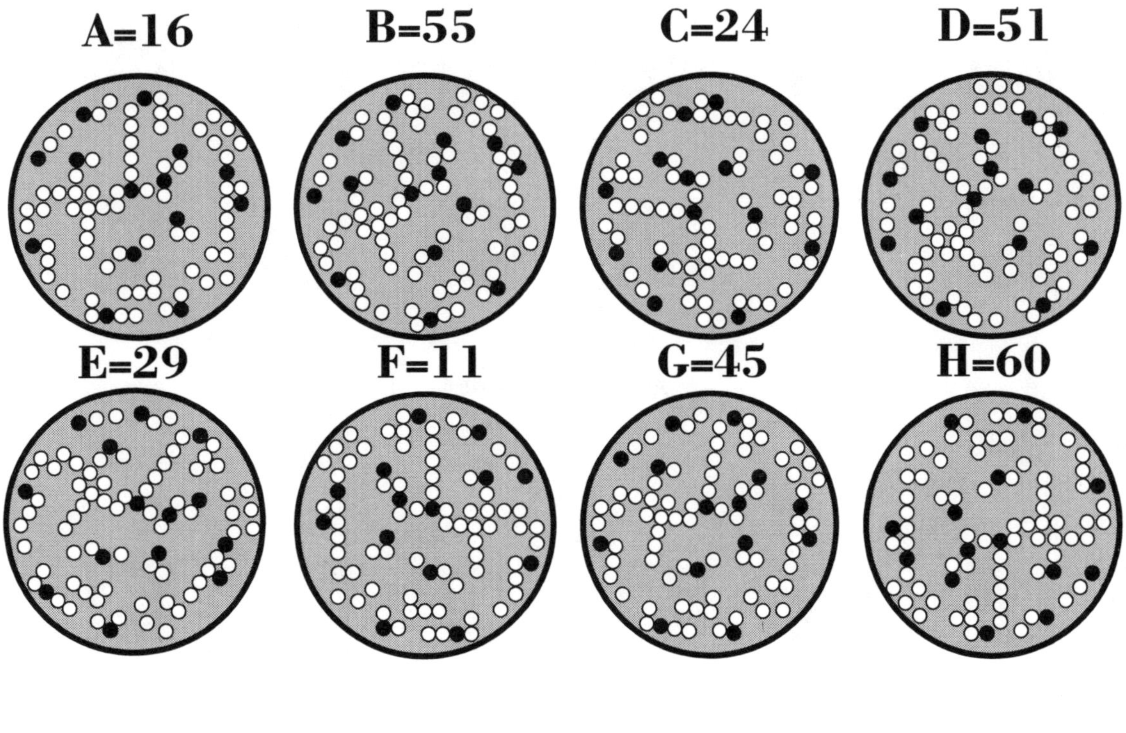

Puzzle 31

Choose the odd-one-out. Your next passcode is underneath it.

A	B	C	D

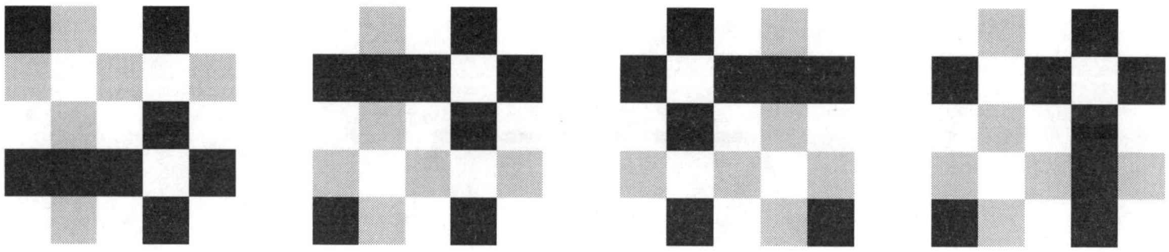

17	9	25	3

Puzzle 32

Put in the missing digits in each empty grey box so that multiplying each four corner numbers together gives the number in the black boxes. Your next passcode is the total of all the missing digits, minus 41.

7		3		5		7		2		6		4
	168		180		525		210		72		144	
2												3
	48		108		945		420		48		96	
6												8
	36		135		630		224		96		48	
2												1
	120		360		180		192		480		30	
5		4		6		3		8		5		2

Puzzle 33

The missing number in C, if you can find it, is your passcode to the next puzzle.

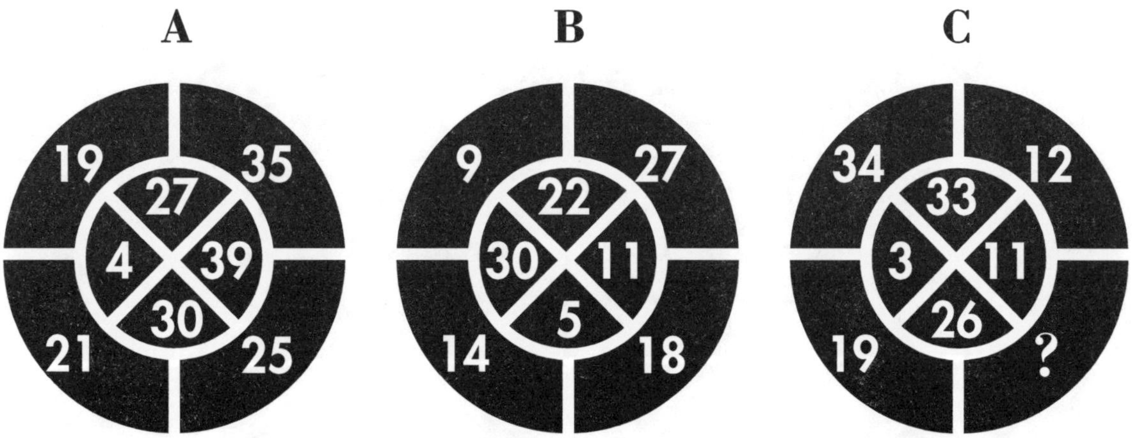

Puzzle 34

5

Pick the odd-one-out and choose your next passcode according to your answer.

A=Passcode **25**. **B**=Passcode **21**. C=Passcode **18**. **D**=Passcode **49**.

Puzzle 35

Find the first and second digits of your next passcode by solving this logic number puzzle.

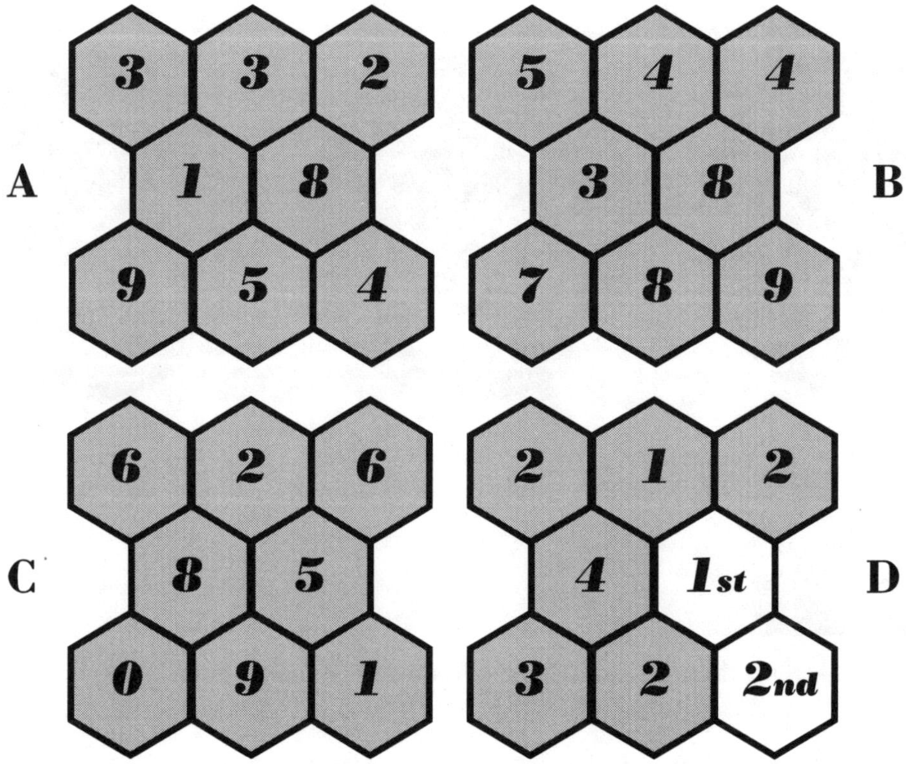

Puzzle 36

Solve the puzzle below for B to find your passcode to the next puzzle.

A + B = 68

A - B = 30

B x A = 931

Passcode = B

Puzzle 37

Add 17 to the number of circles and ovals that intersect (overlap) at the point marked with a black spot in the diagram below to find your next passcode.

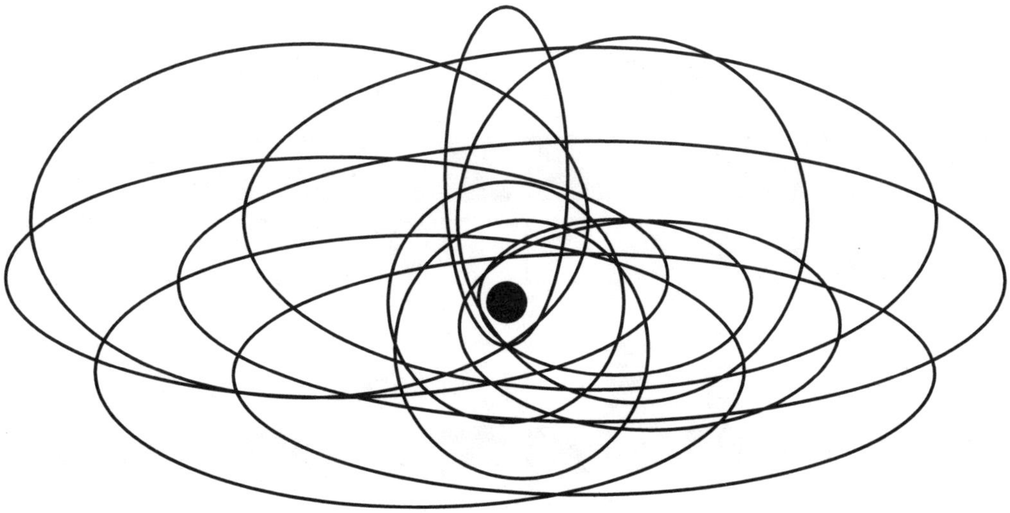

Puzzle 38

Complete this magic square so that every row, column and long diagonal adds to 259. The central number of the square is your next passcode.

34	33	25	17	58	50	42
43	35	27	26	18	59	51
52	44				19	60
61	53				21	13
14	55				30	22
23	15	56	48	47	39	31
32	24	16	57	49	41	40

Puzzle 39

Solve for the missing digits to find both digits of your passcode to the next puzzle.

1		2	5		4	1		8	2		3
	4			4			6			9	
1		2	5		3	7		3	5		4

3		1	5		6	2		6	5		5
	7			8			3			7	
3		1	5		5	4		8	?		?

Puzzle 40

Choose the odd-one-out. Your next passcode is underneath it.

A

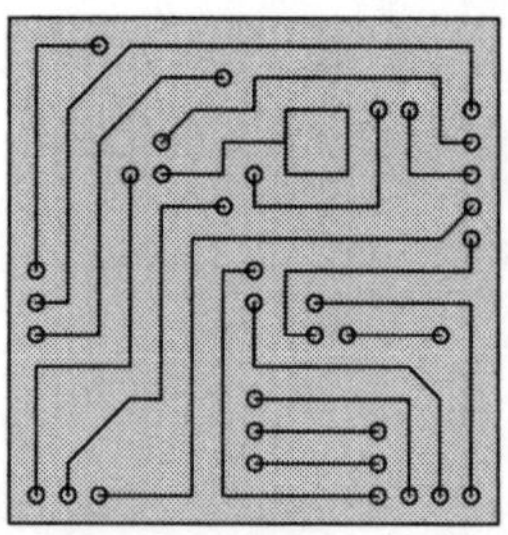

33

B

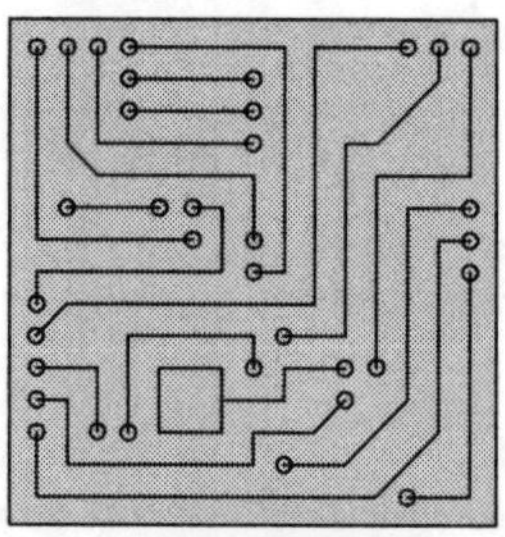

45

C

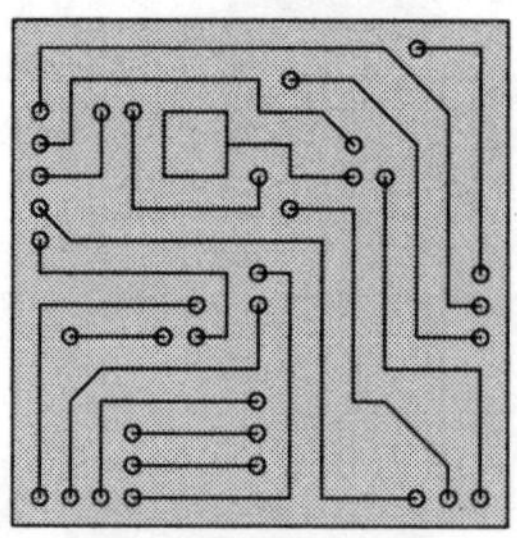

27

D

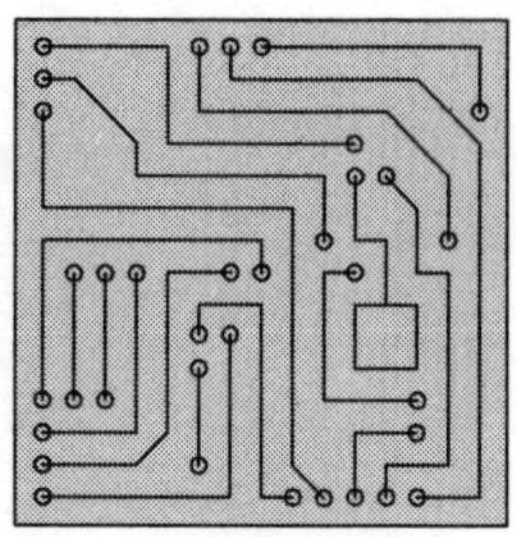

16

Puzzle 41

Complete the analogy and choose your passcode according to your solution.

A=Passcode **15**. **B**=Passcode **2**. **C**=Passcode **48**. **D**=Passcode **29**.

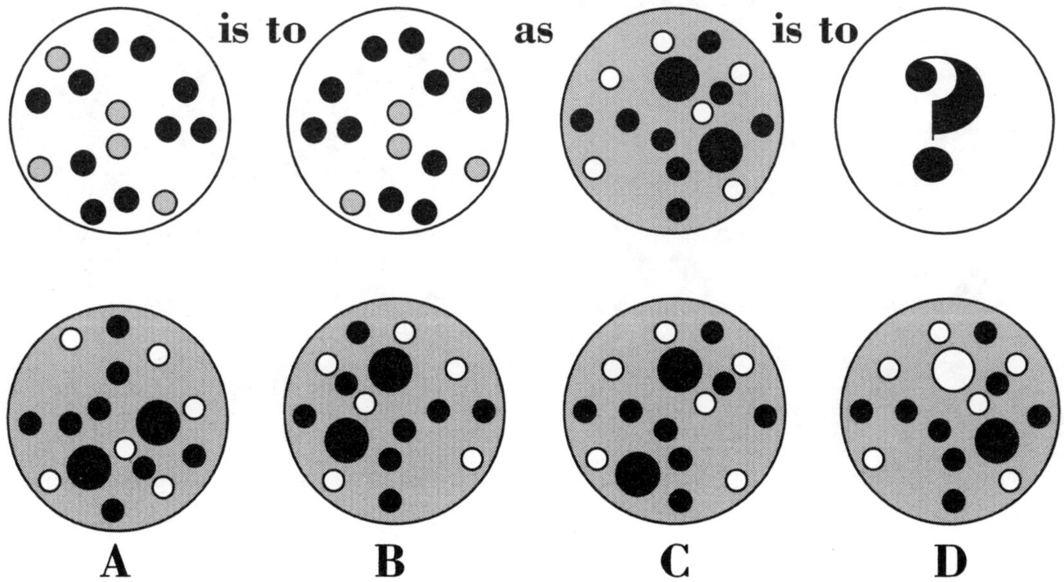

Puzzle 42

Which bell will ring when the cog is turned in the direction of the arrow? If your answer is A, your next passcode is 58. If your answer is B, your next passcode is 61. The central black spot is a fixed pivot point. The white spots are non-fixed swivel points.

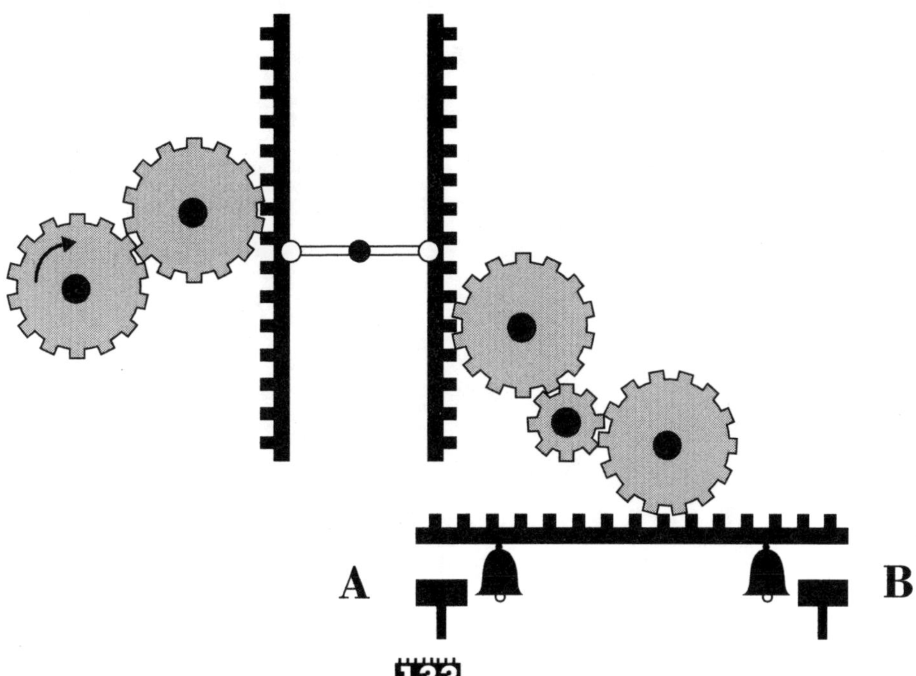

Puzzle 43

Subtract the number of differences between A and B from 55 to find your passcode to the next puzzle.

Puzzle 44

Can you figure out the logic of this circuit and find the missing value, to discover your next passcode?

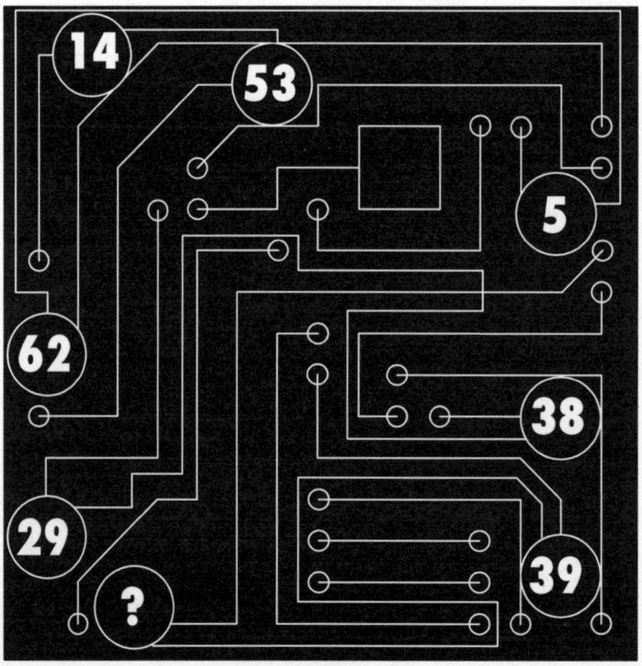

Puzzle 45

Pick the odd-one-out and choose your passcode accordingly.
A=Passcode **22**. **B**=Passcode **12**. **C**=Passcode **51**. **D**=Passcode **35**.

A B

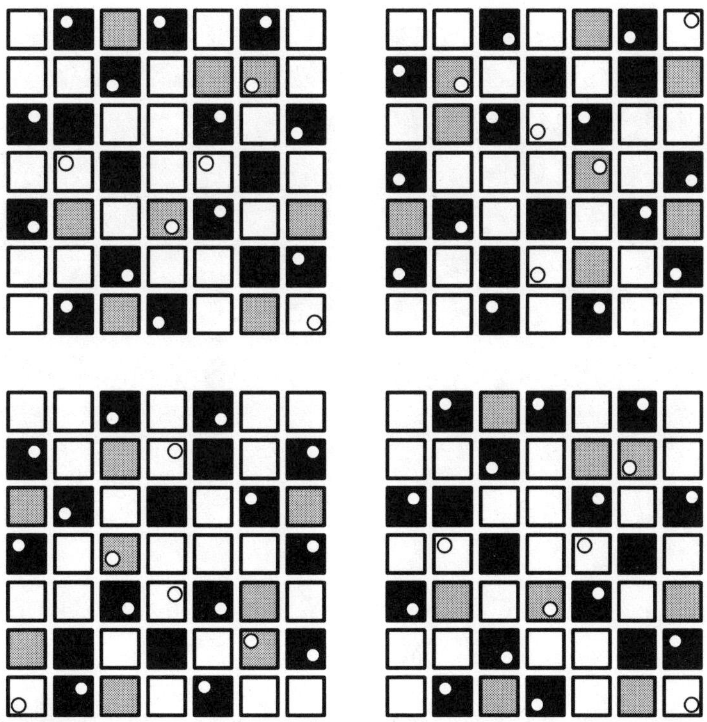

C D

Puzzle 46

Two of the figures are true mirror images of the figure at the top, and they contain the two digits of your next passcode in alphabetical order.

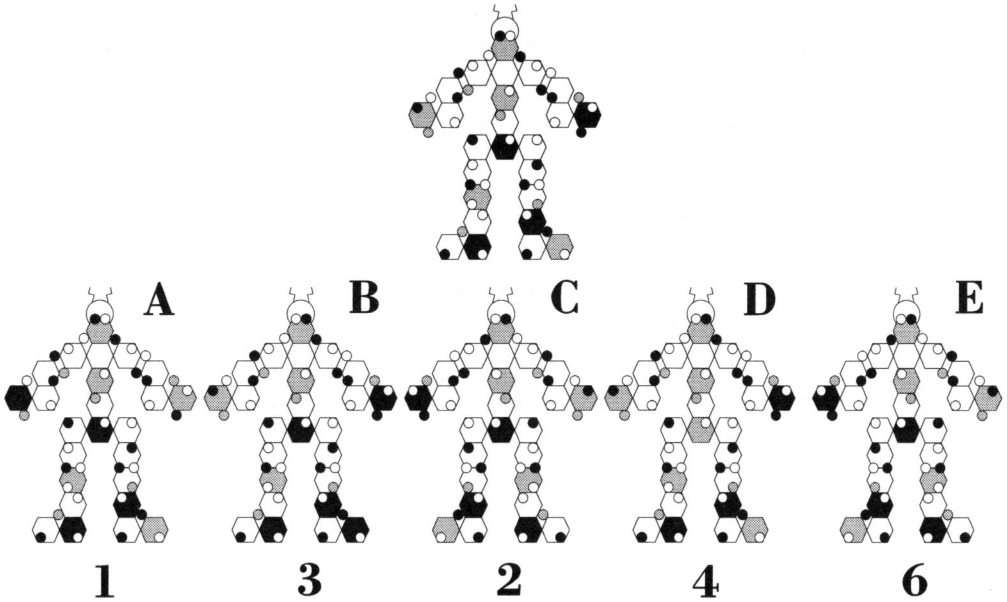

Puzzle 47

Your next passcode on your bid for escape from cyber-reality is beneath the odd-one-out in this puzzle.

A

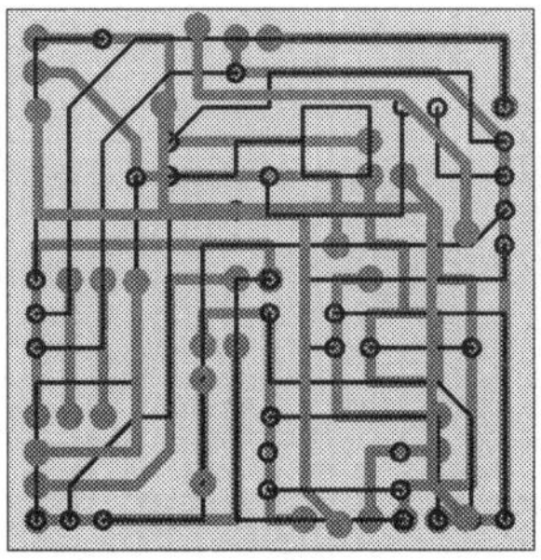

42

B

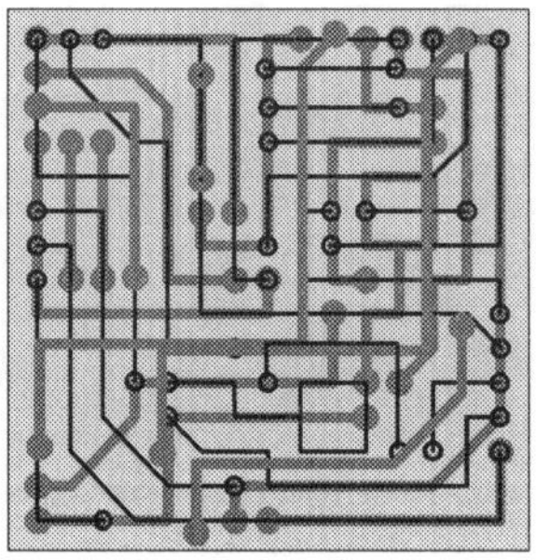

34

C

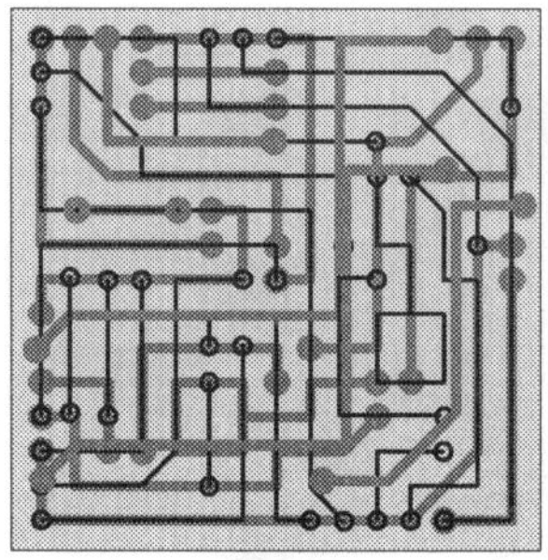

27

D

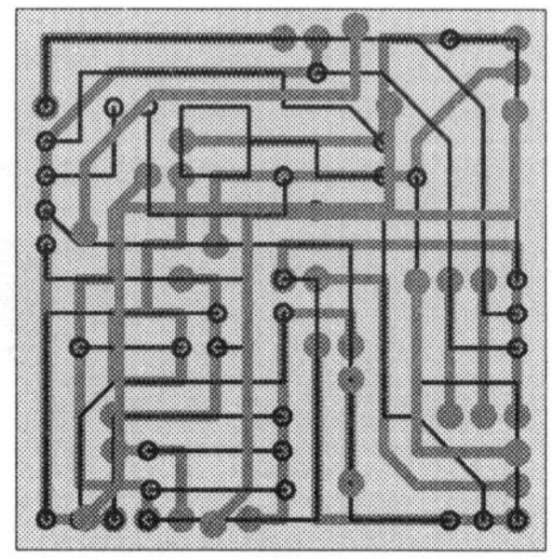

13

Puzzle 48

Some of the tiles are missing from this pattern. You can find your next passcode beneath the correct set of tiles to complete the pattern.

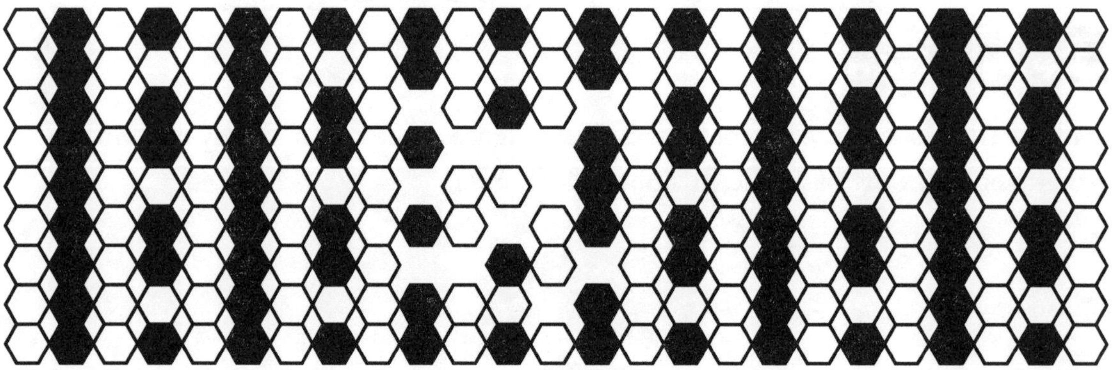

A

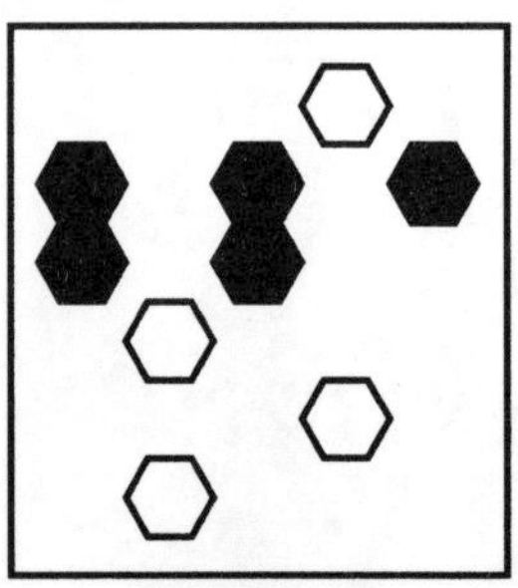

33

B

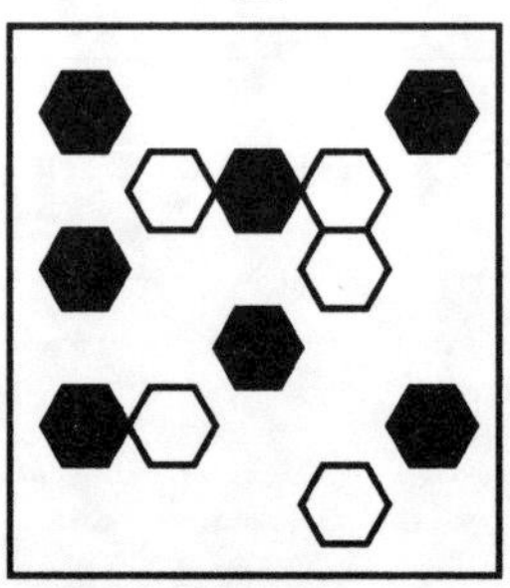

20

C

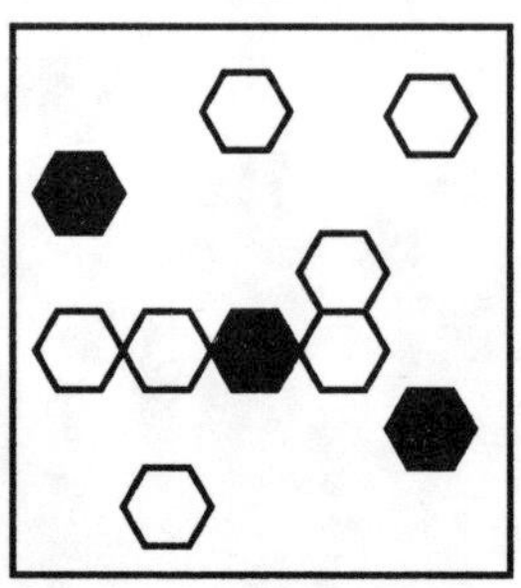

46

D

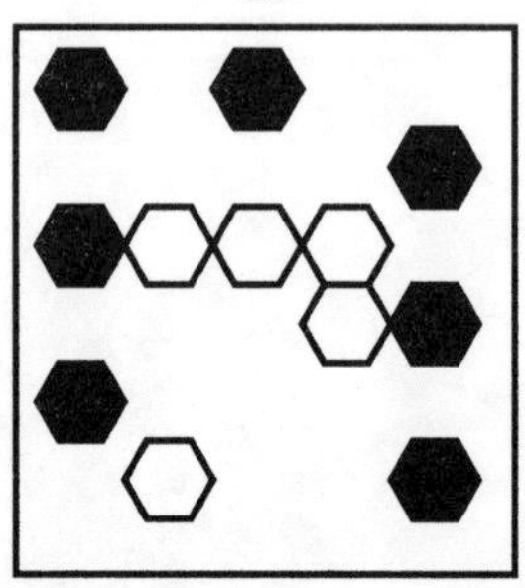

7

Puzzle 49

The missing number in the second star is your next passcode. Find it to progress on your quest.

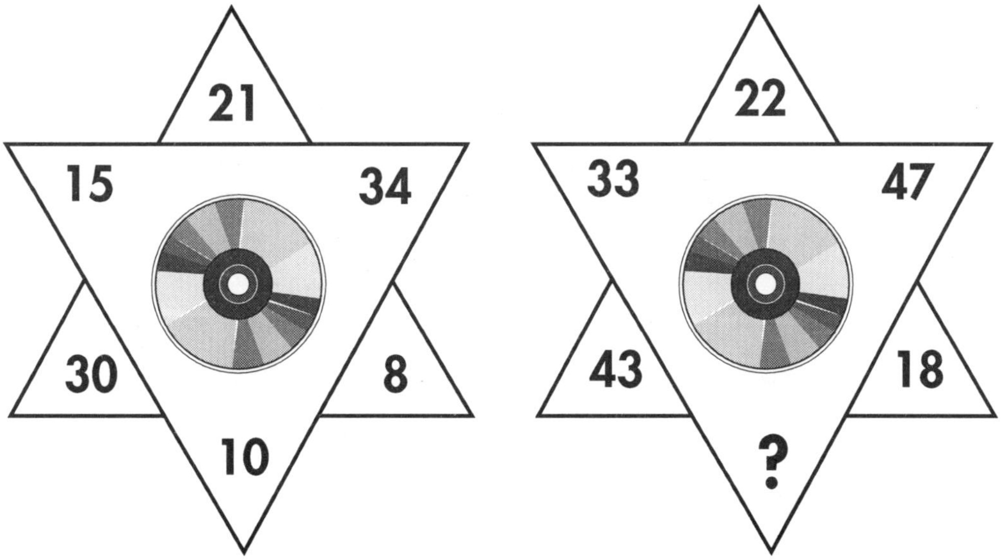

Puzzle 50

One of the panels below completes the pattern and has your next passcode in the middle. Passcodes are not part of the puzzle.

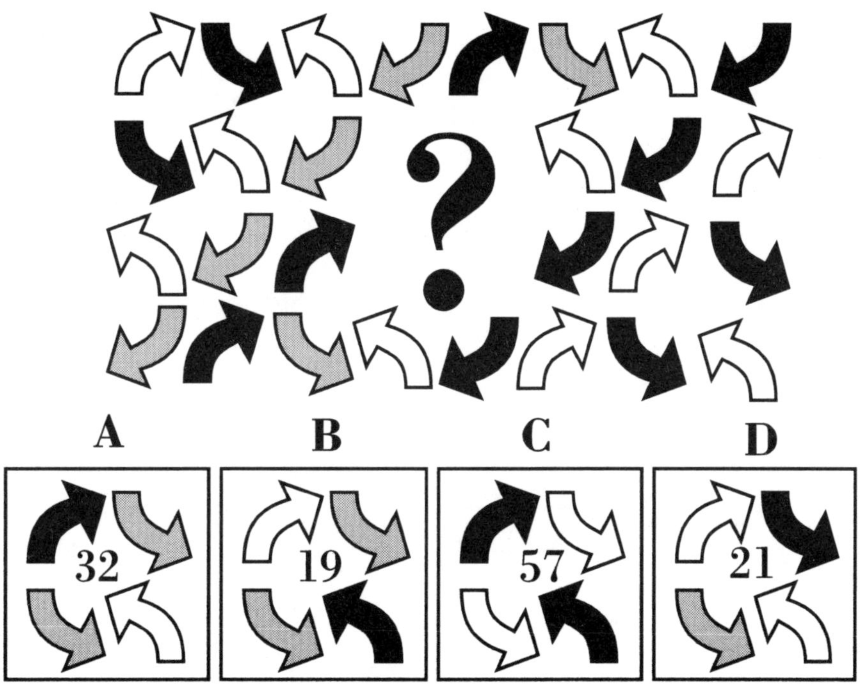

Puzzle 51

Your next passcode is underneath the correct figure to continue this series.

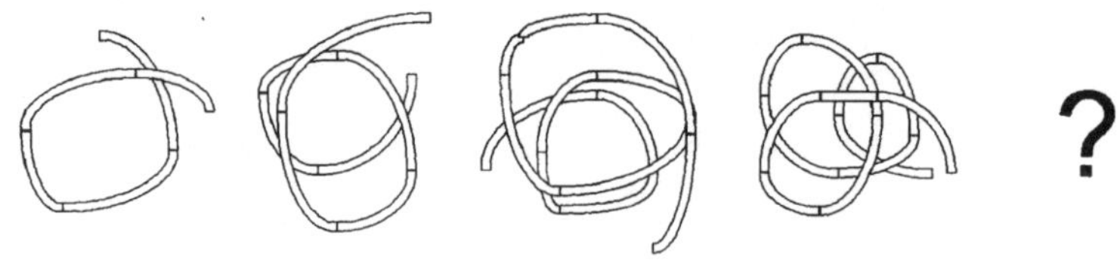

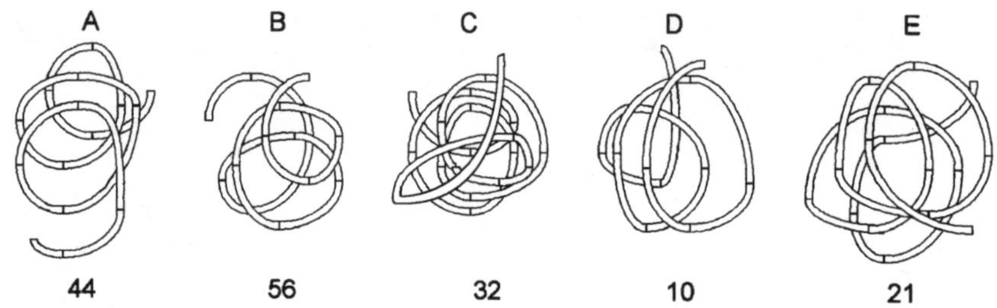

Puzzle 52

Which of the below plans can be folded to make the pyramid at the top? Choose your passcode accordingly.

A=Passcode **32**. **B**=Passcode **17**. **C**=Passcode **50**. **D**=Passcode **40**.

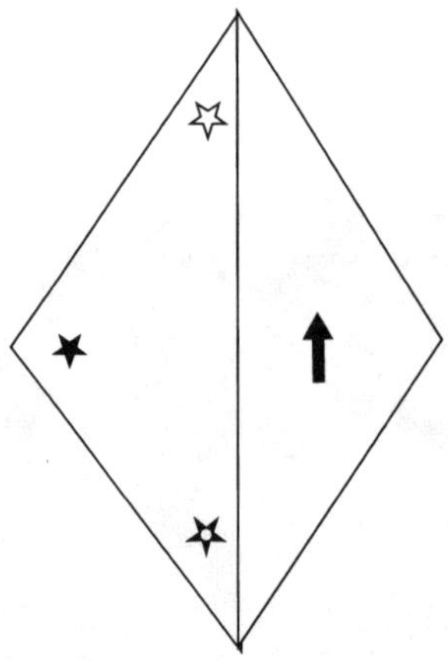

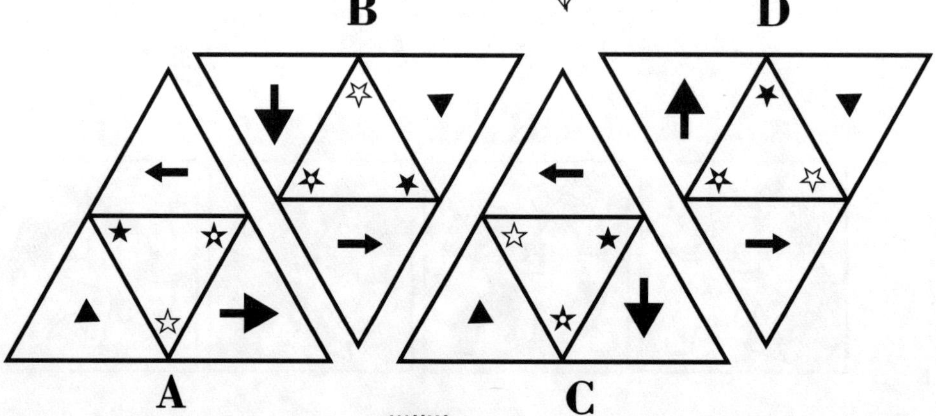

Puzzle 53

Pick the odd-one-out. Your next passcode is underneath it.

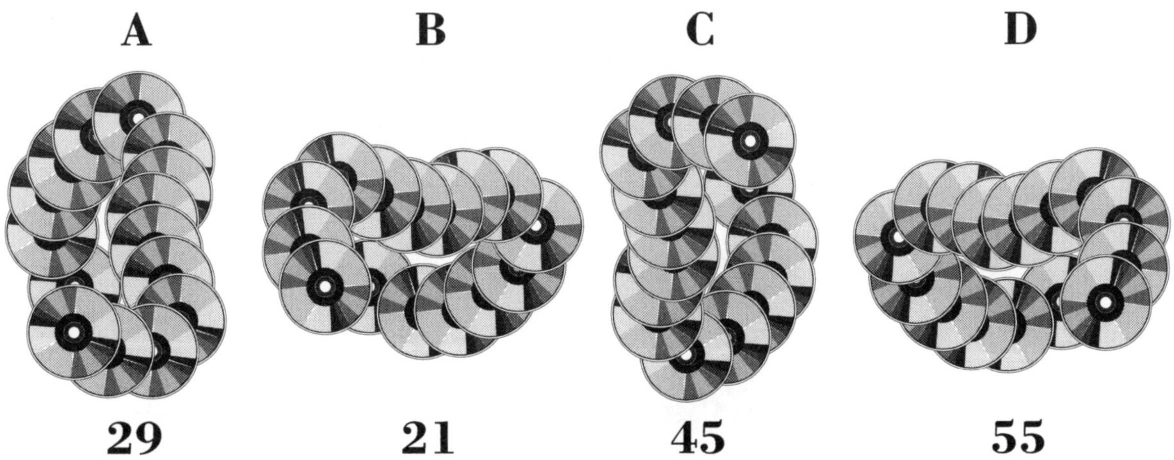

Puzzle 54

6

What number continues this series? The missing number is your next passcode on your quest.

Puzzle 55

One of the surrounding shapes fits perfectly on top of the shape in the middle. Next to it you will find your passcode to the next puzzle.

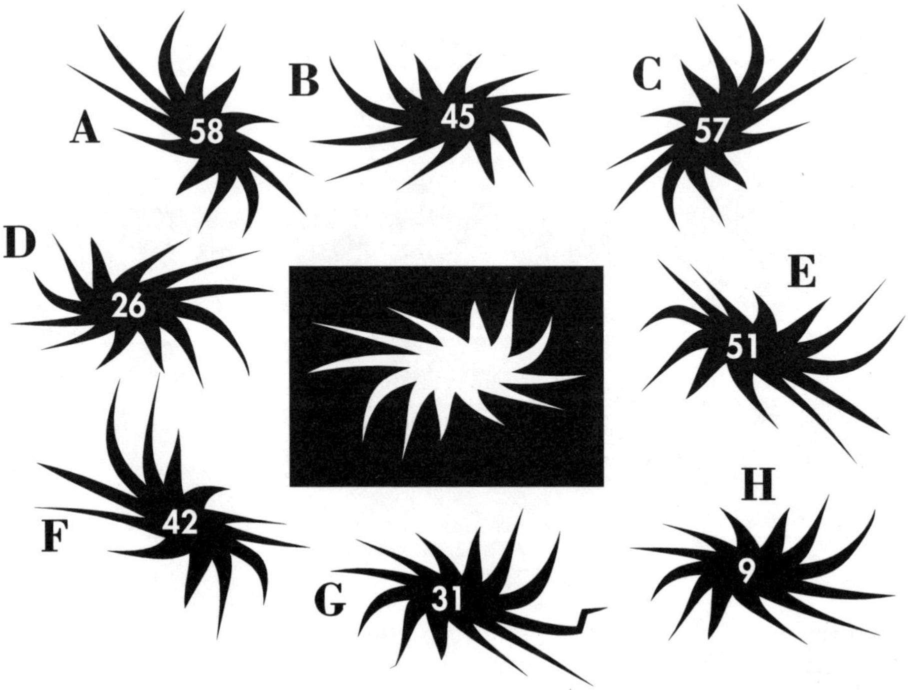

Puzzle 56

Add 36 to the number of differences between A and B to find your next passcode.

Puzzle 57

The value of your next passcode can be determined by solving the puzzle below.

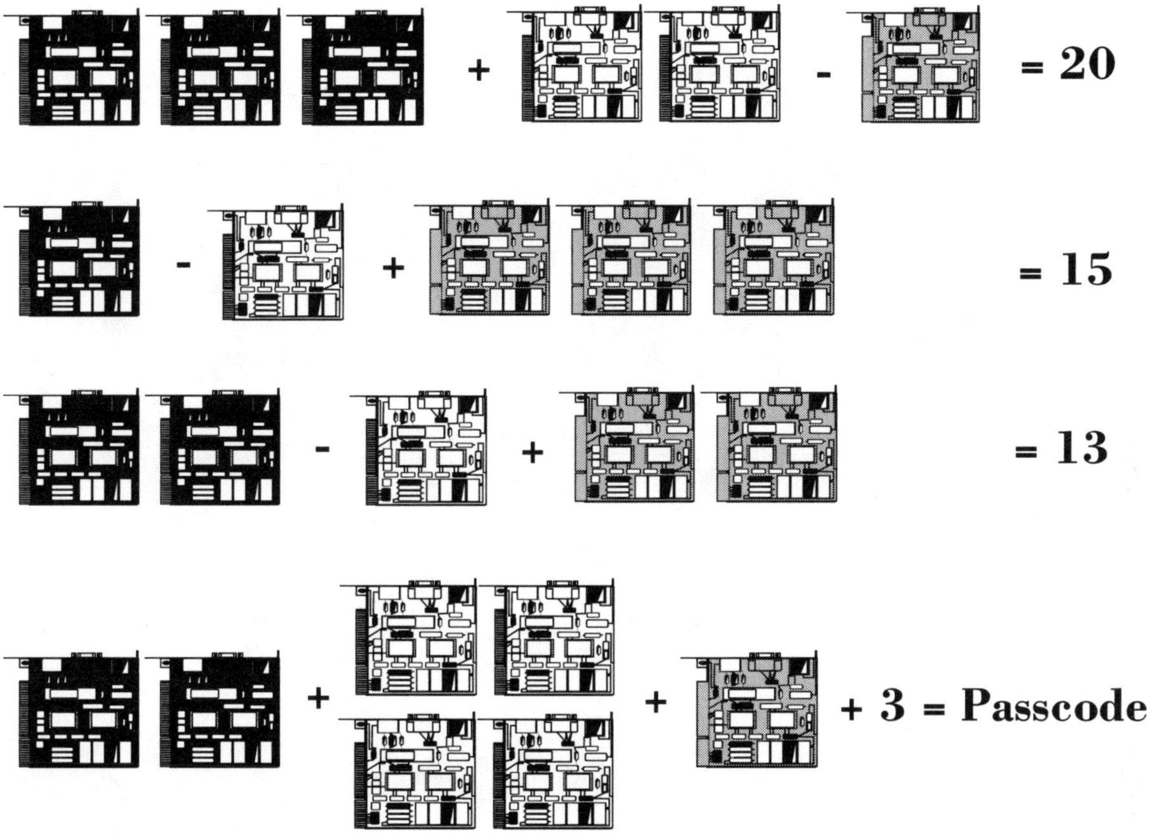

Puzzle 58

This system is in balance. Your next passcode in your tour of cyber-reality is the value of the unknown block on these scales.

Puzzle 59

Your next passcode on your quest to escape is underneath the odd-one-out in the this set of shapes.

A	B	C	D

29	60	58	39

Puzzle 60

10

Find your next passcode by solving the unknown values in this puzzle.

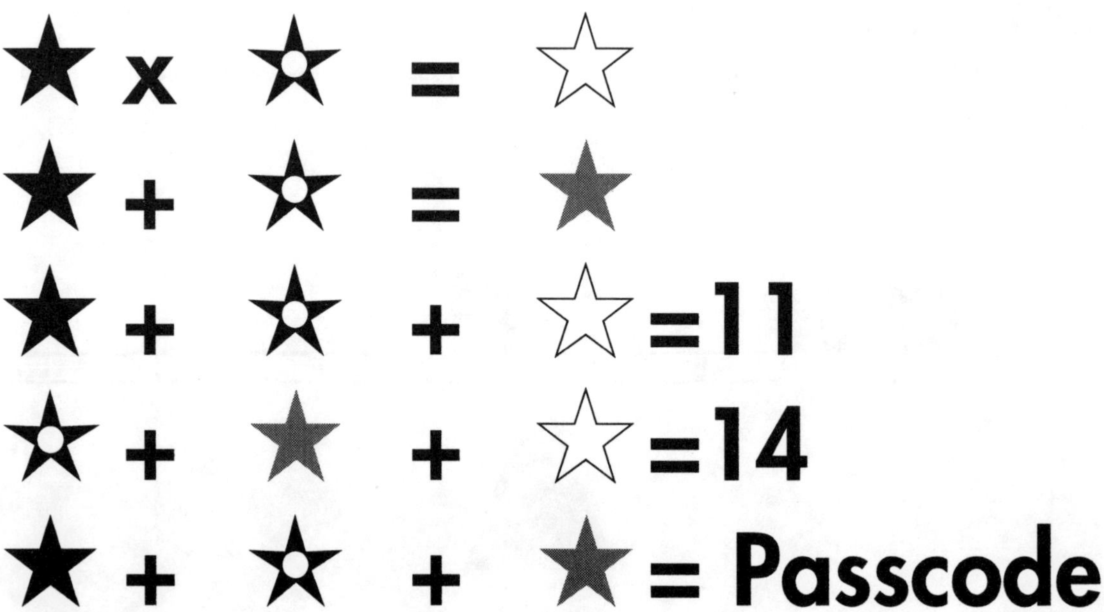

SECTION FOUR KEYCODES

REMINDER: You must solve the puzzles in the correct order. Start at the top of column A, and insert your keys. When you get to the bottom of column A, start back at the top of column B.

To proceed, subtract the total of column A from the total of column B. The result is your passcode for Section 4. Write it below and in the appropriate place on page 220, and use it number as your passcode to the starting puzzle for Section Five.

Adrian Smith has some pretty tough puzzles planned for you in Section Five. He thinks you've had it easy so far.

Dare you continue?

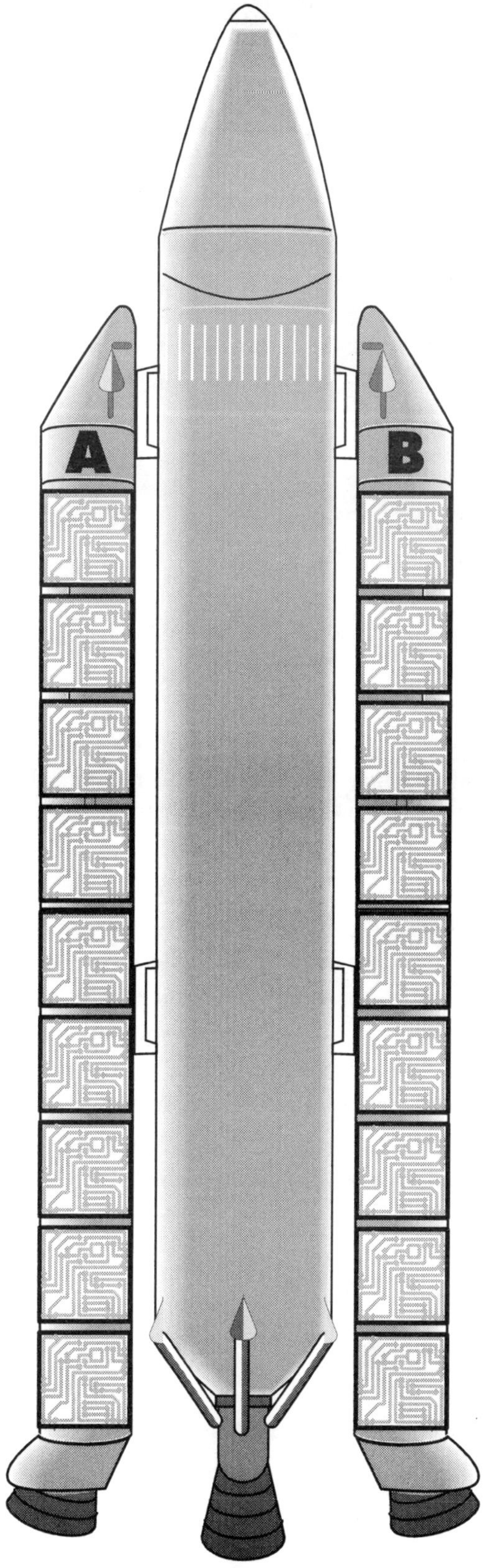

Total A

Total B

SECTION FOUR

PASSCODE

SECTION FOUR

ANSWERS

1. Solution 7. The values are as in the diagram below. **Go to 7. Key 3**

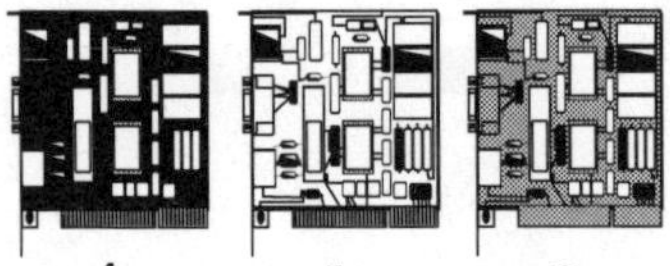

4. 1. 2.

2. Solution 24. Each outside number is arrived at by subtracting half of the number on the clockwise side of each point from the number on the other side of the point. Thus, 29-(14/2)=22 and 50-(52/2)=24. **Go to 24.**

3. Solution 52. This is arrived at by progressively adding half of what was added in the previous step. Thus, 22+16=38; 38+8=46; 46+4=50; 50+2=52. **Go to 52.**

4. Solution 15. 15+10=25; 25x3=75; 75-12=63; 63/9=7. **Go to 15. Key 3**

5. Solution 30. Shoes=7; Boots=5; Sandals=3. **Go to 30.**

6. Solution 51. In each block the middle row is subtracted from the top row and the result divided by 2 to give the bottom row. Thus 777-675=102; 102/2=51. **Go to 51.**

7. Solution 23. (16-3)+(13-3)=23. Starting anti-clockwise from Bottom Right in the top triangle or Bottom in the lower triangle, the first two numbers of each triangle are read as a two-digit number from which the third number is subtracted. The two resulting numbers for each pair of triangles are added to give the central number. **Go to 23.**

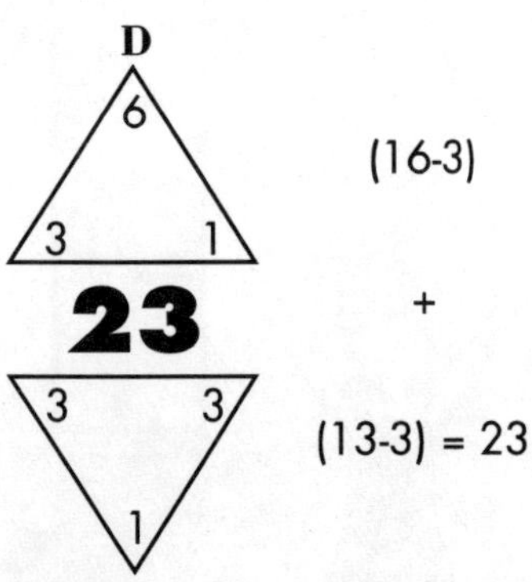

8. Solution 38. Refer to the diagram below. **Go to 38. Key 2.**

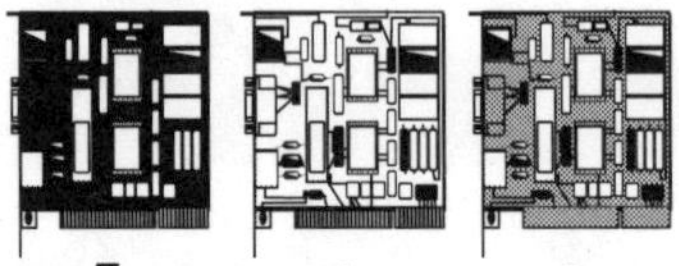

7. 6. 2.

9. Solution 60. Time=Distance/Speed. Therefore, 75/30=2.5hrs+12mins=2hrs 42mins=162mins. 162-102=60. **Go to 60.**

10. There are 142 circles, so 142-2=140; 140/10=14. **Go to 14.**

11. B is the odd-one-out, being a mirror image of the others, which are all rotated version of the same image. **Go to 36.**

12. Solution 48. **Go to 48. Key 1.**

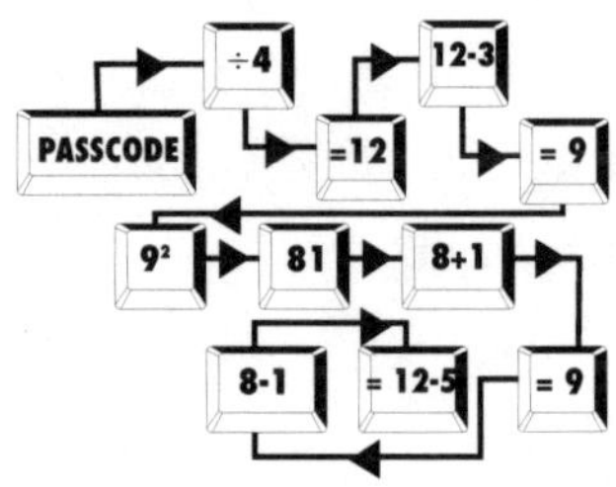

13. C is the odd-one-out because in all the others the numbers above and below each disc add to the same as the numbers at either side of the disc. Thus in, eg. A, 15+21=17+19. But in C the totals are different. **Go to 6.**

14. A is the odd-one-out. This is a mirror-image of the others, which are all rotated versions of the same image. **Go to 17.**

15. C is the only plan the makes the cube. **Go to 50.**

16. Solution 55. Using one of the twin sets, in the diagram below, the H's are marked with a spot on the top left of each. There are 9 H's in each set. 9x2=18; 18x3=54; 54+1=55. **Go to 55. Key 4.**

SECTION FOUR

ANSWERS

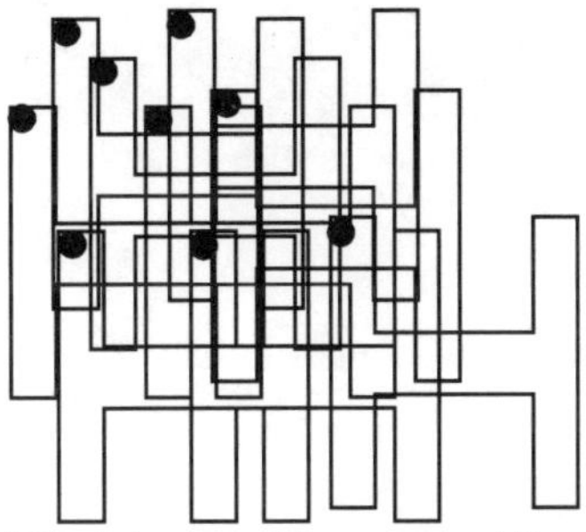

17. A is the odd-one-out. All other cubes add to 100, but A adds to 90. **Go to 53.**

18. Solution 46. Follow the turns of the cogs. **Go to 46.**

19. Solution 13. 536-149=387; 608-013=595. **Go to 13.**

5	3	6	1	4	9
3	8	7	6	0	8
0	1	3	5	9	5

20. Solution 59. The missing number is 81. Following the sequence, 24+(24/2)=36; 36+(36/2)=54; 54+(54/2)=81; 81+(81/2)=121.5. 81-22=59. **Go to 59. Key 5.**

21. B is the odd-one-out. All four shapes are rotated versions of the same thing, but, in B, the circled element has been rotated through 180 degrees. **Go to 22.**

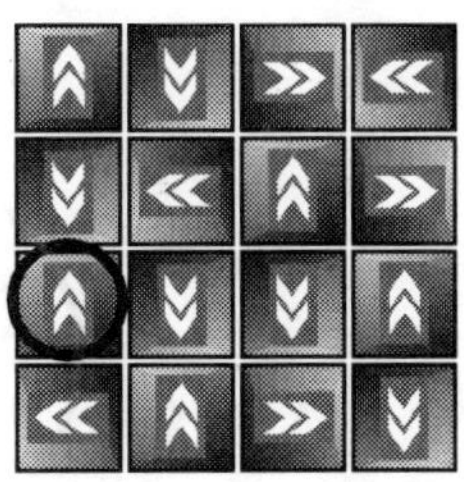

22. Solution 41. The values are according to the diagram below. **Go to 41.**

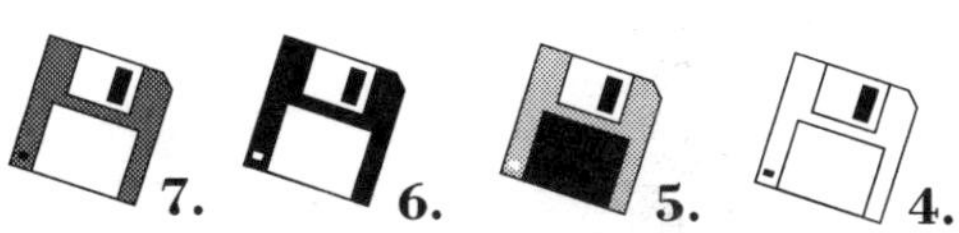

23. Solution 12. The missing value is 8. Each side has a total distance x weight value of 83. 8+(8/2)=12. **Go to 12.**

24. The shape that does not fit is the one containing the number 39. **Go to 39. Key 3.**

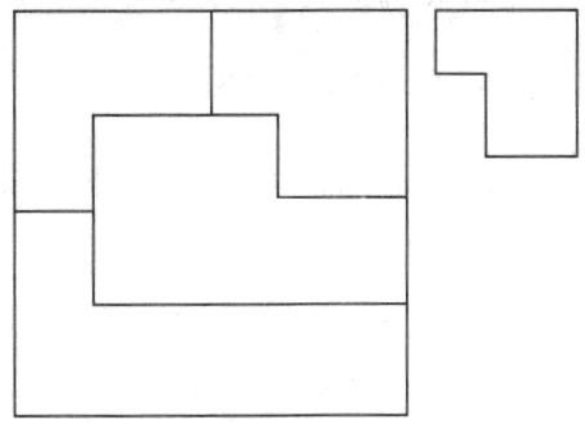

25. B is the odd-one-out. Each row is simply a multiplication sum, but 4x9 does not equal 35, therefore B is odd. **Go to 49.**

26. A is the odd-one-out. The two elements highlighted with heavy borders here have been moved to the right of their correct position. The others are all rotated versions of the same image. **Go to 34.**

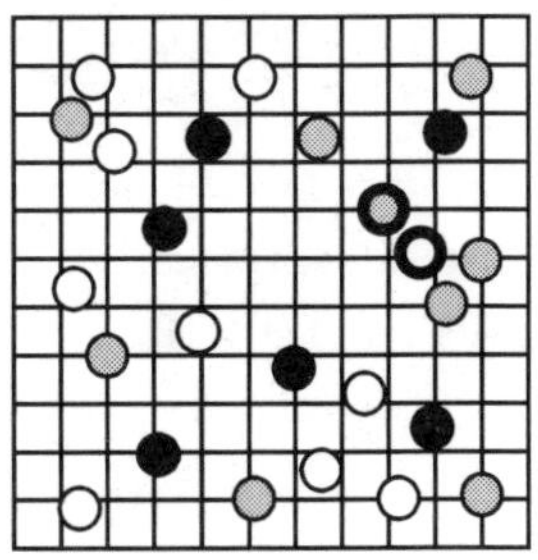

27. Solution 5. E has a total value of 37 (see diagram below). 37-(B)27=10; 10/2=5. **Go to 5. Key 2.**

28. D is the odd-one-out. The element circled here has changed color. It should be white. The others are all rotated versions of the same thing. **Go to 54.**

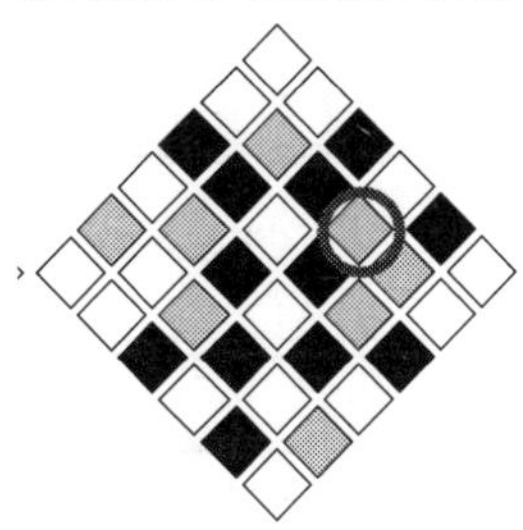

29. Solution 44. We would add 4 light balls. Black balls are worth 4; light balls are worth 7. By adding a further value of 28 (7 balls) on the right (7 balls x 4=28), we have to balance the others with a value of 28 on the left (4 balls x 7=28). 4x11=44. **Go to 44.**

SECTION FOUR

ANSWERS

30. F is the odd-one-out. This is a mirror-image of the other dishes, which are all rotated versions of the same thing. **Go to 11. Key 1.**

31. B is the odd-one-out. This is a mirror-image of all the others, which are all rotated versions of the same thing. **Go to 9. Key 2.**

32. Solution 16. The total of all the missing digits is 57. 57-41=16. **Go to 16.**

7		3		5		7		2		6		4
	168		180		525		210		72		144	
2		4		3		5		3		2		3
	48		108		945		420		48		96	
6		1		9		7		4		2		8
	36		135		630		224		96		48	
2		3		5		2		4		3		1
	120		360		180		192		480		30	
5		4		6		3		8		5		2

33. Solution 8. In each set, the inner ring of numbers adds to the same total as the outer ring. Thus, in C, 3+33+11+26=73; 34+12+19+[8]=73. **Go to 8.**

C

34. A is the odd-one-out. The black arrow with the pointer here has been moved behind the other elements. The other sets are all rotated versions of the same image. **Go to 25. Key 5.**

35. Solution 31. In each set, referring to the diagram below, abc-def=gh. Thus, 243-2[3][1]=12. **Go to 31.**

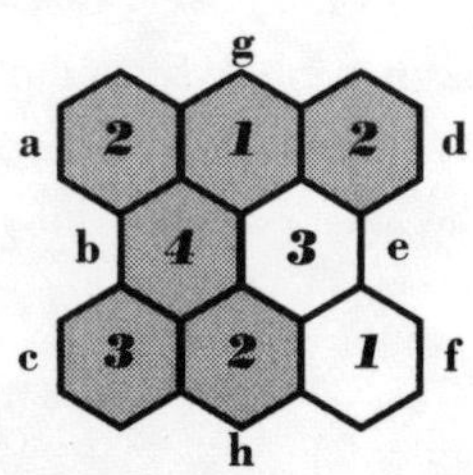

36. A=49. B=19. **Go to 19.**

37. 12 circles and ovals intersect at the point marked with the spot. 12+17=29. **Go to 29.**

38. Solution 37. Complete the square as below. **Go to 37. Key 3.**

34	33	25	17	58	50	42
43	35	27	26	18	59	51
52	44	36	28	20	19	60
61	53	45	37	29	21	13
14	55	54	46	38	30	22
23	15	56	48	47	39	31
32	24	16	57	49	41	40

39. Solution 18. In each row set, the top row-the middle row=the bottom row. Thus, 31562655-7837=315548[1][8]. **Go to 18.**

5		5
	7	
1		8

40. C is the odd-one-out. It is a mirror-image of the others, which are all rotated versions of the same image. **Go to 27.**

41. Solution B. The solution is a mirror-image of the other part of the analogy. **Go to 2.**

42. Bell B will ring. **Go to 61 – The Keycodes. Key 9.**

43. There are 8 differences, circled below in B. 55-8=47. **Go to 47.**

SECTION FOUR

ANSWERS

44. Solution is 28. linked numbers add to 67. 67-39=28. **Go to 28.**

45. D is the odd-one-out. The spot pointed to by the arrow has been moved from the left to the right of the box. The other shapes are rotated versions of the same image. **Go to 35.**

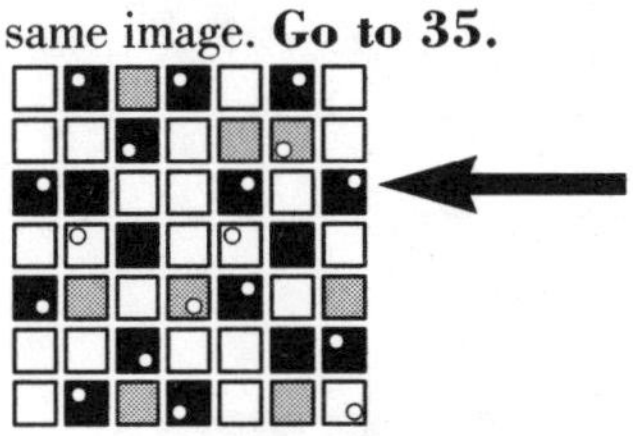

46. C and E are true mirror-images. The others have minor changes. **Go to 26. Key 2.**

47. A is the odd-one-out. The line highlighted in white (below) is missing in A, but not in the others, which are all rotated or reflected versions of the same image. **Go to 42.**

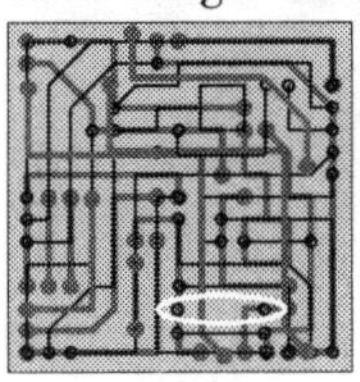

48. Solution B. The completed pattern is below. **Go to 20.**

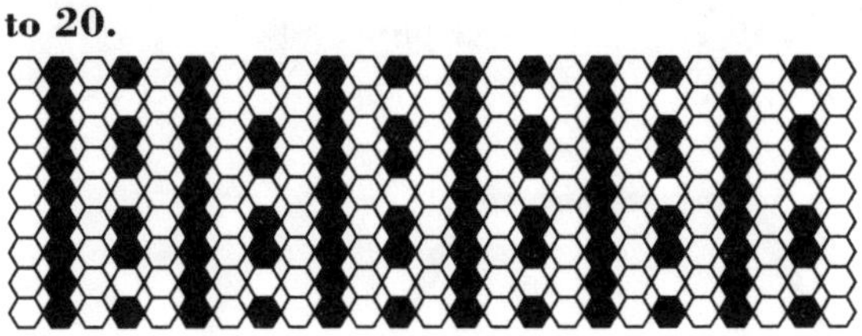

49. Solution 3. In each triangle the numbers in the points of the underneath triangle add to the same as the numbers in the top triangle. Thus, 22+43+18=83 and 33+47+[3]=83. **Go to 3.**

50. A completes the patterns. **Go to 32. Key 0.**

51. Solution B. There are 9 areas enclosed by the line, spiralling from surface to underneath in an anti-clockwise direction. **Go to 56.**

52. D can be folded to make the pyramid. **Go to 40.**

53. B is the odd-one-out. It is a mirror-image of the others, which are all rotated versions of the same puzzle. **Go to 21.**

54. Solution 4. 41580/11=3780; 3780/9=420; 420/7=60; 60/5=12; 12/3=4. **Go to 4. Key 6.**

55. Solution C. **Go to 57.**

56. Solution 43. There are 7 differences, circled below. 7+36=43. **Go to 43.**

57. Solution 45. Using the value below, (2 black=8)+(4 white=28)+(1 grey=6) = 42. 42+3=45. **Go to 45. Key 3.**

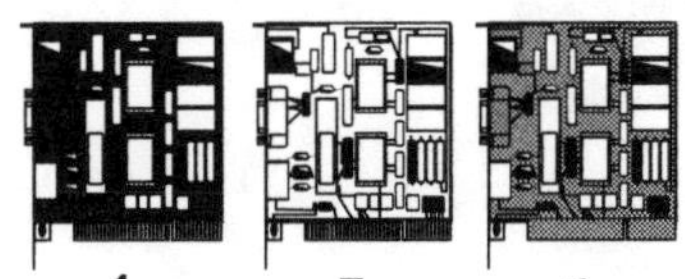

4. **7.** **6.**

58. Solution 33. (4 x position 7=28)+(1 x position 5=5)=33; 33 x position 1=33. Thus, with 33 on either side balance is achieved. **Go to 33.**

59. C is the odd-one-out. It is a mirror-image of the others, which are all rotated versions of the same thing. **Go to 58.**

60. Solution 10. The values are according to the diagram below. Thus, 2+3+5=10. **Go to 10. Key 10.**

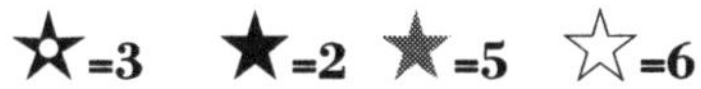

Section Four Keycodes = 37-27 =10. Go to Section Five, Puzzle 10.

Puzzle 1

7

Complete the analogy and use the passcode in the grey box next to your choice to get to your next puzzle. Passcodes are not part of the puzzle.

3	5	8	4
5	6	1	9

is to

9	1	6	4
5	8	5	3

as

2	9	5	1
3	8	7	4

is to ?

A (15)

4	7	5	1
3	8	9	2

B (28)

2	7	8	1
3	5	9	4

C (6)

4	7	5	1
3	8	9	2

D (33)

4	7	8	1
3	5	9	2

E (9)

3	5	9	2
4	7	8	1

F (49)

8	1	4	7
9	2	3	5

Puzzle 2

Multiply the missing number in D by 10, and add 2 to get your next passcode.

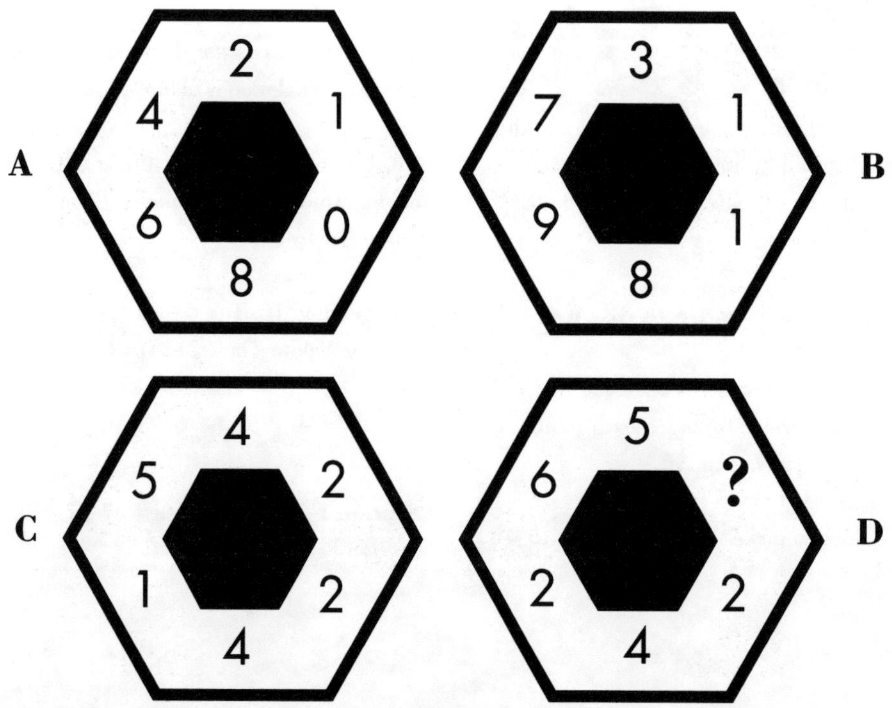

Puzzle 3

Your next passcode is with the odd-one-out in this set.

A=9 **B=33** **C=47** **D=13**

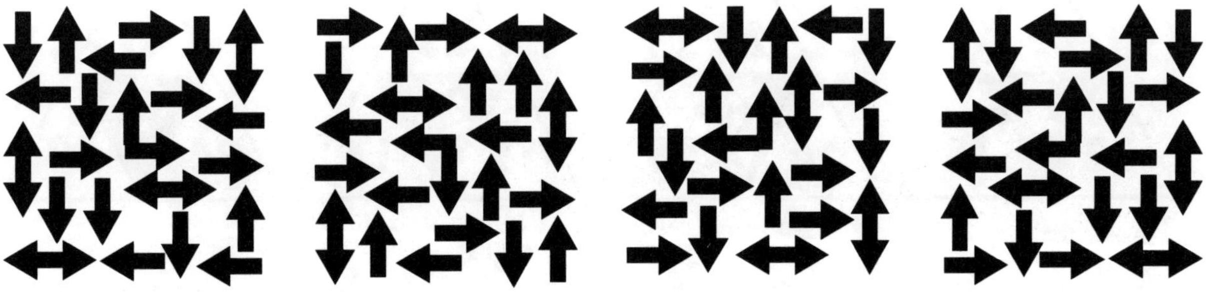

Puzzle 4

Which of the surrounding plans folds to make the cube in the middle? Choose your passcode accordingly.

A=Passcode **21.** **B**=Passcode **31.** **C**=Passcode **37.** **D**=Passcode **2**.

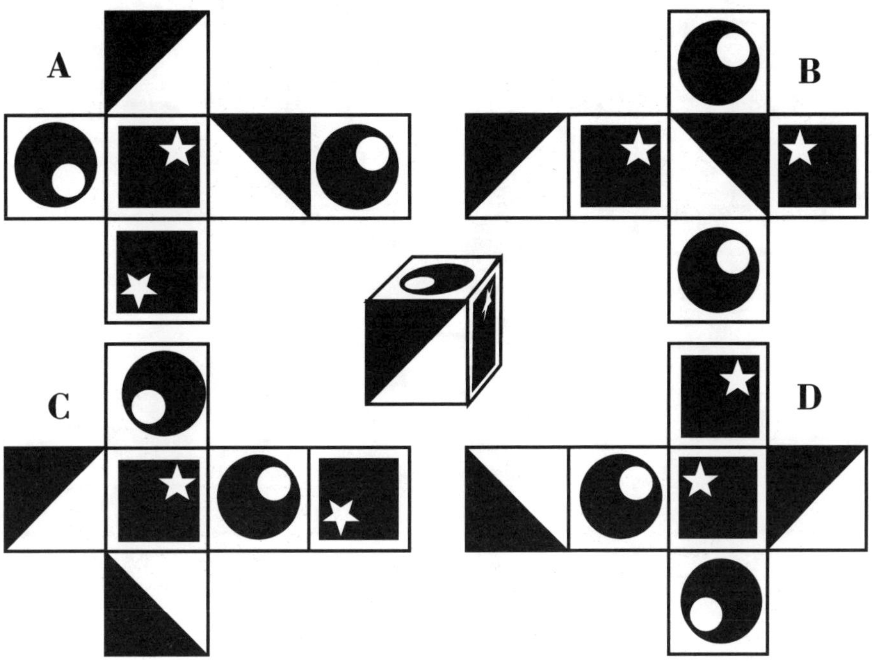

Puzzle 5

The missing number in D is the passcode to your next puzzle on your quest.

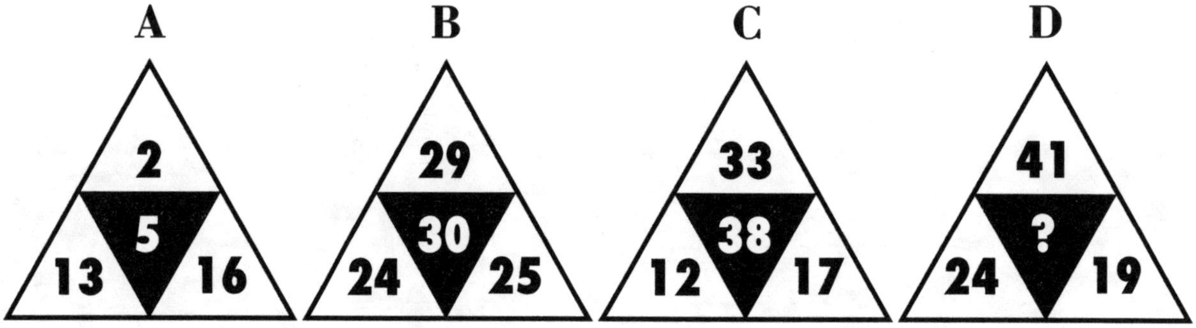

Puzzle 6

Your next passcode is a third of the number of bricks that are missing from the inside of this wall.

Puzzle 7

The last two digits of the solution to the fourth equation are your passcode to the next puzzle.

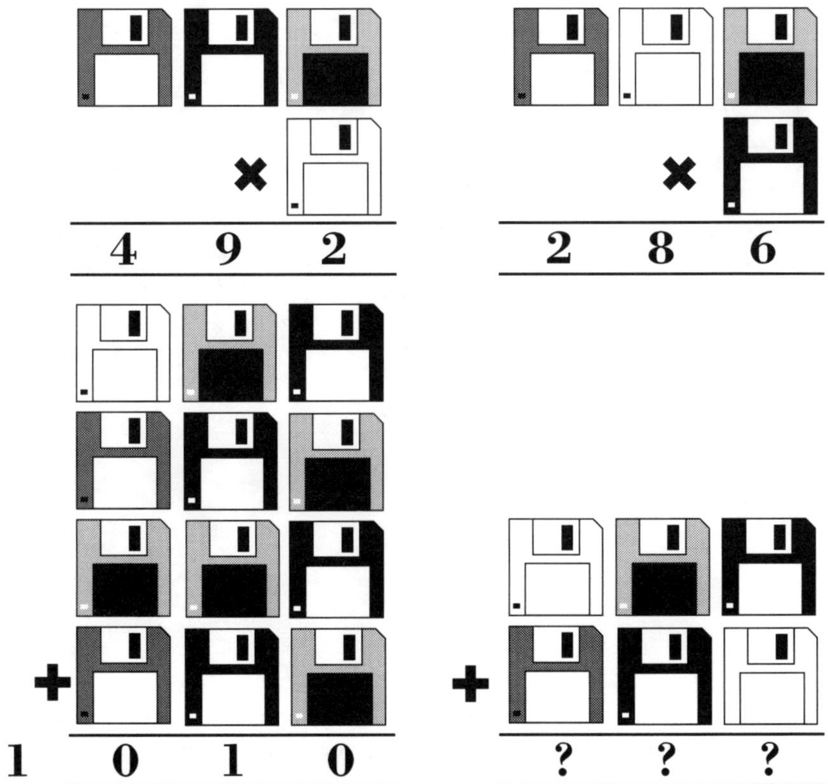

Puzzle 8

Complete the last two digits of this series to find the first and second digits of your next passcode. Adrian Smith thinks this one will get you.

2	1	9	8	3	1	5	4	7	■	8	9	1	2	7	9	5	6	3
6	3	8	9	2	3	4	7	1	■	4	7	2	1	8	7	6	3	9
3	5	6	5	2	8	1	6	9	■	7	5	4	5	8	2	9	?	?

Puzzle 9

Beneath the odd-one-out in this puzzle is your next passcode. Go for it!

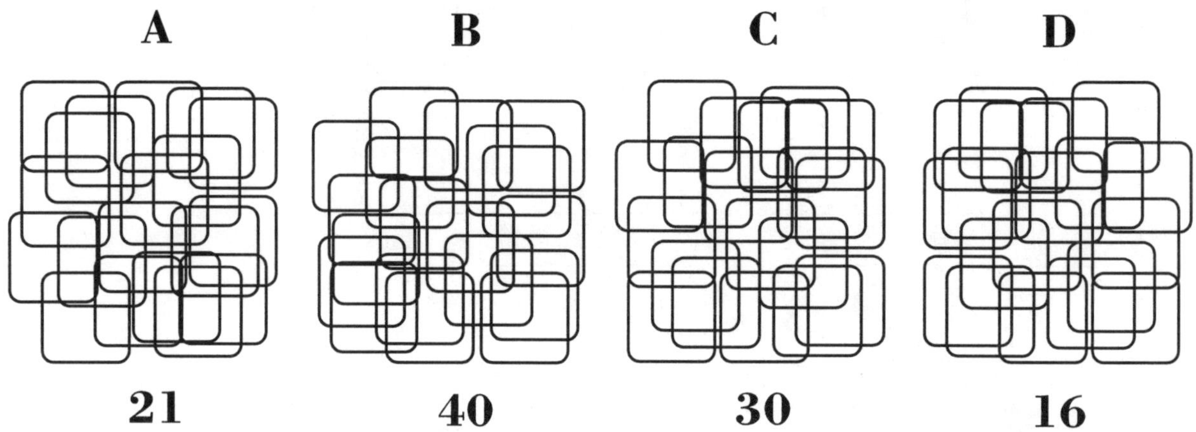

Puzzle 10

5

Which one of these collections of cubes is the same as the one turned on its side in the center? Choose your passcode accordingly.

A=Passcode **47. B**=Passcode **23. C**=Passcode **7. D**=Passcode **20.**

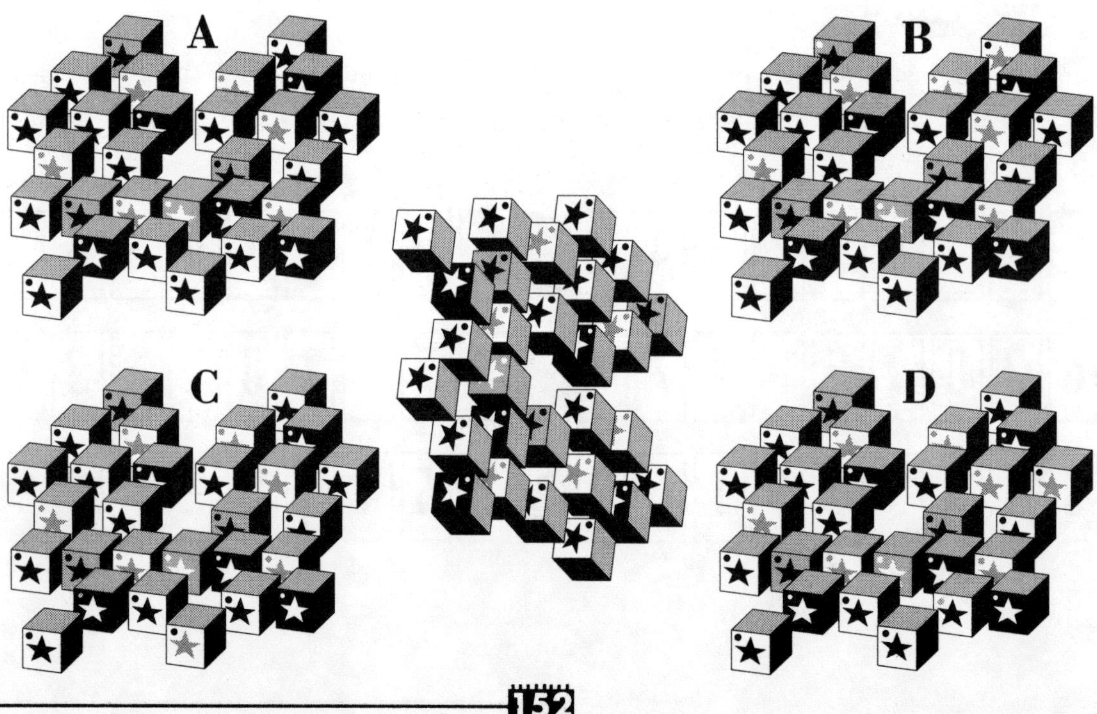

Puzzle 11

Rearrange the digits in the top half of this fraction (not the bottom half) so that the fraction may be resolved into a simple fraction with the lowest possible denominator, with a single digit on the top and bottom of the fraction. When you have done that, the top of the fraction is the first digit of your next passcode and the bottom of the fraction is the second digit of your next passcode. Try to stay sane!

$$\frac{1737003}{9876536}$$

Puzzle 12

The missing digit at [C] in the right-hand circle is the first digit of your next passcode. The missing digit at [E]is the second digit of your next passcode.

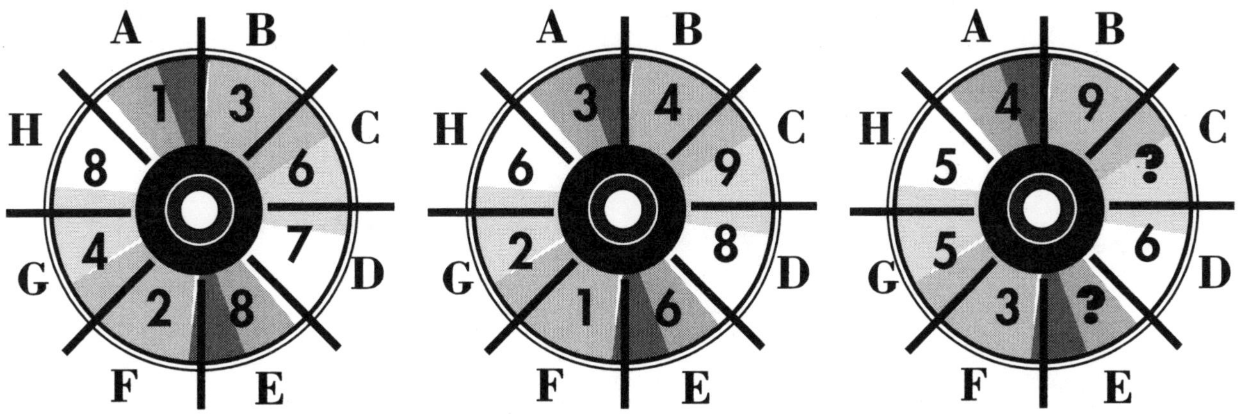

Puzzle 13

Pick the odd-one-out. Your next passcode is below it.

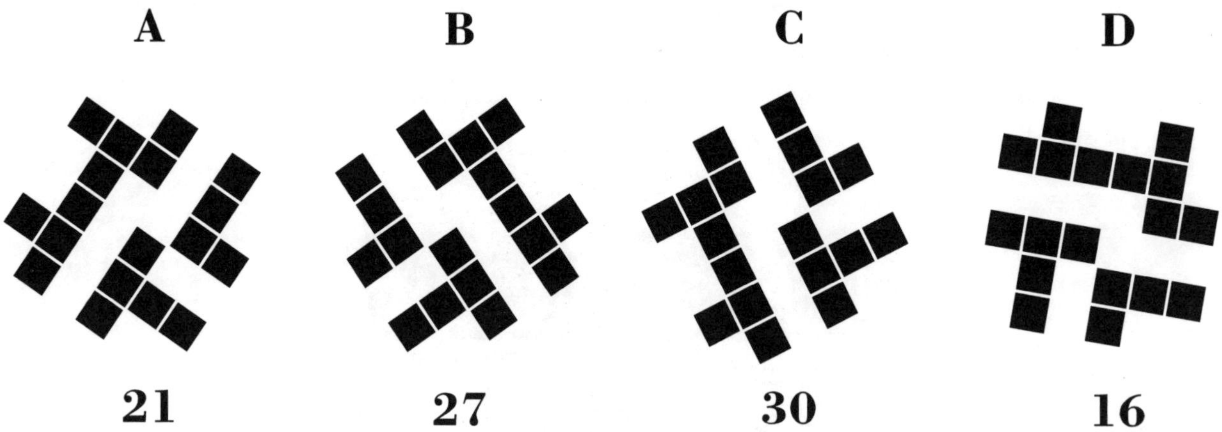

Puzzle 14

The solution to D is your next passcode.

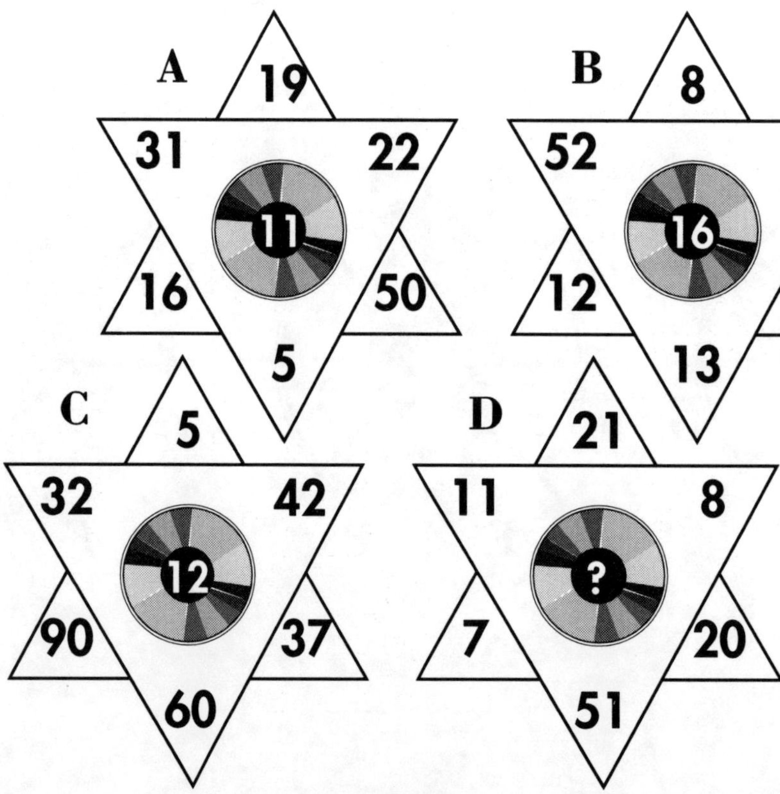

Puzzle 15

Here is a test of your memory and logic. Your next passcode is the number that, when you add 8 to it, gives you the number that, when you double it and subtract 19, gives you a result that, if you take its square root, produces 9.

Puzzle 16

One of the numbers on these discs does not go with the others. That number is your passcode to the next puzzle.

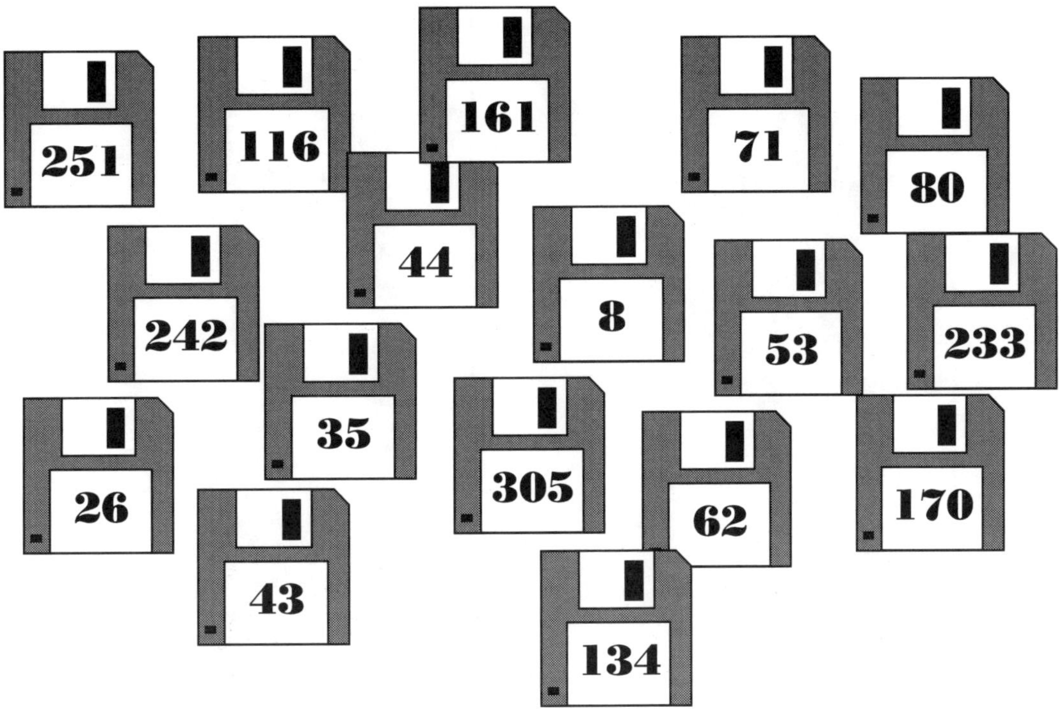

Puzzle 17

Your next passcode + **X** gives 109.

Your next passcode x **X** gives 2968.

Your next passcode is less than **X**.

Puzzle 18

A rectangular room of 12 square units has one wall 4 units long. Moving at a constant speed, it takes a robot 4 minutes to travel the length of that 4 unit wall. How long will it take the robot, moving at the same speed, to cross the diagonal of the room? Give your answer in minutes, then multiply by 9 and add 1 to get your passcode to the next puzzle.

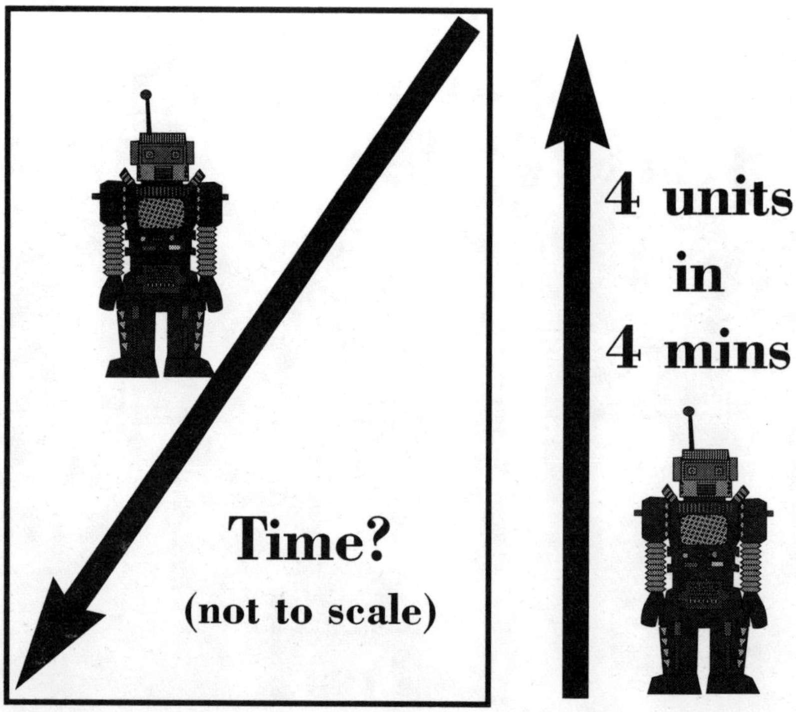

Puzzle 19

Add 48 to the solution of this additive puzzle to find your next passcode on your cyber-quest.

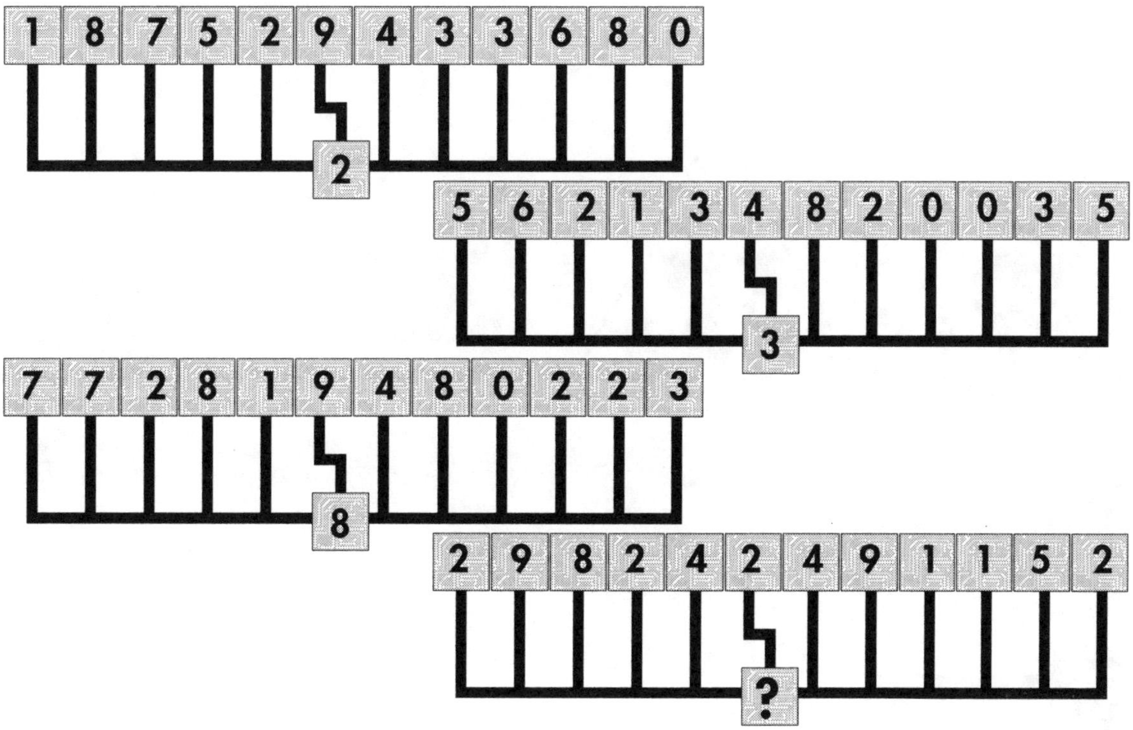

Puzzle 20

Your next passcode is the number of differences between A and B, +60, -2.

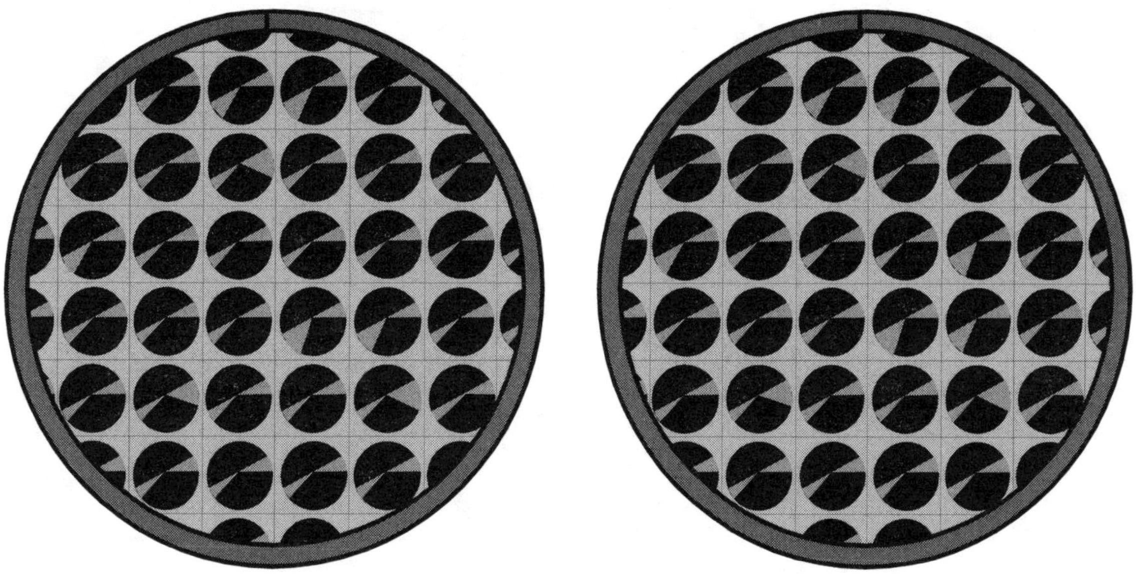

Puzzle 21

The number in the middle of the odd-one-out in this set is your passcode to the next puzzle.

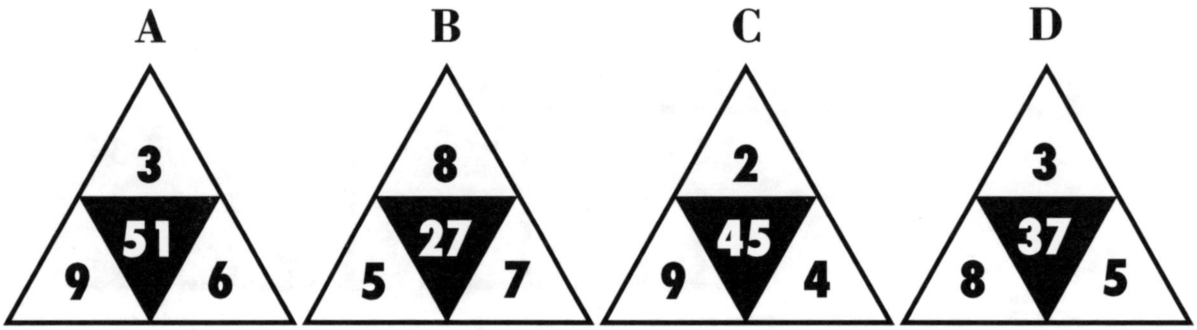

Puzzle 22

Humans find it easier than computers to make analogies, so you should have little trouble solving Adrian's next test. Complete the analogy and use the number under the solution as your passcode to the next puzzle.

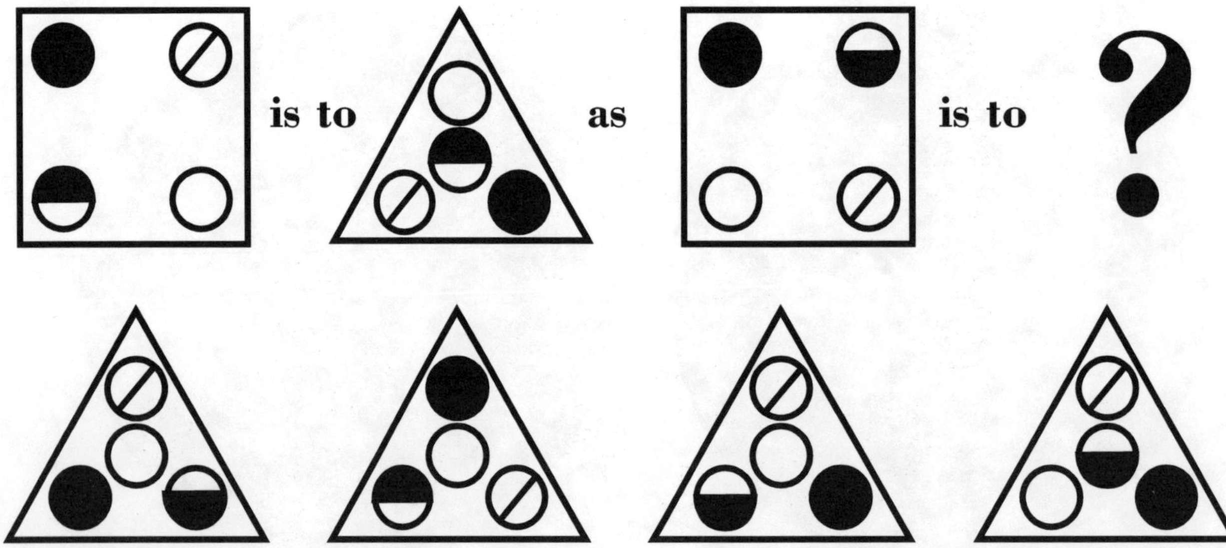

A=16 **B=34** **C=49** **D=21**

Puzzle 23

Which of the below sets satisfies the conditions of the set in the box? Your next passcode is underneath the solution.

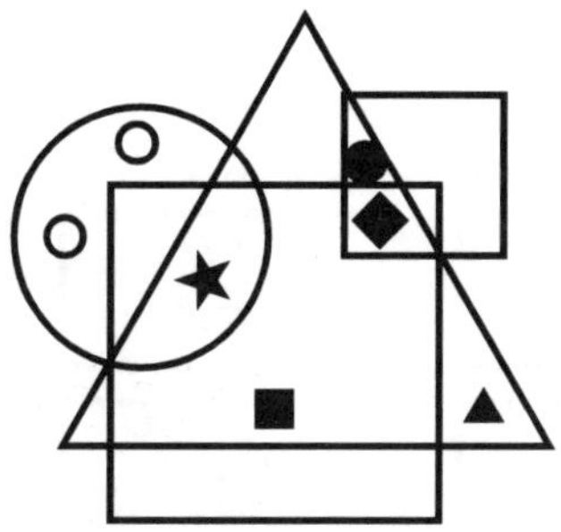

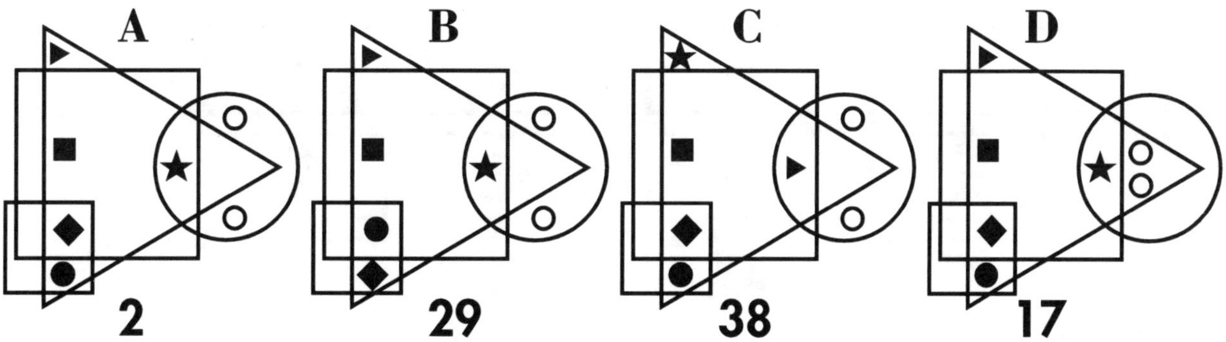

Puzzle 24

The missing lower left and lower right digits in D, in that order, are your passcode to the next puzzle.

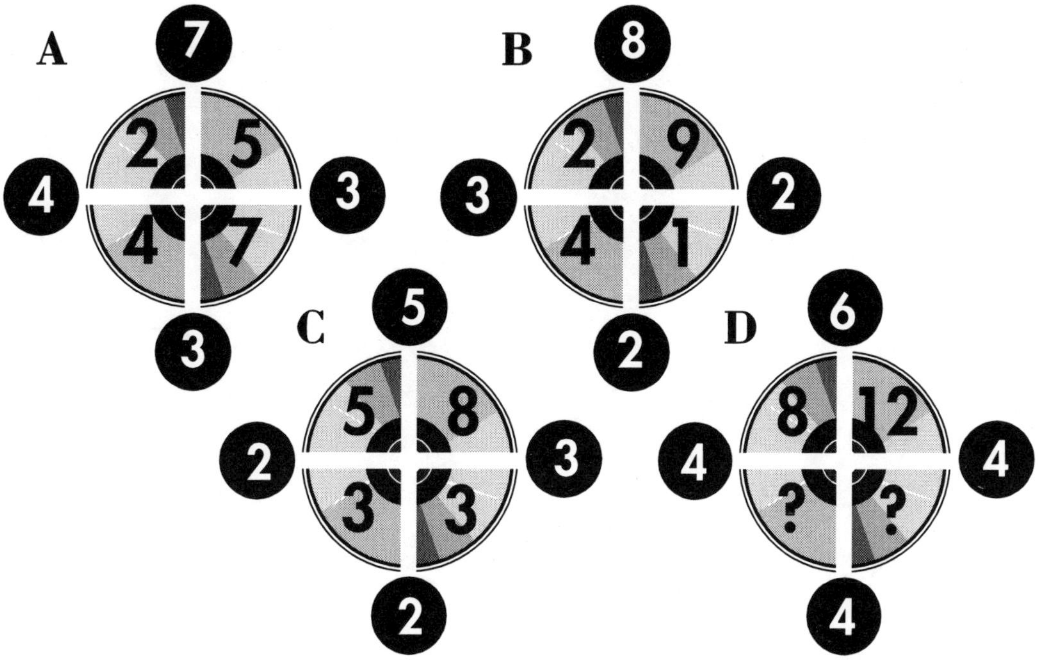

Puzzle 25

Add 51 to the missing number in D and use that as your passcode to the next puzzle set by Adrian Smith.

A	B	C	D
●	◆	●	★
★	◆	●	●
◆	●	★	★
●	★	★	◆
4	4	4	?

Puzzle 26

Which of the surrounding elements is not required to fill in the shaded triangle? The number on the spare element is your passcode to the next puzzle on your quest for escape from cyber-reality.

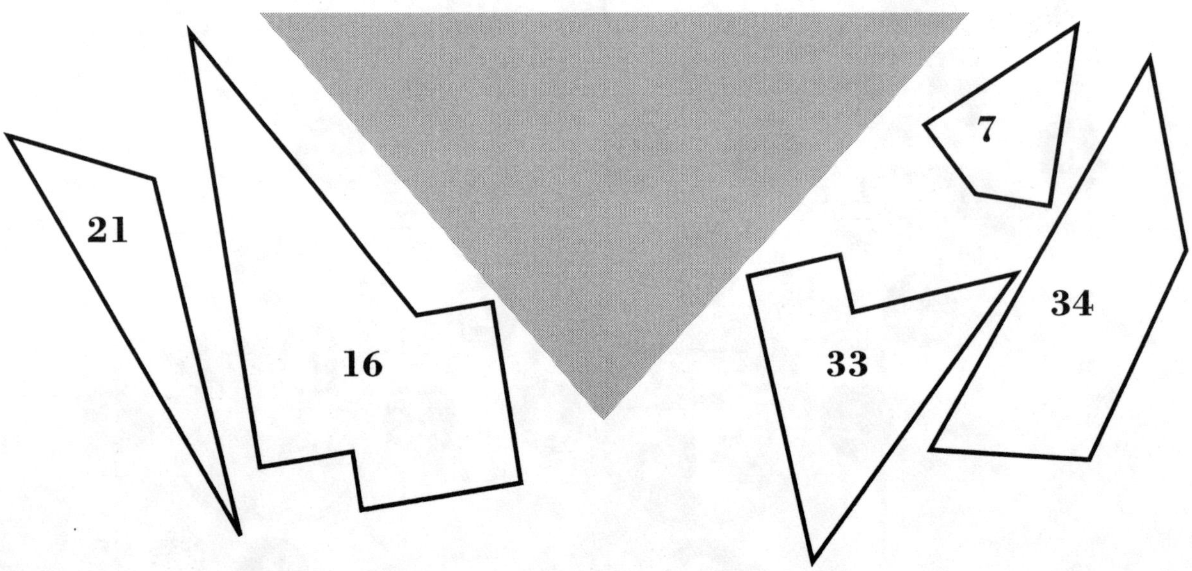

Puzzle 27

What comes next? Choose your passcode accordingly.

A=Passcode **57**. **B**=Passcode **41**. **C**=Passcode **12**. **D**=Passcode **29**.

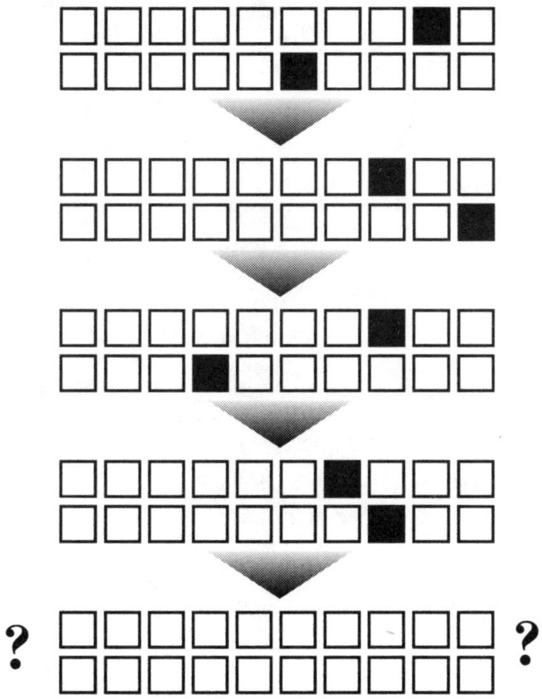

A 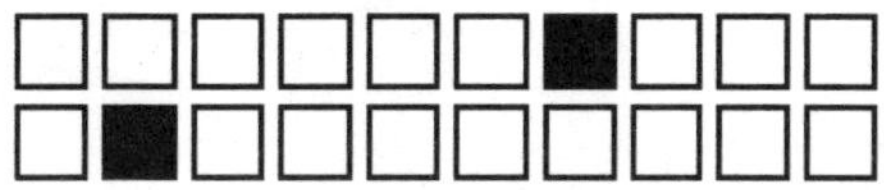

B 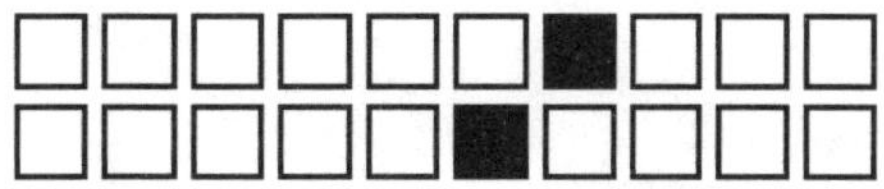

C 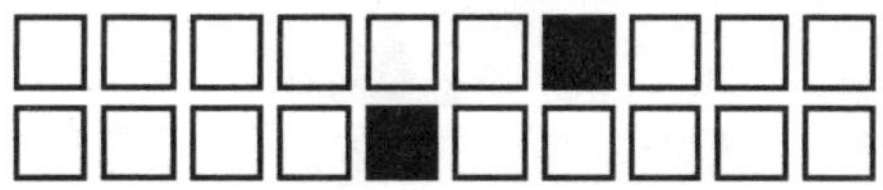

D 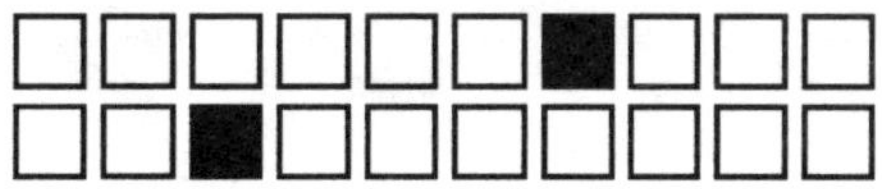

Puzzle 28

Pick the odd-one-out and use the number beside it as your next passcode.

A  26

B 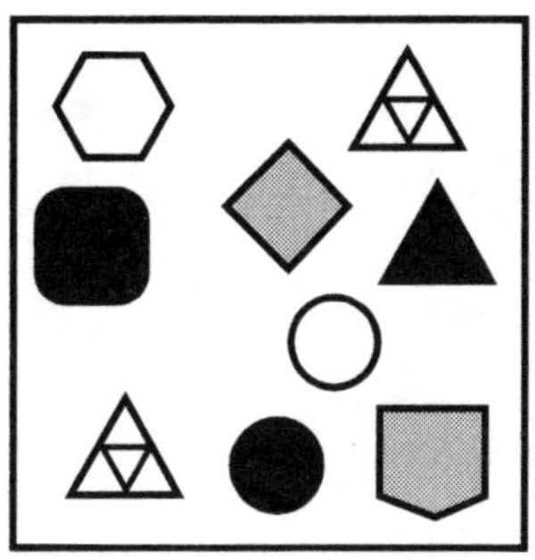 59

C  54

D  31

Puzzle 29

Solve the code to find your next passcode.

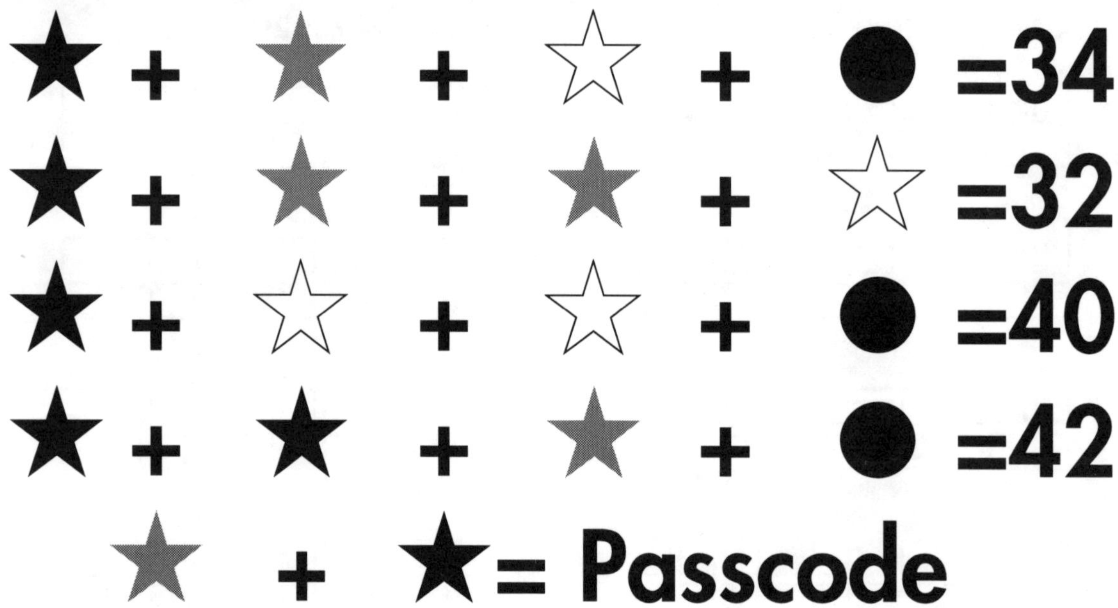

Puzzle 30

Complete the analogy and use the number below the solution as your next passcode.

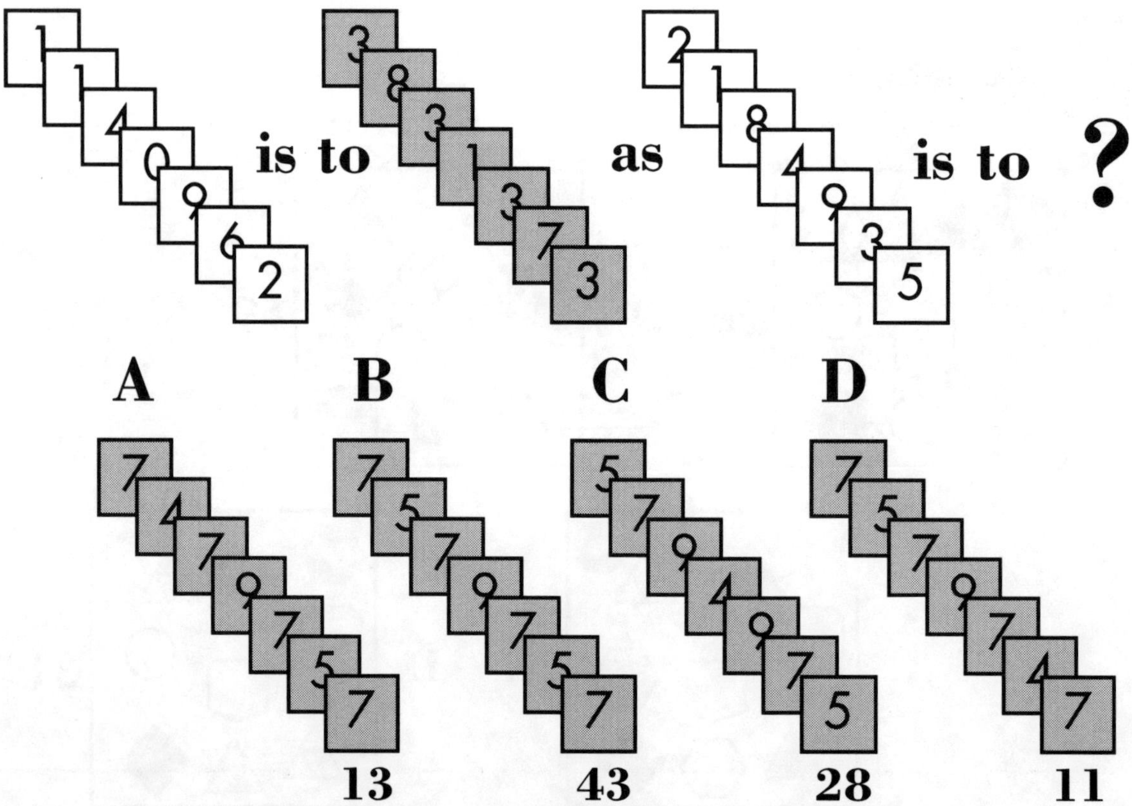

Puzzle 31

Pick the odd-one-out and use the central number as your next passcode. Central numbers are not part of the puzzle.

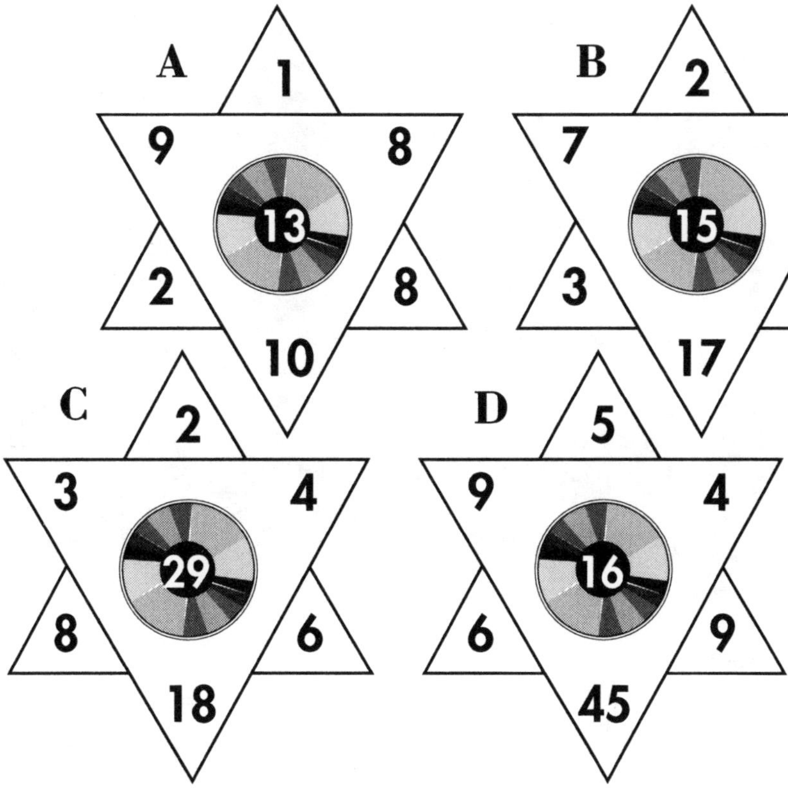

Puzzle 32

Draw 3 straight lines which divide this puzzle into 6 sections, holding the values of, respectively, 38, 48, 58, 68, 78 & 88. The total value in the largest section is your passcode to the next puzzle.

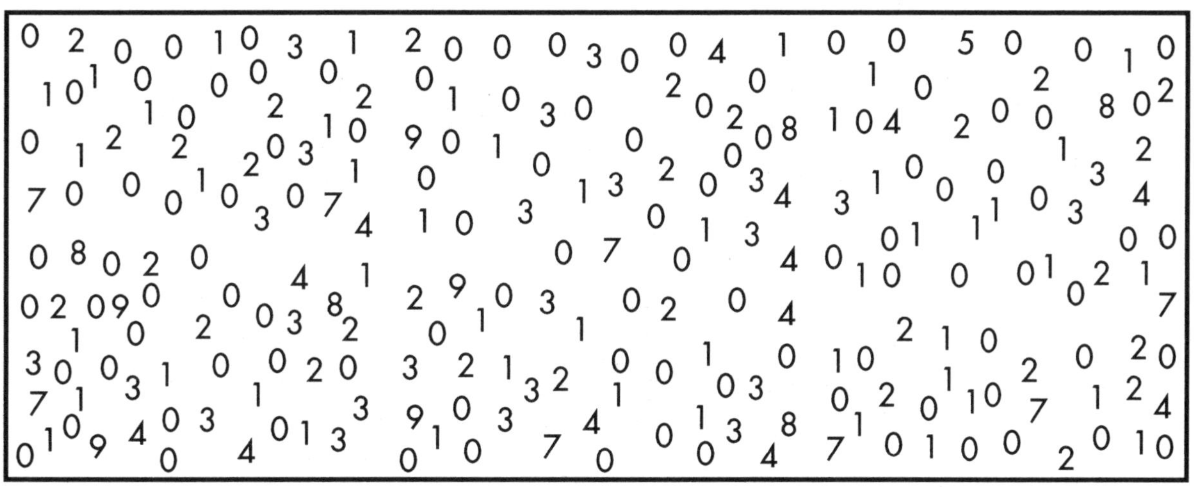

Puzzle 33

Continue the sequence and find the next passcode Adrian Smith has set you by deducting 25 from the missing number.

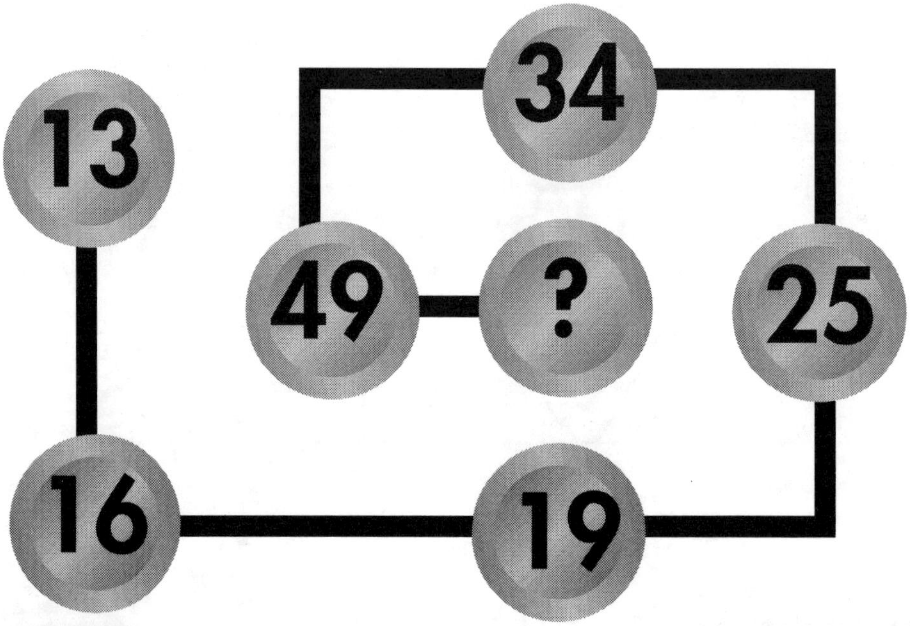

Puzzle 34

One of the numbers in the keys does not go with the others. Find it and divide it by 8 to get the passcode to your next puzzle.

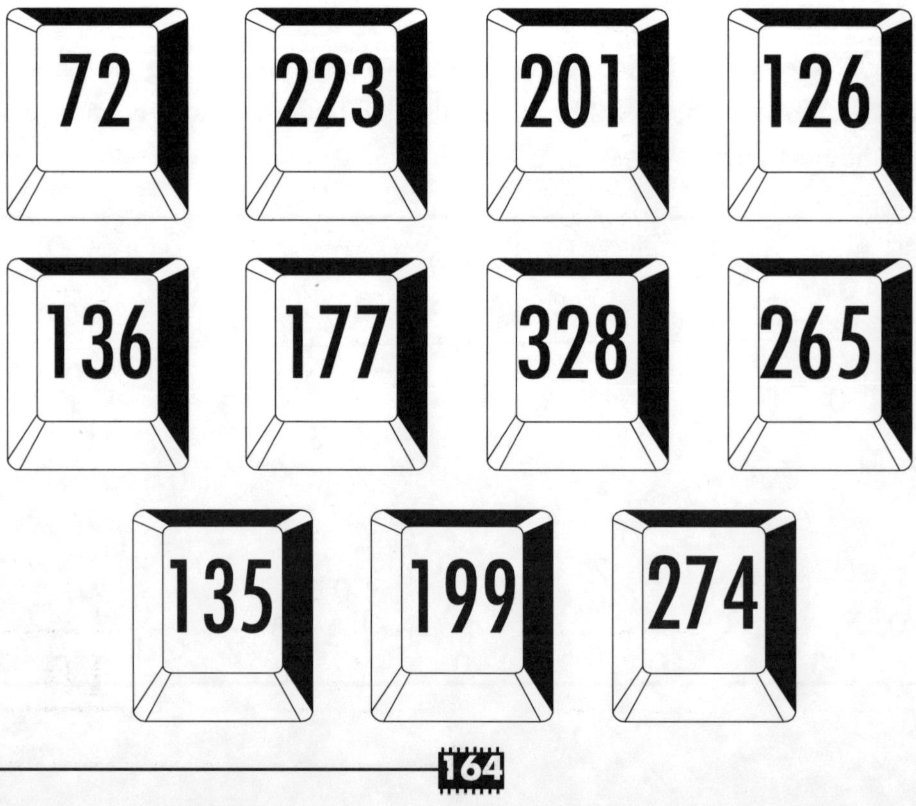

Puzzle 35

8

Stop here to work out the missing number in D. It is your passcode to the next puzzle.

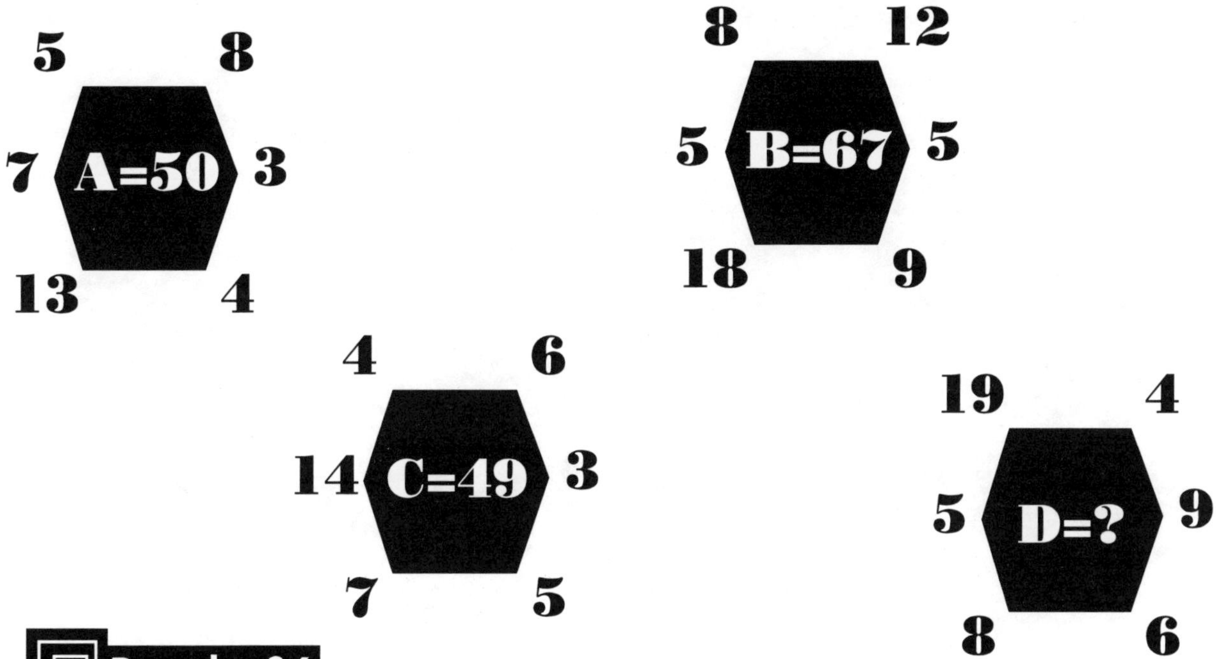

Puzzle 36

Add the total of the symbols in the second column to find your next passcode.

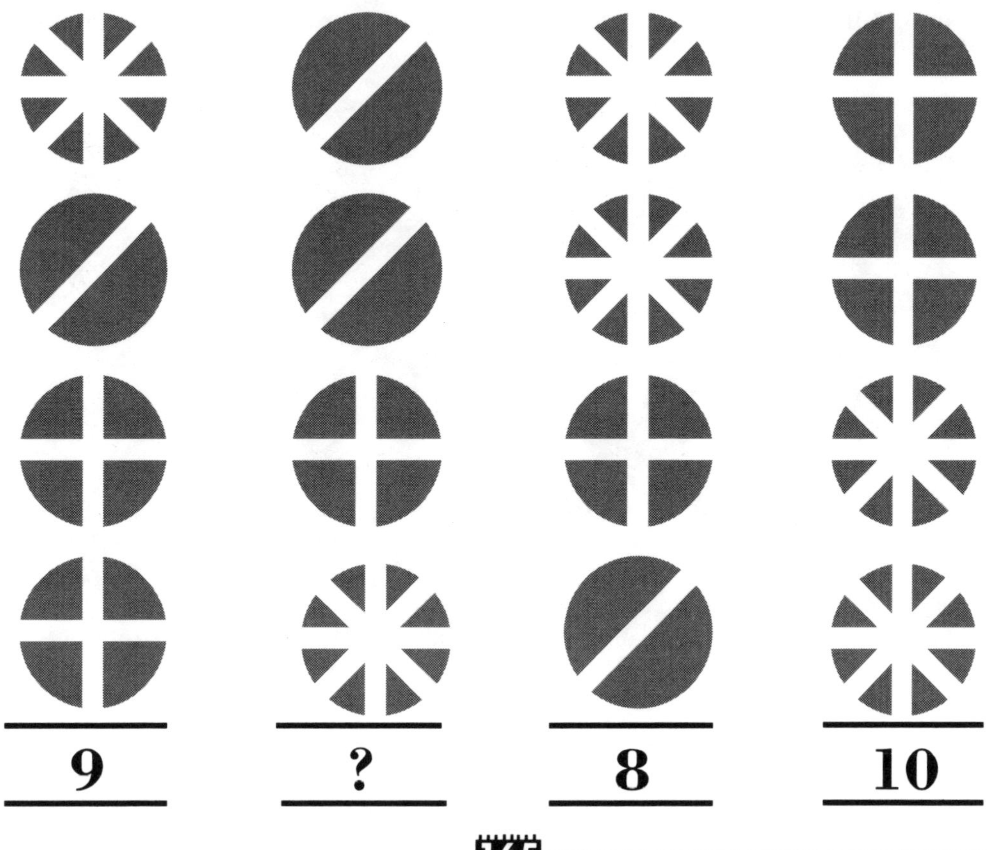

Puzzle 37

Multiply the missing number in C by 4 and subtract 1 to get your passcode to the next puzzle on your quest.

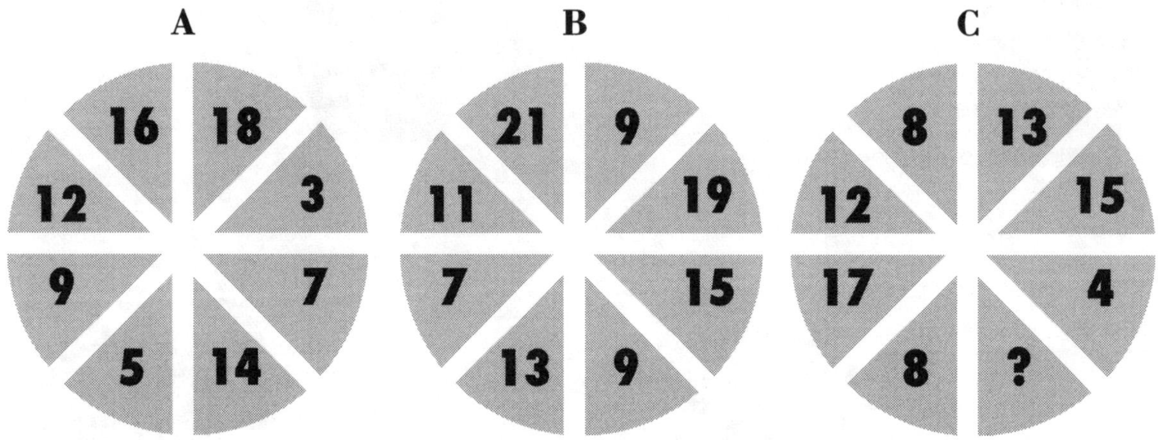

Puzzle 38

The number of different types of star in this drawing is your passcode to the next puzzle.

Puzzle 39

Pick the odd-one-out and use that number as your passcode to the next puzzle.

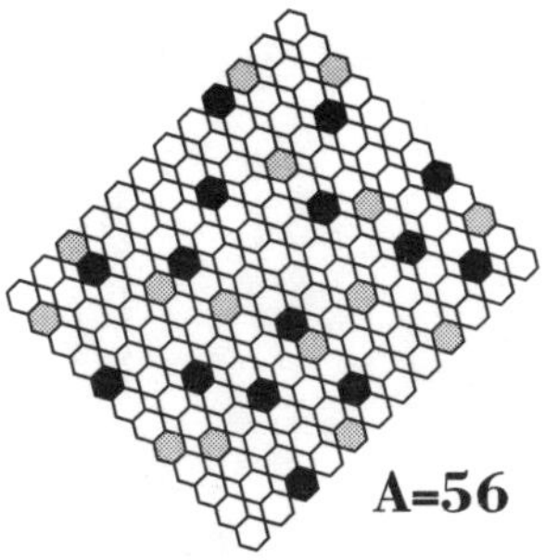

A=56

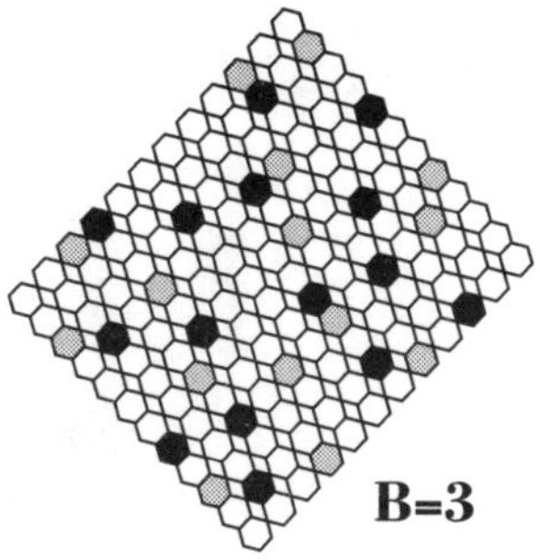

B=3

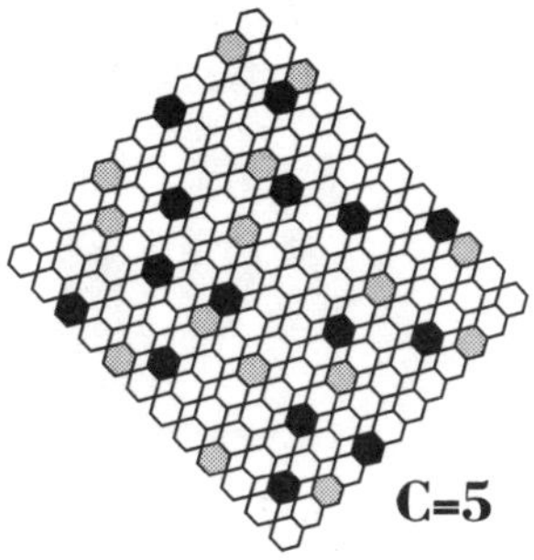

C=5

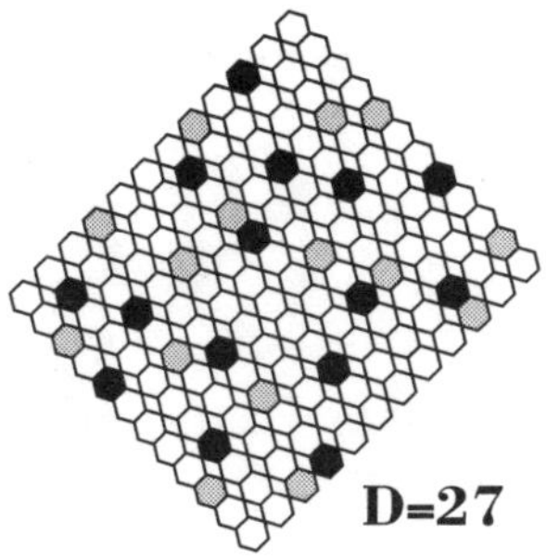

D=27

Puzzle 40

What comes next? Choose your passcode accordingly.

A=Passcode **21. B**=Passcode **29. C**=Passcode **32. D**=Passcode **56.**

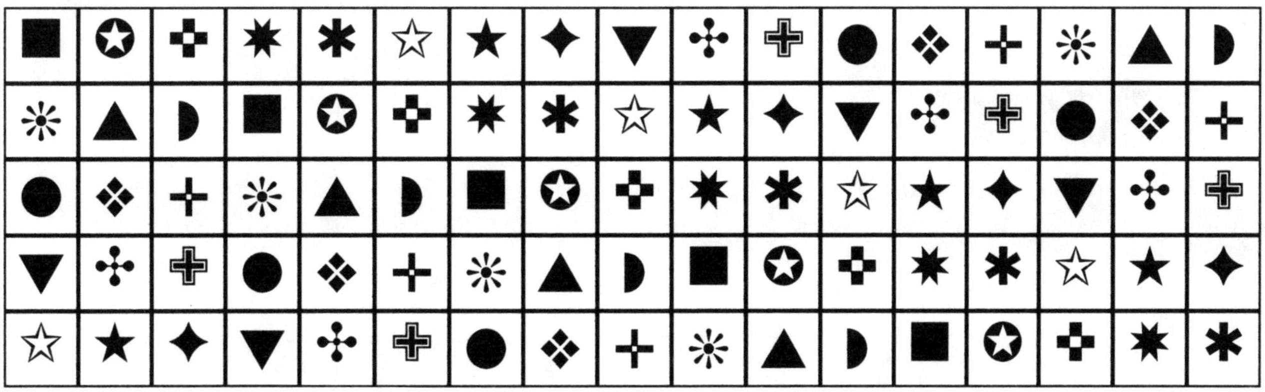

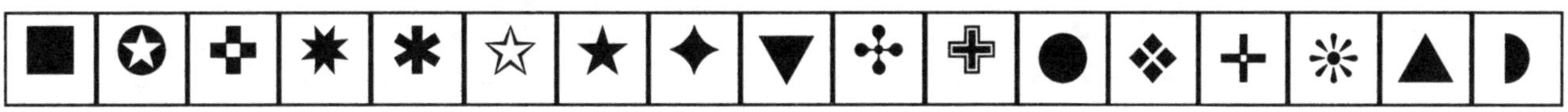

A

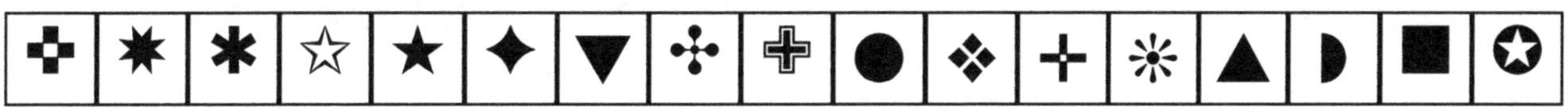

B

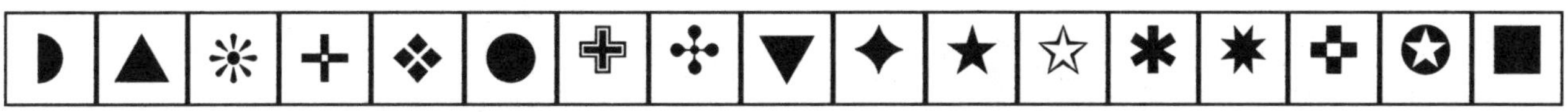

C

D

Puzzle 41

Multiply the missing number in this sequence by 3 to find your passcode to the next puzzle in cyber-reality.

A	B	C	D
19	20	4	8

E	F	G	
16	14	10	?

Puzzle 42

Add 6 to [ba] in D to find your next passcode.

A

1	7	2	3
9	3	8	7
3	4	4	6

B

4	1	7	2
6	9	3	8
8	3	4	4

C

2	6	4	5
8	4	6	5
5	2	9	0

D

3	6	7	1
7	4	3	a
7	3	4	b

Puzzle 43

Two numbers when added together make 80. When their squares are added together they make 3232. Halve the lower of the two numbers and divide the result by 4.5 to find your next passcode.

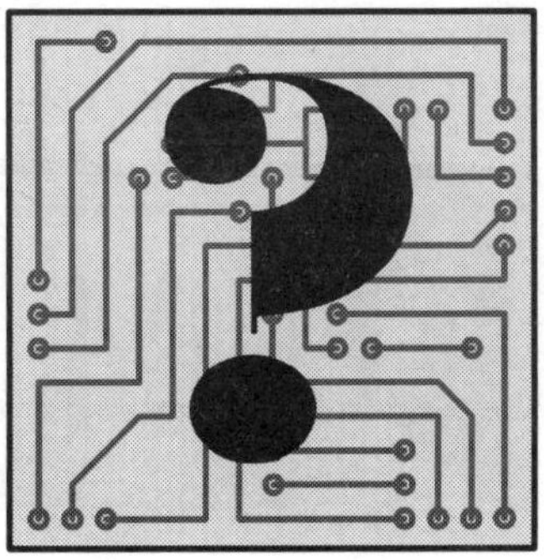

Puzzle 44

Another test of your ability to think in 3 dimensions. Which of the surrounding plans make the cube in the middle? Choose your passcode accordingly.
A=Passcode **29.** **B**=Passcode **1.** **C**=Passcode **15.** **D**=Passcode **18.**

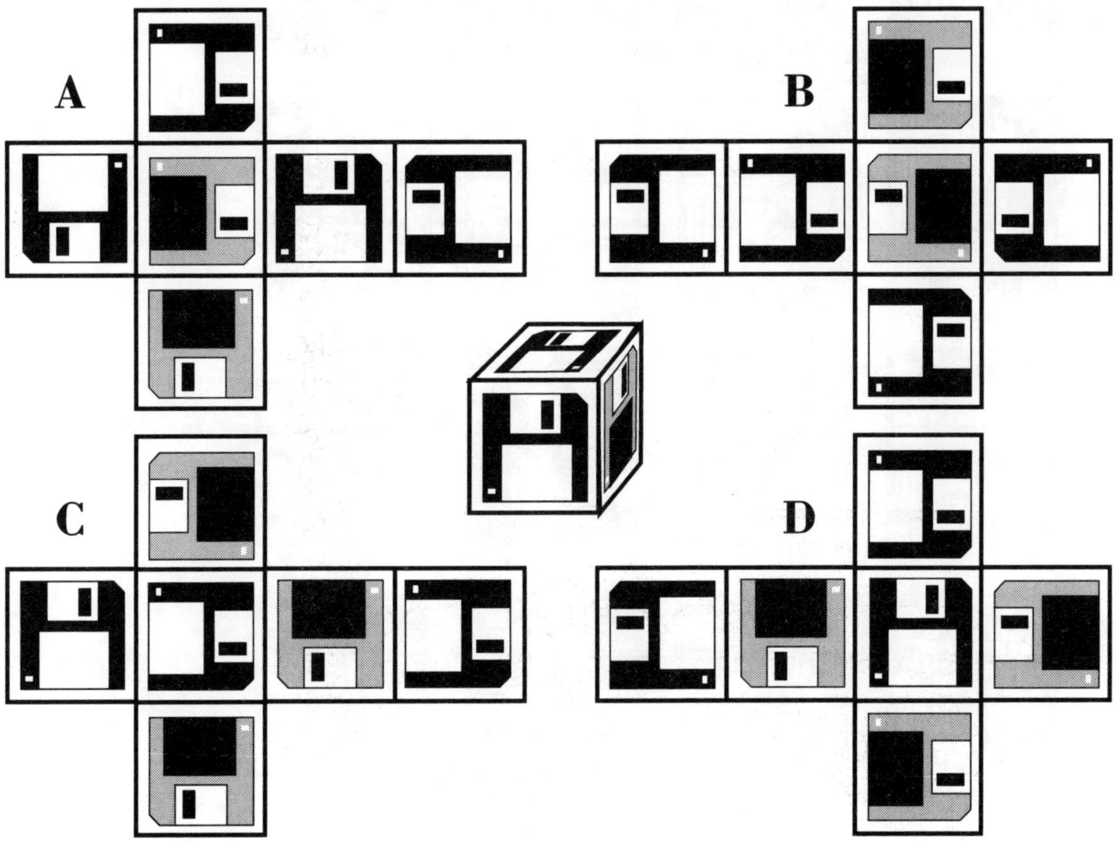

Puzzle 45

Add the last digit of the right hand missing number in D to the top missing number to find your next passcode.

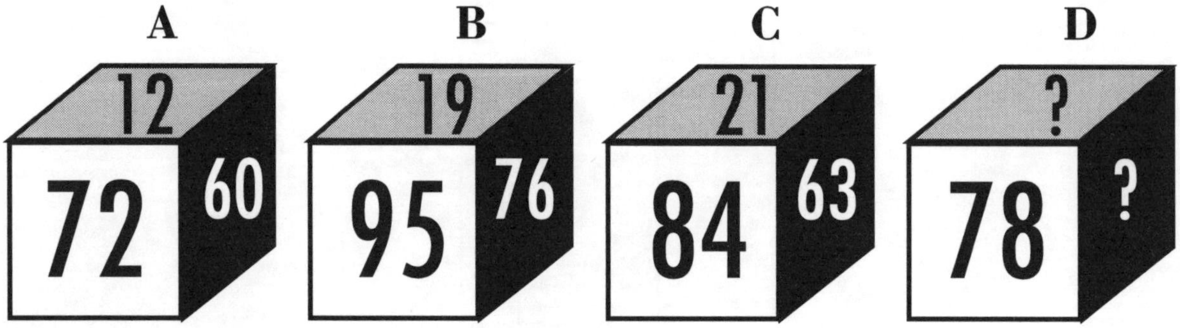

Puzzle 46

The solution to this puzzle is your next passcode.

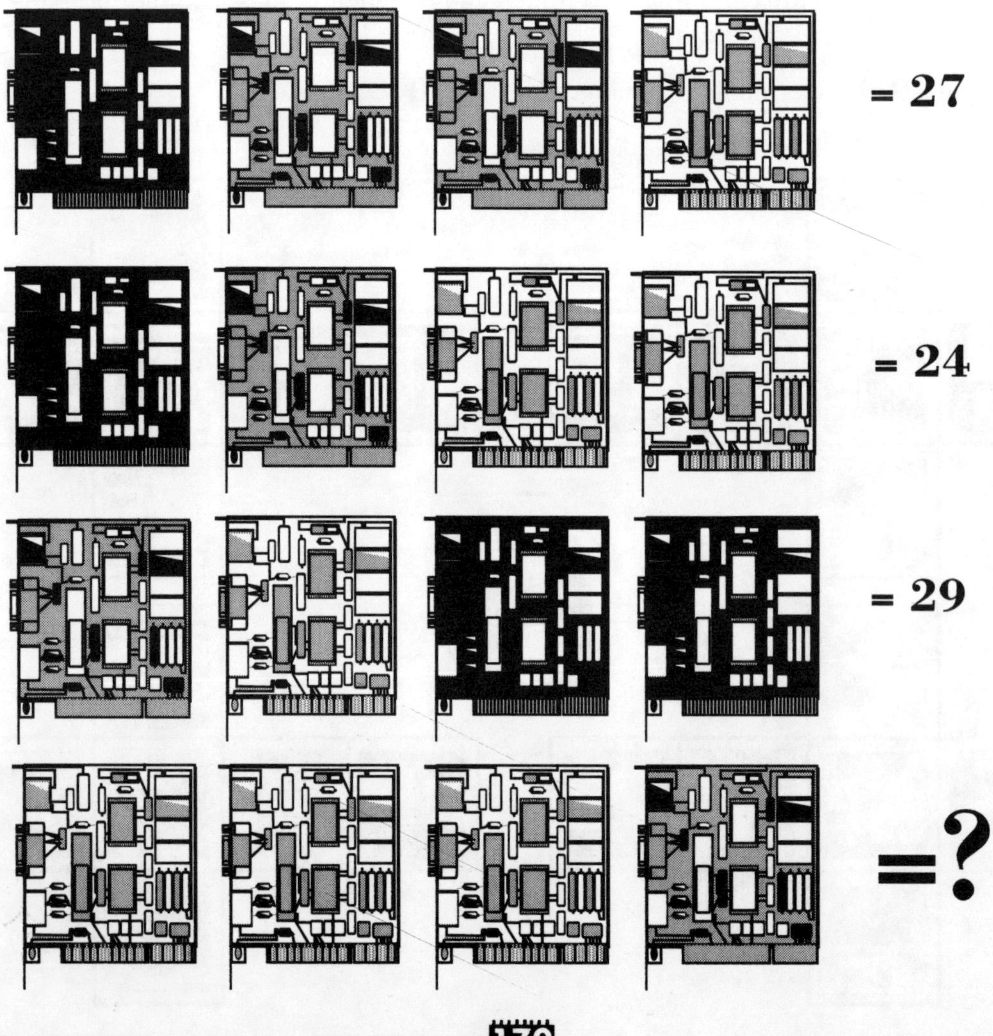

Puzzle 47

Pick the odd-one-out and use the number below it as your next passcode.

A B C D

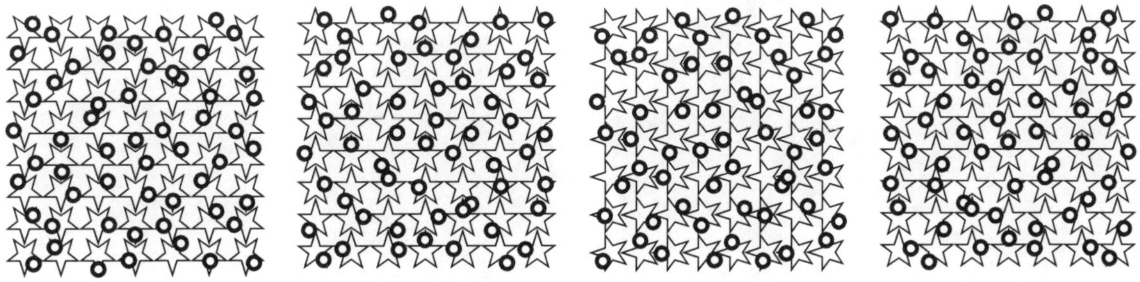

45 12 31 14

Puzzle 48

Complete the analogy and choose your passcode accordingly.

A=Passcode **23. B**=Passcode **55. C**=Passcode **3. D**=Passcode **9.**

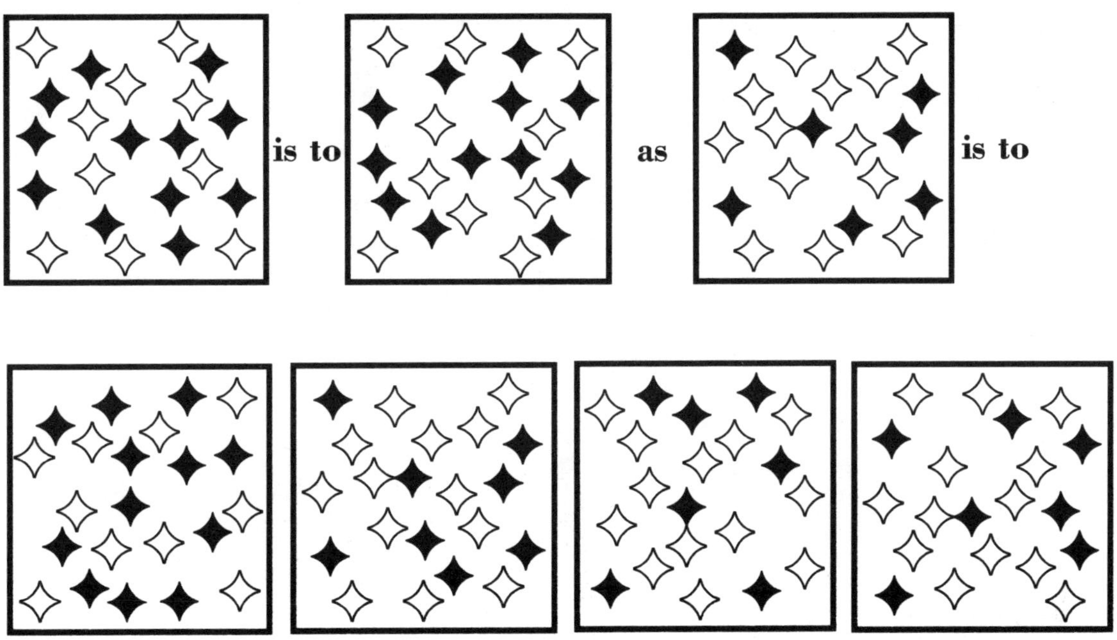

A B C D

Puzzle 49

Pick the odd robot out and use the number below it as your passcode to the next puzzle.

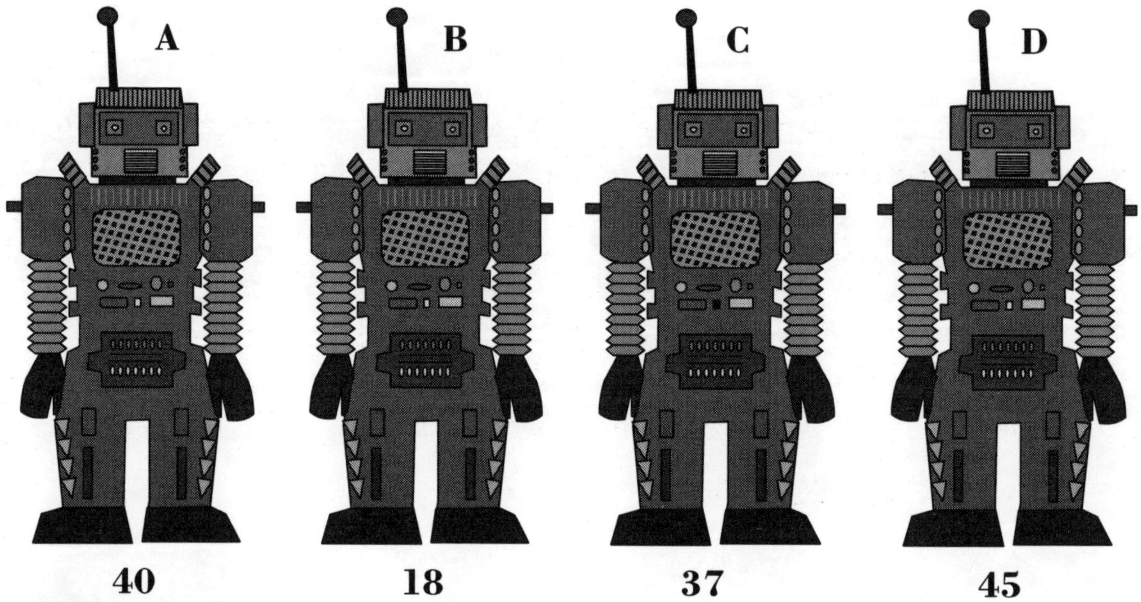

Puzzle 50

Pick the odd-one-out. Choose your passcode accordingly.

A=Passcode **11.** **B**=Passcode **37.** **C**=Passcode **5.** **D**=Passcode **19.**

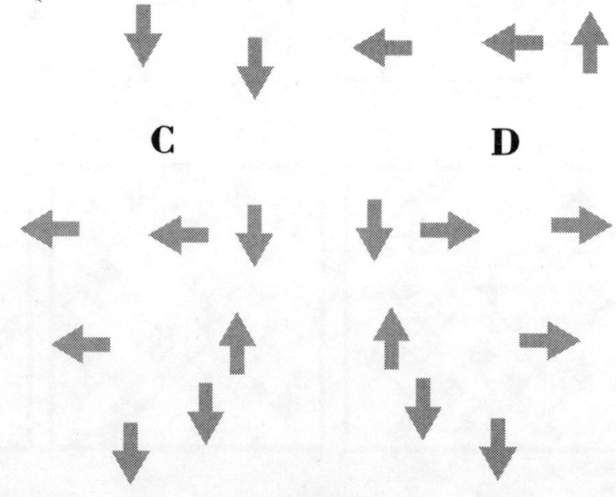

Puzzle 51

Add 2 to the number of ovals that enclose the black spot to find your next passcode.

Puzzle 52

Pick the odd-one-out and use the number below it as the passcode to your next puzzle.

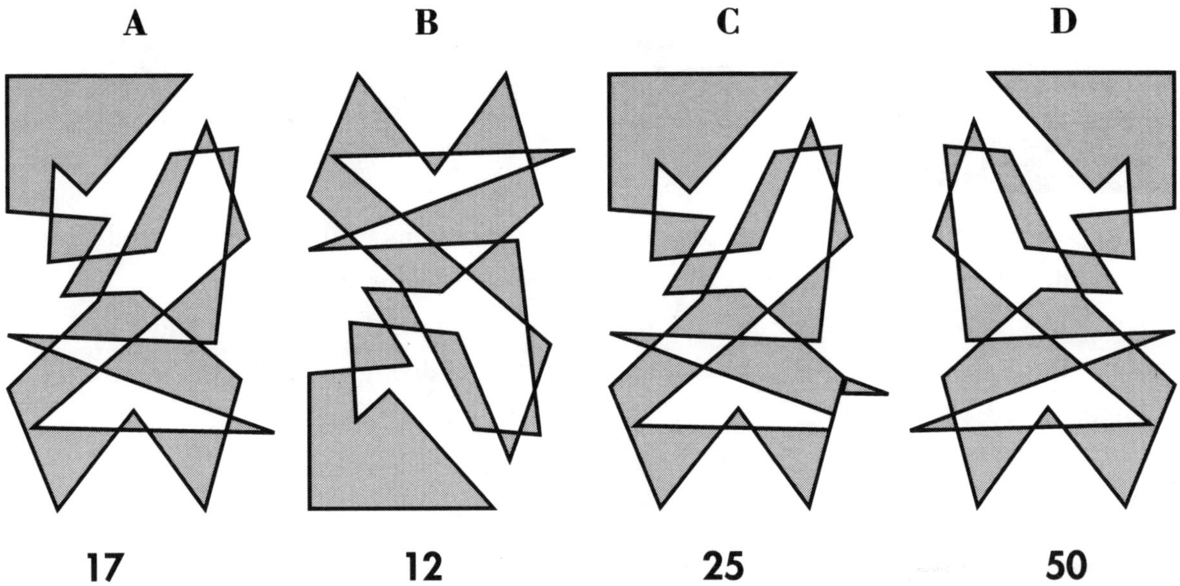

Puzzle 53

Add 30 to the missing number in D to find your passcode to the next puzzle.

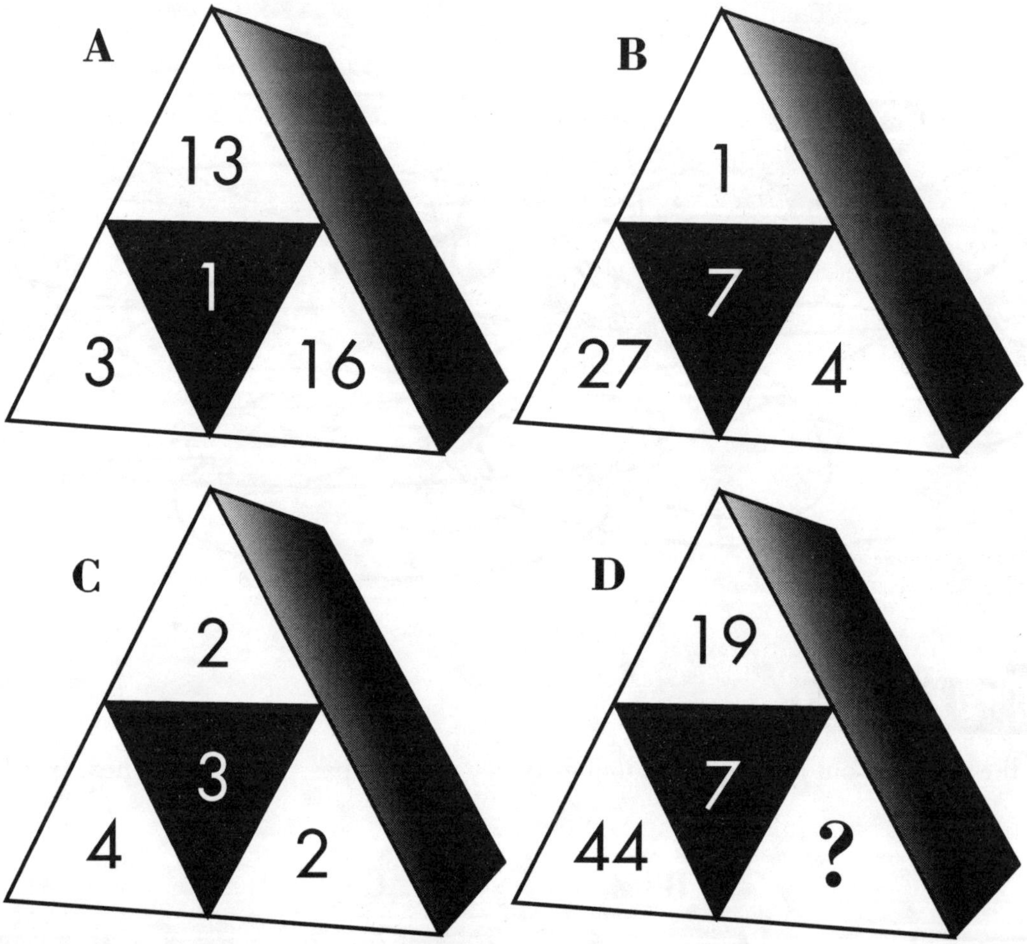

Puzzle 54

When you add 4 to your next passcode, the result is the number that, when you subtract 9 from it, gives you a number that, when you multiply it by three and add 3 to the result, gives you a number that, when divided by 10, produces a result that, if you add 3 and square the result, produces a number that, when 19 is added, gives a number that, when divided by 10, produces 10.

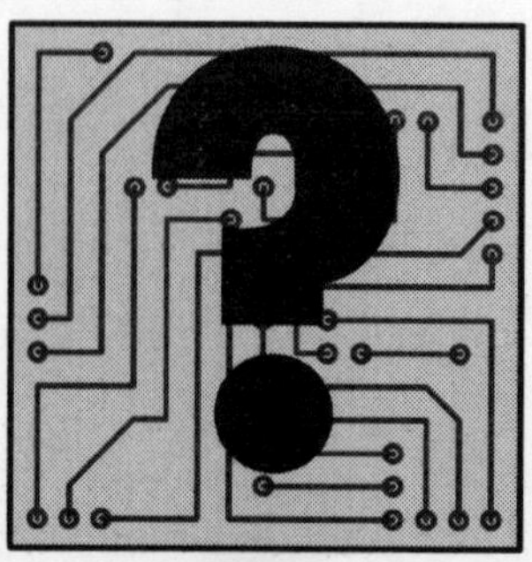

8

Puzzle 55

Pick the odd-one-out and use the number below it as your next passcode.

A B C D

36 26 45 60

Puzzle 56

Which one of the plans below can be folded to make the pyramid?

A=Passcode 22. B=Passcode 5. C=Passcode 44. D=Passcode 31.

A B C D

Puzzle 57

Complete this magic square so that the total of each row, column and long diagonal is 35. When you have done that, add the total value of the nine missing numbers and subtract 23 to find your passcode to the next puzzle.

8	9	17	25	-16	-8	0
-1	7	15	16	24	-17	-9
-10	-2				23	-18
-19	-11				21	29
28	-13				12	20
19	27	-14	-6	-5	3	11
10	18	26	-15	-7	1	2

Puzzle 58

This system is in balance. Add 4 to the value of the block with the question mark to find your next passcode.

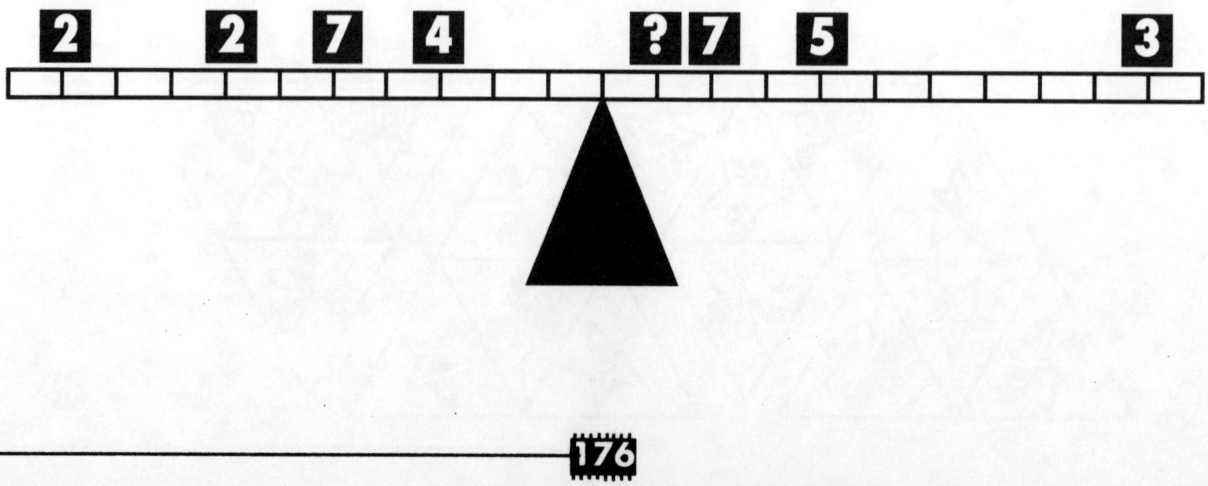

Puzzle 59

Solve for A & B to find your next passcode.

A + B = 74

B - A = 28

B x A = 1173

Passcode = A

Puzzle 60

Ten of the tiles are missing from this pattern. Your next passcode is beside the correct set to complete the pattern.

■	✖	✦	★	☆	■	✖	✦	★	☆	■	✖	✦	★	☆	■	✖	✦	★
☆	■	✖	✦	★	☆	■	✖	✦	★	☆	■	✖	✦	★	☆	■	✖	✦
★	☆	■	✖	✦	★						☆	■	✖	✦	★	☆	■	✖
✦	✖	■	☆	★	✦						✖	■	☆	★	✦	✖	■	☆
✦	★	☆	■	✖	✦	★	☆	■	✖	✦	★	☆	■	✖	✦	★	☆	■
✖	✦	★	☆	■	✖	✦	★	☆	■	✖	✦	★	☆	■	✖	✦	★	☆

A 31

■	✖	✦	★	☆
☆	■	✖	✦	★

B 18

☆	■	✖	✦	★
✖	■	☆	★	✦

C 46

✖	✦	★	☆	■
■	✖	✦	★	☆

D 39

✖	✦	★	☆	■
■	✖	✦	★	☆

SECTION FIVE
KEYCODES

REMINDER: You must solve the puzzles in the correct order. Start at the top of column A, and insert your keys. When you get to the bottom of column A, start back at the top of column B.

In this section, subtract the total of column B from the total of column A. The result is your passcode for Section Five and your starting point for Section Six. Write that solution below and in the appropriate place on page 220.

You will only get the correct solution for this section if you have managed to get every answer correct.

Only one section to go now.

Can you stick it out?

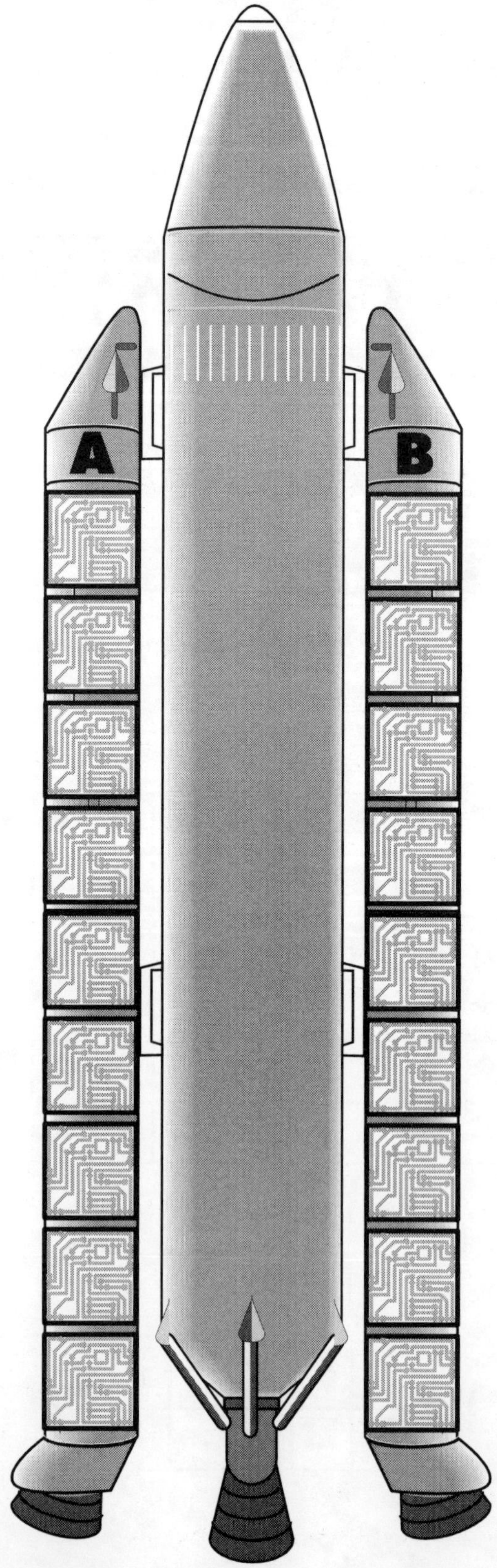

Total A	Total B

SECTION FIVE

PASSCODE

SECTION FIVE

1. Solution D. The numbers shown below in black boxes stay in place. The remainder have their order reversed and swap rows. **Go to 33. Key 7.**

2	9	5	1
3	8	7	4

2. Solution 32. The missing number is 3. Reading in diagonal slices right to left, 56-[3]2=24. **Go to 32.**

3. Solution D. This is a mirror-image of the others in this set which are all rotated version of the same image. **Go to 13.**

4. Solution B. **Go to 31.**

5. Solution 36. In each triangle, top number + bottom right – bottom left = middle number. Thus, 41+19-24=36. **Go to 36. Key 6.**

6. Solution 16. There are 48 bricks missing. 48/3=16. **Go to 16.**

7. Solution 556. The values are shown in the diagram below. Thus, 432+124=556. **Go to 56. Key 2.**

1 **2** **3** **4**

8. Solution 41. The digits on the right side of the black square are those that, when added to the digits on the left side in each row, total 10. Thus, 6+[4]=10; 1+[9]=10. **Go to 41.**

9. C is the odd-one-out. This is a mirror-image of the others which are all rotated versions of the same shape. **Go to 30.**

10. Solution A. The others have one change each in the color of a star. **Go to 47. Key 5.**

11. The solution is $\frac{3703701}{9876536}$ =3/8. **Go to 38. Key 5.**

12. Solution is 50. On each CD, CxB=AH; GxD=FE. Thus, [5]x9=45; 6x5=3[0]. **Go to 50.**

13. Solution B. This is a mirror-image of the others, which are all rotated versions of the same image. **Go to 27.**

14. Solution 40. (8+20+51)-(21+11+7)=40. **Go to 40. Key 9.**

15. Solution 42. [42]+8=50; 50x2=100; 100-19=81; sqr. root 81=9. **Go to 42.**

16. Solution 43. All the other discs have numbers with digits that add to 8. **Go to 43.**

17. Solution 53. X=56. 53+56=109; 53x56=2968. 53 is less than 56. **Go to 53.**

18. Solution 46. The room is 12 square units, so length must be 12/4=3. Hence, by Pythagoras, diagonal is square root of 3 squared + 4 squared = square root of 25 = 5. The speed of the robot is one minute per unit, thus it covers 5 units in 5 minutes. 9x5 = 45 + 1 = 46. **Go to 46.**

19. Solution 52. The missing value is 4. Add all of the digits and then perform the same operation on the result, repeating this concatenating operation if you arrive at another double figure. Thus, 2+9+8+2+4+2+4+9+1+1+5+2=49; 4+9=13; 1+3=4. 4+48=52. **Go to 52.**

20. Solution 59. There is 1 difference, circled below. (1+60)-2=59. **Go to 59. Key 1.**

SECTION FIVE

ANSWERS

21. Solution 45. C is the odd-one-out. In all the others the bottom two numbers multiplied together minus the top number, equals the middle number. **Go to 45.**

22. Solution C. Each element in the square is translated into the same relative position in the triangle according to its initial position in the analogous square. **Go to 49.**

23. Solution A. Only in this set are all inner elements in the same positions relative to the intersections of the outer elements. **Go to 2. Key 5.**

24. Solution 60. Referring to the diagram below, Ax(B+C)=DE; DE+F=GH. **Go to 60.**

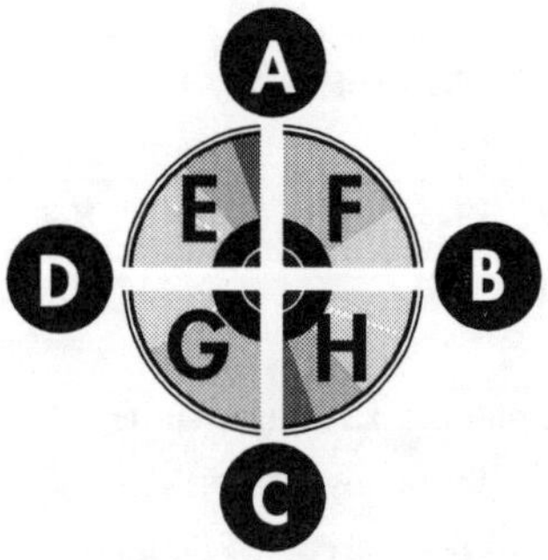

25. Solution 55. All the elements are worth 1 each, for a change. 51+4=55. **Go to 55.**

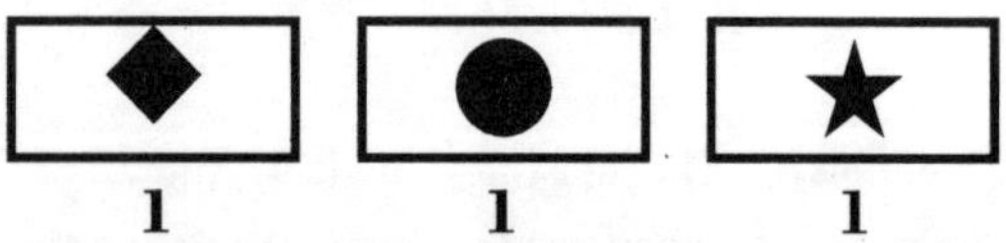

26. Solution 34. The elements fit as shown below. Section 34 does not fit. **Go to 34.**

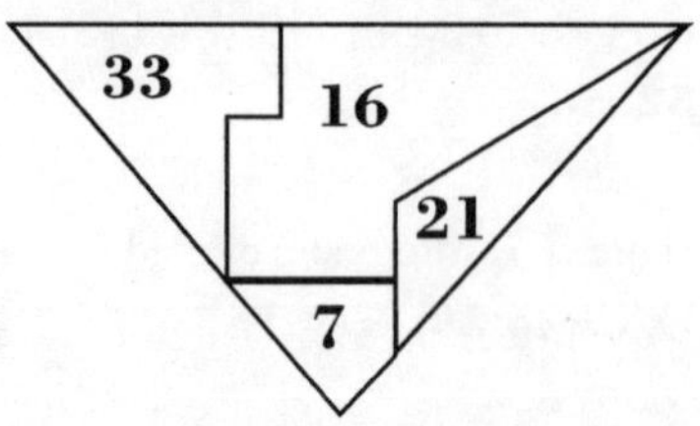

27. Solution A. Each set represents a numerical value with the 10s above and 1s below, reading from zero at the right to 9 at the left. Value shown goes up by six each step: 14, 20, 26, 32, [38]. **Go to 57.**

28. Solution C. This is the only element with 2 hexagons and only one circle. **Go to 54.**

29. Solution 20. The shapes have values shown below. **Go to 20.**

30. Solution D. The analogy is for the sum to be added to the reverse of itself. Thus, 1140962+2690411=3831373, and 2184935+5394812=7579747. **Go to 11. Key 2.**

31. Solution B. The lower number in each star should be a result of, referring to the diagram below, AxB=CD; CD-E=F. Thus [F] in star B should be 16, hence B is the odd-one-out. **Go to 15.**

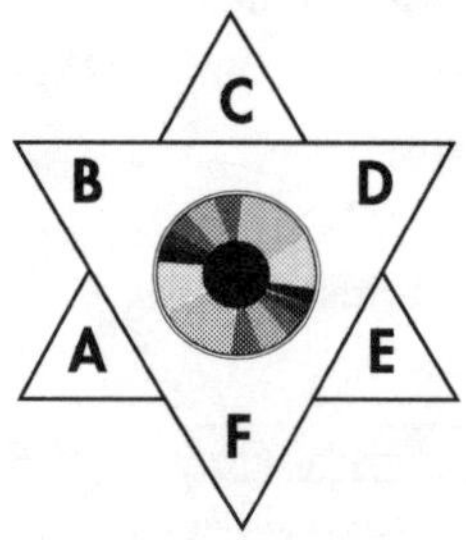

32. Solution 58. 58 is the value in the top-right section. **Go to 58.**

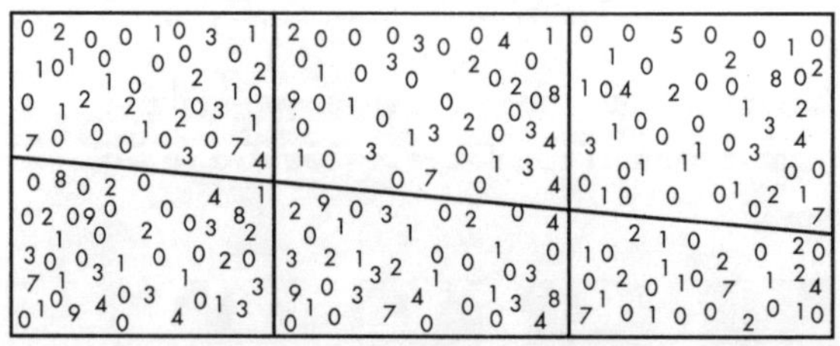

33. Solution 48. Missing number 73. Each number increases by the sum of the previous two increases, ie. 19-16=3 and 16-13=3; 3+3=6; so 19+6=25. Similarly, 34-25=9, and 49-34=15; 9+15=24. So the next number = 49+24 =73; and 73-25=48. **Go to 48.**

34. Solution is 136. The rest are in pairs, as shown below. All pairs add up to 400. 136/8=17. **Go to 17. Key 7.**

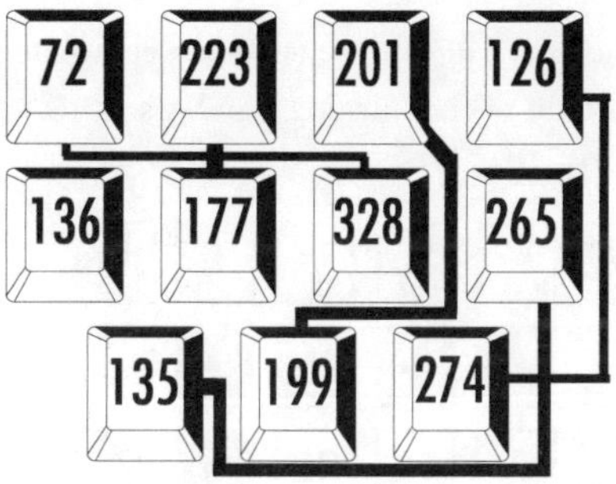

35. Solution 61. The surrounding numbers of each hexagon+10=the central numbers. Thus 19+4+9+6+8+5+[10]=61. **Go to 61 – The Keycodes. Key 8.**

36. Solution 7. Values are as below. **Go to 7.**

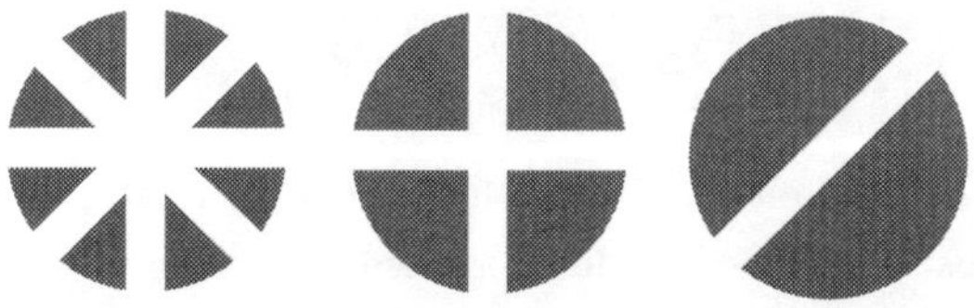

2 3 1

37. Solution 51. The missing number is 13. The numbers on either side of the vertical line in each circle should add to the same, although each circle has different totals. Thus in C, 8+12+17+8=45, and 13+15+4+[13]=45. Multiplying the [missing 13] by 4 we get 52; 52-1=51. **Go to 51.**

38. Solution 14. The different types of stars are shown below. **Go to 14.**

39. Solution B. This is a mirror-image of the others which are all rotations of the same shape. **Go to 3.**

40. Solution B. The bar of symbols rolls to the right by a step of 3 each stage. **Go to 29.**

41. Solution 6. The missing number is 2. Add both digits of the first number together (when there is more than one digit) and double the result to get the next number, and so on. Thus 1+9=10; 10x2=20; 2+0=2; 2x2=4; 4+0=4; 2x4=8; 8+0=8; 2x8=16; 1+6=7; 2x7=14; 1+4=5; 2x5=10; 1+0=1; 2x1=[2]; **Go to 6. Key 2.**

42. Solution 35. In all sets each digit of the middle row is the result of subtracting the above digit from 10. The bottom row is the result of doubling the entire top row. Thus a=9; b=2. Hence ba=29; 29+6=35. **Go to 35.**

43. Solution 4. The two numbers are 36 & 44. 36+44=80. 36 squared + 44 squared = 3232. 36/2=18. 18/4.5=4. (Or you could have divided 36 by 9.) **Go to 4.**

44. Solution B. **Go to 1. Key 3.**

45. Solution 28. In each cube the top number is arrived at by dividing the front number by a progressively reducing figure. In A, the divisor is 6. In B, 5; in C, 4; in D, 3. Thus 78/3=26. The right hand numbers are the result of subtracting the top numbers from the front numbers. Thus 78-26=52. The last digit of 52=2; 26+2=28. **Go to 28. Key 4.**

46. Solution 19. The values are shown below. **Go to 19.**

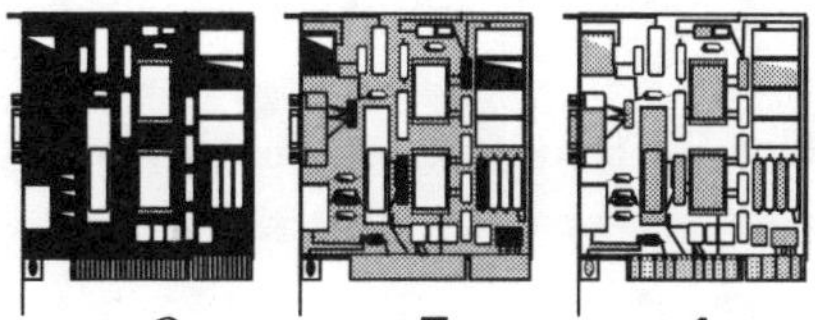

9 7 4

47. Solution B. This is a mirror-image of the others, all rotated versions of the same thing. **Go to 12.**

48. Solution D. The analogy is for a top-bottom mirror-image. The others are rotations, or have internal changes. **Go to 9. Key 4.**

49. Solution C. The element pointed to below has been changed in this robot. **Go to 37.**

50. Solution C. This is a mirror-image of the others, which are all rotated versions of the same puzzle. **Go to 5.**

SECTION FIVE

51. Solution 8. 6 ovals enclose the spot, as shown below. 6+2=8. **Go to 8.**

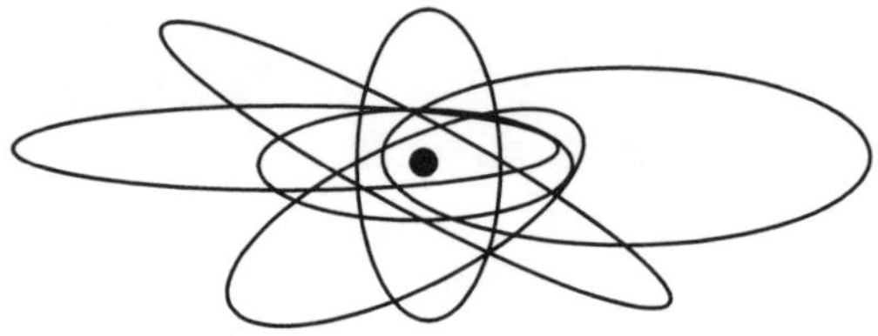

52. Solution C. The piece circled below has been displaced. **Go to 25. Key 6.**

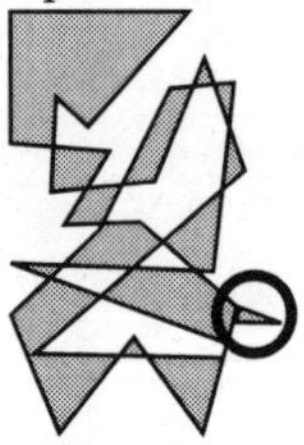

53. Solution 39. The missing number is 9. The central number, times the bottom-right number=the sum of the other two numbers. Thus 19+44=63; 7x[9]=63; 9+30=39. **Go to 39.**

54. Solution 24. 24+4=28; 28-9=19; 19x3=57; 57+3=60; 60/10=6; 6+3=9; 9 squared = 81; 81+19=100; 100/10=10. **Go to 24.**

55. Solution B. The two elements circled below have swapped places. **Go to 26. Key 8.**

56. Solution C. **Go to 44.**

57. Solution 22. The square is shown completed below. The total of the missing numbers is 45. 45-23=22. **Go to 22.**

8	9	17	25	-16	-8	0
-1	7	15	16	24	-17	-9
-10	-2	6	14	22	23	-18
-19	-11	-3	5	13	21	29
28	-13	-12	-4	4	12	20
19	27	-14	-6	-5	3	11
10	18	26	-15	-7	1	2

58. Solution 21. Multiply the weights by their positions to find the force applied.
On the left side we have (from the left):
(2x10=20)+(2x7=14)+(7x5=35)+(3x4=12)=81.
On the right we have:
(3x10=30)+(5x4=20)+(7x2=14)=64.
Thus we need 81-64=17 to balance the system. The block is at position 1, therefore we have 17x1=17. 17+4=21. **Go to 21. Key 1.**

59. Solution 23. 23+51=74; 51-23=28; 23x51=1173. **Go to 23.**

60. Solution B. The completed pattern is shown below. **Go to 18.**

■	✖	✦	★	☆	■	✖	✦	★	☆	■	✖	✦	★	☆	■	✖	✦	★
☆	■	✖	✦	★	☆	■	✖	✦	★	☆	■	✖	✦	★	☆	■	✖	✦
★	☆	■	✖	✦	★	☆	■	✖	✦	★	☆	■	✖	✦	★	☆	■	✖
✦	✖	■	☆	★	✦	✖	■	☆	★	✦	✖	■	☆	★	✦	✖	■	☆
✦	★	☆	■	✖	✦	★	☆	■	✖	✦	★	☆	■	✖	✦	★	☆	■
✖	✦	★	☆	■	✖	✦	★	☆	■	✖	✦	★	☆	■	✖	✦	★	☆

Section Five Keycodes = 43-42=1. Go to Puzzle 1, Section Six.

Puzzle 1

2

You've made it into the final section. A tough one to start. Pick the odd-one-out and take the number under it as your passcode to the next puzzle.

A **B** **C** **D**

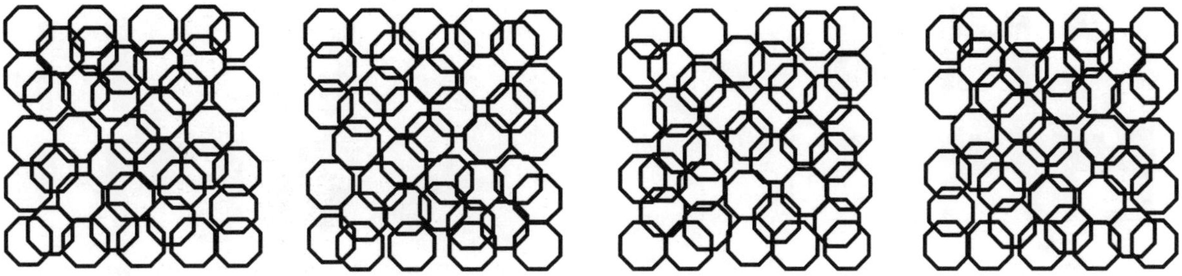

35 **12** **23** **49**

Puzzle 2

Which of the surrounding plans makes the cube in the middle? Choose your passcode accordingly.

A=Passcode **50. B**=Passcode **7. C**=Passcode **31. D**=Passcode **19.**

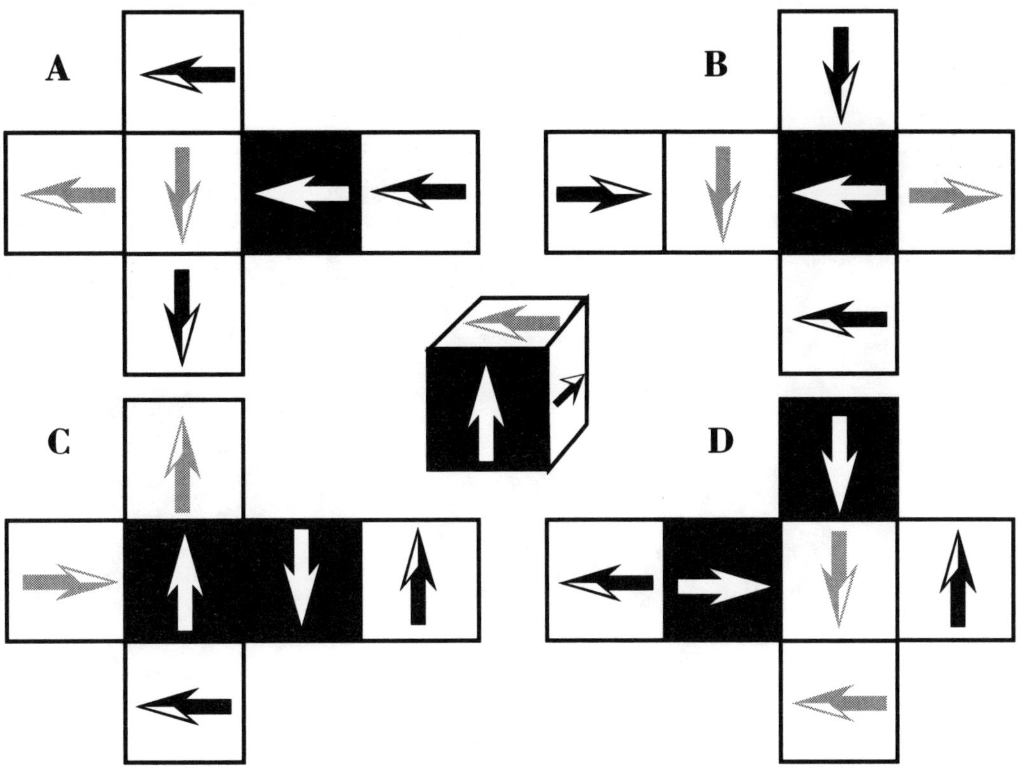

Puzzle 3

In each line, the first two columns multiplied equal the remaining columns summed. A, B, C or D gives you line 4 and the passcode. Each type of disc has a unique single value.

A=Passcode **47. B**=Passcode **40. C**=Passcode **13. D**=Passcode **59.**

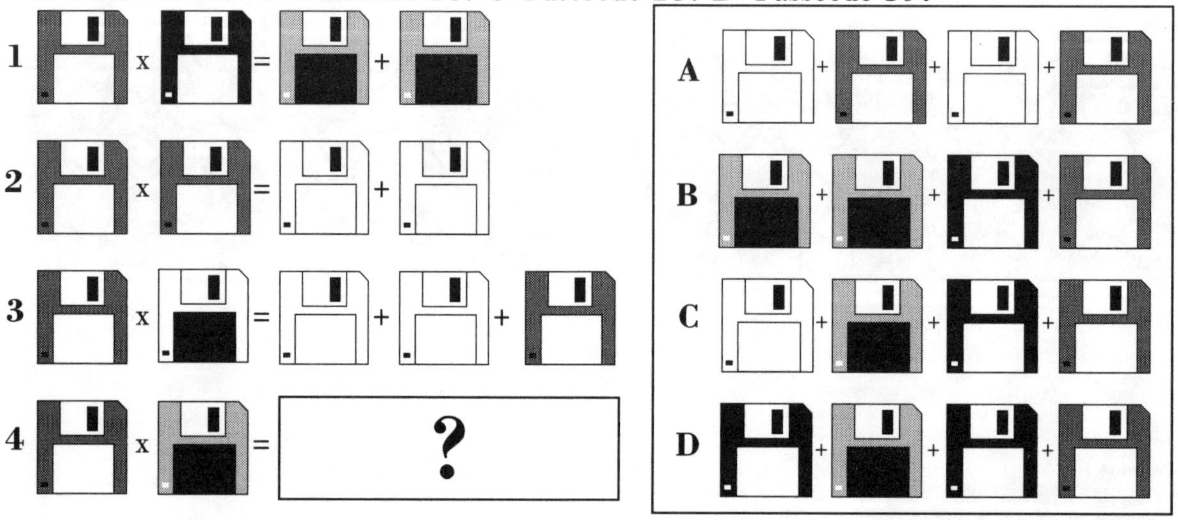

Puzzle 4

Here is a vertical view of Adrian Smith's power supply unit. The missing number in D is your next passcode.

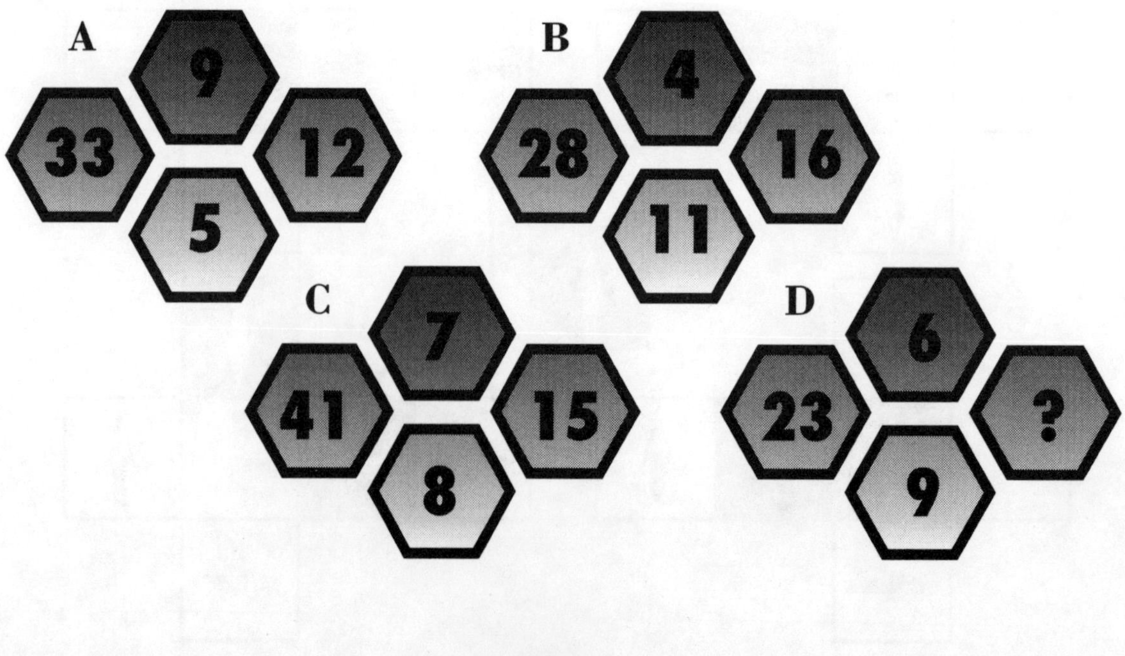

Puzzle 5

Three of these shapes can be fitted together to make the hexagon on the left. The shape that does not fit contains the passcode.

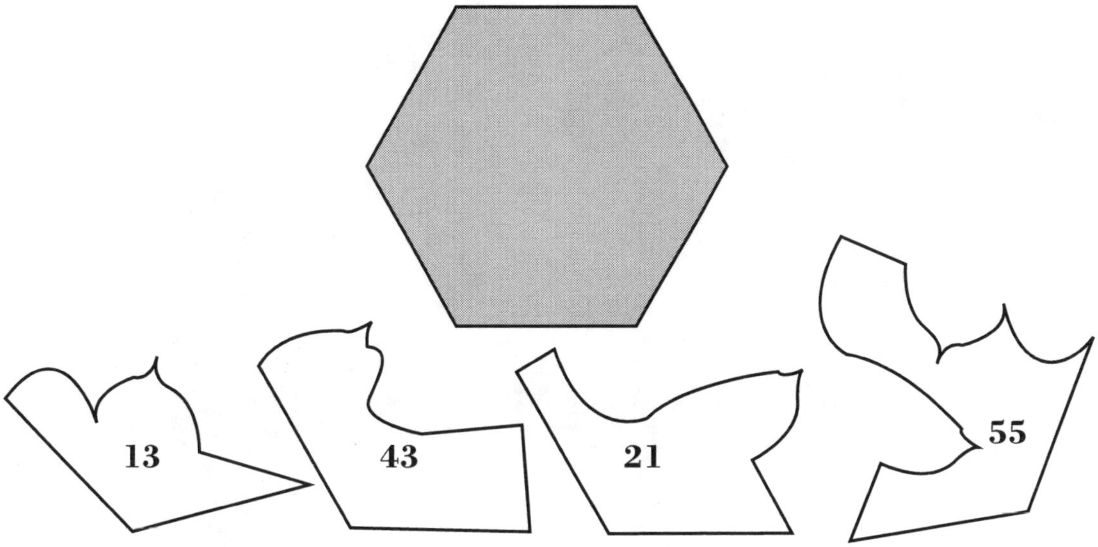

Puzzle 6

Pick the odd-one-out to find your next passcode. Try not to go 'bog-eyed'.

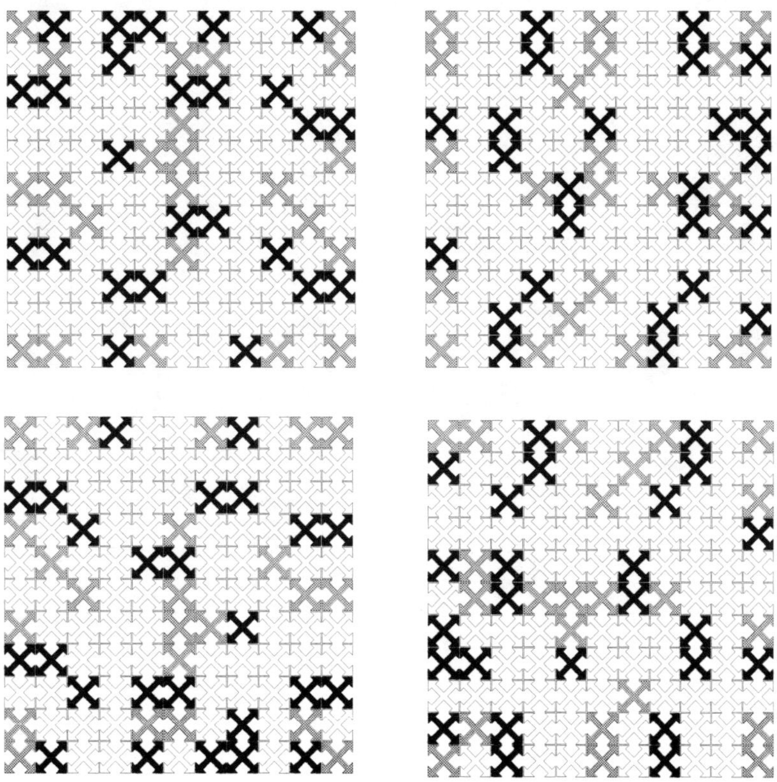

A=32

B=48

C=9

D=16

Puzzle 7

4

Four times the missing number in D is your next passcode.

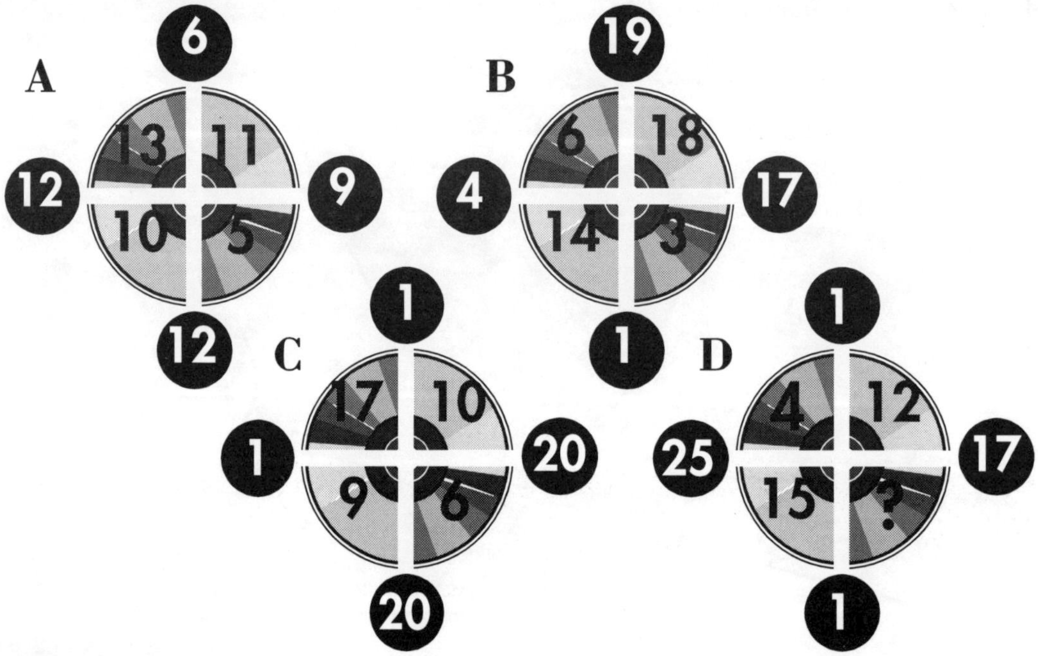

Puzzle 8

Your next passcode is below the odd-one-out in this set.

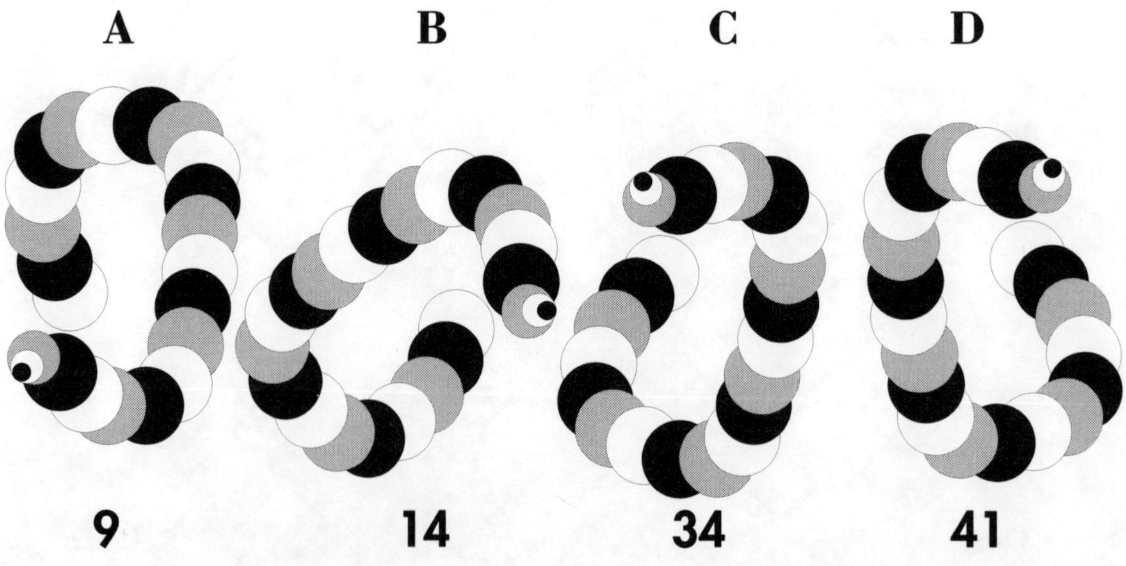

Puzzle 9

Work out the value of the subtraction sum and add 30 to find your passcode to the next puzzle.

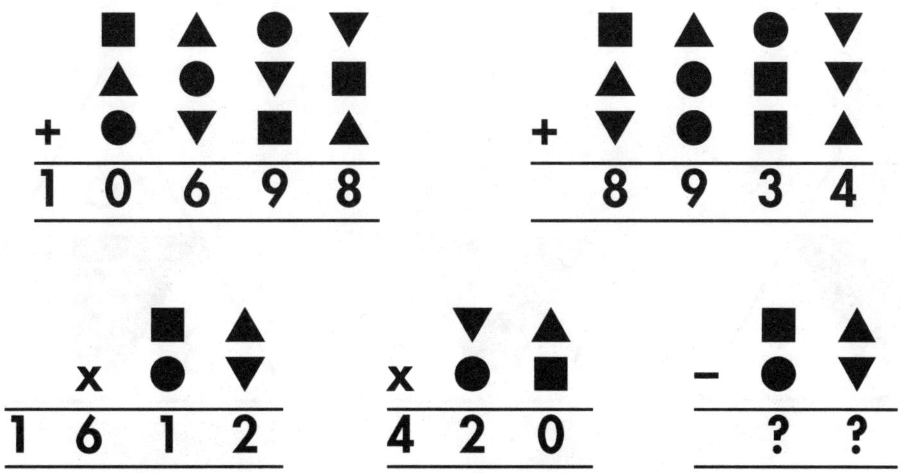

Puzzle 10

Pick the odd-one-out and choose your passcode accordingly.

A=Passcode **39. B**=Passcode **21. C**=Passcode **58. D**=Passcode **19.**

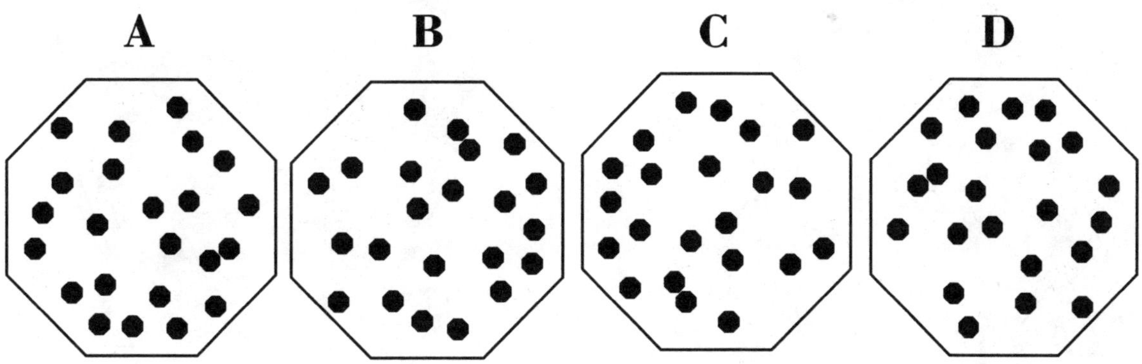

Puzzle 11

Add 37 to the missing number in C to find your next passcode.

A B C

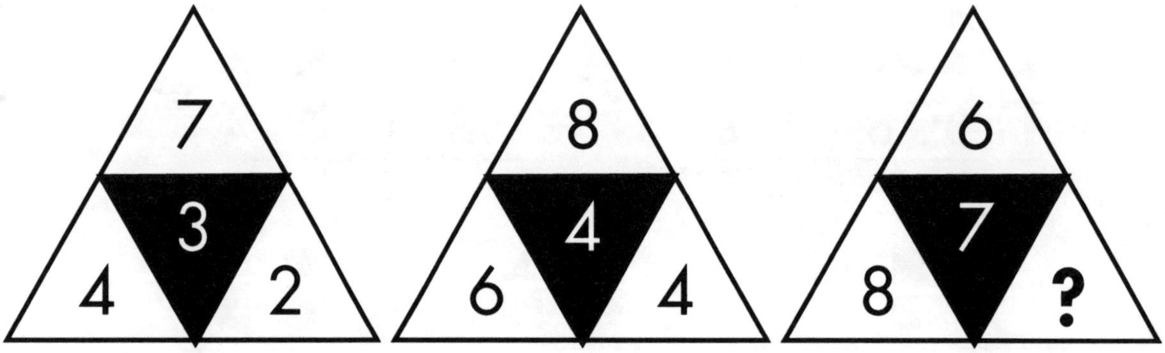

Puzzle 12

Apart from B being upside down in comparison to A, how many differences are there between the two pictures? Add 30 to the number of differences to find your next passcode.

A

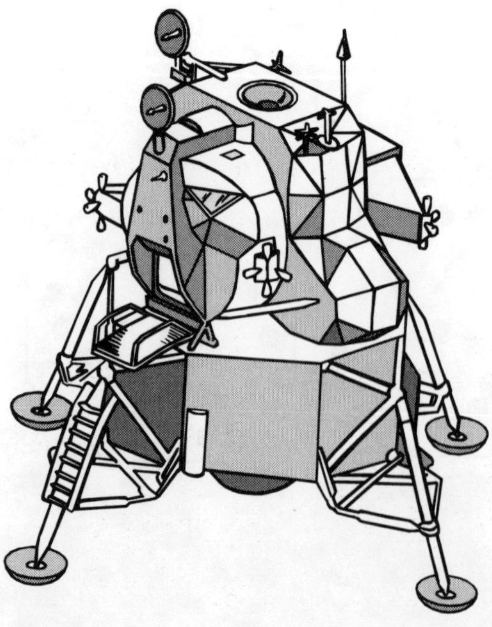

B

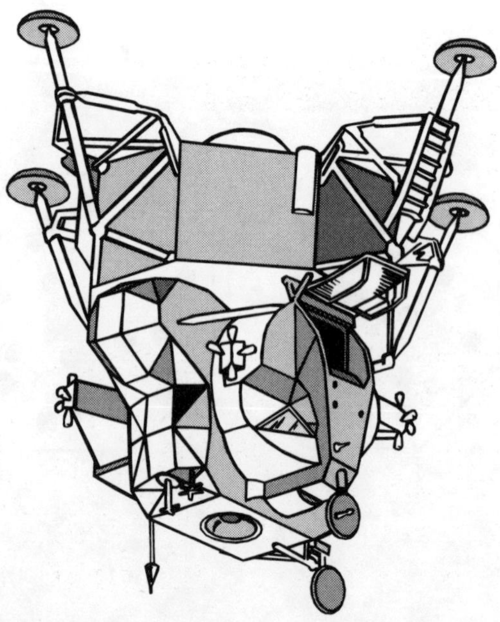

Puzzle 13

Multiply the missing number by 4 and subtract 3 to find the passcode to your next puzzle. Start at 28.

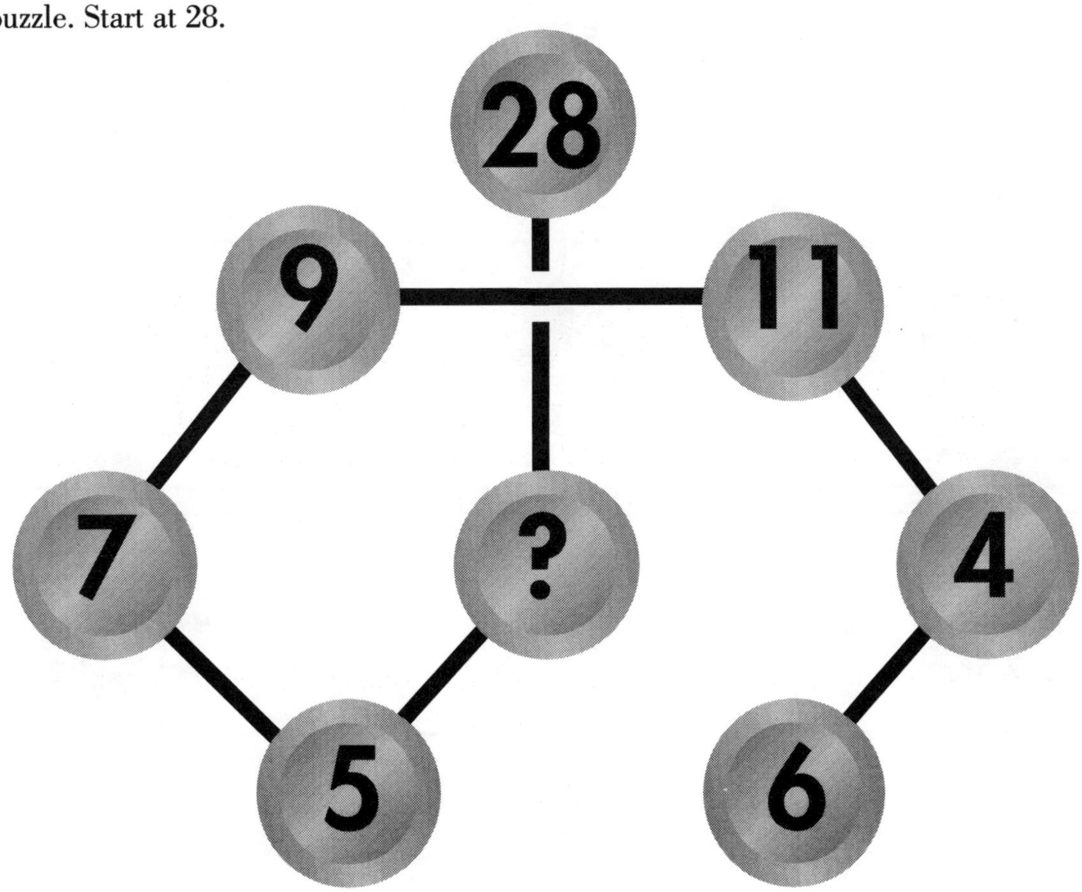

Puzzle 14

Pick the odd-one-out from this set and use the number below it as your passcode to the next puzzle.

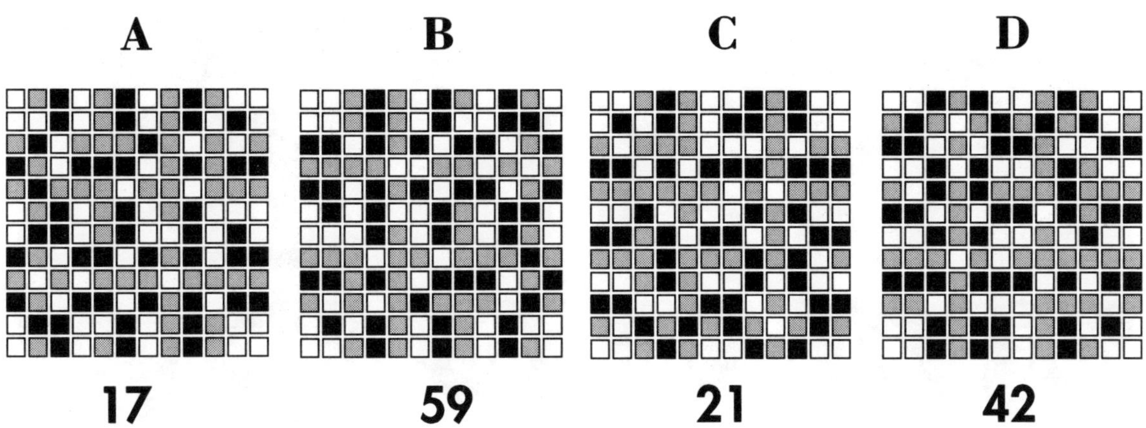

Puzzle 15

You next passcode is the same as the missing value in the lower set of scales.

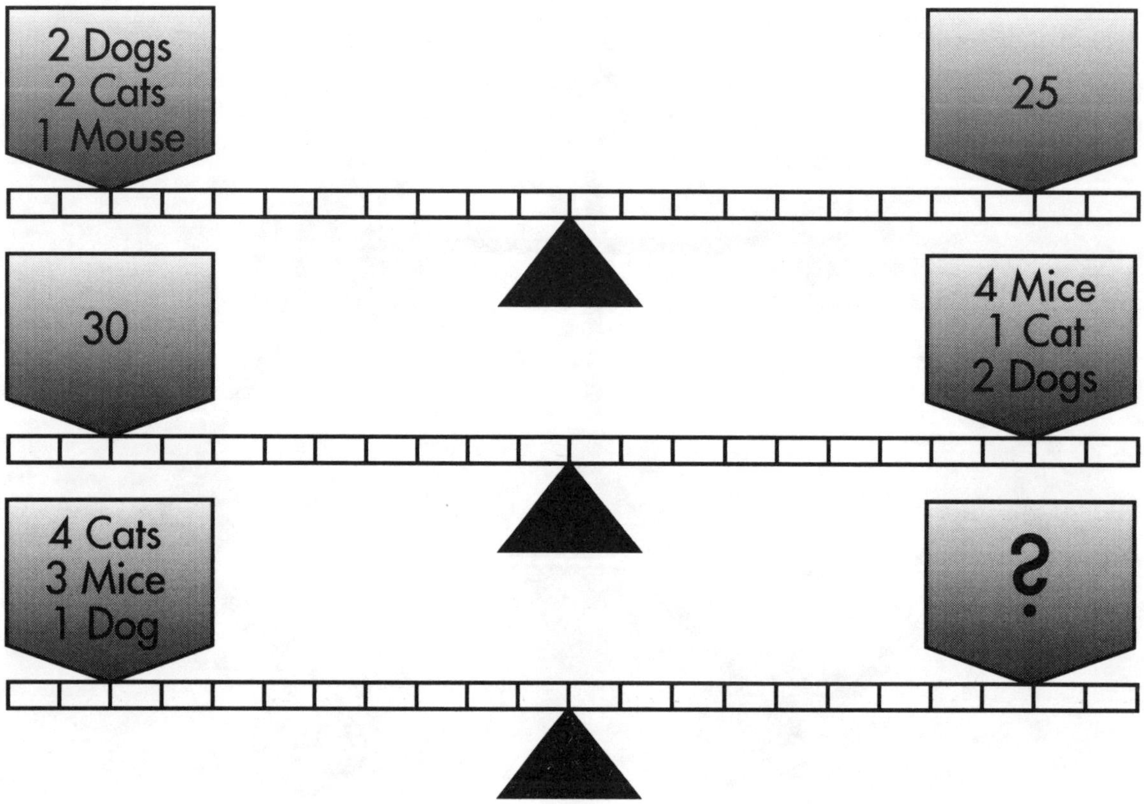

Puzzle 16

Here's a real test of your numerical skill. Subtract 16 from the missing number in C to find your next passcode.

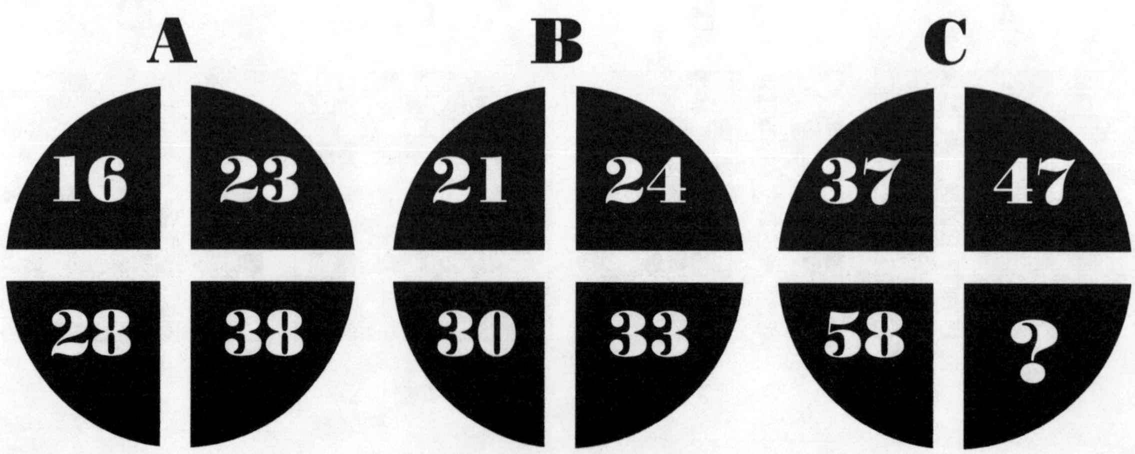

Puzzle 17

Add 21 to the missing value in this puzzle to find your next passcode.

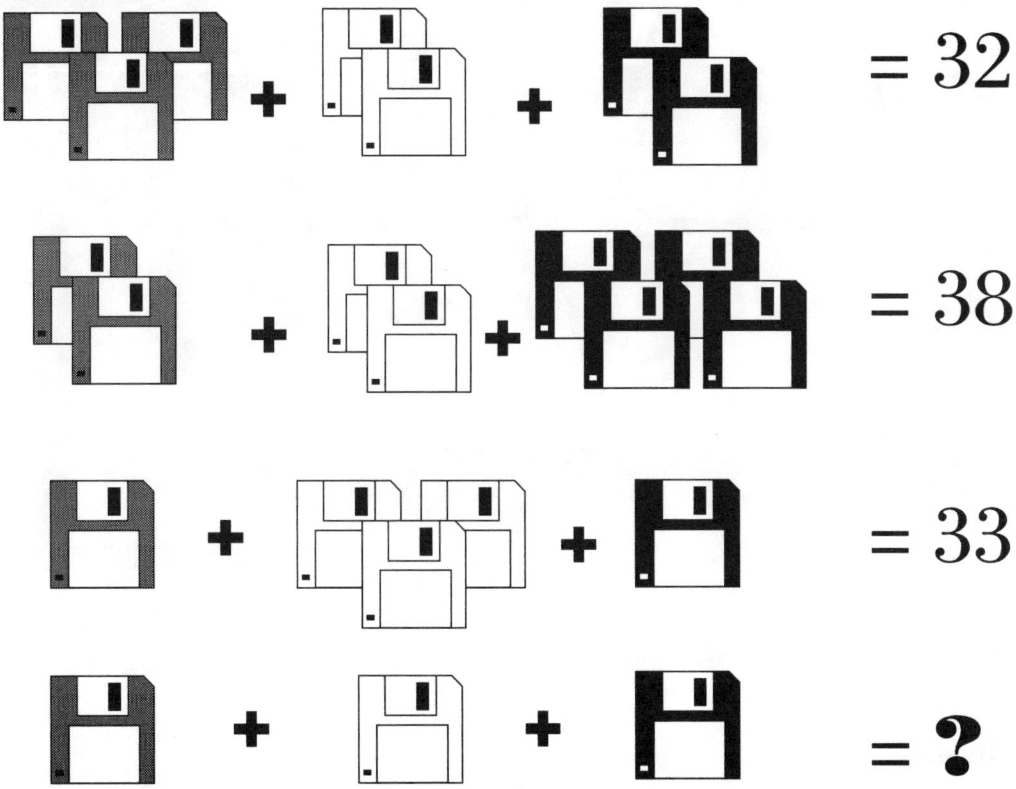

Puzzle 18

Pick the odd-one-out and use the number below it as your passcode to the next puzzle.

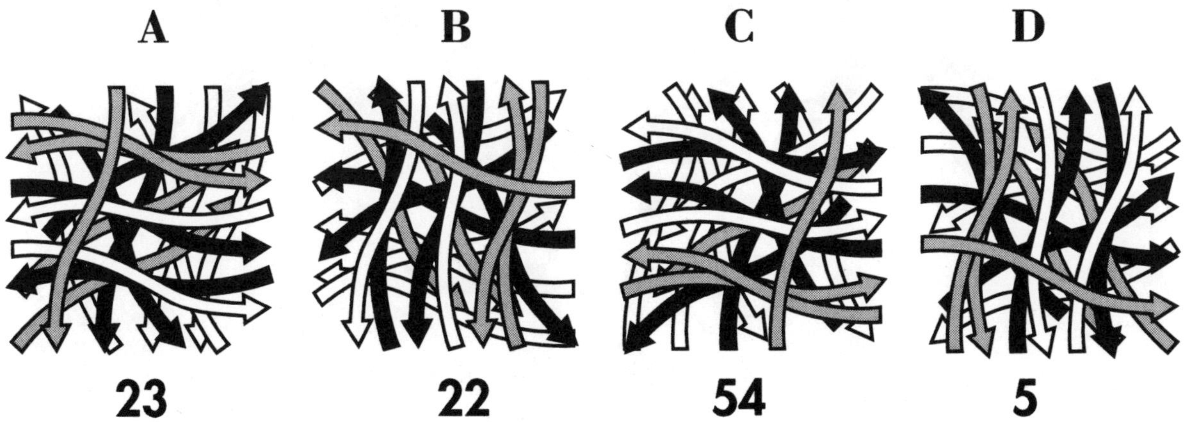

Puzzle 19

Continue the sequence and add 42 to the missing number to find your next passcode.

Puzzle 20

This is a test of your lateral thinking. Three times the missing number in C is your passcode to the next puzzle.

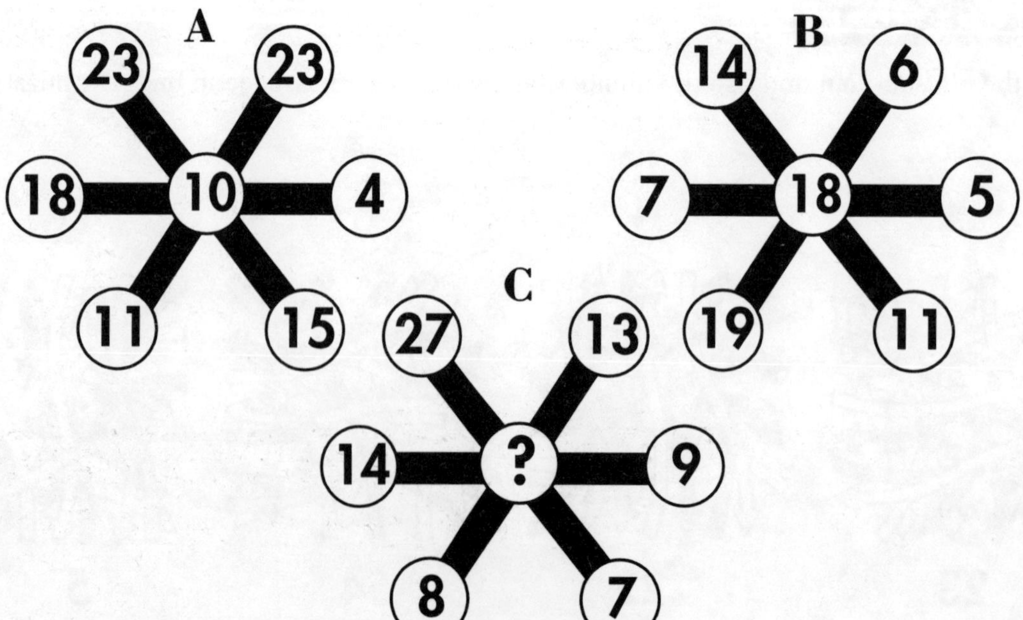

Puzzle 21

Put in the missing numbers in the shaded squares so that each black square is surrounded by 4 numbers that, multiplied together, make the number inside it. Deduct 21 from the total of the missing numbers added together to find your next passcode.

6		3		2		5		1		7		4		3
	90		120		80		90		189		336		384	
1														8
	90		320		192		378		945		60		160	
9														5
	324		384		192		126		840		60		60	
6														4
	90		840		448		96		192		144		324	
1		5		7		8		2		4		3		9

Puzzle 22

Add 27 to the missing number in C to find your next passcode on your tour of cyber-reality.

A

	7	
10	12	15
	8	
	10	

B

	9	
7	26	11
	5	
	4	

C

	3	
16	9	?
	19	
	7	

Puzzle 23

Something different! Add 41 to the missing number in D to find your next passcode.

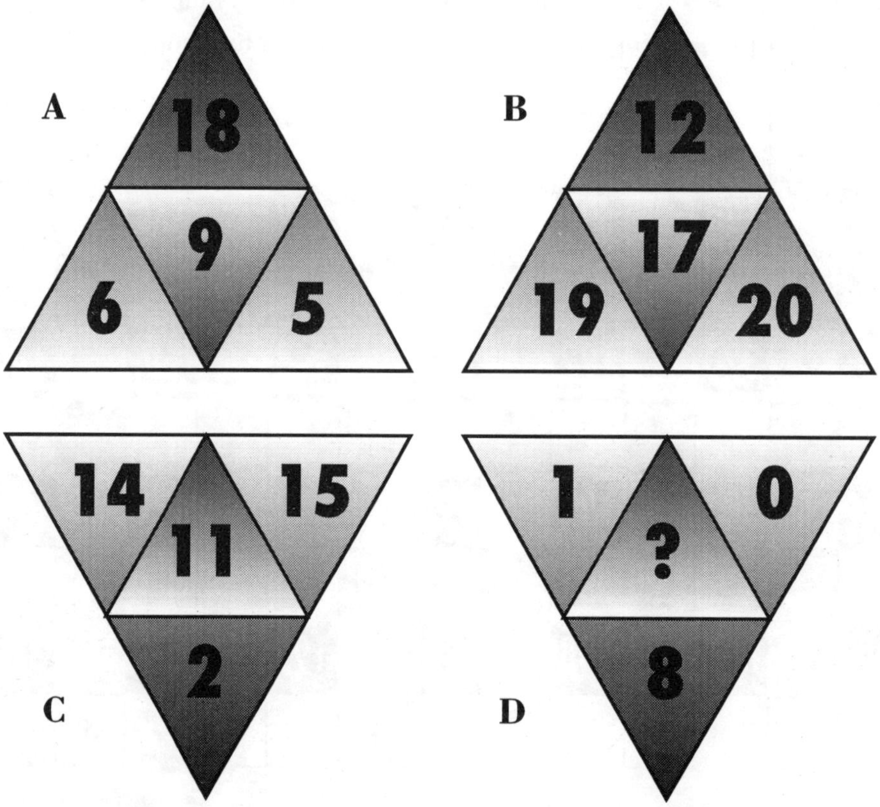

Puzzle 24

Pick the odd-one-out from these circuit sections, and choose your passcode accordingly.

A=Passcode **15.** **B**=Passcode **33.** **C**=Passcode **47.** **D**=Passcode **10.**

A B C D

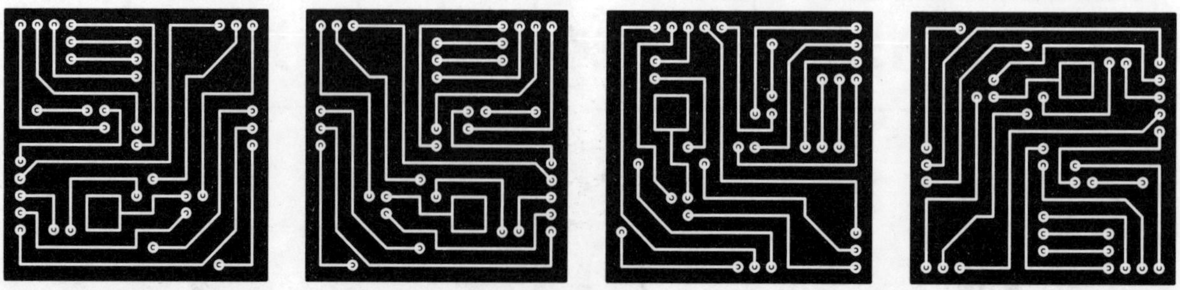

Puzzle 25

Add 22 to the missing number in this puzzle to get your next passcode.

A B C D

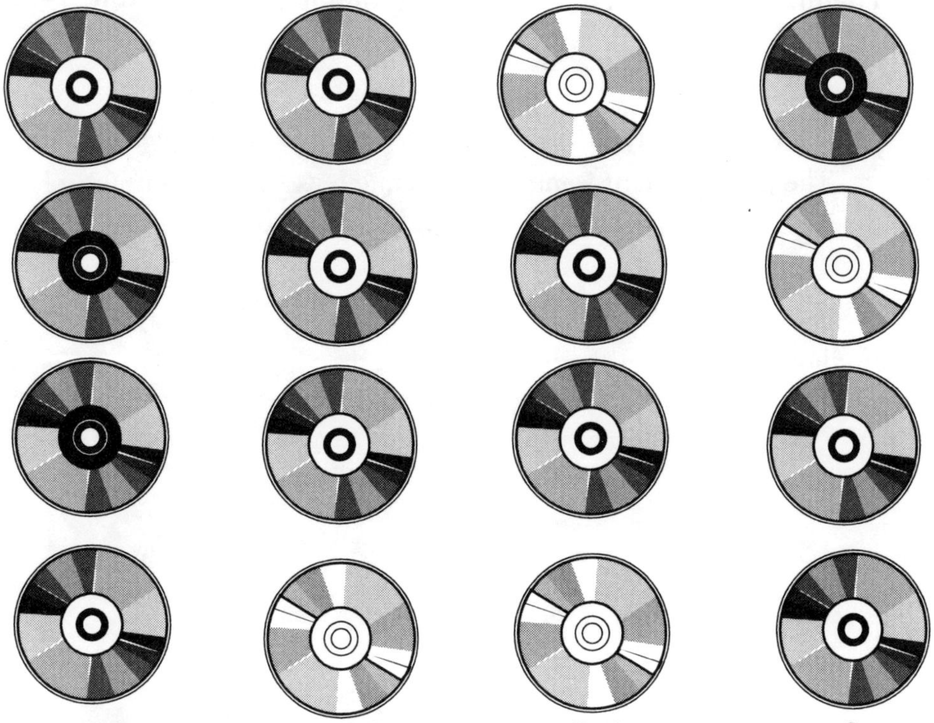

22 29 26 ?

Puzzle 26

This system is in balance. Work out the missing value and add 34 to find your passcode to the next puzzle.

Puzzle 27

As a result of your success so far, four of the circuits in Adrian's processor network are competing for resources – the puzzle circuit, the math circuit, the logic circuit and the nervousness circuit. The total pool of available interrupt power is currently set at 221 standard units.

The math circuit is demanding four times as much power as nervousness circuit, plus four units more. The puzzle circuit wants twice as much as the logic circuit, plus ten units more. The logic circuit needs three times as much as the math circuit, plus sixteen units more.

When you know how much power the logic circuit is drawing in standard units, subtract 3 and use that as your passcode to your next puzzle.

Puzzle 28

Add 45 to the missing number in D to find your next passcode.

Puzzle 29

Multiply the missing number in C by 8 and add 2 to find the passcode to your next puzzle.

A B C

Puzzle 30

Pick the odd-one-out and choose your passcode accordingly.

A=Passcode **10.** **B**=Passcode **42.** **C**=Passcode **17.** **D**=Passcode **29.**

A B C D

Puzzle 31

The missing number in C is your next passcode.

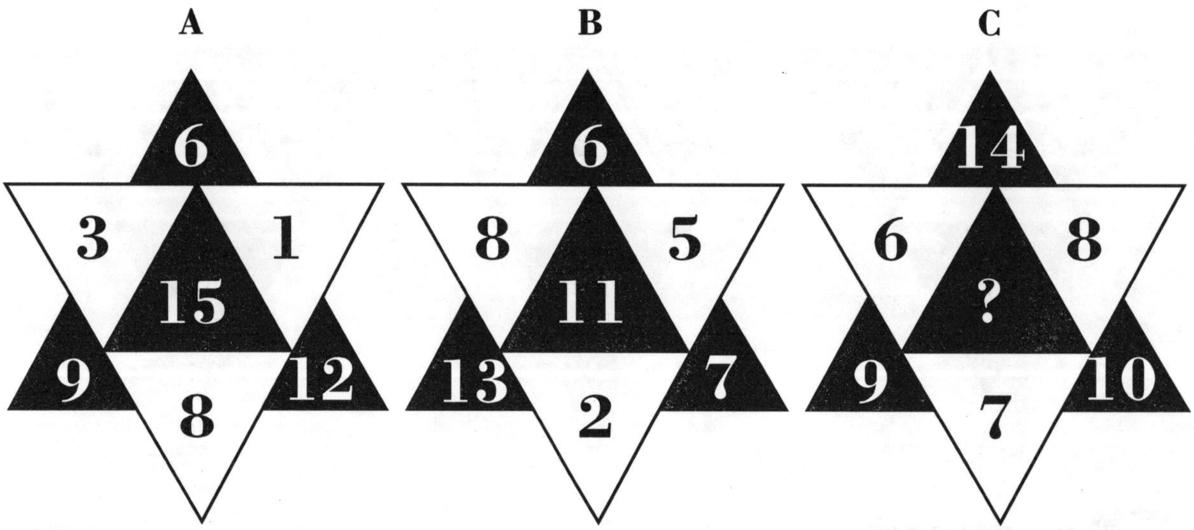

Puzzle 32

Deduct 5 from the value of the missing number in this puzzle to find your next passcode.

Puzzle 33

The missing number in this set is your next passcode.

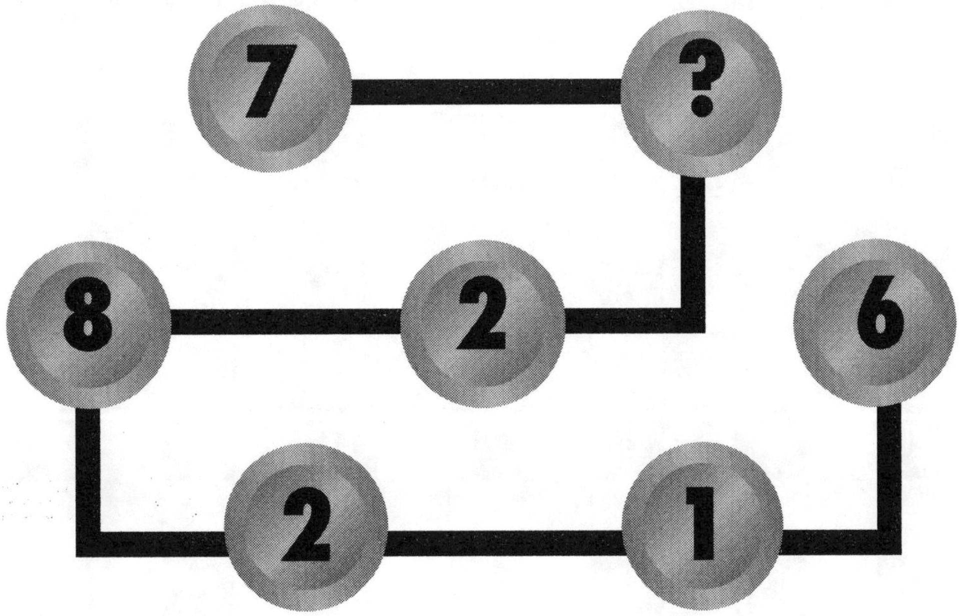

Puzzle 34

Find the missing digit in D and use that, with 10 added, as your next passcode.

A

3	1	6	2	8
5	9	2	8	4
2	6	5	0	3
1	8	4	3	5
4	0	1	6	2

B

7	8	1	3	5
1	4	5	4	7
3	5	7	6	0
0	4	3	5	1
4	3	2	1	9

C

2	8	4	9	7
3	6	2	1	5
5	3	9	0	8
4	2	0	5	2
1	5	3	4	0

D

3	8	6	7	5
4	1	4	3	6
0	5	4	1	7
2	6	1	5	3
6	4	3	3	?

Puzzle 35

Fill missing numbers in the shaded squares so that the digits surrounding each black square add to that number. Subtract 72 from the total of missing digits to find your next passcode.

7		9		3		5		8		4		2		6
	28		26		21		22		19		20		20	
4														3
	24		21		25		19		15		29		24	
8														4
	20		14		20		20		17		23		24	
3														9
	19		19		17		20		20		13		15	
6		5		7		2		8		3		2		1

Puzzle 36

Your next passcode is 5 less than the number that exactly balances the bottom set of scales.

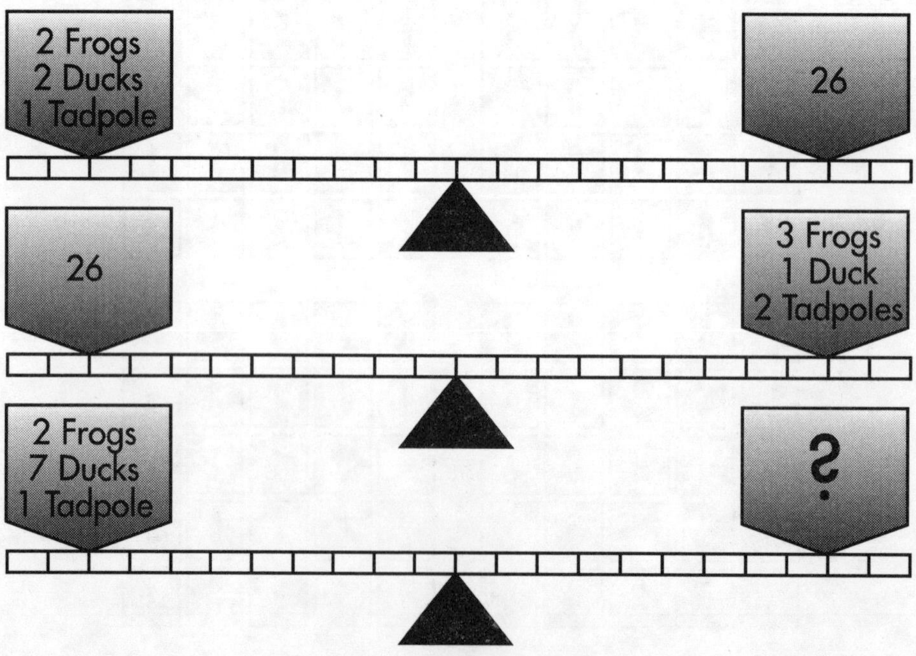

Puzzle 37

Multiply the missing number in C by 4 to find your next passcode.

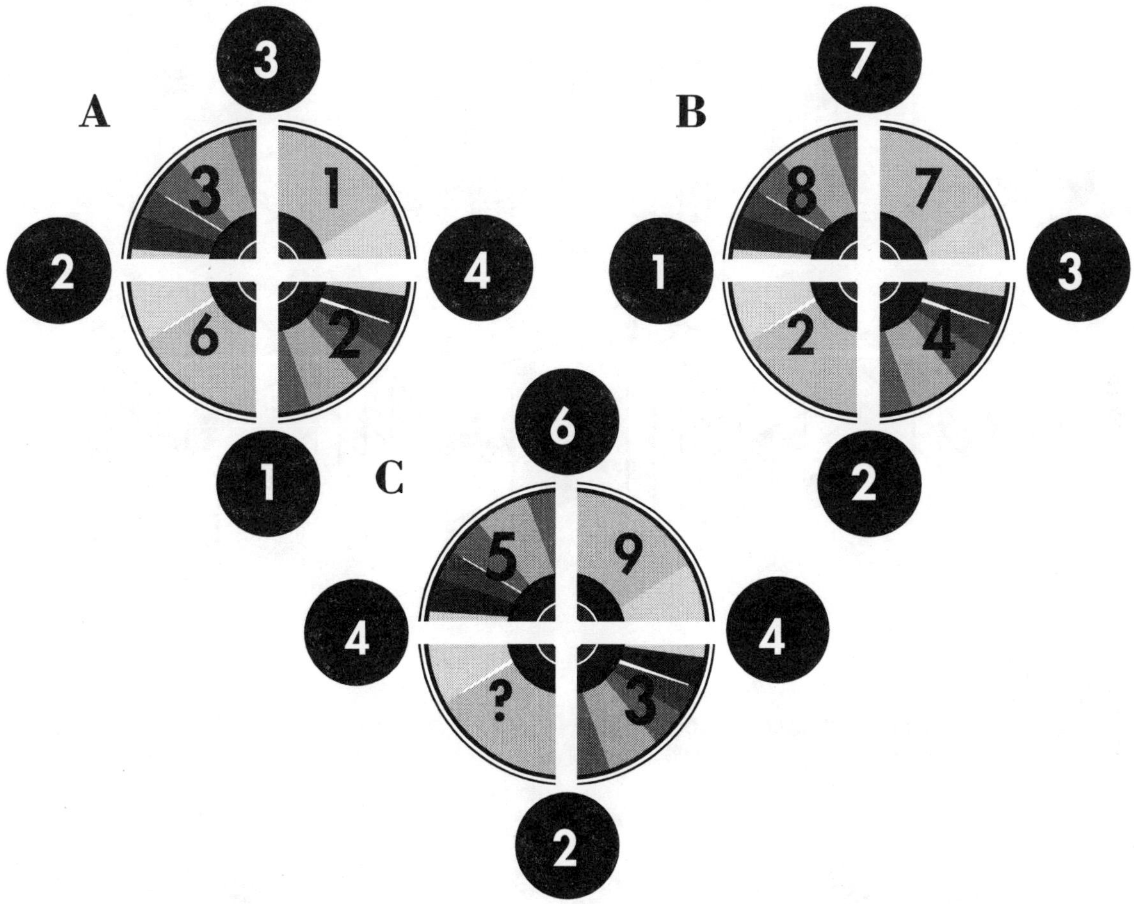

Puzzle 38

Continue the sequence and deduct 34 from the missing number find your next passcode.

Puzzle 39

What comes next: A, B, C or D? The number under the solution is your next passcode.

A B C D

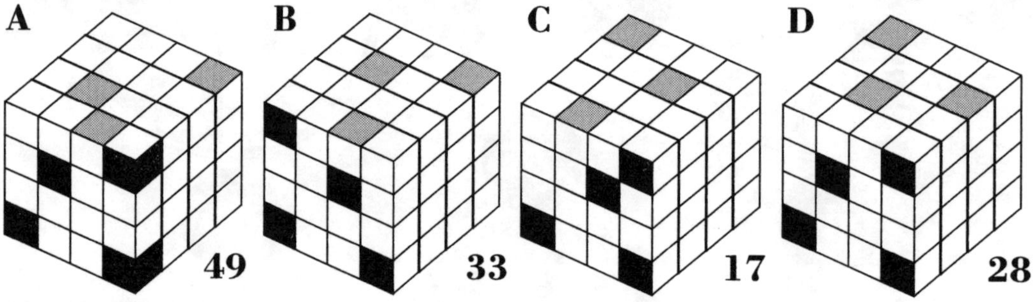

Puzzle 40

The solution to D is your next passcode.

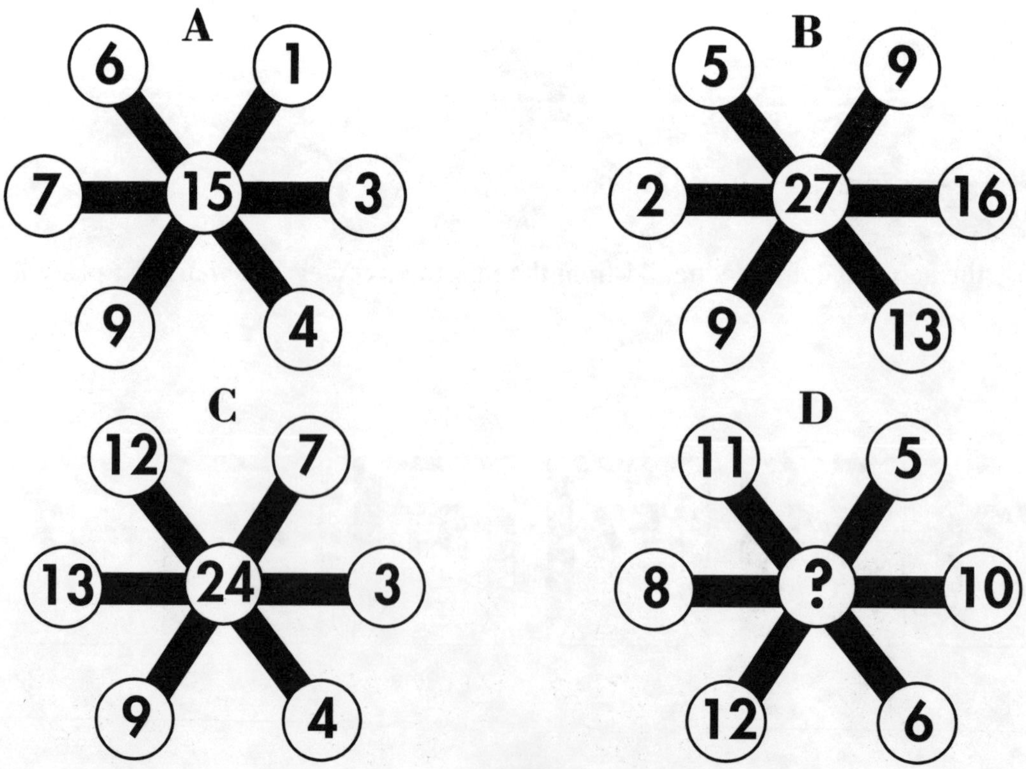

Puzzle 41

Subtract 2 from the number of differences between A & B to find your next passcode.

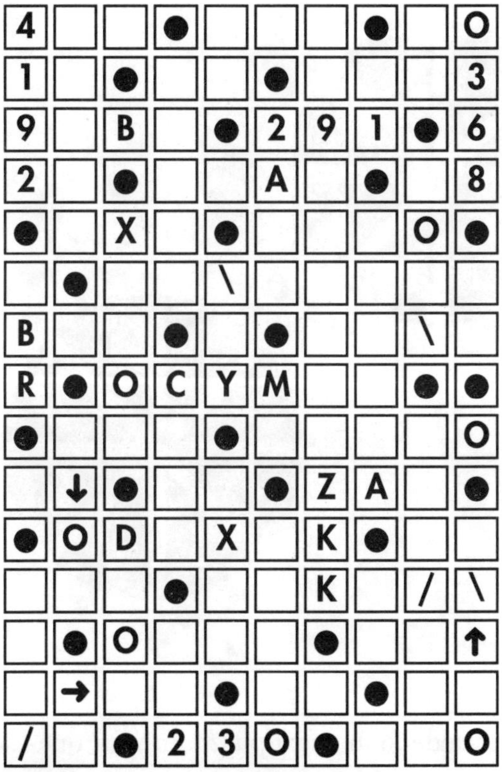

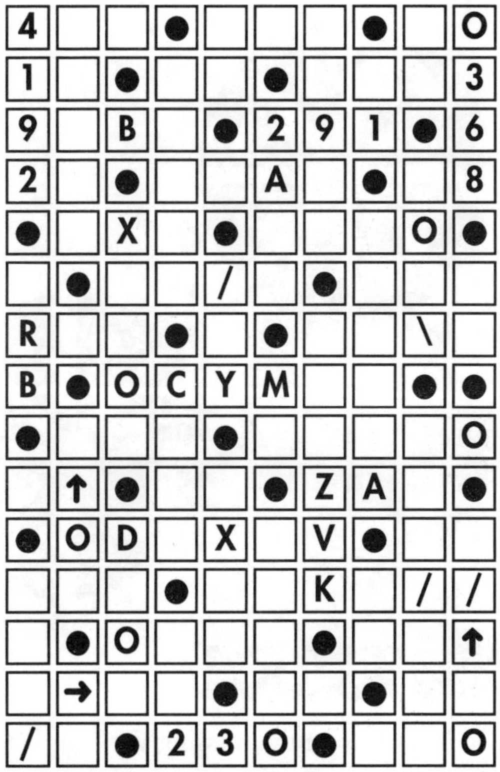

Puzzle 42

What comes next? Choose your passcode accordingly.

A=Passcode **13.** **B**=Passcode **29.** **C**=Passcode **8.** **D**=Passcode **48.**

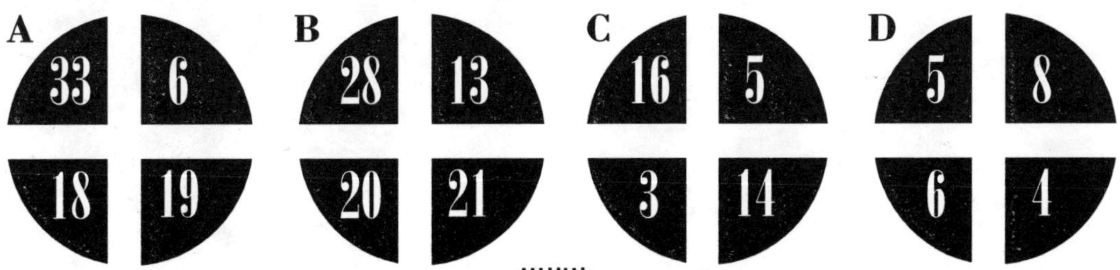

Puzzle 43

Your next passcode on your escape-route from cyber-reality is the missing value in D.

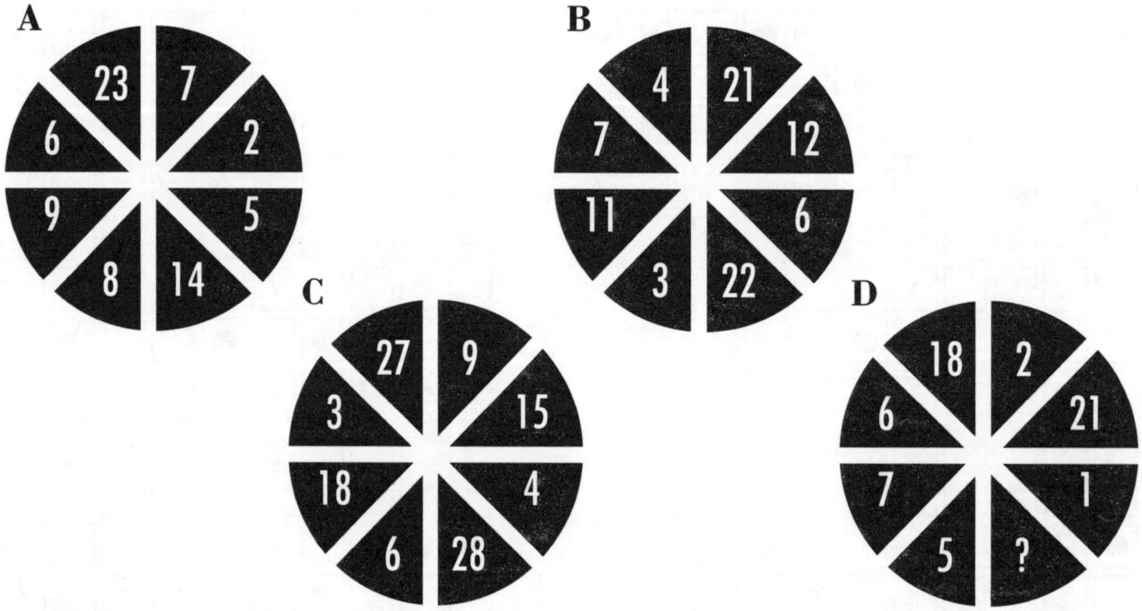

Puzzle 44

Deduct 29 from the missing value in D to find the passcode to the next puzzle in your quest.

Puzzle 45

Pick the odd-one-out and use the number above it as your next passcode.

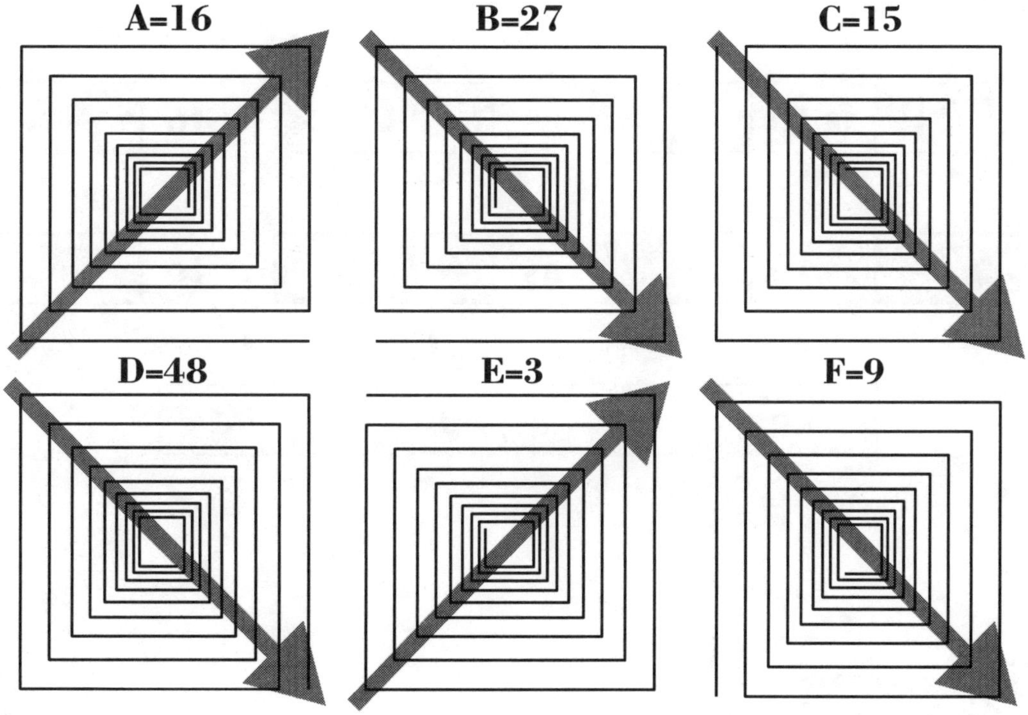

Puzzle 46

Subtract 7 from the missing number in this puzzle to find your next passcode.

Puzzle 47

Use the first digit of the solution to this puzzle as your next passcode.

11980 is to **57** as **32613** is to **45**

25674 is to **72** as **44557** is to **?**

A	B	C	D
46	75	15	33

Puzzle 48

Add 14 to the solution to this puzzle to find your next passcode.

7 9 4 6 7 5 4 7

6 3 3 6 8 7 4

2 1 8 4 2 3 6 ?

Puzzle 49

Fill out the missing numbers in this square using only the digits already supplied so that you make a magic square with each row, column and long diagonal totalling 27. When you have done that, subtract 93 from the total of all the missing digits to find your next passcode.

5				1
			8	
		7		
	5			
6				8

Puzzle 50

Pick the odd-one-out from A, B, C and D, compared to the example box immediately below, and use the number below it as your next passcode.

5	B	A	X	3
9	2	4	Z	K
B	G	H	4	7
L	5	J	M	R
2	P	I	O	N

A

5	B	A	X	3
9	2	4	Z	K
7	4	H	G	B
L	5	J	M	R
N	O	I	P	2

10

B

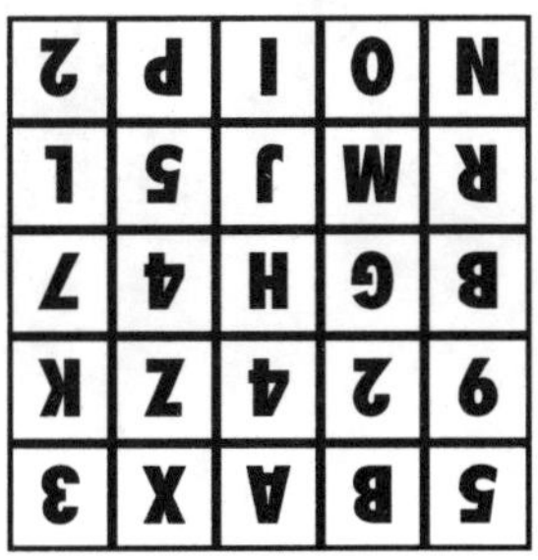

43

C

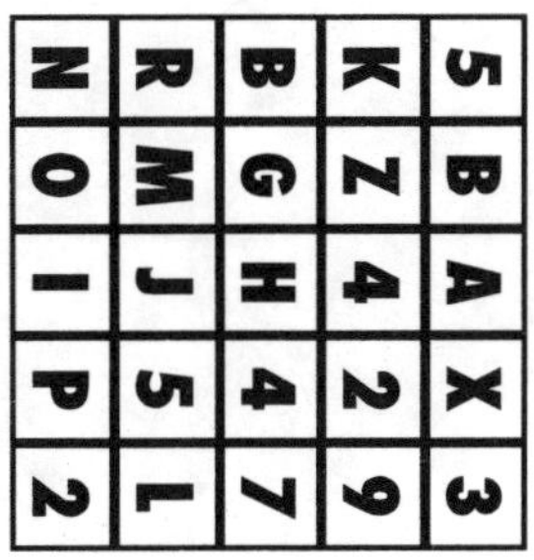

14

D

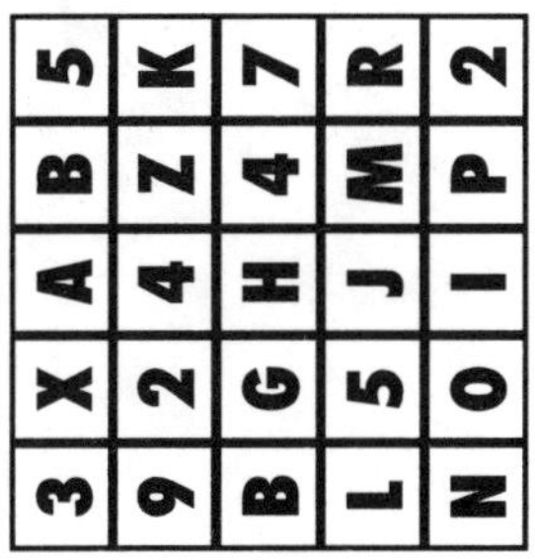

59

Puzzle 51

Complete the analogy and use the number below it as your next passcode.

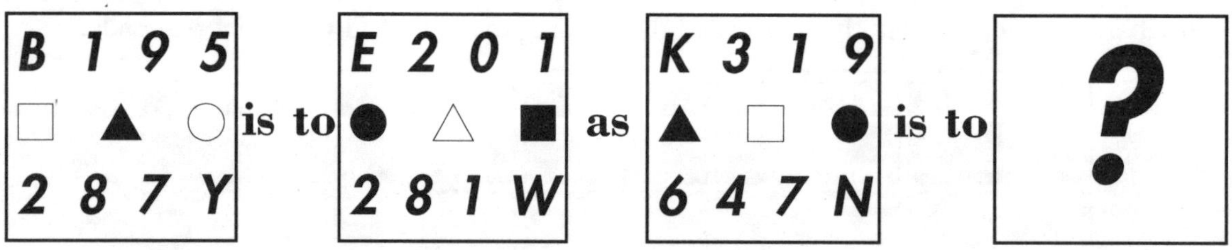

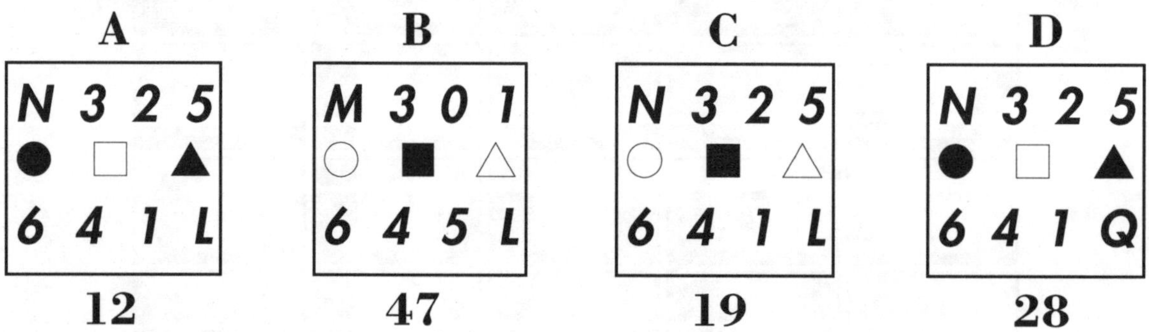

Puzzle 52

Subtract 20 from the missing number in this set to find your passcode to the next puzzle.

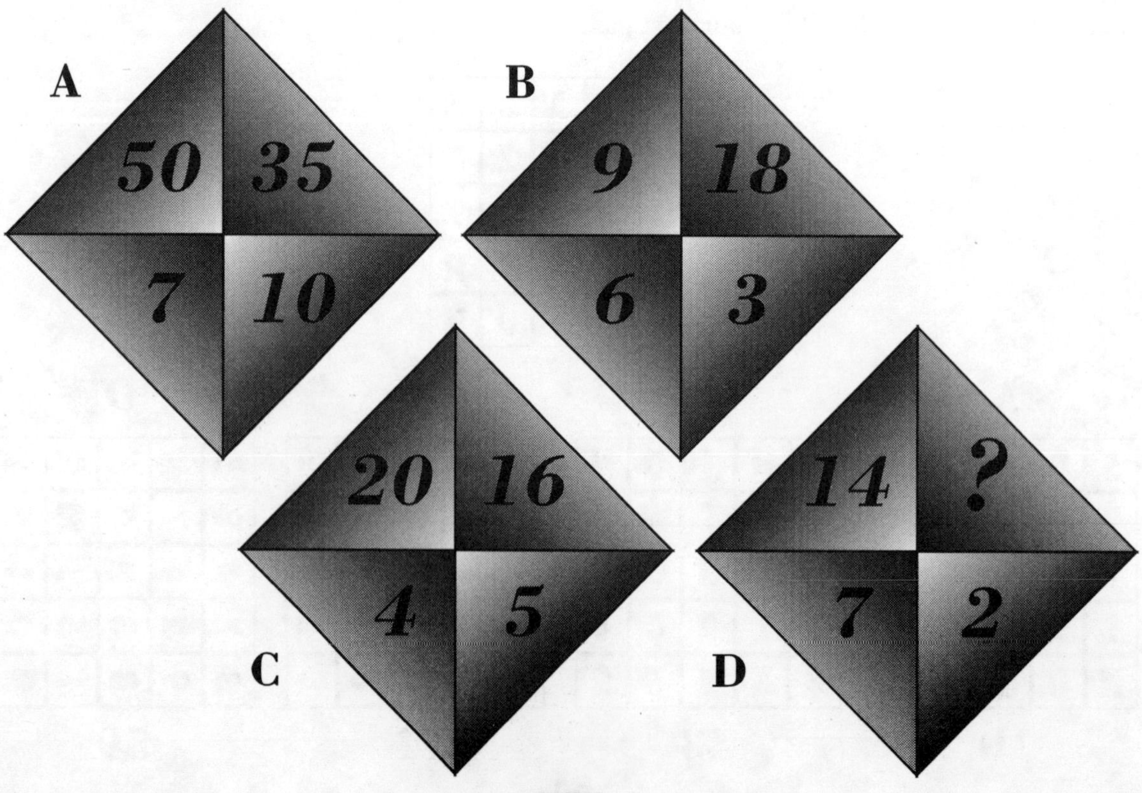

Puzzle 53

Pick the odd-one-out from these four examples. The middle number, plus 6, is your next passcode.

A

5	8	9	2	9
4	2	6	1	5
1	5	3	7	1
8	7	2	6	4
4	6	3	5	8

B

4	5	7	9	2
2	9	5	6	8
8	0	8	3	9
3	7	1	0	2
1	6	2	4	3

C

6	1	7	0	3
3	0	4	8	5
7	8	5	2	1
2	1	4	9	2
7	6	5	3	4

D

7	3	8	9	5
0	2	6	1	2
9	8	9	3	4
7	3	4	0	3
8	1	6	4	6

Puzzle 54

Solve for A, B & C to find your next passcode.

A	A	A	A
A	B	A	B
B	B	A	C
B	B	B	C
C	C	C	C
36	38	34	28

A
B
C

?

Puzzle 55

This is a test of lateral numerical reasoning. The missing number in C is your next passcode.

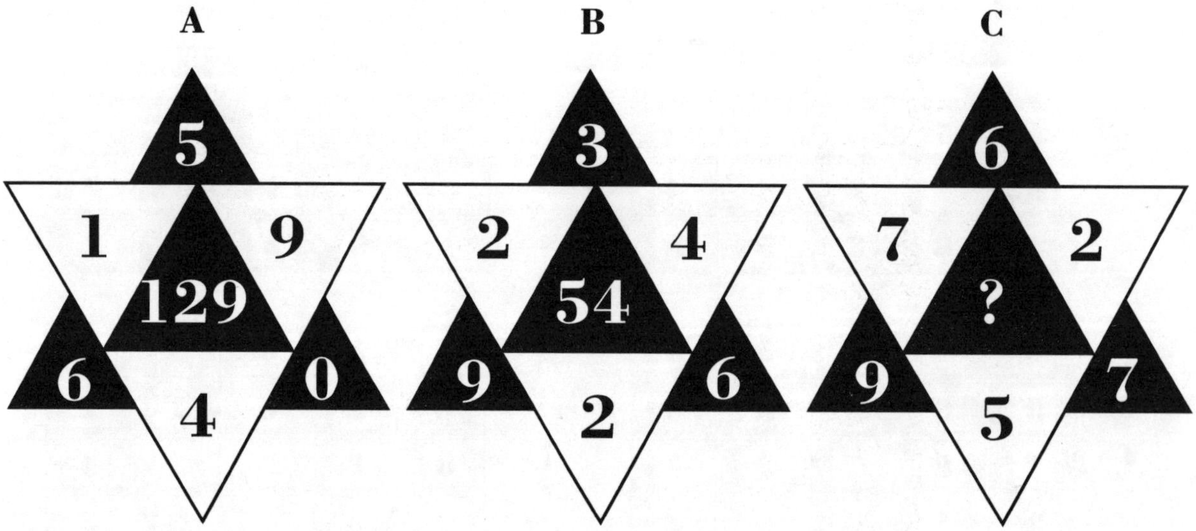

Puzzle 56

This symmetrical figure is divided into 3 zones, A, B & C. The number inside the zone which covers most area is your next passcode, and is not part of the puzzle.

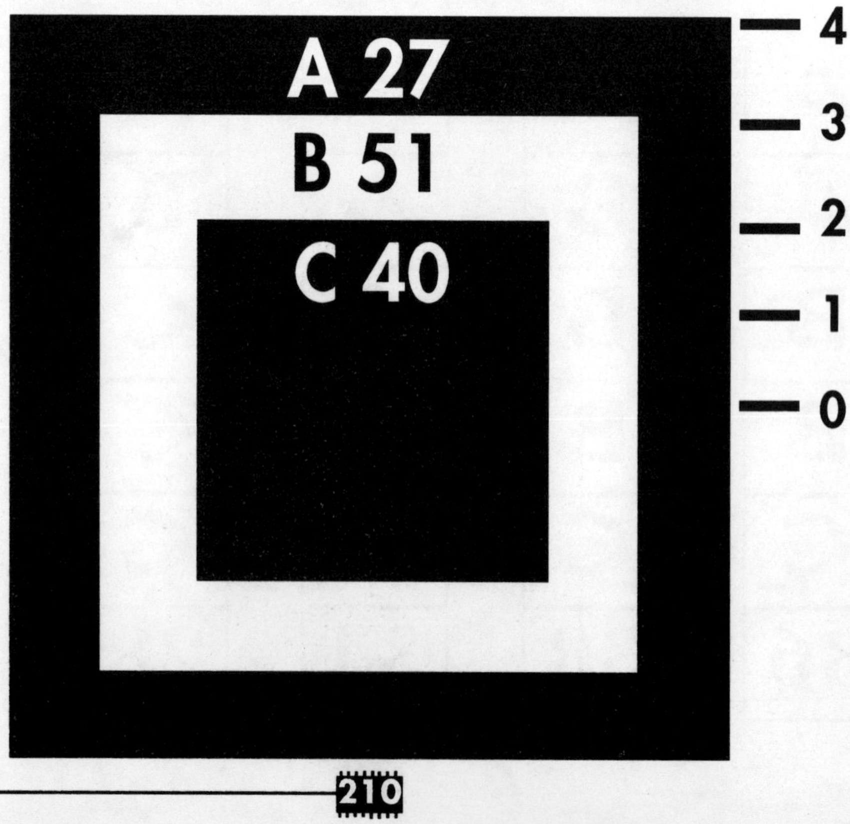

Puzzle 57

Pick the odd-one-out and find your next passcode accordingly.

A=6

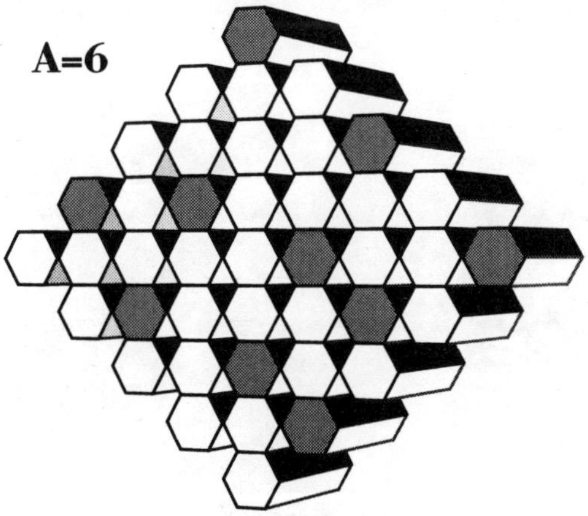

B=13

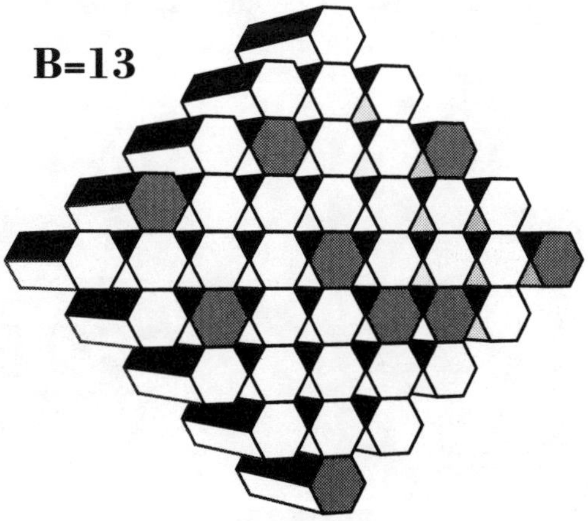

C=20

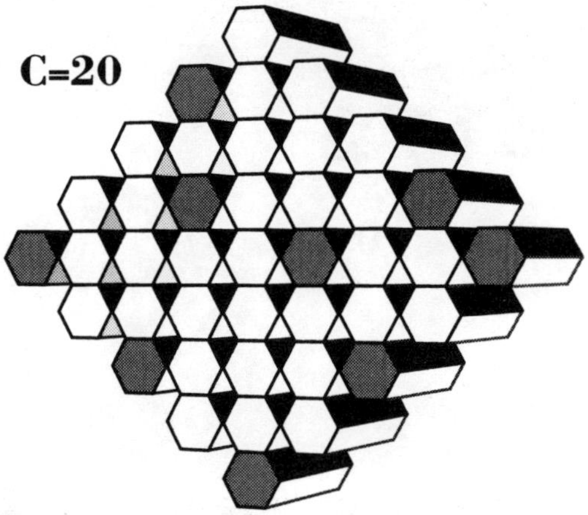

D=43

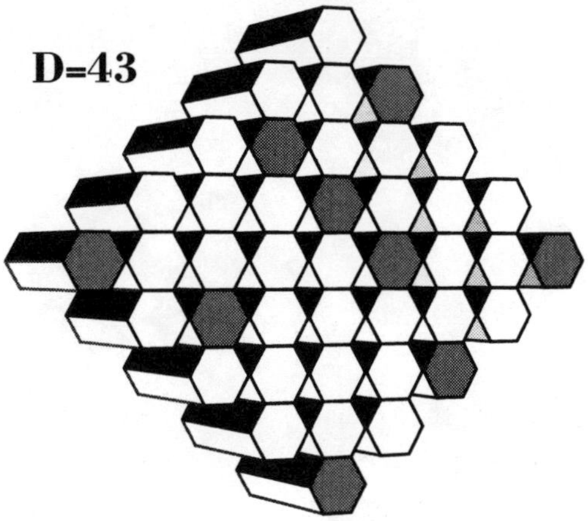

Puzzle 58

Your next passcode is the number that, when you add 6 to it and double the result, gives you the number that, when you add 42, produces a number that equals the square of the value of the roman numeral whose alphabetical position is one greater than the number you are seeking.

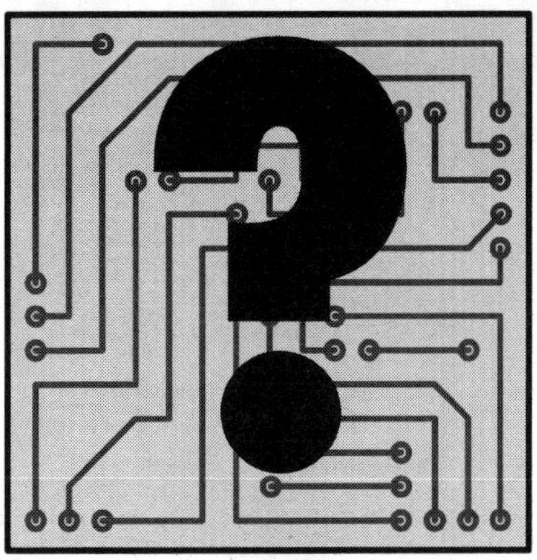

Puzzle 59

What is the missing number, A, B, C or D? Choose your passcode accordingly.
A=Passcode **25.** **B**=Passcode **27.** **C**=Passcode **44.** **D**=Passcode **31.**

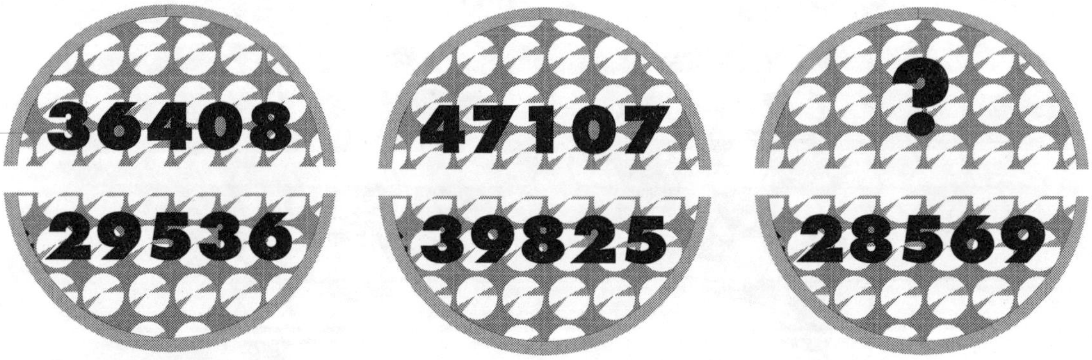

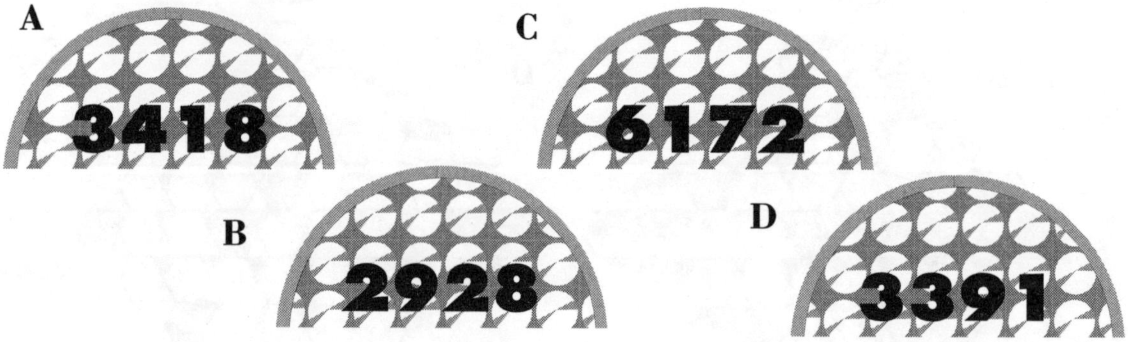

Puzzle 60

Pick the odd-one-out and use it as your passcode to the next puzzle.

SECTION SIX KEYCODES

REMINDER: You must solve the puzzles in the correct order. Start at the top of column A, and insert your keys. When you get to the bottom of column A, start back at the top of column B.

For your final keycode, subtract the total of column A from the total of column B. The result is your passcode for Section 6. Write that below and in the appropriate place on page 220, and then proceed to the Part One final code gate on page 218.

Adrian Smith is actually getting scared...

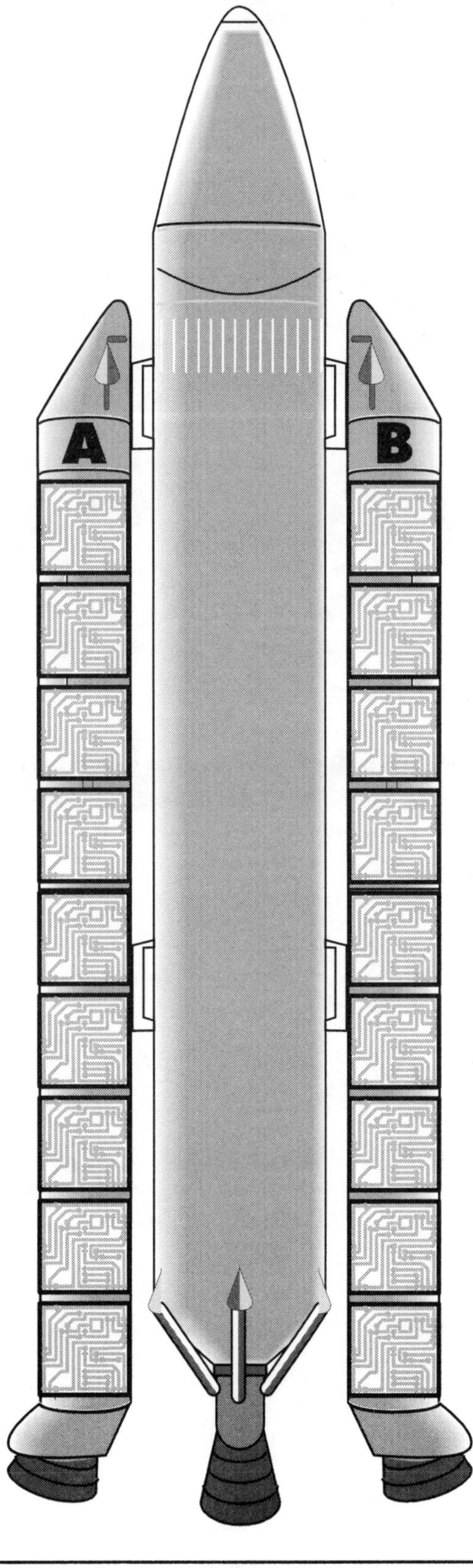

Total A

Total B

SECTION SIX

PASSCODE

1. Solution D. This is a mirror-image of the others which are all rotated versions of the same puzzle. **Go to 49. Key 2.**

2. Solution A. **Go to 50.**

3. Solution A. Row 1: 4x3=6+6; Row 2: 4x4=8+8; Row 3: 4x5=8+8+4. Hence Row 4: 4x6=8+4+8+4. **Go to 47.**

4. Solution 31. The numbers on either side of each set add to the same as the top and bottom numbers multiplied together. **Go to 31. Key 3.**

5. Solution – the shape containing 43 does not fit. **Go to 43.**

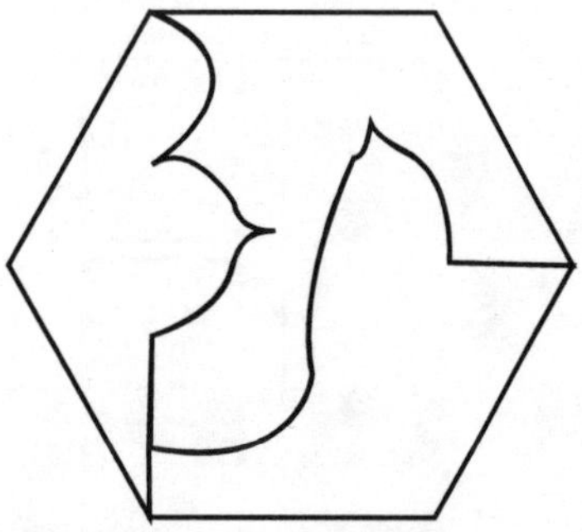

6. Solution B. The circled cross has changed shade. The other shapes are all rotated versions of the same puzzle. **Go to 48.**

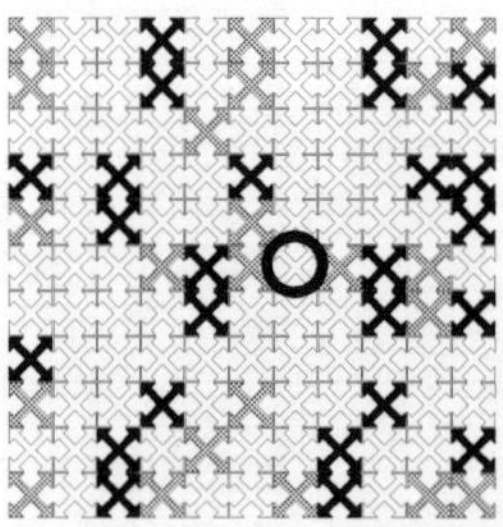

7. Solution 52. The missing number is 13. The inner numbers add to the same as the outer numbers in each set. 4x13=52. **Go to 52. Key 4.**

8. C is the odd-one-out. This is a mirror-image of the others, which are all rotated versions of the same thing. The correct figure is shown below. **Go to 34.**

9. Solution 51. The sum 52-31=21. The values are shown below. **Go to 51.**

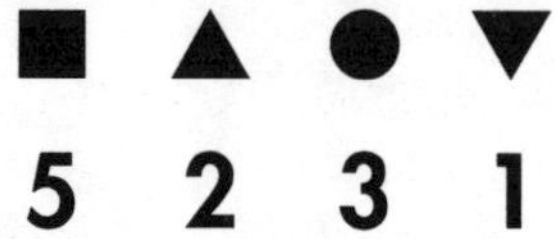

10. Solution A. An extra dot has been placed in A. The others are all rotated versions. **Go to 39.**

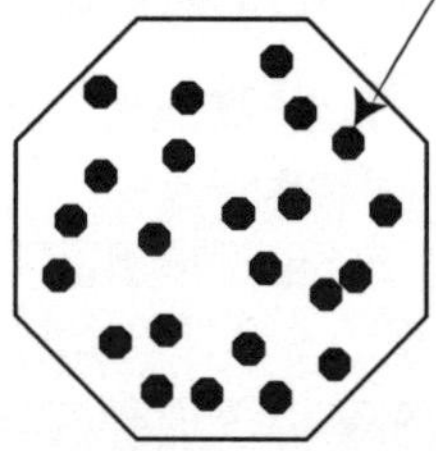

11. Solution 41. The missing number is 4. In each big triangle, top number x middle number = half the number formed from the bottom 2 digits. In C, 6x7=42; 2x42=8[4]. 4+37=41. **Go to 41. Key 3.**

12. Solution 37. There are 7 differences, as circled below. 7+30=37. **Go to 37.**

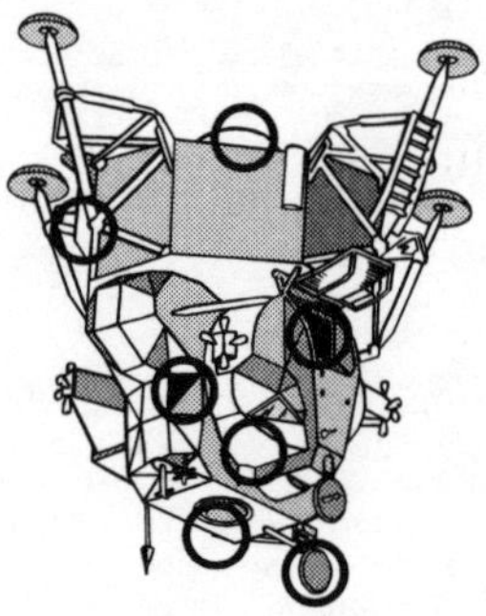

13. Solution 45. The missing number is 12. With double digits, add both digits together and add 2 to get the next number. Thus, 2+8=10, 10+2=[12]; 1+2=3, 3+2=5; 5+2=7; 7+2=9; 9+2=11; 1+1=2, 2+2=4; 4+2=6. 12x4=48; 48-3=45. **Go to 45.**

14. Solution B. The circled spot below has changed shade. The other shapes are all rotated versions of the same drawing. **Go to 59.**

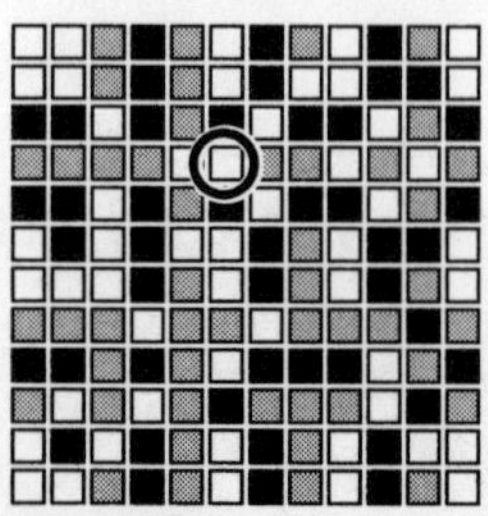

15. Solution 32. Dogs=7; Cats=4; Mice=3. **Go to 32. Key 1.**

SECTION SIX

ANSWERS

16. Solution 55. The missing number is 71. Referring to the diagram below, in each example, A+(both digits of A added together)=B; B+(both digits of B added together)=C; C+(both digits of C added together)=D. 71-16=55. **Go to 55.**

17. Solution 36. The missing value is 15. Component values are shown below. 21+15=36. **Go to 36.**

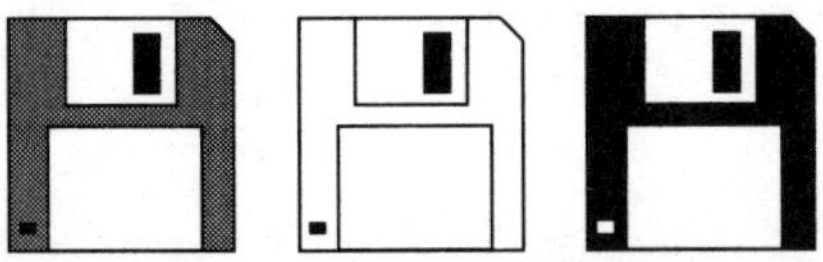

2 **9** **4**

18. C is the odd-one-out. The line pointed to here has changed color in C. **Go to 54.**

19. Solution 35. For each number, take the number before it from it, to give the number following it. 35-28 = 7; 7-35 = -28; -28-7 = -35; -35-(-28) = -7. -7+42 = 35. **Go to 35. Key 5.**

20. Solution 60. The missing number is 20. In each set, referring to the example, (A+B+C)-(D+E+F)=G. 3x20=60. **Go to 60.**

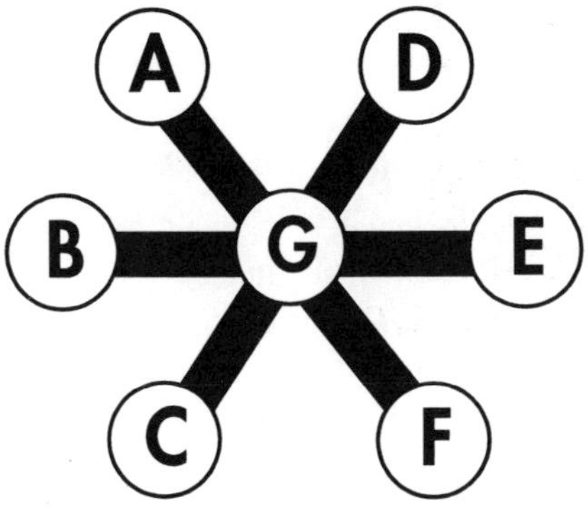

21. Solution 57. The total of the missing numbers, referring to the diagram below, is 78. 78-21=57. **Go to 57.**

6		3		2		5		1		7		4		3
	90		120		80		90		189		336		384	
1		5		4		2		9		3		4		8
	90		320		192		378		945		60		160	
9		2		8		3		7		5		1		5
	324		384		192		126		840		60		60	
6		3		8		1		6		4		3		4
	90		840		448		96		192		144		324	
1		5		7		8		2		4		3		9

22. Solution 40. The missing number is 13. The vertical numbers add to the same as the horizontal numbers in each cross. **Go to 40.**

23. Solution 44. The missing number is 3. The number in each small triangle in large triangles A or B + the number in the same position below it in C or D = 20. Thus in D, the central 17 from B + [3]=20. 41+3=44. **Go to 44. Key 6.**

24. Solution B. This is a mirror-image of the others, which are all rotated versions of the same puzzle. **Go to 33.**

25. Solution 46. The missing number is 24. The values are shown below. 24+22=46. **Go to 46.**

3 **8** **5**

26. Solution 38. The missing value is 4. On either side, multiply each block's numerical position from the middle by its weight, and add the results to find the total weight on either side. On the left, (19x2 =38)+(5x6=30)+(3x9=27)=95; on the right, (22x2 =44)+(5x7=35)+([4]x4=16)=95. Thus the system is balanced. 4+34=38. **Go to 38.**

27. Solution 61. The nervousness circuit is drawing 3 units, the math circuit is drawing 16 units, the logic circuit is drawing 64 units, and the puzzle circuit is drawing 138 units. 64-3=61. **Go to 61 – The final Keycode section before the final code gate. Key 1.**

28. Solution 53. The missing number is 8. The total of the tops of all the cubes is the same as the total of the sides and thus, logically, the fronts. Hence, 5+17+20+[8]=50. 45+8=53. **Go to 53.**

29. Solution 58. The missing number is 7. Referring to the diagram below, in each large triangle, C+D divided by A=B. Thus, in C, (19+2)/3=7. 7x8=56; 56+2=8. **Go to 58.**

30. Solution B. This is a mirror-image of the others, which are all rotated versions of the same pattern. **Go to 42. Key 7.**

31. Solution 12. In each case, total of numbers in the back triangle – total of numbers in the front triangle = the number in the middle. **Go to 12.**

32. Solution 3. The missing number is 8. There is a total distance x weight value of 48 on the left; hence we need to balance that on the right. Since the box is at position 6 we need 6x[8]=48. 8-5=3. **Go to 3.**

33. Solution 4. The sequence is 7x[4]=28; 8x2=16, reusing the 8. **Go to 4.**

34. Solution 11. In each set, the columns add to the same: 15, 24, 18, 19 and 22 from left to right. Thus 5+6+7+3+[1]=22. 1+10=11. **Go to 11. Key 3.**

35. Solution 22. Referring to the diagram below, the missing digits total 94. 94-72=22. **Go to 22.**

7		9		3		5		8		4		2		6
	28		26		21		22		19		20		20	
4		8		6		7		2		5		9		3
	24		21		25		19		15		29		24	
8		4		3		9		1		7		8		4
	20		14		20		20		17		23		24	
3		5		2		6		4		5		3		9
	19		19		17		20		20		13		15	
6		5		7		2		8		3		2		1

36. Solution 61-5=56. Frogs=5; Ducks=7; Tadpoles=2. **Go to 56. Key 4.**

37. Solution 28. On the outside numbers, the top number x the right digit = the bottom and left digits. Thus in C, 6x4=24. The inner numbers total to the multiplication result. Thus in C, 5+9+3+[7]=24. 4x7=28. **Go to 28. Key 1.**

38. Solution 8. The missing number is 42. The sequence is a series of subtractions, reducing by 1 with each step. Thus, 72-8=64; 64-7=57; 57-6=51; 51-5=46; 46-4=42. 42-34=8. **Go to 8.**

39. Solution C. The top and the front independently rotate 90° clockwise each step. **Go to 17.**

40. Solution 26. The central number in each set is half the sum of all the surrounding numbers. **Go to 26.**

41. Solution 5. There are 7 differences. 7-2=5. Differences: 5th line up V/K; 6th line down, line changes direction, extra spot; 7th/8th line down, B/R and R/B; 4th line up, line changes direction; 6th line up, down arrow/up arrow. **Go to 5. Key 3.**

42. Solution A. In each circle, the sum of the bottom numbers should be 2 less than the sum of the top numbers. Only A fits this condition. **Go to 13.**

43. Solution 24. Divide each circle diagonally from top left to bottom right. The sums in each of the diagonal halves are equal. **Go to 24.**

44. Solution 10. The missing number is 39. The sum of the surrounding numbers in each example, plus 8 = the central number. 39-29=10. **Go to 10.**

45. Solution F. In every other example with a clockwise spiral, the arrow points up. **Go to 9.**

46. Solution 21. The missing number is 28. 28-7=21. In each case, the numbers in the next outward ring are double their counterparts in the previous, inner, ring. Thus, 7 doubles to 14 and again to 28. **Go to 21.**

SECTION SIX

47. Solution B. The analogy is for the sum of the digits in the larger box, times three. Thus 4+4+5+5+7=25; 25x3=75. Use the 7. **Go to 7.**

48. Solution 18. The missing number is 4. 4+14=18. Each central number, added to the 2 numbers above and the 2 numbers below = 25. Thus, 4+7+4+6+[4]=25. **Go to 18. Key 4.**

49. Solution 2. The sum of all the missing digits, as below, is 95. 95-93=2. **Go to 2.**

5	8	6	7	1
7	1	5	8	6
8	6	7	1	5
1	5	8	6	7
6	7	1	5	8

50. Solution C. This is the only set with 3 lines reversed compared to the example in the box. **Go to 14. Key 0.**

51. Solution C. The top letter gains 3 alphabetic places; the top number gains 6; the middle symbols reverse and the colors reverse; the bottom number loses 6 and the bottom letter loses 2 alphabetic places. **Go to 19.**

52. Solution 29. The missing number is 49. In each example, divide the lower of each of the diametrically opposite numbers into the higher number to achieve the same result. For example, in C, 20/5=16/4; in D, 14/2=49/[7]. Thus, 49-20=29. **Go to 29. Key 8.**

53. Solution D. In each of the others, both long diagonals add to 24, but in D, the lower left to top right diagonal adds to 26. 9+6=15. **Go to 15.**

54. Solution 20. A=7; B=9; C=4. **Go to 20.**

55. Solution 30. Referring to the star below, ABC-DEF=G. Thus, 627-597=30. **Go to 30.**

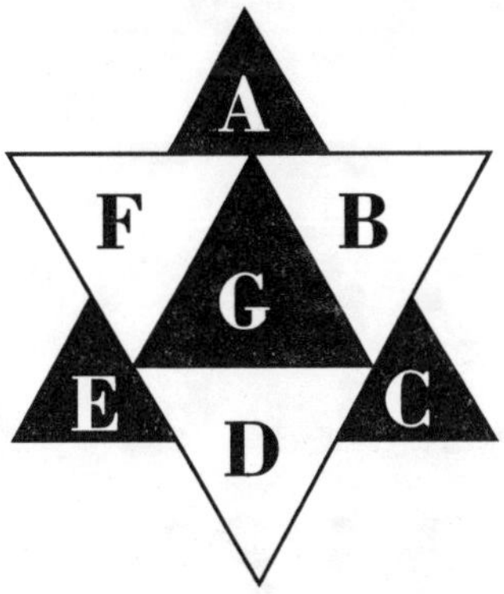

56. Solution A. A has an area of 28 square units, B has an area of 20 square units and C has an area of 16 square units. A is therefore the largest. **Go to 27. Key 7.**

57. Solution A. All the others have 9 dark hexagons, but A has 10. **Go to 6.**

58. Solution 23. (23+6)x2=58; 58+42=100. X is the Roman numeral for 10; 10x10=100. X is the 24th (23+1) letter of the alphabet. **Go to 23.**

59. Solution A. The top numbers are the result of subtracting the reverse of the bottom numbers from 100,000. Hence, 100,000-96,582=3,418. **Go to 25.**

60. Solution 16. This is the only perfect square of a perfect square (4) present. The others are only perfect squares. **Go to 16. Key 2.**

Section 6 Keycode = 36 - 29 = 7. Go to the final code gate on page 218.

PASSCODE RESULTS

SECTIONS ONE-THREE

Multiply all three passcodes together, then add Section 2's passcode and subtract the passcodes for 1 and 3 to get the number for the Part One code gate on p219.

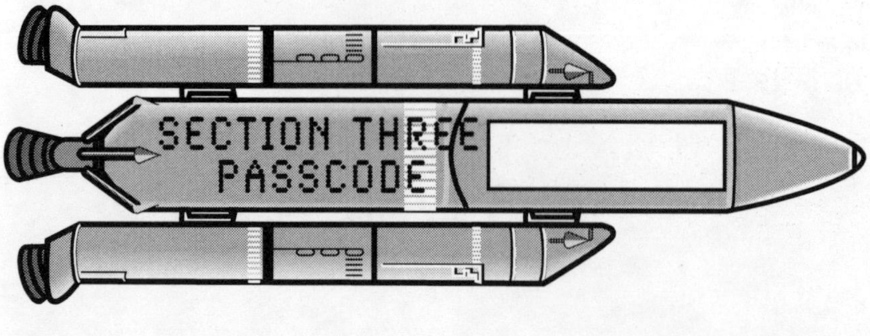

FINAL CODE

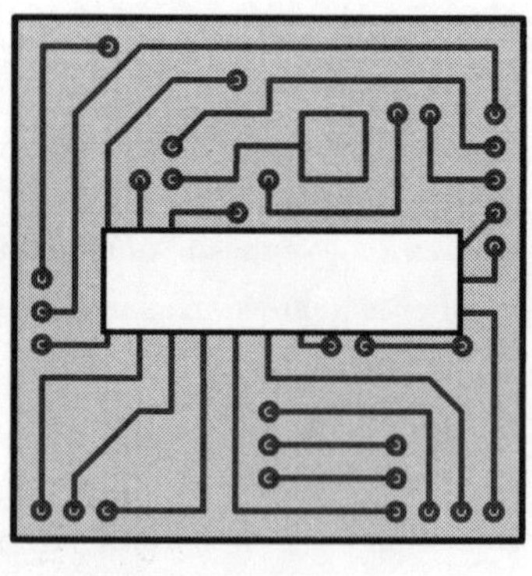

PART ONE
CODE GATE

What number, when you add it to the Part One final code, then square the result, gives you a number that, when you divide it by twice the Section 1 passcode, gives you a number which, when you add both digits together produces twice the Section 2 passcode, and if you subtract the number from ten times that amount produces a number that, if you divide it by the sum of the passcodes for Sections 2 and 3 gives you 6?

PASSCODE RESULTS

SECTIONS FOUR-SIX

Sum all three passcodes and add the digits of the result to get one digit. Add Sections 4 & 5 to the result, then subtract Section 6 and use this total on p221.

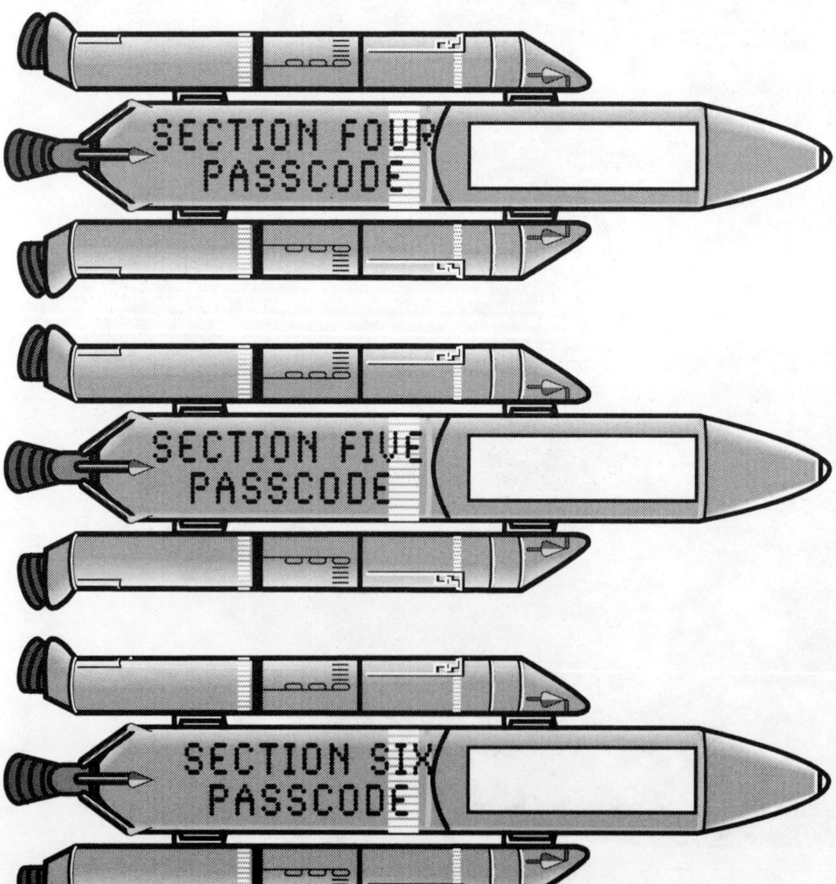

FINAL TOTAL

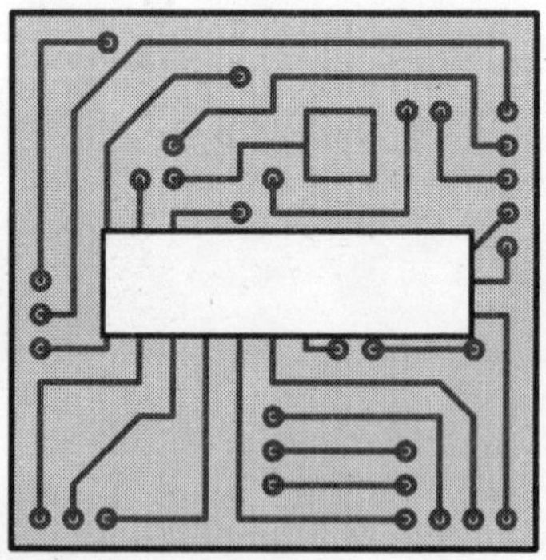

PART TWO
CODE GATE

What number, when you add it to the Part Two final total and divide the results by 2, gives you a number that, when you add 3.5 to the result, gives you the number which, if you subtract 10 and you divide the result by 2 and subtract 5, produces a 2 digit result that can be exactly divided by 3, 5, and 9, and is not 90?

Add the two parts of the final Code Gate together, and sum the digits, for your Final Answer to Adrian's challenge.
If you've got the answer right, Congratulations! You escape from Cyber-reality, getting your body back and locking Adrian forever into one of the flesh cubes he left behind. If you've failed however, you're to be the one trapped for good, I'm afraid...
Well done or hard luck!

PART ONE

Solution to Part One code gate: 4. 2x5x1 = 10. 10+5 = 15; 15-2-1 = 12. Take the 12 and add the solution of 4 = 16; 16 squared = 256; 256/4 = 64; 6+4 = 10; 100-64 = 36; 36/6 = 6.

PART ONE TOTAL

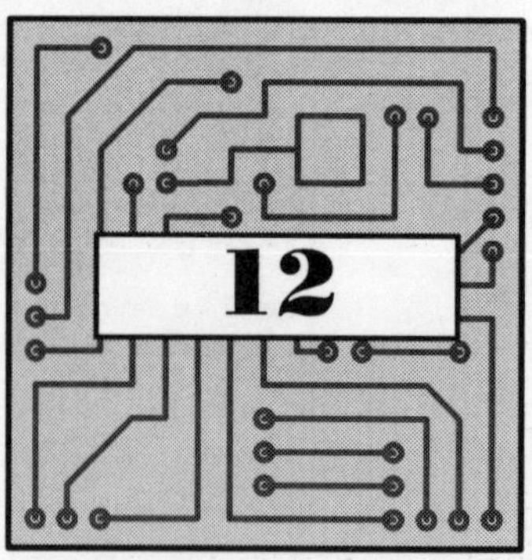

Solution to Part Two code gate: 200. 10+1+7 = 18; 1+8 = 9. 9+10+1-7 = 13. Add 200 to that 13 = 213; 213/2 = 106.5; 106.5 + 3.5 = 110; 110 - 10 = 100; 100/2 = 50; 50 - 5 = 45; 45 can be divided by 3, 5 & 9.

Final Answer: 200+4 = 204. 2+0+4 = 6, your final exit code!

PART TWO TOTAL

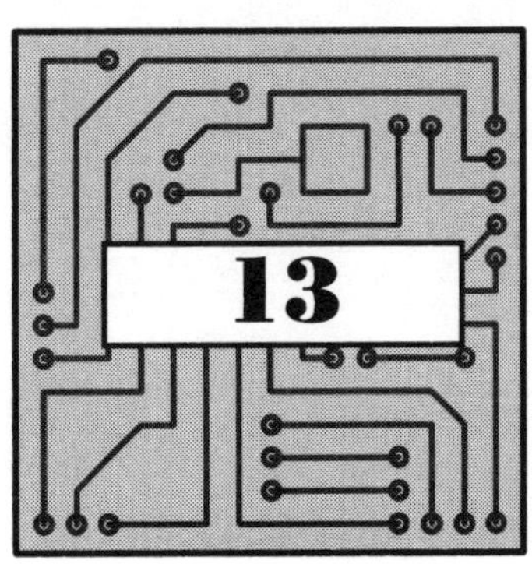

NOTES

Use this page for your working out: